D0078282

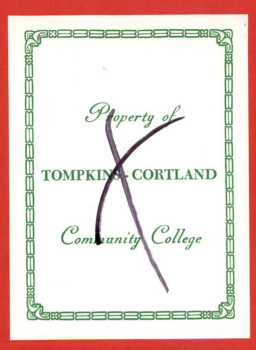

PITTSBURGH SERIES
IN SOCIAL AND LABOR HISTORY

THE SPEECHES AND WRITINGS OF MOTHER JONES

The Speeches and Writings of
MOTHER JONES

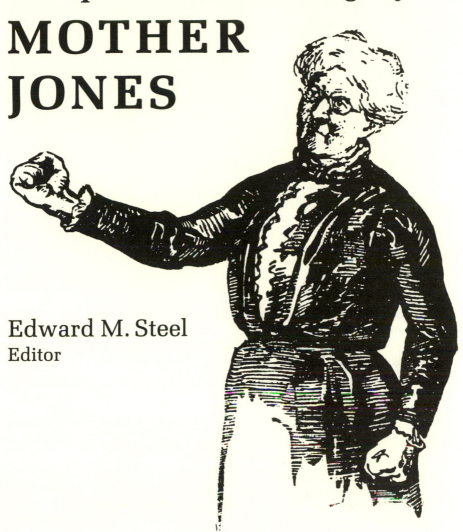

Edward M. Steel
Editor

UNIVERSITY OF PITTSBURGH PRESS

Published by the University of Pittsburgh Press, Pittsburgh, Pa. 15260
Copyright © 1988, University of Pittsburgh Press
All rights reserved
Feffer and Simons, Inc., London
Manufactured in the United States of America

Library of Congress Cataloging-in-Publication Data

Jones, Mother, 1843?-1930.
    [Selections. 1988]
    The speeches and writings of Mother Jones / Edward M. Steel,
editor.
           p.   cm. — (Pittsburgh series in social and labor history)
    Includes index.
    ISBN 0-8229-3575-9
    1. Labor and laboring classes — United States — History. 2. Miners —
United States — History. 3. Trade-unions — United States — History.
I. Steel, Edward M. II. Title. III. Series.
HD8072.J7832 1988
331.88'0973 — dc19   87-25192
                                                    CIP

This volume was supported by research and publication grants from the National Historical Publications and Records Commission.

Contents

Acknowledgments   xi

Introduction   xiii

SPEECHES

UMWA convention, 25 January 1901   3
UMWA convention, 19 July 1902   15
IWW convention, 27 June–8 July 1905   22
UMWA convention, 27 January 1909   24
UMWA convention, 29 January 1909   32
UMWA convention, 26 January 1910   35
UMWA convention, 24 March 1910   40
UMWA convention, 21 January 1911   44
Public meeting, Charleston, West Virginia, 1 August 1912   56
Public meeting, Montgomery, West Virginia, 4 August 1912   70
Public meeting, Montgomery, West Virginia, 4 August 1912   73
Public meeting, Charleston, West Virginia, 15 August 1912   88
Public meeting, Charleston, West Virginia, 6 September 1912   106
Public meeting, Charleston, West Virginia, 21 September 1912   115
District 15 UMWA convention, 16 September 1913   121
District 15 UMWA convention, 16 September 1913   122
District 14 UMWA convention, 30 April 1914   129
District 15 UMWA convention, 15 September 1914   150
Public meeting, Pittsburg, Kansas, 7 August 1915   156
UMWA convention, 20 January 1916   167
UMWA convention, 29 January 1916   174
UMWA convention, 17 January 1918   185
Public meeting, Peoria, Illinois, 6 April 1919   194
UMWA convention, 16 September 1919   200
UMWA convention, 17 September 1919   208
Public meeting, Williamson, West Virginia, 20 June 1920   211
Public meeting, Princeton, West Virginia, 15 August 1920   224
Pan American Federation of Labor, 13 January 1921   232
UMWA convention, 26 September 1921   238
UMWA convention, 29 September 1921   251
UMWA convention, 18 February 1922   254
Afterword   259

Contents

WRITINGS

Civilization in Southern Mills, January 1901   265
The Strike in Scranton, 13 April 1901   268
A Picture of American Freedom in West Virginia,
        September 1901   269
The Coal Miners of the Old Dominion, February 1902   272
The Dawning of a New Era, 23 February 1907   276
The Grave of Martin Irons, 11 May 1907   279
Governor Comer's Alabama Cotton Mills, 24 October 1908   281
Oh! Ye Lovers of Liberty!, 23 January 1909   285
Mexico and Murder, 23 October 1909   288
Girl Slaves of Milwaukee Breweries, 4 April 1910   290
A Sacred Call to Action, 16 April 1910   293
What I Saw in the Anthracite Fields, 14 November 1910   294
How They "Histed" the Sheriff Over the Fence, 2 April 1912   296
Papa, Don't Cry, 3 April 1912   298
Miners' Strikes in the Kingdom of West Virginia, 5 April 1912   300
How a Little Girl Put Deputies to Flight with a Big Gun,
        6 April 1912   302
Fashionable Society Scored, 1 April 1915   304

Addenda to *The Correspondence of Mother Jones*   309

Biographical Notes   313

Index   327

Acknowledgments

The editor would like to thank the many scholars who have assisted him by answering inquiries and helping to pursue clues, sometimes successfully, to the whereabouts of Mother Jones's speeches, especially Maier B. Fox at UMWA headquarters, Jane Lee Garrison, Gene de Gruson at Pittsburg State University, A. D. Mastrogiuseppe at the Denver Public Library, and Mari Tonn.

Introduction

The speeches and writings of Mother Jones throw significant light on the first twenty-five years of American history in the twentieth century. These speeches, like *The Correspondence of Mother Jones,* are a mere sample of a much more extensive body of material which has been lost. In the spring of 1906, for instance, Mary Harris Jones was known to have had thirty-four speaking engagements in Texas, of which only brief journalistic notes have been found. The record of preservation of speeches in other years is similar.

All the speeches in this collection are or purport to be complete transcriptions taken by stenographers who were present on the occasions. Most of them were preserved because the United Mine Workers of America printed full transcripts of their national convention proceedings and frequently of district conventions. These volumes have served as the principal sources for the texts of speeches. The coal operators of the Kanawha Valley hired a stenographer to take down Mother Jones's remarks at a series of public meetings in 1912, and the transcriptions were preserved both in manuscript and in public documents. Three speeches have been retrieved from the notes of military intelligence agents who reported on Mother Jones during or immediately after the First World War.

Friends and foes agreed that Mother Jones was an effective speaker. The lengths to which her opponents were willing to go to prevent her speaking — injunctions, threats, deportation, quarantine, imprisonment — are testimony enough from her enemies. Friends and neutral observers emphasized her ability to carry a crowd irresistibly, or rouse an audience to a frenzy, "the marvelous power she possesses over an audience," "oratory of the agitator type almost unexcelled," "an expert in the subtle use of words." "Men in the audience wept," said a report of a meeting in Wheeling, West Virginia; "She could talk blood out of a stone," reminisced P. J. Conroy. When Nathan Goff of West Virginia denounced her on the floor of the United States Senate as the grandmother of all the agitators, she welcomed the title and said she hoped to live to be the great-grandmother of agitators. One of her "granddaughters," Kate Richards O'Hare, gave Mother Jones primary credit in turning her to her long career as an agitator, and another, Elizabeth Gurley Flynn, called her simply "the greatest woman agitator of our time."[1]

Rather surprisingly, some of the most widely publicized speeches of

1. UMWA *Journal,* 25 April 1901; *Blossburg Advertiser,* 8 December 1899; *Charleston Gazette,* 2 August 1912, 16 August 1912; UMWA *Journal,* 26 September 1912; *Greensburg*

Introduction

Mother Jones have not been preserved in their entirety. In May, 1913, right after being released from jail in West Virginia, she spoke at Carnegie Hall in New York at a meeting sponsored by *The Masses* and presided over by Max Eastman, editor of that journal. In his introduction, Eastman called her the most heroic woman in the nation, and the audience greeted her with a standing ovation and demonstrations in the aisles. "When the applause had subsided," a reporter for the *New York Call* wrote, "She said that people ought to use their hands less and their heads more."[2] Then she reviewed the main events in the West Virginia strike, her own arrest, trial, and imprisonment, and her refusal to recognize the jurisdiction of the military court. The meeting concluded with a collection for West Virginia miners, which Mother Jones asked instead to be sent to the striking silk mill workers in Paterson, New Jersey. Other major speeches in New York, Boston, Washington, and San Francisco are known only from such newspaper notices. No attempt has been made to include these journalistic accounts in this volume, but numerous instances can be found in Philip Foner's *Mother Jones Speaks,* along with many of the speeches reproduced here. A complete collection of newspaper reports of speeches would be virtually impossible, given the number of engagements and the extensive coverage; furthermore, the partial reports of the same speech vary widely, depending on the sympathies of the reporters or of the editors of their newspapers.

In print, Mother Jones's speeches lack the force that her strong personality and skillful presentation gave to her actual performances. Observers over twenty-five years are remarkably consistent in their descriptions of her and her oratory.

Reporters nearly always commented on Mother Jones's small stature, snow-white hair, finely wrinkled face, bright blue eyes, and fine complexion. Her expression was usually described as kindly or benevolent. For public appearances she dressed invariably in the style of the mid-nineteenth century, in a black dress, usually with lace at throat and wrists. Her hat, if she wore one, was often trimmed with pansies or lavender ribbons to lend a touch of color.[3] Once on stage, however, earlier perceptions of fragility were submerged in the impression of enthusiasm, energy, and vitality, with great variations in emotion as she strode about the stage in "a towering rage," or "has the audience clapping and bursting with

---

Tribune Review, 26 June 1977; Kate Richards O'Hare, "How I Became a Socialist Agitator," in *The Socialist Woman* 2 (October, 1908), 4–5; Elizabeth Gurley Flynn, *I Speak My Own Piece* (New York: Masses and Mainstream, 1955), p. 79.

   2. *New York Call,* 28 May 1913.

   3. *Greensburg Tribune Review,* 26 June 1977; *Gary Daily Tribune,* 24 October 1919; *San Francisco Call,* clipping [1924?] in the Mother Jones Papers, Catholic University of America.

laughter." Again and again, reporters made the contrast between the mild-looking old lady and her speech which turned out to be "pyrotechnic, enthusiastic, spectacular. She knows how to tell a good story well and presents it in a way that thrills." She excelled in invective, pathos, and humor ranging from irony to ridicule.[4]

She was equally at home and used the same techniques on a street corner in Douglas, Arizona, or the formal setting of Carnegie Hall. She seems to have been able to establish rapport with her listeners immediately, and to maintain a confident stage presence under almost any circumstances. Her speeches usually lasted an hour and a half to two hours, and many reporters noted that she spoke with a slight Irish brogue. Her enunciation was clear and her English usually correct, but she was sometimes profane, and very occasionally bawdy. Exchanges with her audiences were common. To make a point, she might single out an individual who could confirm a statement, or she would break off to urge a reporter: "Put that in your story, but I know the editor will blue pencil it." She frequently made use of machines or stage properties. One of her prized possessions was an early phonograph on which she used to play patriotic airs when no band was available. As early as 1914 she was the principal speaker at a showing of motion pictures of the Ludlow tent colony. A favorite technique was to wave a photograph, a sheaf of papers, or a telegram which contained proof of what she was saying, sometimes reading passages for emphasis. There is no indication that she used prepared scripts in any of her speeches. Where she acquired her skills she never said; one writer said she was "by nature an orator," and, in the give and take of her days as an organizer for the Knights of Labor, "became a debater."[5]

One of her greatest assets was her voice, which Carl Sandburg characterized as "a singing voice." "Nobody else," he wrote, "could give me a thrill just by saying in that slow solemn orotund way, 'The kaisers of this country are next, I tell ye.'" Observers agree that her voice was clear and strong, "audible in every part of the crowded hall," or reaching five thousand gathered in the rain on the steps of the capitol in Denver. Her voice carried "to the outermost listener" in an open air meeting at Cleveland Square, according to the *El Paso Herald*. "The old enthusiasm for the cause shines in her eyes; the fury of the struggle sounds in the deep, vigorous tones of her voice." "Clear and commanding," said the *Calumet*

---

4. *New York Call*, 16 May 1914; *Calumet Copper Country Evening News*, 10 April 1905; for a detailed study, see Carol A. Downing, An Examination of Rhetorical Strategies Used by Mary Harris "Mother" Jones, (Ph.D. diss., Ohio University, 1985).

5. *Chicago Socialist*, 17 December 1904; Mother Jones to William B. Wilson, 4 October 1905, *The Correspondence of Mother Jones* (Pittsburgh: University of Pittsburgh Press, 1985), p. 55; *New York Call*, 16 May 1914; UMWA *Journal*, 25 April 1901.

(Michigan) *News.* "Mother Jones made the other speakers sound like tin cans," reported the *Charleston Gazette.*[6]

A majority of the speeches collected here were addressed to coal miners in conventions of their national or district unions, though not always on miners' business. On some occasions, Mother Jones was self-invited to ask for aid for brewery workers, or to report on the progress of the steel organizing drive, or to plead for funds for Mexican revolutionaries. More frequently, the leaders of the UMWA brought her on stage to unify the delegates after divisive presidential campaigns or policy disputes. She could break the monotony of long business sessions with her lively reminiscences, tirades, or pep talks. Her humor could clear the air. Surely no other woman speaker of the day would have begun an address with: "I know a lot of you here want to go out and get a drink."

Yet the officers of the UMWA knew that a speech by Mother Jones was no mere entertainment. She gave the men a sense of their own history. She could single out by name a delegate whom she remembered as a breaker boy in West Virginia years earlier and weave him into an anecdote that stressed the need for paying special strike assessments. She could conjure up the names of union leaders long dead whom she had known even before the UMWA was formed. She could give her listeners the sense of being part of the wider world of organized labor as she related her experiences with the garment workers, the smeltermen, or the streetcar men.

For over two decades, Mother Jones was to the coal miners both a symbolic figure and a very familiar personality who knew them intimately. They prized her because she was one of them — fearless in the first rank whenever they engaged in confrontation, and tireless in giving comfort or rallying support behind the lines. They delighted in her irreverence for authority, as when she derided ex-President Theodore Roosevelt as "the monkey-chaser," ridiculed President William Howard Taft for his obesity, or, nearer to home, interrupted her speech to chide their presiding officer, Philip Murray, for a lack of militancy. They knew that in her they had an independent voice who spoke to the whole country for them, an advocate who pleaded the same cause at a street corner in El Paso or in the corridors of power in Washington. They listened to her year after year as she preached the gospel of solidarity to them.

6. Carl Sandburg to Negley D. Cochran, 5 April [1919?], *Letters of Carl Sandburg* (New York: Harcourt, Brace and World, 1968), p. 128; *St. Louis Labor,* 11 March 1905; *Denver Daily News,* 17 April 1914; *El Paso Herald,* 17 August 1916; *Arizona Labor Journal,* 28 March 1919; *Calumet News,* 5 August 1913; *Charleston Gazette,* 2 August 1912. In this speech, and in four others that he took down, stenographer S. P. Richmond estimated that Mother Jones ordinarily spoke at a rate of seventy-five to eighty words per minute, dropping to sixty words per minute in dramatic or emotional passages. See his testimony in *Conditions in the Paint Creek District,* 63rd Cong., 1st sess., 1913, S. Doc. 631, pp. 1181–91.

Speech, not writing, was Mother Jones's forte, and her occasional writings are neither extensive nor of great significance. Those reproduced here are minor examples of the muckraking journalism of the turn of the century; they differ from others principally in that she had worked with and lived among the people whom she wrote about, rather than merely observing conditions as a reporter from outside. As few as these writings are, they sound the same themes, use the same rhetoric, and bear the stamp of the same personality as her correspondence and speeches. All of these articles were discovered in printed versions in Socialist publications or daily newspapers; no manuscript sources were found.

Since all of these items appeared in typescript or print, the editor has intervened only minimally. Minor typographical and spelling errors have been corrected without notice, and varying practices of stenographers in using single or double quotation marks have been standardized. Parentheses enclose stenographers' comments; brackets indicate editorial remarks. The source of each speech or composition is indicated at its conclusion.

To identify people mentioned in the speeches, a brief biographical directory is supplied.

SPEECHES

Speech at the convention
of the United Mine Workers of America
Indianapolis, Indiana

January 25, 1901, marks the first of many appearances of Mother Jones before the annual (later biennial) conventions of the United Mine Workers of America. For the past year she had been on the payroll of the organization, participating in successful strikes in Maryland and Pennsylvania, and visiting the coal fields of Virginia, West Virginia, and the anthracite district of eastern Pennsylvania, where trouble was brewing that would lead to a major strike and presidential intervention the following year. Her earlier participation in miners' strikes and organizing in Colorado, Kansas, Alabama, and Pennsylvania had not been as an employee of the international union.

In the past four years, the United Mine Workers, led by John Mitchell, had enjoyed great success and had become the largest American union, but unorganized miners and lack of recognition in some areas demanded a continuation of its membership drives on all fronts. One suggestion that had been discussed in executive board meetings was the admission of women to membership, or the founding of a women's auxiliary organization. Mother Jones may have been employed to head such an effort, but the project was in abeyance, and she had proved to be so effective in her work with strikers during the past year that Mitchell reappointed her, this time with the official title of International Organizer, which the board had denied her on her first employment.

In her first speech before the miners, she ignores almost all current events—the forthcoming inauguration of William McKinley for a second term as president, the decisions on American policy toward Cuba, Puerto Rico, and the Philippine islands—to speak in general terms of the role of the worker in the new industrial America and of the need for the miners to consolidate their power. Her only specific reference to current policy matters was to the need for preserving the Chinese Exclusion Act, and she mentions her own earlier involvement in the anti-Chinese movement in California. Most American labor leaders of the day shared her hostility toward the immigration of Asiatic workmen to the United States.

§   §   §

Speeches

President Mitchell: Ladies and gentlemen: There are few persons in the Industrial movement who have impressed themselves upon the toilers as has the one who will address you this afternoon. During the long years of struggle in which the miners engaged they have had no more staunch supporter, no more able defender than the one we all love to call Mother. I don't believe there is a Mine Worker from one end of the country to the other who does not know her name. It gives me great pleasure to present to you this afternoon Mother Jones.

Mrs. Mary Jones: Fellow toilers, it seems strange that you should have selected the month of January for your conventions. It has a lesson by which you may well profit, and no craft needs more to profit by that lesson than the miners. The month of January represents two seasons, a part of the dead winter and a part of the beautiful coming spring. I realize as well as you do that you have traveled over stormy paths, that you have rubbed up against the conflict of the age, but I am here to say that you have come out victorious, and in the future you will stand as the grand banner organization. My brothers, we are entering on a new age. We are confronted by conditions such as the world perhaps has never met before in her history. We have in the last century solved one great problem that has confronted the ages in the mighty past. It had ever been the riddle of the people of the world. The problem of production has been solved for the human race; the problem of this country will lie with the workers to solve, that great and mighty and important problem, the problem of possession. You have in your wisdom, in your quiet way, with a little uprising here and a little uprising there solved the problem of the age. You have done your work magnificently and well; but we have before us yet the grandest and greatest work of civilization. We have before us the emancipation of the children of this nation. In the days gone by we found the parents filled with love and affection. As the mother looked upon her new-born boy, as she pressed him to her bosom, she thought, "Some day, he will be the man of this nation; some day I shall sacrifice myself for the education, the developing of his brain, the bringing out of his grander, nobler qualities. But, oh, my brothers, that is past, that has been killed! Today, my friends, we look into the eyes of the child of the Proletariat as it enters into the conflict of this life, and we see the eyes of the poor, helpless little creature appealing to those who have inhabited the world before it. Now when the father comes home the first question he asks is "Mary, is it a boy or a girl?" When she answers, "It is a boy, John," he says, "Well, thank God! he will soon be able to go to the breakers and help earn a living with me." If it is a girl there is no loving kiss, no caress for her for she cannot be put to the breakers to satisfy capitalistic greed. But my friends, the capitalistic class has met you face to face today to take the girls as well as the boys out of the cradle. Wherever

4

you are in mighty numbers they have brought their factories to take your daughters and slaughter them on the altar of capitalistic greed. They have built their mines and breakers to take your boys out of the cradle; they have built their factories to take your girls; they have built on the bleeding, quivering hearts of yourselves and your children their palaces. They have built their magnificent yachts and palaces; they have brought the sea from mid-ocean up to their homes where they can take their baths — and they don't give you a chance to go to the muddy Missouri and take a bath in it.

My friends, we are here to tell you that the mothers of this nation will join hands with you in the mighty conflict ahead. We are here to tell you that no more will the mother reach down into the cradle and take the babe out of it and sell it for so many hours a day to their capitalistic masters. You older men here today can go back in memory with me to the time of chattel slavery, when the babe was torn from his mother's breast and sold; how she wailed and mourned and pleaded with the God of justice to give her a chance to save her child. But, my friends, when that child was taken from her she had no other redress than to lay down on Mother Earth and ask if it was for this reason and purpose her babe was sent to her. But, my friends, we have abolished that, so far as the chattel is concerned; but we have transferred it all to the little white slave. When I look into the faces of the little toiling children and see their appealing eyes, it touches the tender chord of a mother's heart. Think of these helpless little things with no one to fight their battles but labor's hosts! No church, no charity organization, no society, no club takes up the war in their behalf; it is only labor and labor's force that come to their rescue. I stand here today to appeal to you in behalf of the helpless children. I want all of you to go to your homes and act as missionaries in their behalf. Get your brothers into your organization, bring them up under the banner of a coming civilization where we can take the little children and put them in the school room and educate them for the benefit of the nation.

One stormy night at Coleraine I went down to see the little breaker boys as they came into the schoolroom. The little fellows came to me and said they wanted to get organized, because they had a mighty mean boss and they wanted to lick him. I explained to them that they are in bondage owing to the indifference of their own fathers and mothers. I told them that there was a glimmer of light for them, and that I hoped their condition would soon be better. Then I said to them, "In all the years your father has worked what has he now as a compensation for his years and years of labor?" One little fellow, whose face was old and withered with the hard tasks he had to perform, stood up and looked me in the face and said, "Mother Jones, all my father has is the hump on his back and the miner's asthma." It occurred to me that that child was a far better philosopher than the father was. The father had not stopped to think what his compensation would be, but the child had reasoned it out. We are in an age of reason, we are in an age when men and women are thinking. You know as well as I that a way back when women started out to compete with men, when the machine came in, you stood appalled at that machine, and your first thought was to smash it, not to own it, there came with the machine another competitor — women. You tried to close your doors against her; your colleges and universities were closed against her; she had no ballot to pave the way; she had no way of advancing herself but that true grand character implanted in her by the hand of nature and her confidence in the everlasting future. She loved the human race, she perceived the wrongs that one part of the race was suffering under, and she took down the bars and made you let us in. My friends, it is often asked, "Why should a woman be out talking about miners' affairs?" Why shouldn't she? Who has a better right? Has she not given you birth? Has she not raised you and cared for you? Has she not struggled along for you? Does she not today, when you come home covered with corporation soot, have hot water and soap and towels ready for you? Does she not have your supper ready for you, and your clean clothing ready for you? She doesn't own you, though, the corporations own you, and she knows that well. She is well aware that she is as yet needed as a tool; but she is rapidly, steadily breaking down the bars, she is entering every avenue. She did not have to go to war, she did not have to take up a gatling gun and a bayonet to do it: She did it by love, by reason, and appeal. When the Galilean was here did he appeal to men for sympathy, for love? No. When all the world looked dark around him, when men said "Hang him" Mary and the others stood by him and said "We love you." Woman's mission here below is that of love, not that of war, and when the whole world turns you out, you come home to your loving wife, or mother, or sister, and they take you in.

My friends, I am not the only woman who is going to take up the battle of the miners. We propose to organize every mining camp in this country, we propose to get our women together and keep them together. We were with you in your battles, we were with you in your darkest hour, we were with you in your prosperity, and I believe we should be with you in your organization. Of course some Smart Aleck will say, "O, but the women talk too much; they tell everything they know!" Let me tell you that if the women had half so glib tongues as some of you men I would hate to be a woman. If you know anything after you have met in the union at night, it simply burns you until you can run over to the boss by the back door and tell him about it. If you can get a smile from these worms of the earth it is the greatest compensation you can get. I read in the papers this morning about your tendering a vote of thanks to an operator who addressed you yesterday. I want you to stop this. You have nothing to thank them for. I want you to know that they are the fellows who should thank you, not you thank them. What right have you to thank them? When I saw that in the paper this morning I was indignant, and I said to myself, "Those fellows have not got over being serfs yet, and I will have to get after them." You are living in America, in America where Patrick Henry and Jefferson lived, those heroes of days gone by, and they are the ones you ought to thank. I want to see an awakening among you. I don't want to see any more strikes; I want strikes done away with. We have come out of one great and mighty battle. I watched with an eagle eye your chief as he sat in that old room in Hazleton weary and worn, thinking hard, and making a friend of no one but his God and himself, thinking only of the 145,000 human souls that he had in his care. Let me say that I looked upon him and I thought, "Your mother is dead, but she has left to the human race God's noblest work, an honest man." In the dark hours, my friends, when they brought the militia in — by the way it was that corporation dog of an officer that you fellows elected by your votes that did that — in those times he felt that there was a just God, and that the battle we were in was for justice and that we would win. When I looked at your leader I thought of another man of the years gone by. The other day I took up my paper and read a notice that Martin Irons was dead, and I thought, "You good, you noble soul, you fought the battle of labor well. You died in poverty, you died alone, died deserted as the Galilean died; but you left behind you a record of worth and goodness and honesty that the whole Gould system could not buy." But he died in poverty. Yes, he died in poverty, but he left a wealth of honor, right and justice behind. I would rather be Martin Irons dying alone and in poverty, and know that there wasn't a single thing to mark my grave, than to be McKinley or Mark Hanna, or anyone else in the world. Now I want to say a warning note to you. I have not entered the labor movement today. I have seen it rise and fall. I have seen many of your leaders walk over your backs into high positions and leave you behind in the struggle. I have watched the movements of the capitalistic class. Martin Irons could not be bought, and he went down in defeat. The American Railway Union could not be bought, because Eugene V. Debs would not sell out. My friends, when the capitalistic class cannot buy one of these, its next work is to ruin them. This is their work before you now. They were not able to buy your leader, they could not touch him with their millions. But they will send into your ranks their minions in order to bring on trouble, and they will make it their aim to ruin him. But I want to tell you now that they have a job on their hands. We have lived a few years since Martin Irons, and we will look behind us now. We have our pickets out, and there isn't a traitor in the camp that we cannot put our hands on tonight if we want to. I will

7

say here that when the men of this organization sell it out to the corporations there will be women enough in the country to sell you out so you will not live any more. I am warning you to take care of yourselves. Women and children, my friends, are not going to be bartered away any more. Sitting here on my left, as Mr. Mitchell is on my right, is one near my heart. In the great conflict we passed through last year for three long months not a dollar came into the home for his wife and children. He walked in highways with his feet out through his shoes while he was fighting labor's battles; and when the Erie Company could not back him down in any other way they thought to buy him. They went to him with their offers. He said to them, "Gentlemen, if you have come to pay me a friendly visit you can have the hospitality of my house; but if you came to ask me to sell my fellow men, there is the door." That man was W. B. Wilson. I stand here to shake hands with such men; I thank God such men are here. I thank God that you fellows have such men at the helm. Where they are I have no fear of the future. I believe we will get together and stay together and bury all personalities. We will join hands together for the emancipation of the human race. We do not live for ourselves alone. We are not building here today for now; we are building for long years to come, and the foundation which you lay with aching backs and your bleeding hands and your sore hearts will not perish with the years. It will grow and grow and live, and when the enemies of this organization shall lie mouldering in the grave and the world will have forgotten that they ever lived, your organization and your work will live. The men and women that are with you are with you because they know you are right. Just think of it! While over in Virginia I got a statement from some of the miners at the Red Ash mine. I got this from the person who heard it read from the books. Fifty human souls were murdered inside that mine. One morning they went from their homes down into that mine, after bidding their wives and children goodbye they never saw those wives and little ones again. They were slaughtered, murdered, and when they were about to be buried the corporation which murdered them had the list of the men called out from the books, and the clerk said, "Two dollars for a suit of clothes, five dollars for a coffin, five cents for a necktie, ten cents for a pair of stockings, fifteen cents for a bosom to cover his breast." That was all that poor miner was worth to that corporation. Mind you, that did not come out of their pockets. That man had worked four years and a half for them and during all that time he had to pay twenty-five cents a month into a burial fund, yet when they came to bury him the corporation, like the robber it was, put half of the amount into its pockets. Of course it is a crime to offend the dignity of the gentlemen who compose the corporation by calling them robbers. You must call them gentlemen, I suppose I will be told, but here is one who is going to call them robbers.

8

In New York they are going to give a charity ball. I suppose it is a kind of restitution to the people they have been robbing for years. They will spend thousands and thousands of dollars for decorating their old carcasses, and they go into a hall and admire one another; and if we were to sit up in the gallery and venture to look at them they would wonder what such a lot of Wops wanted in the world anyhow. Then some smart newspaper man will take his gilt pen and sit down and write of the beautiful Mr. So and So who was there, and of the beautiful Mrs. So and So who was there, and how they were dressed, and how splendid it all was. Splendid! Yes, my friends, but they are dancing on the minds and hearts of the men and women they have robbed, dancing on the hearts of the little children who are working in their factories and of the boys and girls working everywhere. In Freeland I held a meeting for the boys and girls from the silk mills. They were on a strike and one morning they tried to keep the scab children from working. The children went into the factory to work, and the poor little outside ones entered a protest and called them "Blackleg," and "scab," and a burly policeman took one girl by the hair of the head and dragged her to the police station and she was put under three hundred dollars bond. The bond was furnished and they took her home, but the fright and ill treatment had made her ill, and she had three hemorrhages of the lungs. There was not a dollar in the house to get food or medicine or a doctor for her. Think of that. When the children stood on the platform of a hall we had hired for them to expose the corporations one little boy of twelve came to the front and told us that he worked thirteen hours at night, that they paid him one cent an hour; but that these same people had gone to the church and put in a magnificent stained glass window in it. Did you ever hear a minister say one word about the condition of these children? We did not find one minister to defend these children. In the Scriptures they can see where the Master said, "Suffer little children to come unto me." My friends, I believe we should clasp our hands and come out together in defense of these little children. I can see an appeal in their eyes which seems to ask what they have done that they should be battered and knocked about as they are. There are children under age in those factories. You know they have factory inspectors that are like some of your mine inspectors. The inspector, you know, walks in with the superintendent, and down Avenue A in the mine, but never enters Smoke A at all. He would not go in there at all, because the superintendent has put a bottle of champagne into his stomach and the gas might not agree with him. Then he goes out and writes his report in this fashion, "Everything in good condition. The mine is entirely free from gas." That was what the inspector said of the Red Ash mine two days before those fifty men were murdered. That is what the factory inspector does. While the factory inspector is being taken over the mill there are children hidden in closets and locked up there until he leaves. These things are all wrong. We don't believe in the murder of these helpless little children. This is the reason we are joining hands with you. Take your women as an auxiliary organization; let them help you out; with their assistance you can solve the problem. You know that no business man in days gone by succeeded in business when he kept his business from his wife. The trusts have got ahead of us there, however. Your wives and your daughters can make your organization much more entertaining and interesting than it is.

I will stop here to say that you have reached the danger point in your organization. You have grown to be one of the greatest organizations of labor in the world. Now every grafter is going to begin looking to you for offices. Don't you know that? They will all be out, and they will want the offices. Watch those fellows! Watch them in your organizations, and if you don't watch them I will. Keep your eye on the grafters. Sometimes they will put their names down for four or five offices, so that if they lose one they will be sure to get another out of you. Be sure, my friends, the man who is true to you is not after every office you have to give. The man who is sincere does not care whether you give him an office or not. He is willing to work out his own salvation and help you work out yours. When I see those grafters reaching out to take from you, who go under the earth and delve ten and twelve hours a day, those offices, I am one of those who want to take them by the throat and choke them. I believe that the time is here for us to work. I believe the time is here to throw aside our own personalities. You must go out and work for the benefit of the whole and for the love we bear the children. It saddens me when I see your little boys going out in the early morning and going down into the mines as I saw them in Virginia. I asked one miner why he took such a little fellow into the mine, as he was not able to work, and he said, "No, he is not able to work, but he can get a turn." I want to say to you that the man or woman who would undertake to sell and rob and plunder those children is not fit to be classed with human beings. The man or woman who would witness such scenes as I have witnessed in West Virginia would betray God Almighty if he betrayed those people. Ah, my brothers, I shall consider it an honor if, when you write my epitaph upon my tombstone, you say, "Died fighting their battles in West Virginia." You may say what you please about the West Virginia miners being "No good." Every dirty old miner out there is not a Virginian. He is very apt to be an old scab that the rest of you hunted out of your fields. I met in Virginia some of the noblest men I have met in the country. I wanted to hold a meeting at Red Ash, and stood on the track just above the place. A fellow there said I could not cross over, and when I asked him why he said because he owned half the river, and I told him God Almighty owned the other half and I stood in with Him. Well, we went over and we held a meeting and as those big fellows stood around I felt as though I wanted to take every one of those twenty-five young drivers and caress them. I wanted better conditions for them; that it would make them nobler men, and I determined that every effort we could put forth must be put forth there. I realize that the robbers there don't want us to organize. They did not want me to help organize those young men, but they could not prevent us from organizing; we organized anyhow. They locked the school houses and the churches against us, but we got the boys together and organized them. We brought them together there, and it can be done in other parts of the state, and I feel that before another year West Virginia will be lined up and every miner in it will be with you. Those poor fellows in West Virginia realize that they have been neglected. You have not dealt fairly with them; you cannot find fault with them; the conditions that surround them are very unfavorable. We have to go over the hills and mountains to find some of the bands of slaves. I wish you could see how some of them live. The conditions that surround them are wretched. The women have to take their buckets and bring coal down from the pit mouth; and when they want water they have to go three blocks for it and pay a dollar a month for it at that. They have pluck-me stores and every invention known to robbery and rascality to contend with. Why, the Czar of Russia, tyrant that he is, is a gentleman compared with some of the fellows there who oppress these people. Now, my friends, we propose to go back there again. They told us to go out; but you know that when a woman is ordered to do anything she will do just the reverse. Those operators are not slick at all, for if they were they would say, "Stay in." But they told us to go out, and said their courts were issuing injunctions. I am going back there. Do you understand that? I will tell you why. Patrick Henry said in that old State House in Philadelphia that I was guaranteed the right of free speech while I lived; I am not dead yet. If those fellows put me in jail, I trust I have friends enough in the United States to see that the law is tested, and maybe we will put the judge in jail before we get through. That is more than you fellows will do. You know you will run when they tell you they will put you in jail. No battle was ever won for civilization that the jails and the scaffolds did not hold the salt of the earth. And it is because there were women enough true to the race. They said, "Build your scaffolds if you want to, and hang us; but our dangling bodies will tell the people that we died for principle." We live in America, and we are going to fight for American principles.

Before you meet here again it may be that I shall have gone home; that I may be at rest in my grave. I may never again meet you in convention; but I plead with you to be true, to be men, not cringing serfs, and above all, not traitors to your organization. Go deep down into your heart and

11

look into its secret recesses, and if you have betrayed your organization swear on the altar of this convention that you will go home and undo the wrong you have done, and try to do something in the future for the benefit of the human race. Stop a moment and think of what I say before you become traitors to your organization, before you give the secret workings of your organization to the enemy. Think of the thousands and thousands of children you are helping them to slaughter, and think that you will be held more guilty of their murder than the capitalistic class you are aiding. The man who betrays his organization is a demon incarnate. The man who sells those children into slavery has not a particle of manhood in him. When you find one of those traitors in your organization, one of those who are in there for the benefit of the corporations, you just give him a coat of tar and feathers and march him down the streets with the word "Traitor" on him, and he will never sell you out again.

This is the most important convention in your history, and it is the greatest. I want you to be reasonable. I don't want you, on account of the victories you have won, to get up and think you have it all. It took thirty years to get that victory for you. Don't be in a hurry; be a little slow. Use your reason and your better judgment. Don't ask for too much — not but that I want all I can for you — but I know we cannot get it all at once; that we have to get at the capitalists a little slow because they are consolidating and organizing their forces, they are getting together everywhere and controlling everything. Why, they are even discharging the professors in the colleges who dare to speak for the right. I had a letter from California. The letter said that Mrs. Stanford had discharged some of the professors because they had been teaching socialism. The boy who wrote the letter said, "Say, Mother Jones, will you bring your McAdoo women here with their brooms to sweep the scab professor when he comes?" You see the students are beginning to think. It is an industrial revolution, my friends, that has been going on for one hundred and fifty years unnoticed by the masses and the classes; but now the pressure has been brought to bear so hard upon the shoulders of the toilers that they are beginning to think and reason; they are putting away their prejudices and saying to themselves, "Why is it? We produce and yet we have nothing." When they have solved that question they have solved the riddle of the ages. The people the world over are thinking. In Austria not long ago they had a textile strike, an enormous strike. They called the militia out, as they sometimes do in this country. The leader of the strike said, "You are iron men, we are human men; we made those irons, we call on you to lay those arms down," and they did lay them down, and all the crowned heads in Europe trembled. That did not get out through the press, however, but the result was that the strike was settled. We made those fellows at Panther Creek ground arms the morning we met them; they didn't

12

bayonet anyone that morning. We are the bayonets; we are the people. We produce the wealth of the nation; we support the President and the Cabinet and the National Government — and you bet your life that gang that are in there now won't be there when we women can vote. We will have Mark Hanna digging coal.

Now, boys, listen to me. This year the Chinese Exclusion Act expires. The politicians took good care that your attention was not called to it before election. Let me tell you, my friends, that you are up against it. If you don't get your organization solidly in line you are going to be confronted with the conditions that confronted you before, and for that reason I plead with you to stand by your organization, and each and every one of you go home shaking hands with each brother saying, "By the eternal stars of heaven, we are cemented together, never to separate until we win out!" I know something of the Chinese. I was in California when that question was agitating the people there, and I have had the hose turned on me for helping to agitate it. Five or six of us used to get together and keep talking, and gradually more joined us, a few at a time, and at last it became a national question. Then the fight went on at that end of the nation to save you; now you have got to do the fighting at this end of the nation, and you will have to save yourselves. Notwithstanding that you are paying Powderly an enormous salary they are sending in the Italians in enormous numbers. They go through by the thousands, and his old "Nibs" never says a word about it. I want you to pass a resolution asking him to either give up his salary or attend to his business.

Now, my boys, I want you to be good, and I want you to be true, and I want you to be men. I have seen the rise and fall of organizations; I know the danger [several words illegible]. I know the capitalistic class looks upon us with a little bit of fear. I know they feel they could buy your leaders; that you are secure as far as they are concerned; but I also know that they will put in your midst those who will try to disrupt your organization and get up factional fights. Let me tell you one thing to do. When men get up factional fights in your organization expel them immediately. They are dangerous; they have wrecked organizations in the past; they will do it in the future. I believe in you, and I believe that at heart the great majority of you are right, and I believe that you want your organization to go on, and grow, and I believe that nearly all of you will stick to it or die. Bear this in mind, however, my boys, that the men who fought your battles bravely have always stood alone while you have thrown at them stones of calumny. They stood serene, because they saw down the future. I want to say to you younger men here, and I say as one who stands here for perhaps the last time, that I plead with you to build your organization and to stay by it at the risk of your lives. It is for the future civilization. I don't say that it will do everything for you; but it is the school, the college, it is where you learn to know and to love each other and learn to work with each other and bear each other's burdens, each other's sorrows and each other's joys. I say again, be true to your leaders and to your organization.

[Minutes of the Secretary. Typed copy courtesy AFL-CIO Library, Washington, D.C.]

Speech at a convention
of the United Mine Workers of America
Indianapolis, Indiana

John Mitchell reluctantly called a special convention of the UMWA in July, 1902, to consider a general strike of all coal miners in support of the strike in the anthracite coal fields of Pennsylvania and a simultaneous strike in the bituminous fields of West Virginia. Mitchell was adamantly opposed to a general strike, insisting that UMWA contracts in other districts must be honored. He proposed, rather, that the full resources of the international union be used to support the anthracite workers, and that the West Virginia struggle be continued at the same rate as during the past year. His views eventually prevailed.

Since her last speech, Mother Jones had spent nearly all of her time in West Virginia, first in the southern Kanawha field, and then in the Fairmont field in the north. In both areas she was assisted by other international and specially appointed organizers, and in both had sometimes been the ranking union official in charge. Some success had crowned their efforts in the Kanawha field, but in the Fairmont field early progress had been halted by the issuance of injunctions by state judges or by Judge John J. Jackson of the federal district court in Parkersburg. All of the union leaders in the northern field, including Mother Jones, were eventually charged with violating one or more of the injunctions. It was her first arrest as a UMWA organizer, and she was unrepentant at her trial. The confrontation between her and the white-haired judge, who had been appointed by President Abraham Lincoln, attracted national newspaper coverage. Judge Jackson held her guilty, but refused to "make a martyr of her" by imposing a jail sentence. Her fellow organizers were not so lucky. After the trial she continued her work in West Virginia, interrupted by trips to the anthracite field.

A settlement was worked out in the anthracite strike, largely because President Theodore Roosevelt intervened, and, from the negotiations, John Mitchell emerged in the eyes of many as a labor statesman. The operators' intransigence infuriated President Roosevelt and probably drew public opinion to the side of the UMWA. In the almost unnoticed simultaneous West Virginia strike the union made substantial gains in the Kanawha field, but the northern field and most of the rest of the state remained unorganized.

§ § §

Speeches

President Mitchell: The first order of business, under a motion made at the last session yesterday, is an address by Mother Jones.

The work of Mother Jones in the interests of the miners, the sacrifices she has made in their behalf, are so well known to the miners of the United States as to require no repetition from me. I therefore take great great pleasure in introducing to you our friend, Mother Jones.

Mrs. Mary Jones: Mr. Chairman and Fellow Delegates: I have been wondering whether this great gathering of wealth producers thoroughly comprehended the importance of their mission here today; whether they were really clear as to what their real mission was. I realize, my friends, that the eyes of the people of the United States, from one end to the other, are watching you; but you have again given a lesson to the world and a lesson to the statesmen that a general uprising is the last thing you called for; that you will resort to all peaceful, conservative methods before you rise and enter the final protest.

I realize, my friends, what your mission is; but I am one of those who, taking all the conditions into consideration, had I been here would have voted for a gigantic protest. I wanted the powers that be to understand who the miners were; to understand that when they laid down their picks they tied up all other industries, and then the operators would learn what an important factor the miner is toward his support. But, my friends, I believe you have taken the wisest action, that action which the world at large will commend, and which I now commend, believing it is right. I think, my friends, when you go home from this convention it is not the promise you have made here that will be the important thing, but the carrying out of that promise, the doing of your duty in the matter, the fulfillment of your duty as man to man, that is of the greatest importance.

These fights must be won if it costs the whole country to win them. These fights against the oppressor and the capitalists, the ruling classes, must be won if it takes us all to do it. The President said I had made sacrifices. In that I disagree with him, though I do not usually do that, for I hold him very dear. None of us make sacrifices when we do our duty to humanity, and when we neglect that duty to humanity we deserve the greatest condemnation.

There is before you one question, my friends, and you must keep that question before your eyes this fall when you send representatives to the legislative halls. Your instructions to these representatives must be: "Down forever with government by injunction in the American nation." This generation may sleep its slumber quietly, not feeling its mighty duty and responsibility, and may quietly surrender their liberties. And it looks very much as though they were doing so. These liberties are the liberties for which our forefathers fought and bled. Things are happening today that would have aroused our Revolutionary fathers in their graves. People sleep quietly, but it is the sleep of the slave chained closely to his master. If this generation surrenders its liberties, then the work of our forefathers, which we will lose by doing this, will not be resurrected for two generations to come. Then perhaps the people will wake up and say to their feudal lords "We protest," and they will inaugurate one of those revolutions that sometimes come when the slave feels there is no hope, and then proceed to tear society to pieces.

My friends, it is solidarity of labor we want. We do not want to find fault with each other, but to solidify our forces and say to each other: "We must be together; our masters are joined together and we must do the same thing."

I want to explain to some of the delegates here why eleven of my co-workers in the field and myself were arrested and thrown into jail. We had the Fairmont Company practically licked, and as we did our marching and got our camps established the injunction machine began to work, and we had injunctions served against us, and they can grind injunctions out there in daylight and in the dark — it is no trouble to them at all. The Marshal served one on me, and I said to him: "I shall do my duty regardless of injunctions. I am here to do a work and I am going to do it; I think also that my co-workers intend to do their duty. We were not arrested on that injunction, but they served another. You know there is an amendment to every injunction. Well, we discussed the matter, and I said to the boys: "I don't believe there is any government in the world that can make us go blind; and if the company's tipple is a certain distance away I am not going to shut my eyes and go blind for the sake of the Fairmont Coal Company." We went to the meeting that was held there. There were eight of the organizers there. We held our meeting. I was the only speaker there, and I will confess that I felt particularly irritated that day; in fact, I felt pretty sore. I shall tell you why. One of our boys was beaten nearly to death by their bloodhounds as he was coming home from a meeting. A night or two before that three of our organizers and myself were coming home, and we met a boy with a buggy. I was tired, so the boy drove me to the streetcar while the men walked. The company's store was at the other end of a bridge we had to cross. The guards around the store asked if that was Mother Jones, and I said, "Yes, boys; be good and watch the slaves and don't let one of them get away or you will lose your jobs in the morning." It was a covered bridge, and a very dangerous place. It ought to be torn away. I went through it in the dark and sat down. It then dawned on me what an unsafe thing I had done. There isn't a house there, there wasn't a human being with me, and six thugs there who might have thrown me into the river and no one would have been the wiser for it or would have known what happened to me. Just then one of our men came out from the covered bridge yelling "Murder, Murder!" I said, "What

17

is the matter?" It was Barney Rice, and I asked him what had happened to the rest of my boys. He still kept calling for the police, and directly one of the comrades from Indiana came out, and I said: "Where is Joe and John?" and they said, "Mother, they are killing Joe." I ran towards the bridge, and Joe [Poggiani] staggered out all covered with blood, weak, and almost exhausted from loss of blood. I put him on the car and asked the car driver to take us to town as quickly as possible. When we got him to town and examined his injuries we found that he had eighteen cuts with knuckles on his head.

I said at that meeting, "We are on a peaceful mission, and I don't see why the judge should issue injunctions against us. Why does he not issue injunctions against those thugs who are beating our people to death? We are not armed; no one carries arms, and yet we have injunctions served on us."

It was weeks before poor Joe was able to get up again. Then we were arrested and taken to Parkersburg at twelve o'clock at night; and the Marshal [Charles D. Elliott], intending to be very courteous to me, said he had engaged a room for me at the hotel. I thanked him very kindly, and he told a deputy to go there with me, and when we got to Parkersburg he said, "Come this way with me," and I said, "Come with me, boys." He said, "No, they are going to jail, and you are going to the hotel." I said, "No, I am going wherever my boys go," and we all went to jail. Next day, we were all taken before the judge [John J. Jackson], and I was kept on the witness stand for seven long hours, for seven long hours they were questioning me, and the old judge and I made friends with each other. He asked me: "Did you say there was an old gray-headed judge on the bench up there at Parkersburg who thought he was running everything?" I said, "I said to the crowd there is an old gray-headed judge back there in Parkersburg, and he is growing old just as I am myself; we are both getting childish and some day soon we will both die, and then the whole world will miss us."

Then the judge told me that if I would go out of the state and stay out, and be a good girl generally, he would leave me alone. I asked my lawyer to tell him for me that I said all the devils in hell would not get me out of West Virginia while I had my duty there to perform. I said I was there to stay, and if I died in West Virginia in jail it made no difference with my decision. There would be no going out of the state, however; that thing was settled. I was there and I intended to fight whether in jail or out until we won. We all felt the same about that.

Let me warn you right here and now that any fellow who is not willing to go up against all these forces had better stay out of West Virginia; don't go over there, for we don't want you unless you are willing. We want fighters, although we are conducting our business on peaceful lines and according to the Constitution of the United States.

I have wondered many times recently what Patrick Henry would say, Patrick Henry who said, "Give me liberty or give me death," and who also said, "Eternal vigilance is the price of liberty," if he could witness the things that are done in West Virginia in this day and age, in a state that is supposed to be under the Constitution of the United States? I say with him, "Give me liberty or give me death, for for liberty I shall die, even if they riddle my body with bullets after I am dead."

My friends, you must emancipate the miners of West Virginia; they should be the barometer for you in the future. You have a task; go bravely home and take it up like men. Each one of you should constitute himself a missionary, each one should do his duty as a miner and as a member of this organization. Do your duty also as citizens of the United States, do your duty as men who feel a responsibility upon you, and remember, friends, that it is better to die an uncrowned free man than a crowned slave. You and I must protest against this injustice to the American people that we are suffering under in West Virginia and in Pennsylvania, and in other fields.

In West Virginia the attorney for the company in his argument said, when my case was up, "In strikes of the past we got the deputies, the marshals and the Federal troops out, and still the strikers won the strikes; but the moment the court came out with an injunction, then the strikers were whipped." He said further that the injunction was the barricade behind which the operators can stand.

There is an acknowledgement that we have no show; that the injunction is used for the benefit of the ruling classes. Now remember when your candidates get up and tell you what good friends they are to the laboring class, you ask them to sit right down and take an oath that the first thing they will do when they get to Congress is to introduce a bill entitled, "No government by injunction."

Now I want to say a word about the West Virginia comrades. A great deal has been said for and against them. Perhaps no one there knows them better than I do. No one has mingled with them more than I have, and no one has heard more of their tales of sorrow and their tales of hope. I have sat with them on the sides of the mountains and the banks of the rivers and listened to their tales. One night a comrade from Illinois [John H. Walker] was going with me up the mountain side. I said, "John, I believe it is going to be very dark tonight," and he said he thought it was, for only the stars were shining to guide us. When we got to the top of the mountain, besides the stars in the sky we saw other little stars, the miners' lamps, coming from all sides of the mountains. The miners were coming there to attend a meeting in a schoolhouse where we had promised to meet them, and I said to John, "There comes the star of hope, the star of the future, the star that the astronomer will tell nothing about in his great works for the future ages; but that is the star that is lighting up the ages yet to come; there is the star of the true miner laying the foundation for a higher civilization, and that star will shine when all other stars will grow dim."

We held a meeting there that night, and a braver band does not live on the face of this earth today than that band of men up there on the mountain top that night. And in their behalf I stand pleading with you here today. They have their faults, I admit, but no state ever produced nobler, truer, better men under the appalling circumstances and conditions under which they work. It matters not whether a miner is robbed in Illinois or in Virginia, in Indiana or in the anthracite region; they are all ours, and we must fight the battle for all of them. I think we will come out victorious in this fight, but it will only be for a while. Both sides will line up for the final conflict, and you must be ready for the fray. We have no time to lose. There is a peaceful method for settling this conflict. Get books; read at home; read to each other; take your boys that go to school and sit down and discuss the labor problem with them. Teach your women and children to not buy anything that has not a Union label on it, to buy nothing that is not made by Union men with Union principles. You will in that way soon drive scabs and blacklegs out of the market; there will be no room for them.

All of us should do our duty in this matter. Go home from this convention and put every dollar you can spare above your living expenses into this fight. If it costs us every penny we have, if we have to sell our clothes to get money to put into this fight we should do it. We have a class in the two Virginias—and they are the only two states in the Union, perhaps, where you can find them—that do not know what freedom means. They are a species of the human race that for ages have been slaves. They have come down from the feudal days, they have never known what freedom was; they were sent out here in the time of George III in order to defeat the Colonists who were fighting for the freedom of their country. There are still remnants of them in the two Virginias, and they will work for twenty-five cents a day and be satisfied with it if their masters will give them no more. But they are in the minority. Think of the New River field, of the Kanawha River, of Loop Creek, and think of the work the boys have done there. Every wheel there is closed down, and that shows to you what good material there is there. One of the best elements there, I am here to tell you, are the colored men. One of the best fellows we have is the black man. He knows what liberty is; he knows that in days gone by the bloodhounds went after his father over the mountains and tore him to pieces, and he knows that his own Mammy wept and prayed for liberty. For these reasons he prizes his liberty and is ready to fight for it. My friends, the most of us have been told that we have liberty, and we believed the people who told us that!

Now, my friends, we should all work together in harmony to secure our rights. Don't find fault with each other; rather clasp hands and fight the battle together. Be true to the teachings of your forefathers who fought and bled and raised the old flag that we might always shout for liberty. Think, my friends! Did the laborers ever take twenty-two capitalists and riddle their bodies with bullets? Did the laborers ever take twenty thousand men, women and children and lock them up in the Bastille and murder them? No, labor has always advanced Christianity. The history of the miner has been bitter and sore; he has traveled the highways and the byways to build up this magnificent organization, and let me beg of you, in God's holy name and in the name of the old flag, let the organization be used for the uplifting of the human race, but do not use it for the uplifting of yourself. Be true to your manhood; be true to your country; be true to the children yet unborn.

Now I want to say to you here that whether I die in jail or outside, I want to feel in the closing hours of my life that you have been true to each other, that you have been true to the principles of our forefathers. If you are true to these things the battle will end in victory for you.

[Minutes of the Special Convention of the UMWA, 1902, John Mitchell Papers, Catholic University of America, pp. 81–91.]

Remarks at the first convention
of the Industrial Workers of the World
Chicago, Illinois

In the spring of 1903 Mother Jones took time out from her duties with the miners' union to organize and carry out a march from Philadelphia to Oyster Bay, New York. Her army consisted of children who were workers in the textile mills in the Philadelphia area, and she hoped by her march to induce President Theodore Roosevelt to support the movement for a national child labor act. The president managed to avoid a confrontation with the general and her army, but the march attracted extensive newspaper coverage.

The remainder of 1903 and 1904 found Mother Jones spending most of her time in Colorado among the striking coal miners, but working also with the metalliferous miners in the Cripple Creek strike. On one occasion she was deported by militia from the state; on another, she was quarantined in Utah on the allegation that she had been exposed to smallpox. The bitter coal strike dragged on for over a year, and Mother Jones disagreed strongly when President Mitchell and other international officers encouraged a settlement that left the southern Colorado coal miners with nothing to show for their sacrifices. She resigned her position as international organizer for the UMWA and turned to a new possibility, a single union for all workers.

Mother Jones was the only woman among the twenty-seven signers of the manifesto which, early in 1905, called for a convention to organize all industrial workers. She served on the organizing committee of the Industrial Workers of the World, nominated Emma Langdon of Denver as the assistant secretary, and presided over the morning session of 28 June 1905. She made no major speech but participated in the business of the convention with a few remarks. One of the founders of the IWW, she had little to do with the organization in later years, although she remained friendly with many of the leaders.

§ § §

Secretary (to Mother Jones): How do you vote on the adoption of the constitution as a whole as amended?

Del. Mother Jones: I was not here when the report of the constitution was read, but I have sufficient confidence in the makeup of the Constitution Committee to commit my destinies to them, and therefore I vote yes.

§ § §

Del. Mother Jones: Owing to the fact that there is no money in the treasury to start this organization with, it seems to me it would be good policy to leave the decision of the salaries to the incoming officers. I for one am not afraid to trust those officers with fixing the salaries that will compensate the officers, and I think it will be satisfactory to the body as a whole. I do not know that this body here could now decide what is best to do with regard to the salaries, as long as we have no funds to begin with. When the funds grow larger and it is worth while making a decision about that, I believe that is time enough for us to begin.

The Chairman: Now Mother, will you please state that motion again? Just make the motion so that I can understand it.

Del. Mother Jones: My motion is to refer the salary question to the incoming officers, the Executive Board. [Seconded; later amended and passed.]

[*The Founding Convention of the IWW* (New York: Merit Publishers, 1969), pp. 29, 114, 127, 508, 555–56.]

Speech at the convention
of the United Mine Workers of America
Indianapolis, Indiana

After resigning as a UMWA organizer in 1904, Mother Jones became a lecturer for the Socialist Party of America, traveling through Indian Territory, Missouri, Texas, and Arizona for several years. From time to time she broke into her strenuous lecture tours to participate in strikes and organizing drives for several unions, including the Western Federation of Miners. But her main concern came to be the plight of Mexican revolutionists in the United States who were being arrested or deported by American authorities. She was particularly involved with Ricardo Flores Magón and his Partido Liberal, one of many movements which worked inside and outside of Mexico for the overthrow of the dictator-president, Porfirio Diaz. Campaigns to raise money for the revolutionaries' legal defense occupied most of her time in 1909 and 1910, and led to testimony before a congressional committee and interviews with President William Howard Taft on their behalf. She was also taking part, though not so intensely, in another legal defense campaign headed by Jane Addams for two radical Russian emigres, Christian Rudowitz and J. J. Pouren, whose extradition was being sought by the czarist government.

To raise money for the Mexican rebels, she came before the annual convention of the UMWA in 1909. Ironically, the president who introduced her to the delegates was Thomas L. Lewis, an old enemy who had been designated to take charge of the strike in northern West Virginia in 1902 after her arrest and who had gone on to become president of the UMWA. She regarded him as insufficiently militant and too accommodating to mine owners, for whom he became a spokesman after his terms as president. In the audience were William B. Wilson and Thomas D. Nicholls, former miners who were now congressmen from Pennsylvania, and William Green, future head of the AFL. She alludes to the Buck Stove and Range case, at that time being appealed to the Supreme Court, in her reference to the sentencing of Samuel Gompers and Frank Morrison to jail for violating an injunction forbidding them to name the company on a "We do not patronise" list in The American Federationist.

From the speech it is clear that Mother Jones was confident of being able to achieve her purpose, despite her years away from the organization.

§ § §

Permit me to extend to your worthy President my appreciation for his introduction. In the days of old when the revolutionists fought against the conditions that King George III was about to fasten upon them, could he have reached his claws in and have put them around Washington he would no doubt have hung him. Today, after a century or more of history in this nation, we find two diabolically tyrannous governments reaching their hands into this country and asking us to deliver men who have taken refuge here and surrender our rights to the czar of Russia and the military despot of Mexico. You will realize, my friends, that international economic interests are back of all this; you must realize that for this change in our nation's history there is a cause. Economic interests, both in Mexico and Russia, are dictating the policy of our government today—I mean the other fellow's government. As the method of production changes, the policy of the government must change to fit into it. Newspapers, magazines, churches, all must fit into the changed order. It governs home life, it governs national life, it governs the newspapers, it governs all avenues of educating the people.

To prove my statement I am going to give you an illustration, and I don't know of a better one to convince you that they have reached into the avenues of religious life to gain their ends. In Texas we had a fight with the Copper Queen Company. They sent to Joplin, Missouri, for scabs. And I want to say to you Missouri boys that you ought to get those scabs organized or lick hell out of them. They got about forty scabs. They were coming over the Rock Island road. I asked the conductor why the train was rocking so much, and he said there was a bunch of fellows on it going to Bisbee, Arizona. I asked him to take me to them, and he did, and I won over thirty-seven of them. The company had only three left. I sent them into Mexico. I said, "Go in there and earn four or five dollars a day and lick the other fellows who are scabbing." I had to stay in El Paso for a while. While I was there three miners from Mexico came along and they said, "Mother, we haven't had anything to eat today, or yesterday, or the day before, and we are dead broke." I said it would be remarkable to find a miner any other way. I said I had enough money to get them plenty to eat, but to be sure and steer clear of the charity organizations. I said, "I can tell you where you can go and get filled up. Go down to the saloon and get a free lunch, and they will give you a schooner of beer to wash it down. I will have a meeting on the street tonight, and as this is the tourist season the collection will be good and I will give it to you." We had a collection of eighteen dollars that night, and I gave them five dollars apiece and kept three dollars to get something to eat.

Then we saw a gang coming down the street and they were hammering each other. I asked a policeman what the trouble was. He said it was a row about Jesus. I said, "Who is in it?" He said, "The Salvation Army and the Volunteers are fighting about Jesus." I said, "That is a hell of a way to fight for Jesus. Why don't you arrest them?" He said it would not do because they were fighting for Jesus. They had beaten each other and the women had pulled each other's hair out. They were fighting to see which side Jesus belonged to. While they were hammering each other the collection that had been taken up rolled on the street. I jumped in and rescued the coin. When I had some coin I didn't have to fight for or talk for, but got it by bending my back a little, I said to the policeman: "Don't you want a drink on Jesus?" He said, "By God, I do!" so we went to a restaurant and got supper and some beer, and if any fellow wanted to get an extra jag on we were ready to pay for it because we had Jesus's money. When we had had our suppers we asked the restaurant keeper how much we owed him, and he said we didn't have to pay anything.

Those things fit into the changed order of things. That month I went up to Douglas, Arizona, to try and organize the smelters for the boys. One evening on the street one of the boys came to me and said, "Mother, there has been some dirty work going on at the jail." I said, "That is none of our business; let the jail take care of itself." Then he said, "But something is going on that is not straight. They brought a fellow there in an automobile and he screamed for his liberty. I think there is something wrong." Then a young fellow came along and said, "My God, Mother, they have kidnapped our young revolutionist [Manuel Sarabia], and they have run him across to Mexico and he will be murdered immediately!" We telegraphed to the governor and to Washington. We got Teddy out of bed that night, I can tell you. The next night we proposed to hold a mass meeting. I needn't tell you it is a very hard thing to wake people up in a town. There is a peculiar stupidity about them, and it is hard to wake them up at once to action. I said we would have to get at the papers in some way or put leaflets into the hands of the people.

I went to a fellow who was fighting the Copper Queen and asked if he could get out an extra. He said he hadn't the money, and I gave him twenty dollars and told him to go ahead. He did, and we flooded the town with them, and when we got to the meeting the crowd was dense all around that neighborhood. I needn't tell you, boys, I suppose, or most of you, that I long ago quit praying and took to swearing. If I pray I will have to wait until I am dead to get anything; but when I swear I get things here. Well, I was not very particular what I said at that meeting. I said, "Boys, if you will go with me we will go into Mexico and bring that fellow back; we will make Diaz give him up." They said they would go with me. I said, "There isn't a Pinkerton between here and hell we won't go hang," and they went and got the ropes. Well, we got the fellow back.

Here is the question you have to bear in mind, my brothers. Owing to international economic conditions this government is becoming officious in this matter. The Southern Pacific railroad, the Standard Oil and the copper interests are all back of this affair. They know if these men win out their doom is registered. Here are some pictures I wish to send down through the audience. These men were in the battle of Cannanea in 1896 when they drove those poor slaves back. These six were missing. Nobody could tell where they were for three or four weeks afterwards, and then they were found hanging as they appear in the pictures, with their flesh eaten off their bodies. The other two that led the strike in the Green mines of Cannanea were sent to prison at hard labor for fifteen years.

I have a letter here which says: "The cause of liberty is going back here every day. The Mexican who has the courage to speak out is arrested and punished to the limit. The Mexican consul is lying every day to his government in order to hold his dirty job of spy. God only knows what will become of those people. They have incarcerated many workers in Sonora for leading the strike." Talk about Russia! Mexico is worse than Russia, because Russia has a parliament but Mexico has nothing but Diaz! They have reached into St. Louis and have the Jeffries Detective agency to hound those men all over the continent, even into Canada. Those men were behind the bars when I was notified of it. They said they had not a dollar for their trials. One of their lawyers said he had been engaged in the last year fighting the case. He said that when he saw me he would tell me many things that would make my blood boil. He said they needed both money and moral support. He asked that whenever I spoke before a gathering to have a resolution adopted asking the government to intercede in their behalf.

I have a bunch of such letters, but as you have been held here a long time, with someone spouting something to you to make you good or bad, I won't detain you. I am not here to spout something to make you good or bad; I know you are good. I have fought with you long enough to know that you are about the best fighters this country has. You miners can revolutionize this whole country if you want to. I will tell you, Comrade Wilson, it is not waterways we need, but the ownership of those means so the boys will only work four hours a day. That is what we are after. You have to work too much.

President Lewis: We are willing to work less.

Mother Jones: Send more fighters to congress. I want to tell you, Wilson, you haven't made enough noise in congress. I have been watching you. You must understand that this government is not in Washington; it is in Wall Street. That is the trouble with those boys. That is why Russia can enter Sandy Hook and find written on the portals of the city, "Leave behind all hope of liberty, you who enter here." Morgan went to Russia last year and made a deal with the czar of Russia, and the czar said: "If you will surrender those refugees we will take care of your interests." Morgan got his order for thousands and thousands of tons of steel rails. Harriman and Morgan were fighting, and Harriman went to Morgan and said: "Let's fix it up," and they did, and instead of charging the Southern Pacific $29.00 a ton for rails they put them down to $23.00 a ton, and reduced the wages of the steel workers. If you fellows cannot make a noise in congress get down and out and we women will go there. If I was in congress I would tell Teddy to shut his mouth, not to be lecturing women about race suicide, when his own daughter has been doubled up with a congressman for three years and he hasn't said a word about race suicide to her yet.

Now, boys, remember that back of all these things is the question of economic interests. The Standard Oil owns the Green mines. Green owns seventy-five square miles of the people's land in Arizona. And we haven't an oligarchy in this country! You ought to be looking after those things, Wilson and Nicholls, not looking after waterways. Those little side-show issues don't amount to anything; what we are after today is to shake them up, because president, cabinet, congress, senate and the courts are simply putty in the hands of the Wall street gang of commercial pirates. If they weren't old Joe Cannon would not be boss and shooting off his bazoo. If there was just one woman in that congress old Joe Cannon would shake on his throne.

Now, I will tell you what I am here today for. I am not here to beg. I hate beggars; I don't want any begging machines; I want to do away with every begging parasite in the world. I want to fight and take what belongs to us. What I want here today with you is this: We have got to get those boys out of jail. We have got to let them live in this land; we have got to let them fight Mexico from here. And I am with those boys because Diaz and Harriman and Rockefeller and the whole push are together down there. They were down there wining and dining, and we paid for it. And while I am on this wining and dining subject I am going to say something about the board member from Pennsylvania, Miles Dougherty. I want to talk to you Pennsylvania fellows. You had an awful fight there. I was out West and took up a paper and read of Mr. Miles Dougherty sitting down with his feet under the table looking Mrs. Harriman square in the eye and putting a bowl of champagne inside of his stomach — "Here's a health to you, Mr. Belmont; here's a health to you, Miss Morgan, and here's a health to you, Mrs. Harriman." And then, when Mrs. Harriman and Miss Morgan walked down the street with Miles Dougherty the fellows over home in Pennsylvania said, "Don't you see how labor is getting recognized?" How labor is getting recognized! That's true, Mr. Lewis, as sure as you sit there, they said that about labor getting recognized! I want to tell you here the trouble with you is this: your skull hasn't developed only to the third degree. You would consider it an honor to go down the street with Miss Morgan, who never worked a day in her life. You would consider it an honor to dine with those fellows that skinned you and your children and murdered you in the mines, and while they were filling you with champagne they murdered us poor devils with bullets.

Now, I want some money. I am not here begging; I am simply here to wake you up and tell you to tell Mr. Lewis and Mr. Ryan—I am not going to say "brother" to him now because he is leaving me and going over to the other fellows. We fellows have got to stick together and fight, and if we get a jag on us we have to get a ten-cent drink of rotten whisky instead of champagne. And they are even trying to get that away from us! What we want to do is to fix things so we can drink the champagne and make them drink the whisky for a while. As I started out to say, I want you to tell Mr. Lewis and Mr. Ryan to give me this money. I want to get those men out of the clutch of Diaz. Down there in Mexico a Canadian and a British syndicate own all the railroads and street cars and the land is being surrendered to them. You must realize when men and women have the spirit of liberty in their breasts, even though for nineteen hundred years they have been trying to carry out Christ's doctrine, "Peace on earth, good will to men," there can be no peace on earth under present conditions. We have no peace on earth today. You are making an awful fuss about Mr. Gompers and Mr. Mitchell and Mr. Morrison going to jail. What is the matter with you? Didn't you build the jails? Didn't you put the iron bars on them? Didn't you pay the judges, and didn't you tell them when you paid them, "You can send us to jail if you want to?" They didn't put Mr. Lewis in jail because he was a good boy. If you weren't, they would have you locked up, too, wouldn't they, Mr. Lewis? But they are not going to; don't worry. Now, I wouldn't fight that injunction. It was perfectly legitimate. What I would do is to take my medicine and go to jail. I ought not to go because I didn't indorse the building of that jail; but the fellows that did ought to go. Do you think I would say a word to Judge Wright? I called the old judge [John J. Jackson] in [West] Virginia a scab. He said, "Did you call me a scab, Mrs. Jones?" I said, "Yes," and he gave me a document to show he was no scab, and I said I was glad an old scab judge didn't try me.

I read in the paper, Mr. Ryan, what you said about recalling the resolution. I don't know whether that was right, because the papers don't always tell the truth. The boycott is the only weapon left to labor outside of the ballot, and I would not only boycott the Buck Stove and Range Company, but I would boycott every minister that didn't have the union label on the outside of his church. We have nothing to take back. We are giving them everything. The parasites couldn't live on this earth without us; they are too lazy to work. The Rio Grande railroad murdered a lot of people the other day. The officials of the road were too stingy to put a man in the tower and pay him fifty dollars a month to watch the trains. They could not pay that, but they could pay a hundred thousand dollars a week before to fill their own stomachs. That's what you ought to bring up in Congress, Mr. Wilson.

Now, boys, I want you to ask Mr. Ryan to give me a thousand dollars out of the treasury. And, Mr. Lewis, if ever you get hard up I will go out and raise a thousand dollars for you. Lawyers are grafters, and they won't do a thing on God's earth unless you pay for it. They are like a lot of blood-suckers hanging around to see where they can get the blood to suck out of us. We have got to make a fight up there in Washington. We must let those fellows know we are alive. I want to say to you here before I close that they are more afraid of the organized body of workers than they are of all the political bodies of the country. If we can thoroughly organize and educate our people we can stop every wheel in the country and we can make those fellows stop eating. When we do that we will spend what belongs to us and they will work as we will rest. If you cannot give me the money out of your pockets — and I don't believe you can, because those old pauper leeches have been here bleeding you — I will get it from the locals. The mine owners bleed you first, and then the people here begin. I saw one of those leeches over at the hotel last night with a nice little basket shaking at you and asking you to put in. She was dressed like one of those parasites. What I want you to do is to vote me a thousand dollars, and then Mr. Ryan will have to pay it to me whether he wants to or not.

I am not going to hold you here any longer. Say, you ought to be out in the country with me. We have great times out there in the West, and I am going to stay there for quite a while. An old fellow said the other day in Pittsburgh, speaking of me, "That old devil ought to die!" What is the matter with him? Why, I am only seventy-three years young and I have a contract with God to let me stay here many more to help clean up that old gang.

[J. H. Walker moved $1,000 for the defense of the Mexicans. Seconded. Amended to $5,000. Laid on the table. Some discussion between William Green and J. H. Walker over need for more information. Mother Jones joined in:]

When Rudovits and Pouren were being tried a strong committee in Chicago was attending to their affair, but no one was pleading the case of the brave fighters on the border line within the clutches of Diaz and Standard Oil. Moyer wrote to me and I said, "Which way will I go, east or west, to stir up sentiment?" He told me to go east. I send this money through Brother Germer and every dollar is registered in East St. Louis. Every dollar goes out to Mr. Moyer of the Western Federation of Miners. I would trust them with the United States treasury, and I wish to God we had it! I don't want any of the money; I am responsible for every dollar I collect. If you don't find it recorded in the miners' magazine, call me up and put me in jail if you want to. I am collecting for those boys in the West, and I propose to get them out if I have to go down to congress and ask for an appropriation. Those boys out on the border line won't go back to Diaz. Now, Mr. Green, if you have any objections to donating the thousand dollars, keep it and I will get the thousand dollars out of your boys in the locals. I have already got $1,200.

[Green denied any implication that the money was not safe; he merely wanted the matter to be considered calmly. More money might be necessary, but it should properly be referred to the Committee on Resolutions. The convention eventually took that course. Mother Jones did not participate further in the meeting.]

[*UMWA Proceedings* (Indianapolis: Cheltenham Press, 1909), pp. 375–82.]

Speech at a convention
of the United Mine Workers of America
Indianapolis, Indiana

Two days later, Mother Jones returned to the platform to thank the delegates for voting to contribute a thousand dollars to the defense fund for the Mexican revolutionaries, but she devoted most of her speech to encouraging the miners to present a united front to outsiders and to the need for the solidarity of all laborers.

§ § §

In behalf of our brothers who are lying in the bastile of capitalism because they dared to raise their voices in behalf of their oppressed and murdered brothers in Mexico, I tender to you my deepest and most heartfelt appreciation of the resolution and donation to them. It is not charity; it is our duty even to go with them and give our lives for a cause so great. Never in human history before were men and women called upon to link hands in the mighty battle for the emancipation of the working class from the robbing class. Our brothers are behind the bars, and it lies with you and with me to do our part to free them. I extend to you my deep appreciation for the generous donation you gave to them. And when your turn comes they will be on deck to do their part for you. They will never surrender the rights of labor to the ruling class, even if they die in its defense.

Now, my brothers, you and I are not going to part. We have fought many battles together, and we have marched the highways together. Brave hearts marched with us then. Lying in lonely graves are some of the men who laid the foundation for this great and magnificent organization that you represent here today. Let me say to you, my brothers, the hand of capitalism is in your convention. The Standard Oil has its tools on the floor of your convention and they are trying to divide the forces. I intended to bring a letter over with me to read to you. I received the letter some time ago from one within the Standard Oil. In writing that letter he said, speaking of the Western Federation of Miners, "The secret service men of the Standard Oil I know were in that organization and kept the members in a turmoil the whole winter. The miners did get the best of the secret service men, but the machinists fell victims to their wiles." I say to you, my brothers, today to be cautious because every eye is on this convention. Down in the state I went to a bank to get a check cashed.

I took a miner with me, and the banker said to him, "You are going to have war up there in Indianapolis at your convention, aren't you?" The miner said, "What about?" "Oh, they are going to have a big explosion there." "I don't know," said the miner, "I haven't heard about it." "Yes, they are going to have war." Of course I had to chip in then, and I said, "If we have a family row it is none of your business. We will settle our row ourselves, and after you are through if you begin to attack us we will fight you into hell, for the whole bunch of us will get together to do it."

Now don't give those fellows the satisfaction of seeing you have a row here. We have made mistakes, and we will make them again; we can't help it, but when this convention closes—and I want this registered by your reporter down there—every one here will be united to fight our masters. We are going to settle our difficulties. No family ever succeeded very well that did not hammer one another once in a while. We must hammer President Lewis once in a while to keep him thin or he will get to look like old Taft. When this convention assembles next year I am going to try to be here, and I am going to try to bring your Mexican brothers with me. I am going to present them to this convention and get them acquainted with you.

Now, my boys, I want you to be good. You know there was a time in our convention here when Indianapolis people thought they had to fill the miners with booze. The corridor used to be lined with beer bottles every time they were going to give us a banquet. The banquet they used to give us was to sell beer for a trust. We concluded that didn't pay, so we made them clean out the beer. And we will make them clean out their smokers by and by and put a stop to all this nonsense. We are not going to take any taffy; we are going to get down to solid business.

Now I want to say something to Missouri about this organizing business. Some of the delegates took exceptions to what I said here the other day, and said that Joplin belongs to the Western Federation of Miners. There must be no line drawn. Whenever you can organize a man bring him into the United Mine Workers, bring him into the Western Federation, bring him into the Carpenters' Union—bring him into any union. Whenever you do that you have taken one away from the common enemy and joined him with you to fight the common enemy. When I am on the street cars with organized men I bring up their conditions before them. I make it a point to get on the cars early in the morning and talk to them and show the necessity of getting together. I try to bring the farmers with us also, because the stronger we grow numerically the weaker the other fellow grows. I have got no pet organization. Wherever labor is in a struggle with the enemy, the name of the organization cuts no figure with me, I am there in the fight. I did speak of Joplin the other day. Why? Because in my experience in the West I found the companies could go to Joplin and get scabs and bring them on to break strikes. Because you live in Missouri close to that region you should do what you can to organize Joplin and bring them with us. You must remember it is the unorganized man and the modern machine that will lick you by and by. It is the brain of the genius working out on modern lines that is going to interfere with your prosperity by and by, and every uneducated, every undeveloped worker will be used by that class to fight us. It is no reflection on you brave boys of Missouri. I simply called attention to that nest of scabs, and I advise you to get them organized and educated. And organize and educate them not only in Joplin, but wherever you find them.

The man who has to be paid for organizing labor — well, I don't care much about him. Each one of us should be an organizer, and we should not wait for any commission from any president. We should all be organizers in every field, and not only organize the workers, but those poor slaves of the pen as well and get them with us. I mean you, you newspaper boys. One of them said the other day he had the headache because he didn't sleep enough. Of course he had, and by and by his skull will get so dumb he won't know what he is writing. Now, boys, I am going down through the State, and probably will go West after awhile. I promised to go to New York State to do some work in some prominent meetings.

In closing I want to say to you, shake hands with each other and let the boys who are here for the paper spread the news that you are the jolliest, most harmonious and loving family there is in the nation. On you and around you are built other organizations. If you become weak the forces of every craft will become weak. When you become strong you strengthen the forces of every other craft. You must not be narrow. For the first time in human history we are able today to touch the wire and even over in Japan we can say, "What are you doing for the workers?" And in the morning you will get the returns, "We held a tremendous meeting last night, and we, too, are marching on to claim our own with you, the workers of America." Don't let the tools of capitalism sit in this convention and tell you to get up and give some one hell! Get up and throw him out! Stop that, my friends. Transact your business and go home. You need the dollars you are spending in Indianapolis. The longer you stay the more the merchants will get and the less you will have. Now, good bye, and God bless you.

A motion was made and seconded that a vote of thanks be tendered Mother Jones.

Mother Jones: You have been trained under the capitalists. We don't owe a vote of thanks to any living being on earth; but we owe a vote of condemnation to every human being that does not rise up and do his duty.

[*UMWA Proceedings,* (Indianapolis: Cheltenham Press, 1909), pp. 517-19.]

Speech at the convention
of the United Mine Workers of America
Indianapolis, Indiana

When Mother Jones returned in 1910 to address the UMWA convention, she reported on some of her activities of the past year, which had been devoted largely to her crusade on behalf of Mexican revolutionaries. She had spoken frequently from Texas to Minnesota and from Denver to New York, raising some four thousand dollars for their defense. In November and December she was in New York speaking for the Mexicans at Cooper Union and the Berkeley Theater, but she took time out from her crusade to lend her efforts to the shirtwaist makers' strike in December. Shortly thereafter she accepted the invitation of the leaders of the brewers' union to conduct an organizing drive among the women who worked in the Milwaukee breweries.

Her speech encompassed these topics but ranged much more widely, touching on the dangers of foreign competition, the influence of manufacturers in government as reflected in the Danbury Hatters decision of the Supreme Court and the current Buck Stove and Range case, the breaking up of the Department of Commerce and Labor, and, in the field of general relations of manufacturers and workers, the National Civic Federation, an organization sponsored by Marcus A. Hanna to encourage cooperation between capital and labor. She opposed the National Civic Federation as a stalking-horse for capitalism; instead, she called the delegates to militant, aggressive unionism.

§   §   §

Mr. President and Fellow Workers: The struggle of the workers down the ages has been that of blood; it has been that of hunger. Today the struggle is reaching its final crisis. The forces are lined up against us. Today we are waiting for the last great battle of man with man, and when this battle is over humanity will be free, there will be no robber class and no working class. I heard a speaker who represented the steel industry portray the conditions of the workers in his organization. It is well to consider where we stand today. We are up against a condition unknown to the industrial bodies of this nation in its past history. Go over to China and you will find 20,000 men working in one mill alone, and for his work each one receives 7 cents a day. You can see they have almost crushed out the organization of steel workers, and they are reaching out to crush other organizations. Therefore it is necessary for us to unite our forces. I agree with the Vice-President of this organization and with the president of Illinois that the time is here when the steel workers, the mine workers and the railroad men must join hands and say to the pirates of the human race that they can no longer rob us and murder us.

When we come to consider that the American capitalists are investing in China with the idea of crushing out the unions of America it is time for us to wake from our slumbers. It is not alone in China they are doing this, but across our borders in Mexico you will find a $50,000,000 steel plant and a million dollar smelter. All along the line they are making moves. They do not go there to establish schools to make good mechanics. Modern ingenuity has made it possible for a child to run some of the machines and the child will get the job while the men must tramp. There are two forces in this and in every other nation of the world today. One force is the taker and the other force is the maker. The taker manufactures criminals and destroys womanhood and childhood.

When I went to the federal prison in Leavenworth this spring to get some documents to carry to the President in regard to an injustice that was done the revolutionists of Mexico, I stood in the corridor with the chaplain of the institution, and before us marched 800 men from their lunch to their different posts. I said to the chaplain, "We are neither civilized nor christianized when we will build an institution and support a condition that manufactures criminals." When I looked into the faces of those men I concluded there were not forty among the whole number who could not have been made good citizens under a proper civilization. You remember that when France turned over her criminals to DeLesseps he was told, "Kill those devils in the trenches! Don't let one of them ever come back alive!" DeLesseps took the chain off the prisoners and said, "Men, you are in a new world under new conditions; you will have no master, and I will give you four dollars a day. All I ask of you is to be men." In four weeks the earnings of those men were going home through the postoffice to their children. It is a wrong form of government we are living under, and we, the workers, stand for the overthrow of the whole damnable institution.

I carried those documents to the President of the United States and presented them to him in the presence of Mr. Powderly. He took them from me, and I made a statement of what they contained. He said, "Mother Jones, if I gave you the pardoning power there wouldn't be any one left in the penitentiaries." I said, "Mr. President, if this nation spent half the money and half the energy to give men a chance to keep out of the penitentiary it does to force them in we would not need any penitentiaries."

When you fellows met in Pittsburgh and talked the steel combination over a few weeks ago Mr. Morgan went up to see Mr. Taft and talked to him. He served notice on Taft of what he should do in the case, and Taft did it. We have been beggars too long. If I had my way about it every blamed one of you would go to Washington today and tell old Joe Cannon to get out and we would get in. I hear you complain about the jails. What is the matter with the jails? Don't we build them? They are the national reception parlors for the working class. A lot of us were in jail and we will go again. A lot of us who are here went to jail but when we came out we did not me-ow about it, we said we would raise the flag of revolt and we would face the guns and the courts and the jails again, and the whole infernal bunch of robbers and thieves and plunderers. We haven't taken any backwater yet and we don't intend to. Put that down, Mr. Newspaper Man.

A Delegate: Tell us about the Civic Federation, Mother Jones.

Mother Jones: Don't mention it! I have been watching it for ten years and I have had the guns ready. All the Civic Federation members have done is to fill their stomachs until every one of them has a paunch on him as big as old Taft's.

A Delegate: You are right.

Mother Jones: Of course I am. Isn't it interesting to see a lot of labor leaders going to Mrs. Harriman's and after they have filled their stomachs hearing Mrs. Harriman say, "I have received such an inspiration from you." Why didn't she send some of the money her husband robbed the people of to Cherry. If you will vacate the chair for two weeks, Mr. President, I will attend to it. I will take the matter to Congress and say, "You have stood for the murder of four hundred of our men; now put up $4,000,000." If you men want to take any more of that medicine go home and put on mother hubbards and we women will go out and give them hell!

Now I can't stay much longer. I have got to take a train. You had a McKees Rocks case, where men were slaughtered and shot down. You had an anthracite strike where men were shot, but Roosevelt came in there and stuck his finger in that pie. Then you had a Colorado strike, but he sent the thugs out there to shoot us down, and your Morgan's Civic Federation never said a word about it; it stood for our being shot. What good is that Federation? Where does the money come from that runs it? It comes from Morgan, Belmont, Harriman and old Oily John. Think of the shirt waist makers, those little girls of sixteen who are on strike in New York, who took the contract the Civic Federation wanted to make for them and tore it up on the platform. That Civic Federation is a job making business. Get a move on you because if you don't you will have to. The government is running a Department of Labor and Commerce in Washington. It was trying to take off the pressure from the cities where scabs were found and put them on the farm, and the Civic Federation stepped in and demanded of the government to surrender the Department of Labor and Commerce. It has been surrendered. You see, step by step, what they are doing. They don't tell those things, but I will if I am hung for it. The trouble with us is this: We put men in office, we pay them, we eulogize them. There never was a labor leader on the face of the earth who won a strike—not even you, Mr. Fairley. I will tell you who win the strikes. The women who go hungry, the men who march into jails, the men who go to jail and do not carry their cases to the Supreme Court. When the representative of the shoe workers said the other day that you went home and gave your money to your wives and they went out and bought scab goods for them, I wanted to ask him how much money the women get to spend whose husbands did not work all last winter in the anthracite region? The operators went to the banks to see who had money there so they could collect their rents. How much money can a woman spend foolishly who gets five or six dollars a week to support five or six children and send them to school. You haven't a banker in this nation who is such a financier as that woman is. Don't find fault with the women. If you stand for a system that robs them and degrades them you are no better than Morgan.

I don't stand for the jails, but I am not grumbling about them, although I am able to go in at any time. I went to Washington at the request of the brewery workers. I went into the breweries and looked after the condition of the women workers. Those women and girls are getting three dollars a week. They put men out of work, but they do not get enough to support themselves. I am going to Milwaukee to organize those girls in the breweries. We are also going to organize them in the breweries in St. Louis. After that I am going into the anthracite region and bring on another war if you don't move up. I want you to pass a resolution here and make a demand and send it to President Taft telling him we cannot be civilized, that we are trampling on all the conditions for which our fathers fought long years ago when we allow conditions to exist such as we have in the Southwest where they are allowed to take those Mexicans and put them in jail without a just cause and keep them there. To the everlasting disgrace of the American people they stood for it, and applauded when Taft shook hands with the greatest tyrant that ever lived on earth. A greater murderer never lived than Diaz.

Turn the jails into school rooms, take the children out of the mills and factories and sweat shops and allow them to develop their bodies and their minds. I am in favor of putting the jailer to do an honest day's work instead of turning keys on us. I want to congratulate you on the step taken here today, the amalgamation of the forces. We are facing a mighty crisis; and it behooves us all to clasp hands together and say we are in one fight. I was not opposed to your discussions here. They were healthy discussions, they cleared up any doubts we had, and when this convention closes every man within these walls should clasp hands and pledge themselves to go forth and fight for a nobler civilization, for a collective ownership of the mines and railroads, the telegraph, telephone, newspapers and everything else. We stand for the ownership of all these things, and then we will get what belongs to us and not until then.

[*UMWA Proceedings* (Indianapolis: Cheltenham Press, 1910), pp. 420–24.]

Speech at a special convention
of the United Mine Workers of America
Cincinnati, Ohio

Two months later, when Mother Jones returned to the UMWA special convention in Cincinnati, she was seeking their aid in her efforts to organize the women brewery workers in Wisconsin. Since January she had been investigating and agitating in Milwaukee, and she was now asking the miners to threaten to boycott Milwaukee beer. She was also threatening the brewery owners with an appeal to the Wisconsin legislature for regulatory legislation. When she asked for, and the miners passed, a resolution for a boycott of Milwaukee beer, they were consciously challenging court decisions of the last few years that had rendered this weapon of union struggle a two-edged sword; Samuel Gompers, Frank Morrison, and John Mitchell were all still under jail sentences for violating injunctions against boycott notices and resolutions in the Buck Stove and Range case.

Whether it was because of the threat of the miners' boycott or for other reasons, the brewery operators gave way, and the women bottle cleaners were organized and recognized by May. It was one of Mother Jones's most successful organizing drives.

§ § §

I am not here today to talk on the mining industry. Another phase of the industrial conflict has brought me here. With the wonderfully rapid changes in the field of economics we have brought in a new condition, something unknown in the history of the nation before. For the last two months I have been in Milwaukee, Wisconsin, going through the breweries studying the phase of the industry that affects women. I have come to the conclusion that the breweries are no place for women workers; but if economic conditions enforce the women to abandon their homes they have to find some place to earn their bread. I went to the head of one of the firms and said to him, "Your foreman uses the most beastly language to those women. You realize as well as I do that in this nation there is growing a terrific sentiment against your industry. You realize as well as I do that your industry is the product of the profit system, and while the profit system lasts your industry will go on, either openly or secretly. Therefore I have come to you to show how you can correct some of the horrors existing in your institution." I told him the language used by those men to the women who worked in the breweries would not sound well in print. He said, "I thank you for coming here."

I went to Milwaukee at the request of the Brewery Workers' organization. There are between 600 and 700 girls and women working in those breweries, and the average wage is from $2.50 to $3.00 a week. They work in the bottle-washing department, where the work is very disagreeable, as their clothing becomes very wet. Many of them are foreigners, but some of them are American born. I tremble for the future of some of the young girls who were driven to such work. Some statesman once said in the early days of this country, "When a nation sends her old to the poor house and her young to the scaffold and to the jails that nation is in its decline, there is something wrong with it." When a nation stands for its women being dragged from their homes and driven to do such work for the master class and to be ground into profit for them there is something wrong.

These breweries are making millions upon millions of dollars. They prohibit the organization of the girls and women that are working for them, and discharge them as soon as they join a union. I have been there for two months, and while some of them are organized, as soon as the bosses get on to it they are discharged under one pretext or another. I went to Blatz's brewery and I said to the proprietor, "I would like to go through your brewery." He said, "We held a meeting of the Brewers' Association when we heard you were in Milwaukee and we concluded we could not allow our girls to be organized. They get married and go away and they don't need to be organized."

I said, "If women have to go into the industries we need to get them together to show them the future stage of civilization. You surely will help me to do that?" He said, "I will not. You cannot go into the breweries." I said, "There is one place you can't keep me out of and that is the legislature of Wisconsin. I will go there and ask the legislators if they can afford to have the women of the state slaughtered to build a monument to you."

Like the mine owners, the brewery owners do not know everything. There is a good deal they don't know. The only thing they are expert in is getting profit and crushing us and degrading us. I wrote an article on this, or rather I gave the points and some one else wrote it — I didn't know enough to write it myself. I belong to the working class and you know we don't have time to go to school. There is only one school we get proficient in and that is the school of hard knocks and hunger.

Now I want to tell you why I am here. I want to ask this body of men to help those girls. You can go into any mining camp — and very few of them I haven't been in — and find that Milwaukee beer is sold there. Those girls working in those breweries tell me how good it would be if they could get only $7 a week. One told me that in two weeks she only earned $5, and another said that in two weeks she only earned $6. Some of them said they only earned enough to pay their room rent, and that they washed dishes and helped the woman where they boarded for their meals. These conditions exist in the Milwaukee breweries. I have tried every way to organize the girls peacefully and without hitting the brewery owners; but I have concluded that the only way to hurt them is to touch their pockets, and therefore I want this convention to help me. If you could see the pictures I have seen there is not one of you who would not rise to your feet and pass the resolution that will be presented to you, not one of you that would not pledge yourselves not to drink a glass of Milwaukee beer or see that not a glass is sold in any mining camp in the country until those girls are organized.

When this nation gives back to her womanhood the economic rights that have been stolen from them; when this nation gives back to childhood the right to be well born and well cared for; when this nation gives back to the motherhood of the nation the time to mold and train the children well, want will cease, robbery will cease, jails will be no more, there will be institutions for the uplift of the race, not for its degradation.

I want you not only to pass this resolution in regard to the brewery workers, but I want you to help the Cigar Workers who are fighting in this city. I honor them for their spirit of revolt. I am going away in a day or so. I am going West. I will be back in Milwaukee when I have touched the brewers' pockets. When we find we have over 500,000 miners who will not drink a glass of Milwaukee beer in any place, north, south, east or west, the breweries of Milwaukee will be brought to time.

A Delegate: Judge Jackson will get hold of you, Mother.

Mother Jones: The old fellow is dead, my friend, and I don't know whether he's in heaven or hell. Now I want you to pass the resolution that will be presented and pass it strong, because I am going to send a copy to the Brewers' Association, and I am going before the Wisconsin legislature to have a bill passed providing that no girls can work in breweries.

Mr. Newspaperman, I want you to print what I have said!

Now you have been here a long time, boys, taking a rest; you have been having a picnic. I want to tell you if they force the fight we are all in trim to give them the damnedest fight they have ever had. One of the boys said I was looking well. Of course I am. There is going to be a racket and I am going to be in it! When I get a lick at them it makes me young again. I am going to watch you! Line up, and if you have got to give those fellows a fight they will regret they have brought it on. There is a different feeling in the country now to what there was a few years ago. We are ready for war now. When I went to see the big gun of the nation, his royal nibs, Taft, I was not able to hit him in the eye, but a bug did it for me. He was out automobiling and all the big guns were shaking hands with him.

I thought, "What a lot of lickspittles!" A bug flew in his eye, and when I saw him he had a curtain over it, but he had one eye he could see me with. After a little conversation I said to him, "You had better not see any one else today, but go home and rest, because before the four years are at an end you will need your two eyes and your two ears, because there will be something doing in this country." And so there will. Get *The Appeal to Reason* and read it. When Turner undertook to show up the American capitalistic combine in Mexico *The American Magazine* closed out the articles immediately. When a man went to California to look over the articles he said, "I cannot get a magazine in America to take them up." I said, "Of course, because the magazines and papers are controlled by the Wall Street gang of commercial pirates and they don't want their crimes known by the people." Now get the paper I spoke of and you will be able to read the articles. They will show how the mine owners of the United States are in league with the Guggenheims and the Standard Oil people getting the peons down there to work cheap. The President's own brother has 250,000 acres in Texas with Mexican peons working on it for a few cents a day. That is the way they protect the American workingman!

Now pass that resolution. Mr. Lewis, when that fight comes on I will be with you to the last ditch—I will help you out.

[*UMWA Proceedings* (Indianapolis: Cheltenham Press, 1910), pp. 60–63.]

Speech at the convention
of the United Mine Workers of America
Columbus, Ohio

The convention of the UMWA in Columbus in 1911 was a homecoming for Mother Jones. The new president, John P. White, was an old friend, and she had made arrangements with him to go back on the payroll as an organizer, with the understanding that she would set her own agenda. She had already gone on a speaking tour in the anthracite field to reinvigorate the union there and had made a foray into the long and bitter strike in the Irwin field in Pennsylvania. She intended to return there and then go out to Colorado, where coal miners were once again on strike. She had had no use for the accommodationist Tom Lewis, who was presiding over his last session of the union before White took over as president. With White, and his successor, Frank Hayes, she was able to work in harmony for the next nine years.

She was also in the process of breaking with the Socialist Party, for whom she had lectured in recent years. After several months of organizing in Milwaukee, beginning in January, she attended a Socialist meeting in Cincinnati in June, where she fell seriously ill for about a week; she recovered in time, however, to testify before a congressional committee on behalf of the Mexican revolutionaries. She had resented and deplored the fact that the Socialists had not officially supported her attempts to assist the Mexicans, and she became embroiled in a quarrel with J. Mahlon Barnes, the party secretary, against whom she filed charges of financial misconduct.

The Socialist investigation of her charges against the secretary were still under way when she attended the miners' convention in January, 1911. The UMWA had been torn by internal dissension, particularly during the last years of Tom Lewis's presidency, but with the militant John P. White at the helm she looked forward to a more unified and aggressive administration where her talents would have full scope. She took up her new duties with the union with no sign of regret that her days as an official Socialist lecturer were coming to an end.

§ § §

President Lewis: Mother Jones is here. A motion was unanimously adopted yesterday to invite Mother Jones to address this convention at

9 o'clock this morning. That carried with it that it would be any time to suit her convenience. I believe most, if not all, the delegates in this convention know Mother Jones and know of her work in behalf of the mine workers and the wage earners of the entire country. I take pleasure now in both introducing and presenting to you Mother Jones, who will address the convention.

Mother Jones: The time is short and I will not wear you out. I know a lot of you here want to go out and get a drink.

President Lewis: There is no time limit to your speech, and when we adjourn we will convene that much later after dinner.

Mother Jones: Brothers of this convention, perhaps never in the history of the mine workers was there a more important convention than this. The eyes of the world are resting today and all other days you are in session on this hall. The master class is watching your convention with keen interest. And so I say to you, be wise, be prudent in your actions. Think before you act. Don't give the master class any weapon to strike you with and laugh about. Let us have the laugh on them.

Now, my brothers, the last year has been a trying year for organized labor all along the line. There have been some wonderful fights on the industrial field. It has not been alone the miners, it has not been alone the steel workers. For the first time, perhaps, the women in the industrial field have begun to awaken to their condition of slavery. In New York and Philadelphia the women arrayed themselves in battle, and they gave battle fearlessly. They were clubbed, they were jailed, they were insulted, but they bore it all for a principle they believed in. Never can a complete victory be won until the woman awakens to her condition. We must realize that the woman is the foundation of government; that no government is greater or ever can be greater than the woman. It was once asked of Napoleon how the French nation could become a great nation. He considered a moment and then said: "Never until you have a great motherhood. When you have that you have a great nation."

And so it is with us in this nation. Never as long as the women are unorganized, as long as they devote their time to women's clubs and to the ballot, and to a lot of old meow things that don't concern us at all and have no bearing on the industrial battle, can we succeed, and the men will have to make the battle alone. But the century is here when the woman is going to take a mighty hand in these battles, and then we will fight it out and fight it to a finish. Put that down, Mr. Reporter!

Now, I want to call your attention to some things. The industrial war is on in this country. Why? Because modern machinery plays a greater part in the production of wealth in this nation than it does in any other nation of the world. The class that owns the machine owns the government, it owns the governors, it owns the courts and it owns the public officials all along the line. There may be an exception, but on the whole it is true. It certainly owns the Governor of Ohio [Judson Harmon]. Put it down, Mr. Reporter, that I said so! First the Governor of Ohio brought out his dogs of war to turn them on the steel workers. That cost this State $250,000. Then he brought them out and turned them on the street car strikers and undertook to lick them into submission. I want to serve notice on the Governor of Ohio that he has never licked labor into submission and never will, and by the eternal gods we will lick him into submission before we are through!

I have not forgotten Harmon. He brought the bayonets out in '94 — not the state bayonets, but the federal bayonets, to shoot us down in Chicago. He was Attorney-General and Cleveland was President. Cleveland was off on a drunk and the other fellow had the job. I generally keep tab on what these fellows do. Well, the steel workers are not licked yet. They are going to come to the front one of these days, and when they do they will be heard from.

Now, you have a fight of the miners in Colorado. You have got to call a strike in the Southern field and lick the Colorado Fuel and Iron Company out of its boots. You cannot win the Northern field until you take a hand in the Southern field. You could have won in Colorado at one time. You had the strike in your own hands, but you undertook to make a settlement in the Northern field and left the Southern field to fight the battle alone. Then they were able to turn their batteries. The Northern field furnished coal for the State institutions, and the result was their rotten carcasses got heated up and they could turn the bayonets on you. I am for making a fight on the whole bunch. If you don't want to do it alone, I will go there and take a hand in it and give them hell.

When I heard those fellows talking about a dual organization here on this floor I was disgusted — it was enough to make a dog sick! Let me say to you the only real dual organization there is in the country is the Civic Federation and the gang of robbers of Wall street. That is the dual organization against labor, and I want to tell you fellows in the central field to bury your hatchet, take a day off and get your skulls to working instead of your jaws. I happened to be in the central field a long time ago, before those fellows who are blowing off hot air here were in the union — they were scabbing. I am glad you are in the union, however. I know how a scab is made up. One time there was an old barrel up near heaven, and all of heaven got permeated with the odor. God Almighty said, "What is that stuff that smells so?" He was told that it was some rotten chemical down there in a barrel and was asked what could be done with it. He said, "Spill it in a lot of bad clay and maybe you can turn out a scab." That is what a scab is made of, and he has been rotten all down the ages. We have a few scabs in Pennsylvania, Mr. President, and once in a while we get hold of one of them and lick him. I have licked lots of them, and I expect to lick more of them before I die.

Now, I am going to speak to you on this question of machinery, and I want to draw your attention to the fact that they have reached into China and are developing the industries there. Capitalism is in business for profit, and wherever it is going to realize the most profit out of human blood there it is going. So they have reached into China, where they can hire men for eight cents and ten cents a day. The result is we are feeling it here all along the line. The merchants in Westmoreland county, at Greensburg, called the Council together and asked them if they would not pass an ordinance demanding that the mounted constabulary be placed in Greensburg, They wanted one placed in each hotel to take care of the hotelkeepers. They said the miners were in a terrible way and the scabs were afraid to come into town. The scabs were not a bit afraid to come into town, but the merchants were so full of greed and avarice they did not realize where they were struck. They wanted the constabulary to protect them against a handful of miners, but they never thought of calling in the constabulary to see after the Standard Oil, that has taken over eighty-four of the great department stores in this country. It is the onward march of civilization. And so it must be with us; we must centralize our forces to one great, mighty column.

If there is an organization in this land or in any other land the master classes are afraid of, if there is an organization they want to split in two, it is the United Mine Workers of America. They are putting up every sort of game to divide our forces, but they are going to get left, my friends. We may have a little housecleaning, we may have a little jawing and chewing the rag; but when the time comes we will line up and give the master class what they have been looking for. In Colorado you have sixteen men in jail. A distinguished judge, owned body and soul and brains — and he never had any too much brains — by the corporations, has put sixteen of our men in jail. Let me serve notice on the judges of this country that the day is not far distant when we will put every capitalist judge in jail and make a man out of him. That day is coming and it is not far away. Put that down, Mr. Reporter, so the judges will know it!

They take our boys and for no cause on earth put them in jail. In Greensburg they hauled them all over the county, and gave them nothing to eat until the miners came along, put up their treasury, bailed them out and they went back again to help their brothers strikers. They are trying to create a riot. Fellows will go out and say, "Why the miners are very peaceful." I wonder what those fellows think? We will be peaceful while they are skinning us. We are at war, and there is no war so fierce as an industrial battle. No war on the battle field of the world's history can equal an industrial battle.

Now, I want to speak on the strike in Westmoreland county. I did not go in there until a little late. I was engaged on the Mexican case, and had to carry it to Washington. I forced it myself without any aid from any human being. Nobody else knew anything about it. I spent nights awake and days alone. I knew if I went and secured counsel it might be bought. It was a grave and mighty question, and I knew its importance to the labor movement, so I worked it out as best I could. I got some documents from the federal prison in Arizona. The men had them stolen out to me. They were forwarded to me and I sat up at night to read them. I said to myself that the liberties of the whole American people were at stake if that thing was not brought into the public eye.

Then I went to President Taft. I did not present the documents to him, but I made statements. He said, "Mother, if you bring me some evidence in regard to this I will go over it myself." I said, "Very well, Mr. President; that is all I can expect you to do." Then he said, "They were not anarchists, were they?" "They don't know any more about anarchy than a dog does about his father, because the real anarchists of this country are the Supreme Court judges, the Wall street gang and the Governor of Ohio. They don't understand the definition of anarchy. I would have told him something about anarchy, but I had a mission there and I thought I would use a little diplomacy and a little taffy. Even if he is President, he will swallow that as well as the rest of us. His eye was hurt and I said he ought not to use it any more that day. He said he had been out in his automobile and a bug got in his eye. I never get hit in the eye automobiling, because I never go riding. I said: "Mr. President, don't see any more people today; that eye needs a rest. Before you are four years in this office you will need the use of your two eyes and your two ears." He said, "Do you think I will, Mother?" I said, "I am sure of it."

I didn't hear very much from the President. I was telegraphed for to go to San Antonio, where they were arresting a lot of those men. I want to show how closely we are watched. The editor of a paper there came to me in the afternoon and said: "Mother, you had better be careful in your speech tonight. The Mexican government has filled the city with secret service men." "I am much obliged for the information," I said, "but I want to tell you that old Diaz, the bloody murderer, can come here himself and I will talk all I want to." I said I was not going to be careful; that I was going to say what I pleased, and even if they hung me for it I would say it before I was hung.

We held five meetings. I went to the United States marshal to get permission to see some of the revolutionists who were in jail. The marshal and the attorney were in the marshal's office. The marshal gave me a permit to go to the jail. While I was there they got to talking about guns. It seems they went into a little Mexican cabin and found a couple of old

48

broken pistols you couldn't shoot a cat with. I said: "I don't see why you are so afraid of guns. Didn't Washington use guns? Wasn't the victory of this nation won with guns? Didn't we make the Southern Confederacy come back into the Union by the use of guns?" Then I said, "If it is necessary to use guns to protect these revolutionists, we will do it." He said, "That is right." He came to the meetings every night, and he threw money into the collection. The secret service men got all the talk they wanted. The night I closed my meeting I told them in my speech I was going to El Paso. I said, "I want all the dogs of war belonging to Diaz and the secret service men to come down there, because I am going to raise a row with old Diaz."

To tell the truth I was going to the Black Hills to speak on Labor Day, but I thought I would throw them off my track. A fellow has a job on his hands to get the best of a woman, even if he is a slick sleuth of a detective. All my mail went to El Paso and I had to write there to have it forwarded to the Black Hills. When I got to Fort Worth I said to the conductor: "There is a bunch of those corporation dogs on my trail. I am going to the Black Hills, but they expect me to go to El Paso. I have only one satchel. If you will take care of it I will walk about five miles out in the country and get on the train." He said, "All right, Mother; I will send you out in a buggy."

Then they arrested one of the Mexicans. I went to Texas and they telegraphed me to come to New York. I carried those documents. I remembered we had two miners in Congress, and perhaps they could frame a bill on the question and bring it before the House. The bill was framed by Congressman Nichols, of Scranton, and he fought a brave battle. I want to tell you it is necessary for you to put your clear-cut men in Congress and in the Legislatures. You will not win until you do. I bring this up to impress upon your minds what can be done. The bill was brought up in the House, sent to a committee and pigeon-holed. I wrote to the different labor papers and trades councils asking them to demand of their representatives that that bill be brought out on the floor of the House, where it could be discussed. I went to Washington and the bill was brought up. The Attorney-General, Wickersham, the Wall street representative of the gang of thieves, made a slight excuse. I asked Congressman Wilson to frame a bill appropriating $25,000 to bring lawyers and witnesses there. The bill was framed.

I was sick in Cincinnati when I heard the bill was coming up for a hearing on the following Friday. I went to Washington and talked to Congressman Wilson. He had read the documents I had in my possession. The question came up to the committee. You should have been there before that committee! There were representatives of the Steel Trust, of the Southern Pacific Railway and of other interests. I sat during the hearing and took it in. Congressman Wilson called on me to give my evidence. I got up and related a little history to the committee. I said, "I do not go into the classics after language to express myself when there is a condition that forces me to pray, and it isn't the prayer that will take me to heaven that I use." Dalzell said, "Mother Jones, where do you live?" "I will tell you. I live wherever there is a bunch of workers fighting the robber. My home is with the workers." He didn't ask any more questions, but I related the whole affair.

Now the miners of this country put up $4,000, and these Mexican refugees are indebted to you for being where they are today. Had we not exposed this affair they would have been arrested again the day they came out of prison. On account of the hearing and the way we exposed it they were not arrested. The morning they came out I sent $75 to each of them. That was your money. I sent $100 later. There is a little more in the treasury of the Western Federation of Miners. We placed the money there because it was nearer the seat of war. That I intend to hold. I have written the warden of the penitentiary to find out when the time of a man who is there now will expire. He has five children and they are without a mother. You have dug down into your treasury and brought out your hard-earned dollars and put them up for that cause. I desire to pay my respects to Comrade Germer, who handled the money and sent it West. Those Mexicans are indebted to the miners of this country for being safe today. A revolution is on in Mexico, and if we didn't have a revolution of our own I would be down there, because I want to send that bloody thief of a Diaz up to God Almighty in a condition that will show how big a rascal he was down here.

Now to come back to the Irwin field. I didn't go in there when I should have gone, because I was not well after the spell of sickness I had. I had been up against two governments and it was a great strain. I went to the anthracite and stayed at Charlie Gildea's home, and Andrew Matti, Martin Flyzik and Angelo Gillotti furnished all the beer I needed until I got well. Now as to the Irwin field. Fourteen years ago I went there with poor Pat Dolan. I think Ed McKay was with us. We pulled out Congressman Huff's mine and the mines all along the line. I said to Pat, "You can get these fellows if we can only take care of them." He said, "That is the trouble; the organization is not in a position to take care of them." I left the Irwin field then and did not go back until last November. Then I surveyed the situation carefully. Now, I am not going to whitewash anything; I am going to tell the delegates to this convention the truth, because you are the men who furnished the hard-earned dollars to win that strike.

No man, no set of men will or ever have owned me except the working class. There is not a more important strike in the history of the Miners' Union than the strike in the Irwin field—not one. I knew that when it started; but the whole industrial body of the miners were in a strike of their own at the time it started. They were not able to take hold of it as they should have done. They have done yeoman work in that field; they are magnificent fighters; but in all strikes there will be the grafters, there will be those who have no conscience, there will be those who sell their homes and come out and live off the organization.

I want to say to you that strike must be won; it will be won, but you have got to center your forces there, and if it takes all the money of your organization, put it there and lick hell out of those operators. Maryland depends on the Irwin field, Central Pennsylvania depends upon it, and the Pittsburgh district depends upon it. If you lose the Irwin field the operators of the Pittsburgh district will give it to you in the near future. There is the Connellsville field, there is Maryland and West Virginia which you must organize, because the coal comes into competition with yours, and if a fellow goes over there who is afraid to go up those mountains, send him home, put a mother hubbard on him and give him a nursing bottle. Many men have lost their lives. Many men want a job of organizing, but they never did any organizing. Put that down, Mr. President! Don't be watching the salary. For God's sake cut that rotten salary out of the deal. Get into the fight, every one of you, because we are up against it.

They have made a fine fight in the Irwin field, but the men were inexperienced in strikes. I saw that the minute I went in there. I wasn't there four days until I took the whole situation in. I have been in strikes for a good many years — not alone miners' fights, but garment workers' and textile workers' and street car men's strikes. I knew that field could be won if we were able to center our forces there. You must stop all conflict and get down to the fight. Instead of fighting each other, turn all your batteries on the other fellow and lick him; then, if there is any fellow in our own ranks who needs a licking, let us give it to him. Let us be true to the organization; let us fight to a finish. That field must be organized, and the Southern Colorado strike must be won. You cannot win that field in the North until you do. You are wasting money. I know that field thoroughly. I was up against the guns there too many months not to understand the situation.

Now, I am talking to you miners. I am not talking to officers. I am talking to you who put up the money to fight those battles and win them. I knew the men who blazed the way. There was no pay, there was no newspaper eulogy, there were no compliments; they slept by the wayside, but they fought the battle and paved the way for this magnificent organization, and knowing them as I did, this organization is dear to me. It has been bought with the blood of men who are scarcely known today.

Now, I want to say a few more words. I want to call your attention to that magnificent dope institution that was formed to get labor, that

51

mutual admiration society, the Civic Federation. The biggest, grandest, most diabolical game ever played on labor was played when that was organized. The Civic Federation! It ought to be called the physic federation, because that is what it really is! I know it all! That Civic Federation is strictly a capitalistic machine. The men or women who sit down and eat and drink with them and become members of the Belmont-Carnegie cabinet are not true to labor. Tell them I said so! I have a letter I ought to have brought with me. It is from one of the leading lawyers of the city of New York. I got it just a day before I left Greensburg. There were eight pages in the letter. I met him during the protest meeting when I was going after the judge, and he was one of the leading lawyers. He said in that letter: "Mother, I should very much regret that your work would be lost. Why don't you tell the workingmen to pull their leaders out from the Civic Federation?" Labor never will progress; it cannot as long as they sit down and eat and drink and fill their stomachs and get their brains filled with champagne. And then Mrs. Harriman will say: "How deah! I get such an inspiration!" Inspiration from a couple of old labor scavengers! "It is so delightful to have labor and capital coming together in a brotherhood." What do you think of such rot? The robber and the robbed, the fellow who brings the militia out to murder my class and representatives of the workingman! Not on your life!

Let the Civic Federation stop the guns. Thirteen men have been murdered in the Irwin field. What has the Civic Federation done there? Sixteen men are in jail in Colorado. What did the Civic Federation do with Roosevelt when he sent 2,000 guns to the Governor [James H. Peabody] of Colorado to blow your brains out? You have an old Mary Ann of a Governor there now [Elias M. Ammons]. He hasn't as much backbone as Peabody had. Make me Governor of Pennsylvania or Colorado just one month, and you will find there will be none of those fellows in jails.

That Civic Federation is a menace to the working movement. The Labor Commissioner of Colorado came to Trinidad during our strike and said: "Mother, we had a delightful time in Chicago. You know there was a banquet of the Civic Federation. It was a charming treat. It was delightful to be there. Here was a labor leader, here was a millionaire, here was a labor leader and here was a millionaire. Why, we had drinks that cost 75 cents a drink and cigars that cost 50 cents apiece! I have one here; the odor of it is beautiful." "It ought to be," said I, "when it is stained with the blood of men that you infernal hypocrites, scavengers, robbers and fakers have wrung out of the labor movement! They pay the bills." You can tell old Easley, the secretary of the Civic Federation, that we know his game; that he has been hoodwinking labor; but labor is awakening. This convention must tell those who represent labor in the Civic Federation to get out of it or get out of the labor movement.

You must look after the Irwin field. I went nine miles one day to where we found a woman with a baby wrapped up in a carpet. There were six other children, cold and hungry. The organization sent them clothing. They had built houses, they have done everything that could be done, but now you must do more. You must send your forces in there. I want to say that the secretary of the Labor Temple in Pittsburgh is deserving of a great deal of gratitude and appreciation from the organization. Besides doing her other labor work, she has tramped over that field. She did not go into the newspapers to say what she did, but her work is there. I refer to Miss [Emmiline] Pitt, secretary of the Pittsburgh Labor Temple Association. We need more women of that type to take up the work.

Now there is a great deal more I want to say, but I know you want to go to dinner, and I know the newspaper men want to go to the office with their news. Some of you want to go out and get a drink and you wish I would shut up. I am not going to do it for a minute or two. Whatever else you do, keep the fight up in the Irwin field. I want to say to the International that it is the miners' money that is to be spent. I know that many of you put up the assessment when your wives need it at home. I was in West Virginia with Ben Davis when he was a boy. Going down the track one day I saw a poor fellow and a little boy carrying the head of a bedstead up the mountain. I said, "Jack, for God's sake where are you going with that bed?" He said he was going up there to live. "Why," I said, "don't you know the children will roll down the mountain and be killed?" He said: "Mother, I get this place for three dollars a month. The company keeps it off. I haven't a dollar, and I thought maybe I could save the other three dollars I paid for the house down the river. With my assessment and dues I haven't a penny."

Next day I went up there. His wife was dying with consumption. The little boy of ten and the father walked in tired, worn and wet. I gave the little ones a few pennies. One little girl said she would go down to the company's store and get some peanuts. The older girl, the little housekeeper, said: "No, Mamie, you can't spend that; we have got to put it away to buy some things for mama." I could tell you stories that would take the roof off this building, but many of you know them all without my telling. I know it is these brave men who are digging down into their hard-earned money to pay for the strikes, to pay for this convention and for everything else, and so for their sakes see that the money is judiciously spent; see that there is an accounting for every penny, and that the man who is low enough and mean enough to take money from this organization and rent out houses and draw the rents — well, you may say he will go and scab. Let him do it, but lick him out of his boots before he does it. He is an imposter, a robber and a thief. There is no bigger rascal walking. I have more respect for Morgan — he doesn't belong to my class; but when our own people rob us there is nothing to be said for them. What about the men in the Hocking Valley twenty-five years ago? What about the men in Illinois? What about the men who have given up their lives for the organization? Look at those unmarked graves, the graves of men who made it possible for us to be here holding a meeting in the capital city of Ohio today and discussing these mighty questions.

Today twenty-one men are to be hung in Japan—twenty-one revolutionists, twenty-one brave souls in that nation that has only come from barbarism within the last forty years. Those twenty-one brave men go to the scaffold today, my friends, for a principle in which they believe, the principle of right and justice, and I want this convention to pass resolutions and notify the Japanese consul in Washington that they will hear from us if they hang any more of those men. Today Fred Warren goes to jail for undertaking to save the lives of the men of the Western Federation of Miners when they were behind the bars. I have a letter here I received from a gentleman who wrote me from New York. He said: "I notice in the papers today that one of the Appeal to Reason men has been tried on a charge of criminal libel." It was a falsehood, but that is the way the capitalist papers give the news. He was tried because he sent a postcard out. He asked the postmaster several times if it was against the federal laws and the postmaster said it was not. He sent the cards out asking that Taylor of Kentucky, who murdered Goebel, be caught and taken back to Kentucky. It was no crime to hang and starve and shoot workingmen, but it was a crime to dare to do anything to defend our people. He asked me if I could get him the data of the case and a copy of the complaint. It is in this sort of thing he is going to specialize, restriction of the freedom of speech and the press. He said: "For years we have been fighting for that. It is the corner stone of our institutions and of all our rights that should be most sacredly guarded." That comes from one of the great attorneys of New York who did not understand the case. I sent for a copy of the complaint and had it forwarded to him. You see how these things are going along.

In reading over the report of the President I noticed statements I want to call your attention to. He said it makes no difference to him if he is the retiring officer, he would stick to the workers anyhow, and would not sell his knowledge and experience and education the miners of the country gave him to the master class. I hope, Mr. President, you will keep your word. That is the particular part of the report I took stock in. It is unfortunate that men whom you have educated and have thrown up against the trained brains of the nation to learn how to benefit labor should give their services to the corporations of the nation. You have paid their salaries, you have paid their expenses, and I can count on my fingers over twenty men that I know have given their experience to the mine owners, to the master class, and are serving them. It is time to call a halt on this thing. You are not educating men to serve the master class. You give them office, you trust them to serve you, and when they do not do so, ostracize them as you would a mad dog. I have gone over this country and I have seen these things until I have become disgusted sometimes with the workers.

You are in the mightiest conflict of the age. Put away your prejudice, grow big and great and mighty in this conflict and you will win. There is no such thing as fail. We have got to win. You have brave fighters, both in Colorado and Pennsylvania. You have warriors there, but you must stand by them. Pay your dues, win that battle in the Irwin field, and then, my friends, turn your batteries on the Colorado Fuel and Iron Company and show them what the United Mine Workers' organization is made of.

[*UMWA Proceedings* (Indianapolis: Cheltenham Press, 1911), pp. 258-69.]

Speech at a public meeting on the levee
Charleston, West Virginia

The Paint Creek–Cabin Creek strike in West Virginia in 1912–13 focused attention on Mother Jones as never before because of the many incidents of violence that produced national headlines. Her imprisonment in February 1913, and her trial and conviction by a military court created such a furor that the U.S. Senate ordered a committee to investigate conditions in West Virginia. Fortunately, a number of her speeches during the first six months of the strike were preserved, giving a picture of her in action over a two-month period.

After rejoining the UMWA in 1911, Mother Jones went to Colorado to organize the coal miners there, staying from February to August, when she returned east to meet speaking engagements in Ohio, Pennsylvania, and New York. She paid no attention to her official expulsion from the Socialist party. In October she journeyed with Frank Hayes, vice president of the UMWA, and Joseph Cannon, of the Western Federation of Miners, to Mexico where they consulted with President Francisco Madero and other officials and received assurances that the new revolutionary government would permit the organization of workers in Mexico. She then made a flying trip to Los Angeles as an emissary of the minister of justice to try, unsuccessfully, to persuade Ricardo Flores Magón to abandon his independent revolutionary course and return to Mexico to become part of a united movement. During the winter of 1911–12 she continued her work among the coal miners. In the spring she shifted her efforts and assisted in a strike of western railroad employees. In the midst of the railroad strike, she decided to return to West Virginia and inject herself into the Paint Creek dispute, remaining involved for nearly a year.

The struggle in the Kanawha coal fields in 1912–13 was, first of all, a fight for better wages and working conditions, for organization and recognition of the union, and for the right to collective bargaining; but the focus quickly shifted to the hiring of armed guards by the operators and the role of the state government in maintaining law and order. On three occasions Governor William E. Glasscock called out the state militia to preserve order in the strike area; over nine months many bloody clashes took place between guards and miners and the death toll reached fifty. The trouble began in April 1912 when the operators in the Kanawha field refused to renew a contract with union miners. A strike ensued, and, although settlements were made by other companies, those on Paint Creek held out against a new contract. To protect their property the operators began importing guards from the Baldwin-Felts Detective Agency who, joined to others on unorganized Cabin Creek, constituted a formidable force. Estimates vary on the number of guards, but several hundred were probably employed. They supervised the eviction of the miners' families from company towns and many took refuge in a tent colony set up by the union at Holly Grove. Violent clashes between miners and guards increased in number and frequency from the end of May into the summer.

Mother Jones plunged into this situation after her train from Butte, Montana, reached Charleston, West Virginia. She proceeded directly to the strike zone some twenty-five miles from the capital and began making speeches. When a battle on 26 July at Mucklow, West Virginia, resulted in the death of sixteen men, Governor Glasscock sent three companies of the state militia into the area to establish order.

To put pressure on the governor, Mother Jones called a public meeting in Charleston outside the strike zone. In her militant address on the levee she insisted that the miners would not tolerate the brutalities and lawlessness of the mine guards, and that no settlement would be possible so long as they remained. The resolutions she presented at the end of her address were conciliatory, however, with promises that the miners would respect property rights and cooperate with the state militia.

The coal operators' association had reacted to Mother Jones's appearance by hiring a stenographer to take down her words, and the following six speeches are transcripts of his records in Charleston and Montgomery, West Virginia, in August and September. She spoke much more often, but other speeches, most of them delivered to miners within the strike area, have not been preserved.

§ § §

[Mother Jones gets up into the back end of a dray wagon while the crowd says first one thing and then another.]

If you would just use your brains instead of your mouths, but you do not.

(Cries of "Take your time, Mother.")

Don't give me any advice. I will attend to you; I will stay with you.

(Voice: "I believe you are right.")

Now, you have gathered here today for a purpose. Every movement made in civilization has had an underlying purpose. You have reached the century in human civilization when the charge of human slavery must forever disappear. (Applause.)

You, my friends, in my estimation, have stood this insult too long. You have borne the master's venom, his oppression, you have allowed him to oppress you. When we said, "a little more bread" he set out to get the human blood-hounds to murder you. Your Governor [William E. Glasscock] has stood for it. He went off to Chicago [to the Republican convention] and left two Gatling guns with the blood-hounds to blow your brains out.

(A voice: "That is what he has done, Mother.")

Yes, that is what he has done. But what did you elect him for?

(A voice: "That is the question.")

Then you elected a sheriff, that began to shake like a poodle dog the night of the trouble on Paint Creek. He began to tremble and ran into a store to be sheltered. I have never in all my life — in all the battles I have had — taken back water, and why should a public officer do it — elected by the people. The best thing you can do is to apply to some scientist to give you some chemicals and put into a nursing bottle, give it to them fellows and tell them to go away back and sit down. (Applause.)

This industrial warfare is on. It can't be stopped, it can't be put back, it is breaking out over all the nation from the city of Mexico clean through to the border of Canada, from the Atlantic Ocean clean across the oceans of the world; it is the throbbing of the human heart in the industrial field for relief. They are preaching appeal to the Legislature, they appeal to Congress — and I must give this Congress credit — I always want to give credit where credit is due — you have had more labor bills passed in the last session than in all the days of your Congress.

I was in Washington not many weeks ago. I sat up in the gallery watching the voters. I was watching the fellows who would vote against your bill. One fellow, when they asked for roll call, he got up among those who didn't want it, but when the vote came he had to be registered on the *Congressional Record,* he took mighty good care that his vote was in your favor Why? Because the whole machine of capitalism realize for the first time in history that there is an intellectual awakening of the dog below, and he is barking. Have you been barking on Paint Creek?

I want to say, without apology, without fear of the courts, without fear of jails, you have done what ought to have been done a long time ago. When — when a corporation which is bleeding you to death, would go and hire, — send over the nation and hire human blood-hounds to abuse your wife, your child, it is time every man in the State should rise.

I saw an inscription on your statehouse, and looked at it, — because I know Virginia. I know the whole machine of capitalism; they locked me up and put me out of the State and shook their fists at me and told me not to come back again. I told them to go to hell, I will be back tomorrow.

You know the trouble with you fellows is that you get weak-kneed, and get a pain in your back, and then go home and are sick for a week.

Now, this fight, the governor can't stop it, the State militia can't stop it, and I want to say something to you—Don't get into conflict with the boys in the State militia.

(Cries of "Amen! Amen!")

I don't want one single man in the State militia hurt. I know what the militia is for. It is organized to shoot down the workers when they protest, in every nation of the world. But there are many workingmen in the militia, and I always deal with them—they are mine, anyhow. I am going to change them from the capitalists' interest over to my interest.

You know the "two-by-four" governor—(Applause)—I am not talking about your governor. He has the Gatling guns. I am talking about the "two-by-four" corporation tool in the State of Pennsylvania.

(A voice: "How about West Virginia?")

I am not talking about West Virginia. When we had a fight in 1900, the governor was going to clean us up, and four thousand women went down at three o'clock in the morning—They weren't ladies, they were women. A lady, you know was created by the parasitical class; women, God Almighty made them. The crack thirteenth were sent down by that governor to meet those four thousand women. Their sleeves were rolled up on their arms, they walked fifteen miles over mountains. What did those women do? They licked the crack thirteenth of Pennsylvania. The "two-by-four" lawyers, the back crooks and corporation rats—they don't know how to fight. So the militia begged for mercy. The Colonel says, "Move back, we are going forward in civilization. I will charge bayonets on you people." "Not on your life, you don't charge bayonets on us, because if you do—I will tell you now, we are fighting the robbers who take our bread and butter; if you go to shoot us we will clean up the highway with the whole bunch of you." You ought to have seen them run! Their moustache wasn't curled that day. They went up and hit the pike and didn't bother us any more. The sheriff said to me, "Take these people away." "No, I didn't come here to take them away, I came to meet them." He said, "I will have you arrested, I will call on the governor for the militia." I said, "We will lick the militia." It is the fighting of the classes. You have today in this country two warring forces, the one the lying oligarchy, the other the crush pin, the breath is taken from them.

Go into the mines—I want to say to you, don't let me hear that you have ever injured a single mine in the whole State of Virginia. These mines belong to you. The outside belongs to the operators, the inside is where your property is, your job is inside, that is your property, you go inside and dig down the wealth, and you are generous enough to give three-fourths of it to the other fellows. You give up three-fourths to the other fellows, then if you say you need a little more bread for your children he sends out after the blood-hounds.

I want to say, my friends, in this age of ours, in this modern conflict we are going to prepare you to stop it. I am eighty years old — I have passed the eightieth mile stone in human history. I will be eighty more, for I have got a contract with God Almighty to stay with you until your chains are broken. (Loud applause.)

We have broken the chains of chattel slavery, we changed his condition from a chattel slave to a wage slave. But you say we didn't make it any better. Oh, yes, we did, we made it better for the chattel slave. Then we entered into industrial slavery. That was one step in advance. We forever wiped out chattel slavery and came into industrial slavery. Now, industrial slavery is the battle you are in.

Let me say to you, I don't want a singe officer of the militia molested in any way. I am not going to say to you don't molest the operators. It is they who hire the dogs to shoot you. (Applause.) I am not asking you to do it, but if he is going to oppress you, deal with him. I am not going to take any back water because I am here in the capital. No back water for me. No man lives on the face of God's earth that is oppressing my class that I am afraid of. (Loud applause.)

I want to say, my friends, here, — (Here the speaker took time to get up on top of a box which was in the bed of the wagon.) I want to see if the guards are here.

You have inscribed on the steps of your Capitol, "MOUNTAINEERS ARE FREE." God Almighty, men, go down through this nation and see the damnable, infamous condition that is there. In no nation of the world will you find such a condition. I look with horror when I see these conditions.

You gather up money to send to China to learn them to know more about Jesus. Jesus don't know any more about you than a dog does about his father. (Loud applause.)

I was in church one day when they raked in $1600.00, and at the same time they were robbing the representatives of Jesus to feed them who robbed them. You build churches and give to the Salvation Army and all the auxiliaries of capitalism and support them, to hoodwink you.

But I want to say they will not be able to get an army in the United States big enough to crush us.

I was speaking to the manager in the ticket office in the Far West, and I said "I am going in to West Virginia." I had been in fourteen states with the strikers in each state. I said, "I am going into West Virginia, and there will probably be hell." He said, "Be quiet, a great many of us will be with you. Get all you can out of these thieves." I say to the policemen, "Get all the ammunition you can, get all the ammunition and lie quiet, for one of these days you will come over with us and we are going to give the other fellows hell."

Now my friends, my brothers, this is a new day for me. I can write a new message to the boys in the Far West. I can write a new message even to my boys in Mexico.

I went into Mexico last October. I want to give you a little incident of how things happened over night. I fought Diaz until I had to leave the country. I made it so blamed hot for the tyrant that I had to get up and get away to be safe. I saw the whole administration in Mexico. I had a talk with them. I walked up into that palace where that tyrant had robbed and murdered millions of human beings—I walked up into that palace that he left, and I said "My God! this is making history fast." He went to Santa Cruz and took a steamer to go into exile; the prison doors were opened the same day and four or five of my brothers that he had incarcerated there went free.

Oh, friends, even castles cannot protect tyranny. Every member of the Mexican administration gave me an audience, and they said to me, "Mother Jones, you can come into Mexico—we want you—and organize the men."

Someone said yesterday in my presence, that when the Panama Canal was finished, their goods would get a tremendous market. Let me say the Panama Canal was not started for your benefit. The gang on Wall Street started the Panama Canal because they said "We will capture Nicaragua and Mexico and get thirty million peons." When the Wall Street oligarchy move, it don't fool me. (Applause.)

You held a convention here the other day, to elect him president again. May God Almighty grant that he may die before election comes. He sent two thousand guns in to blow my brains out in Colorado, and I have got it in for him.

(A voice: "Call his name.")

I did call his name, it is Teddy the monkey chaser. I can give you more.

(From the crowd: "Tell it, tell it.")

I can't tell it from hearing, I can tell it from experience. The Mayor of New York [Seth Low] didn't want to let me in, but I got in. A man is a fool to try and play the game on a woman. The Mayor let me in and then I went on to Oyster Bay. He [Theodore Roosevelt] had a secretary [B. F. Barnes], who died since in Washington—I was glad when I heard it—he was afraid I would dynamite him. That fellow Roosevelt had secret service men from his palace down at Oyster Bay, all the way to New York, to watch an old gray-headed woman.

I don't care whether it is Taft or him, the fight is the same. Mr. Policeman, we will give them hell anyhow.

Now boys, you are in this fight. I want to say to you the governor is sick, poor fellow. I feel sorry for him.

(From the crowd: "I hope he is dead. I do.")

Let the governor alone today. We have arranged a mass meeting in Montgomery, also the citizens, merchants, lawyers, doctors and all—in

Montgomery for four o'clock Sunday afternoon. Come down there and then we will do business with the governor. You must have a system, you must have a force behind you. When you are going to do business with those big fellows you have got to have ammunition. (Loud applause.)

One day I went to see President Taft, spent nearly forty minutes with him. Teddy was scared of me, but I will give Taft credit, he wasn't, he gave me an audience of forty minutes. I know Taft belongs to the Wall Street crowd, but he shows his hand, but the other fellow will talk about referendum and recall but he will recall you with the militia and bayonets.

And don't trust those judges today. I know them. I went down to see a judge in Colorado [Greeley W. Whitford]. He had fifteen of my boys in jail. I first tackled the sheriff and then went to see the governor. I gave him some taffy and then he let all my boys out. He said, "Mother, if you would get them to come down and apologize." I said, "I have been trying to get them to stand up off their knees for many years, and there is no apology to make." I wouldn't have them to apologize under any circumstances. Seven years ago we went to the governor and put the whole matter before him, and he said, "I can't do anything, I am helpless." Then we went to the sheriff, and he said, "I can't do anything, I am helpless." But the governor wasn't helpless when the operators asked him for two Gatling guns to murder the miners. (Loud applause.) He wasn't helpless then. The sheriff wasn't helpless then, my friends. Are we going to stand for the insults of the governors and the public officers and see our children and wives thrown out and insulted by the corporation blood-hounds? I say, no, fight daily until the last minute. (Prolonged applause.)

We are not going to surrender. We are not going to destroy property, but we are going to do business with your blood-hounds (Applause.)

"Mountaineers are always free!" Take that inscription off your Statehouse steps until we have made you free, and then you will be free.

I want to say, boys, take this advice from Mother — I have stood with you in all the years. No Gatling guns, no militia, no courts, have ever intimidated me. There isn't a policeman in any city in America has ever molested me or arrested me. Never! They are every one my friends. When I spoke at the Navy Yard at Brooklyn — when I quit talking I went up to four policemen — I said, "Officers, will you kindly tell me where I will get a car to such a place." They said, "We will go with you, Mother." They said, "Come back next week, and give them fellows hell." (Applause.)

So, you see we have been educating, we are converting the police, and you (operators and officers) haven't got everything with you. I know the Baldwin guards are here, maybe Baldwin is here, but I want to say, you take back water, or by the Eternal God we will make you do it. (Loud applause.) We won't down further. There will be no guards to shoot us down. *We* will watch the property, it is ours, and in a few years we will take it over. And we will say to Taft and Teddy, "You have had a devil of a good time, go in and dig coal."

Boys, go home peacefully (peaceably), and I will go with you. Yes, I will go with you.

(A voice from the audience. "Lord help.")

No, we will help ourselves.

I am like a fellow in Pennsylvania. The Salvation Army was whooping for Jesus. Along came a fellow and one lassie went out and said to him, "Say, brother, did you ever work for Jesus?" "Oh, no, I don't know him." "You don't know Jesus?" "No."

She got horrified, she thought everybody ought to know Jesus. She said, "Well, come in and work for him."

"How much will you give me a day?"

"He will give you a bed in heaven."

He said, "Give me a bed here."

So we want the bed here, not when we die. There it too much preaching to wait until you die in peace. We don't have any peace, there is an industrial war. It isn't politics, it isn't parties, it is industrial war, my friends. There will be no peace until that question is settled and settled right, and until man gets justice.

Look, you operators! You are here. God Almighty, come with me and see the wrecks of women, of babies, then ask yourself "How can I sleep at night?" How can your wife sleep at night? I saw one of them coming down the street the other day in an automobile. She had a poodle dog sitting beside her; I looked at her and then looked at the poodle. I watched the poodle—every now and again the poodle would squint its eye at her and turn up its nose when it got a look at her. (Laughter and applause.) He seemed to say: "You corrupt, rotten, decayed piece of humanity, my royal dogship is degraded sitting beside you." She had lived off the blood of women and children, she decorated her neck and hands with the blood of innocent children, and I am here to prove it to the world.

Do you want any more? If you do I will give it to you. I have got the goods, and I will deliver it, and I have no fear of the courts, no fear of the militia, no fear of the mine owners, no fear of Taft, or of Teddy the monkey chaser.

It takes six billion dollars to take care of the criminals which the system makes. When Mr. Taft, the president of the United States, said to me, "Mother Jones," said he, "I am afraid if I put the pardoning power in your hands, there wouldn't be anybody left in the prisons!" (A voice from the audience: "Great God Almighty.") I said this: "Mr. President, if this nation spent half the money, half the energy to give her people a chance that she does to force them into the prisons, I don't think we would need many prisons."

My friends, I stood in the federal prison at Leavenworth, and saw eight hundred men march before me in the corridors. I looked at those men, and said to the warden — the chaplain, who stood with me — I said, "Chaplain, we are not civilized yet, we are not two degrees away from the savages." A pen like that, in a nation which can create more wealth than the world can consume! There wasn't twenty-five men among the eight hundred that I couldn't take and open wide the Bastille doors, and say to those men, "Go free, I will break your chains, trust yourselves, and then you will trust me." They wouldn't violate the confidence I placed in them because if a man can't live without being robbed he is going to rob and murder to do it. (Applause.)

You are today with the guard system. I will say, Mr. Operators, the day is going to come when you will say you wished you had never seen the face of a guard. We are law-abiding citizens, we will destroy no property, we will take no life, but if a fellow comes to my home and outrages my wife, by the Eternal he will pay the penalty. I will send him to his God in the repair shop. (Loud applause.) The man who doesn't do it hasn't got a drop of revolutionary blood in his veins.

Now, boys, we are approaching the day, we are going on until every man and woman that works, that produces, in this life, he becomes aflame with the same spirit that brought from the brain of England's greatest orator, "Resistance to tyranny is obedience to God."

Now, I want you to be good boys. Don't drink. You haven't got anything to drink on. A good many women will say, "Don't drink, then you will have money in the bank."

I would rather drink than let the banker drink. These women howl Temperance! Temperance! The government says for $12.00 a year for drink — that wouldn't get a jag on a good black cat — Don't drink! No, save it — and the operators will have that much more. You rob them everywhere and then you murder them. Then you think they are going to stand for it? No, by the Eternal God, we are not.

That old fellow Taylor, from Paint Creek, with a couple of guards and a sheriff — if I was that fellow's wife I would lick him every day and on Sunday — he ran into a store and said, "Hide me!" Don't touch the sheriff, there isn't enough in him to touch. Let him go, only when he comes up again tell him to take a walk.

I will tell you something. If the Adjutant General had come and said "Mother, will you come with me, we are going to Peytona, the sheriff can't handle the trouble." I would have said, "All right." We would have settled that thing in twenty-five minutes.

I will give you an instance. We had a fight with the Erie Company. The company said "Bring the militia, hurry up, they are going to eat us up." We were not going to touch them; their flesh is too rotten to eat.

The sheriff met me and wanted us to get off their property. I said, "They want to take our jobs and we are not going to let them. That is our bread and butter, sheriff. We dig down the wealth and the other fellow isn't satisfied. We want to make a day 8 hours instead of 10. We want to spend a little time with our wives and children, we want to study our affairs. Sheriff, come with me and swear the boys in and it will end in twenty minutes." And the sheriff came, and inside of one hour it was settled.

Out in Colorado, the officers were gambling, and one of them lost seven hundred dollars that night. While they had a corporation jag on them they telephoned for the militia. Some one telephoned to me that they were mobilizing the troops. I said, "Let them mobilize the troops." They had a colonel with them. They always had a title, "Colonel," "Major," or something of that sort, to make you fellows believe they are bigger than you. The boys said to me, "You had better go to Utah." I said, "No, I am going to stay and fight it out." Saturday night they pulled me out of bed and landed me out of the state with five cents in my pocket to get a bed and something to eat. Next day the Santa Fe train came along, and I said, "Will you take me into Denver?" When I got there I said, "I am here in the capital, what in the hell are you going to do about it?" When I know I am right fighting for these children of mine, there is no governor, no court, no president will terrify or muzzle me. I see the babies, the children with their hands taken off for profit; I see the profit mongers with their flashing diamonds bought by the blood of children they have wrecked. Then you ask us to be quiet! Men, if you have a bit of human blood, revolutionary blood in your veins and a heart in your breasts, you will rise and protest against it. (Applause.)

I went up where you murder these baby children, and you will see those little boys gather around me in the dead of night and say "Mother, do come back to be with us."

Oh, men of America! Oh, men of human instinct! Oh, men of descendants of the great Patrick Henry and Lincoln, will you stand for it?

(Cries from the audience: "No, No, No, No.")

The only thing in life is at stake. Put a stop to it. Don't go near the governor today, he might have a nervous collapse.

Now, like good boys, go back home. I will go with you. We won't hurt anybody, we will have a good time, and when we get home, if the operators want to come and have a good time with us, we will be good to him — if he settles with us.

Now, boys, you came up here to the capital. It was the proper place to come to. This is the chief executive. So you haven't retired, if the chief executive don't do something, if the sheriff don't do something, then the people *must* do something.

I am not going to talk any more today. I am going to talk Sunday at

Paint Creek. They said that if I went up there last Sunday they were going to riddle me with bullets. Now, I went, and there wasn't a bullet struck me. I am going next Sunday. I am going with you wherever you are.

I have been in the mines twenty-five years ago on the Monongahela River. I went in on the night shift and the day shift. I went to study the conditions and to get posted. You were working long hours then. I talked with you in the mines and got you together, told you what you were facing. I worked on the night shift and the day shift, I put the literature in your hands. I lay on the floor with your baby children. Today we are four hundred thousand strong, marching on to liberty, marching on to freedom. We are the United Mine Workers of America today numbering four hundred thousand. Then you worked 12 or 14 hours. We brought it down to 10, then to 8. Your stores ran and worked their help until 10 o'clock at night. The merchants said if you closed up they couldn't make any money. We brought it down, and you haven't got a merchant who will give up the business on account of making no money. You are now working 10 hours.

(From the crowd: "Nine hours.")

This is 4 hours too much. We are going to keep on and are going to make it 6 hours. When I came in you were working 11 hours and 15 sometimes. I fought those fellows. They gave you 9 hours. You are as much to blame as the mine owners because you didn't stick to your organization. If you were true to your organization, true to your manhood, you would not have to bother with the guards.

A fellow said the other day—Saturday—We are going to have a convention in Charleston, to talk politics. I want to say that the man who is not true to the economical part of his life is not true to the political. The labor movement has two wings. She has the economic wing and the political wing. When you are organized thoroughly on the economic you can march on and make demands of the other fellows what you want.

(At this point "Mother" quoted a poem written by Rudyard Kipling addressed to the crowned heads of Europe.)

I want to say to you mine owners, if you are here, I know you will go home and say we have been false to our homes, to our country, let us shake hands with these miners. Let us have no strike. You will have as much when you die, you will have as much rotten meat on your carcass for the rats to eat. (Loud applause.)

Now, boys, be good and come to the meeting Sunday at Montgomery, there will be no mines to be closed up that day. I want to say to you that these mine owners have contracts, and don't close the mines every day. Let us get together and have concerted action.

(At this point "Mother" began to shake hands with the audience.)

I will always be with you, no court, no judge or deputy can scare me, and if any judge pulls me into court I will tell him what is business.

Good bye, boys. Don't bring them down, because the corporation is here and you will lose your jobs tomorrow.

When the strike is won I will [words omitted by stenographer] for you, and then you can get a jag on. I will get something better than beer for you.

I want to say—I forgot—I intended to pay a tribute to Major Elliott. Of course he has got to take orders. It is the sheriffs and the governor that I am opposed to. I want to say that never in my life did I meet a more perfect gentleman than Major Elliott. He arrested me in Clarksburg, but he was a gentleman in every sense of the word. He didn't want to put me in jail, but he wanted me to go to the hotel and stay until my trial came up. But I prefer boarding with Uncle Sam when he wants me to.

I want to say to you that you need not be afraid of Major Elliott. I know that he will do the best he can with you, and I know, I believe in my own heart that he will tell these troops not to fire on you, and I want to tell you, Mr. Operator, you can't buy him to do it. Of course he is a public officer. As such he has got to obey orders from above, but he won't obey the mine owners. (Applause.)

Before I leave you, I want to say to you there isn't a nation on earth but what brings out the troops when capitalism wants them to murder you.

In France, the government is supposed to be atheistic, when the telegraphers went on a strike the government brought the troops out to shoot the workers back.

In Germany, which is a Protestant nation, they called on the troops to shoot the workers down when they struck.

In Spain, which is a Catholic country, they called out the troops to shoot your back.

Then in Italy, the home of Catholicism, they brought out the troops to shoot you back.

Then here in America out comes the troops.

Don't you believe it is time to stop it? Don't you know you have the same government as when the immortal Lincoln was in Washington? He didn't bring out the troops to shoot you. With machinery you have changed the whole industrial world, you have changed literature, the pulpit in the teaching of religion. Your public press today is run in the interest of the ruling classes. These editors have got to do it. Don't blame the editor. I blame the pirates behind. The poor editors are like you, slaves, and you are slaves.

Nobody can change this but you. The other class will never change it. The ministers will never change it. They will tell you to go up to Jesus, and Jesus will tell you to get back and fight. That is what He will do with you.

Now wait until I read this:

"The miners and workmen in mass-meeting assembled, believing in law and order and peace should reign in every civilized community, call the attention of honest citizens of the State of West Virginia to the fact that a force of armed guards of men belonging to the reckless class, the criminal and lawless class, have no respect for the rights of their fellow man, who have been employed in the coal fields of Kanawha and the New River valley. These lawless men and criminals beat up her citizens on the public highways, a menace to the traveling public."

(Comments): If you are molested you have a right to sue the railroad.

"They insult our wives, our daughters, arrest honest citizens in lawful discharge of their duties, without process of law; they carry on a course of conduct which is calculated to bring about warfare and disturb the peace.

We earnestly insist that the recent trouble on Paint Creek Valley was brought about by the armed criminals against whose depredations we could get no relief from the courts."

(Comments): I will explain the courts to you directly, and I hope the judge is here. He belongs to the corporations if he is here.

(From the audience: "You bet your life he does.")

"We earnestly and sincerely call upon the State administration, men in public life throughout the State, all good citizens, to cooperate with us, to use their influence by enforcing the law, by forcing such guards to disarm themselves and leave the territory where they are now stationed. We believe their presence there will lead to further riot and bloodshed and murder and general disturbing of the peace, a condition to be deplored by all law-abiding citizens.

"We hereby promise and pledge our support and cooperation with Major C. D. Elliott, who is in charge of the State militia, in the interest of law and order, at the same time insist that law and order cannot be restored until the armed guards are discharged.

"We pledge ourselves to abide by the law, doing everything within our power to cause our sympathizers to do likewise, upon the condition that said guards and bloodhounds are disarmed and removed from the State.

"We condemn the action of the Circuit Judge of this county for leaving the bench at the time of the threatened impending danger, at a time when there existed a condition that brought fear and unrest to the members of our families, to our neighbors and friends. We submitted our cause to said court in which the action of said armed guards was clearly set forth, through and by our attorneys, and an injunction and restraining order was asked for, and said restraining order was denied by the judge. We hold that the recent outbreak and riot was due to the fact that said judge refused to grant a proper restraining order against said guards under the condition set forth in the bill and proof filed in support thereof.

"Resolved that a copy of this resolution be forwarded and transmitted to the Honorable William E. Glasscock."

(Comments): What on God's earth did you give him this title for? Did he have any honor when he sent Gatling guns to shoot you? Quit saying "Honor" to those fellows. When I was in the court you have to say "Your Honor." I said, "Who is the court?" I said, "Is the old man on the bench with the long beard the court?" He said, "Yes." I said, "How can I know he has any honor?"

"—and a copy to Major C. D. Elliott."

(Comments): I will bet you if Major Elliott disarms those guards the miners will sit down. But I want to tell you operators that by the Gods you will have to settle with us. We are no slaves, no peons, and we are not going to submit to you. If you want peons, go down to Nicaragua and get them.

(Continuing): Be good, boys, don't drink. I will be down tonight, and we will have a meeting Sunday evening at four o'clock. Then we will decide what steps we are going to take.

The governor is sick now; don't bother with him, poor fellow.

(From the audience: "He is sick in the head.")

He was at the Republican convention in Chicago, and had a pain in his back.

There is a man in this audience, he has a big hat on, and he will now speak to you.

(Calls for J. W. Brown, Socialist organizer, who came and got up on the dray and proceeded to make a speech.)

[George Wallace Papers, West Virginia Collection, West Virginia University.]

Comments on resolutions
presented at a public meeting
Montgomery, West Virginia

Three days later, Mother Jones addressed a mass meeting in Montgomery, West Virginia, the largest town near the strike zone, and gained endorsement of a series of resolutions protesting that the local courts and officials had failed to act effectively in protecting the citizens of the area. Although her speech and her comments on the resolutions were recorded separately by the stenographer, they very likely occurred one after the other on the same platform.

§   §   §

The miners and citizens of Fayette and Kanawha Counties, in Mass-Meeting assembled in the Town of Montgomery, West Virginia, make the following resolution:

Resolved: That we most earnestly denounce certain officials of Kanawha County, State of West Virginia, because they failed to do their duty under the laws of West Virginia, which has resulted in the most cruel, inhuman treatment of the United Mine Workers, of their wives and children by certain Baldwin guards, in the County of Kanawha. Because we know that if the Judge of the Circuit Court of Kanawha County, and the Judge of the Intermediate Court of said county, had, at the time the oppressions were being committed against defenseless miners, their wives and children, had called a special session of the grand jury to indict certain criminals, that if the prosecuting attorney had prosecuted them as they should have been prosecuted, and as other criminals in said county, and sent them to the penitentiary, the trouble would all have been settled and peace would reign.

We declare that said officials have disregarded their sworn duty, that had they regarded their duty it would have saved the state enormous expense.

We denounce the coal operators of Fayette County as unworthy of confidence by the people. They have met in political conventions and denounced in strong terms the guard system of West Virginia. At the same time they are contributing to the salaries of these guards, who have caused such outrages to be committed on many mine workers of this state.

We denounce the candidates for office who have gone into those conventions, because they have not the courage to demand that there should be steps taken to get rid of the Baldwin guards of West Virginia.

Be it Resolved Further: That we now, seeing as never before the vast importance of the laborers of the country vote as one man to elect the officers of this state, that the laborers meet and organize.

These resolutions are drawn up by the citizens and miners of Montgomery, so that they will go to the Governor and state officials.

(Comments): Now, the Judge said if the operators would quit paying the Baldwin guards they would leave the State. The operators don't pay the Baldwin guards, they don't pay them a penny. If it had to come out of their pockets the Baldwin guards would be gone long ago. The miners are robbed in the weighing of coal, in rent, and in the store, they pay the Baldwin guards. (Applause.)

You are the fellows that have got the right to clean up the Baldwin guards because you are the fellows who pay them.

There was a poor black fellow down here at Nashville who couldn't afford to pay the rent in a rotten shack that you couldn't put a hog in. He said he couldn't do it, and went in a coke oven to sleep, and the company charged him $2.50 for sleeping in the coke oven.

What is the matter with you people of West Virginia? What is the matter with the Governor? What is the matter with the whole of you? There isn't another state in the union stands for it — not a one. Poor black wretch, just because his skin is black. It was an accident that the lawyer's skin wasn't black. If you work long for the coal companies you won't have any skin about you.

Stand by the guards, be sure to do that, let them hammer you. Let them put your wives into the creek, and make them walk it. One fellow said the guards haven't troubled me, they never bother me, put every body out of the houses, but let me stay. So his wife was going to give the nation another citizen. They walked in and put the whole bunch out. He was boasting what lovely fellows the Baldwin guards are. Then that gave him a blow. It depends on how you get hit.

They have got to go out of the State. And if the men of the State of West Virginia are too cowardly, if they will give their wives and children up to the blood-hounds to be beaten and abused we will bring enough men in to clean them up, who are not afraid of your guards, who are not afraid of your Governor. When our women are insulted, who are the mothers of the nation, no blackguard will come along to beat them that we will not beat them back. We are not afraid of the Governor.

Don't drink. Go home and be good boys.

Resolved that a copy be sent to the Governor; a copy to Judge Burdett — Don't send a copy to the poor sheriff —

Speeches

(Cries of: "Send him one.")

Oh, the poor fellow, he might take a fit.

Taylor and this Morton up here, who have been telling you what they will do — the dirty cowards — they went into the cellars, and said, "Put the dirty clothes all over my back." God knows there couldn't be anything dirtier than they are.

[George Wallace Papers, West Virginia Collection, West Virginia University.]

Speech at a public meeting at the baseball park Montgomery, West Virginia

Fellow Workers: Let me say this to you, that not one person wins a strike, that it takes the combined forces of the oppressed, the robbed, class to get together and win a strike. The operators, the money power, never in all of human history have won a strike. You have never lost a strike, that is, the workers have not. You have simply rolled up your banners and retreated for a while until you could solidify your army and then come back and ask the pirates, "What in hell are you going to do about it?"

This hero worship must stop. We don't owe any debt of gratitude individually.

Now, we are here today, as we have been — this is the outcome of an age-long struggle. It did not begin yesterday nor today. It is an age-long struggle, and it has crossed the oceans to you. It is about to crystallize, it is about to come aboard. The ship is sailing, it calls for pilots to come aboard. I want to say to you that all the ages of history have been ages of robbery, oppression, of hypocrisy, of lying, and I want to say to you tyrants of the world — (Railroad train whistling) — They got that gang to blow off hot air. (Applause.) I want to say to you tyrants of the world that all the centuries past have been yours, but we are facing the dawn of the world's greatest century, we are facing the dawn of a separate century.

This, my friends, is indicative of what? No church in the country could get up a crowd like this, because we are doing God's holy work, we are breaking the chains that bind you, we are putting the fear of God into the robbers. All the churches here and in heaven couldn't put the fear of God into them, but our determination has made them tremble.

What happened on Paint Creek? Did the church make the operators run and go hide in the cellar? (Applause.)

I don't know who started the racket, but I know that Mr. Operator began to shake, the marrow in his back melted, and he had to go into the cellar to hide himself.

Now, my friends here, twelve years ago I left the great battle that closed in the State of Pennsylvania, and came in here. We had fought a tremendous battle there. We fought that battle until Mr. Hanna said, "These workers are men and women, we have got to do something, we have got to blind them, we have got to hoodwink them some way. Let us start the

Civic Federation." The Republic hurrahed for peace and harmony is coming. Mark Hanna stood at the top of the game. We had them trembling, and they didn't know where to get off at.

And so they got the Civic Federation, they got Morgan, Belmont, and the labor leaders. I said, "That is only a 'Physic' Federation, what are you joining it for?" There are some fellows in the labor movement, when their heads get swelled, they sit down with the thieves. They had their feet under the table, twenty-six thieves and twelve labor leaders, and you stood for it. I begged them not to join it, and some of them left it. They stuck their feet under the table and drank champagne, and the bloody thieves, when we had the women fighting for bread, that gang of commercial pirates were feasting on our blood in New York. And then we stand for it. And when those fellows come along you say "Hurrah" and the whole gang drunk.

Now that wouldn't do. They got the women so as to keep the labor leaders up in tune. They got women to join. They got a welfare department in their Civic Federation, and after a while the leaders and parasites and bloodsuckers they thought they would hoodwink us. One went up to Washington, it was . . . Morgan's daughter. I happened to be in Washington. They were running to the free soup bowls to get a lunch. An Irish machinist ran in and had a piece of bologna that long (measuring on her arm about a foot), and a chunk of bread in the other hand. One of the women said to him, "Oh, my dear man, don't eat that, it will give you indigestion." He said, "The trouble with me is I never get enough to digest, indigestion, hell." The half of you fellows never get enough to digest. You never got a good square meal in your life, and you know you never did. But you furnish the square meals for the others who rob and oppress you.

When I came here ten or twelve years ago, we marched those mountains. The mine owners threatened to kill me, to shoot me. I am never much afraid of their shot. We have some men that will run away, but you will never get me to run, don't worry about it at all. They said I ought to be gotten out, I ought to be shot, locked up in an asylum. We marched the mountains, every one who took up Christ's doctrine — not the hypocrites but the fighters. We organized, you organized, we got together, we fought, we got you double what you had. We made a settlement with these operators. You became friends for the time being. But the mine owners have their tools, their paid lying, treacherous dogs amongst you, and you were betrayed, and you can't deny it for I can prove it. Mind you, I am not looking for office I am looking for your interests and your children's interests, and when you don't have an office you are watching the pendulum of every fellow that has. When I find out that they are false to you they have to get down and out. I don't care who it is that is at the head of your organization, if I find they are false to you they will get down and out, for I won't let up until they do. (Applause.)

You need not give me any advice (to someone in the audience who offered some advice).

It was Aristotle who said to Alexander, many ages ago—he said, "Alexander, don't bother with the outside enemy, your real enemy is inside your own ranks."

And so it is. We could clean up the mine owners overnight if you were true to your standards.

You lost your organization. Scabs and union men work together. You destroyed your charter. Go down to that hell-hole, there isn't another like it in the United States. I went up to that hole one night. I looked at the riches, and wondered at the men who call themselves Christians, who give to the Salvation Army, to the church, to the temperance brigade, to every other shouting gang that comes along—I wondered how those blood-sucking pirates could sleep in their beds, with that horrible outcome of their exploitation. Women sat on the porch, and these pirates said "Keep that burning hell before them to keep them in subjection." They said, "The more hell you keep, the more of their blood will decorate my head and arms." One woman, the wife of one of the blood-suckers, got diamonds to buckle her shoes with. She went to church and said, "Jesus, I made the other fellows give it up." (Laughter and applause.)

And so, if you, who are here, were true to each other, we would not have to have this meeting today. But you have started, and I want to congratulate you. I want to say here, my friends, that is what brought me into West Virginia. I was in a fight all winter. I traveled fourteen states, and fifteen thousand miles in your behalf, inside of seven months. I went down to Mexico, and I made arrangements with the Mexican Government—I want you to listen, Mr. Operator, get your skull ready because there is a very little will go into it—I had an audience with the Mexican governor, and I said, "I want to come in and organize the men that slave, that have been oppressed, crushed. We want to educate, elevate them." The Mexican governor said, "Mother Jones, you can come into this nation and bring any organizers you want. I will take your word, from my experience with you you will not work with those who will not do their duty." I said, "I may be rushed with cannon." Immediately, he had the wires touched, and said, "If they arrest you or your organizers, they will have to be turned loose." That was in despotic Mexico. We chased the President out because he was a tyrant. Not so long ago in this State—I came into your state and found the Baldwin blood-hounds, and find your wives and children thrown out like dogs on the street. They beat you up, put into their hands weapons to beat you with, to beat any of us, yet I didn't find the courts saying, "Stop it." I didn't hear of the Governor saying, "Stop it." No. Why? Because the powers that be are the courts. I want to say, if the judge is here, I know Judge Bennett is. That judge in Charleston went off on a visit. I guess his skull needed a fish to give it something to do. The Governor [William E. Glasscock] went to Chicago, then when he heard there was a racket on Paint Creek, he got sick and went to Huntington. (Applause.)

Now, my friends, I want to say here, I have dealt with courts; I have dealt with the detectives and spotters. I have been from one end of the nation to the other, even in Mexico — I have been in Washington fighting for these poor unfortunate wretches — I have seen more freedom in Mexico than I have seen in America under the Stars and Stripes. We appealed seven years ago to the Governor and he said, "I can't do anything." We appealed to the sheriff, and he said, "I can't do anything." But the State was in jeopardy. We pictured the guards and the outrages to them. Let me say this to you, when the Governor occupies the chair and can't do anything, he ought to get down and out and put somebody in that can. (Loud applause.)

I had business with the Governor [Davis H. Waite of Colorado] in the West. The corporations asked for the militia. The Governor said, "You will get no militia from me." "Give me the job," said I, "and I will attend to them." The Governor said, "You will do it too fast, Mother," said he. He went down himself and surveyed the whole state of affairs. He went to the miners' union and got their story; then he went to the operators and heard their story — he walked twelve miles in the rain and snow. He called to the militia and said, "Take care of those miners, in their jobs, and if the tools of the corporation dare to raise their hands against them, blow their brains out." They went down and the strike was settled in no time. The sheriff called for the troops, like your sheriff did. When you had the trouble here on Paint Creek he got under a table, and said, "For God's sake, hide me." The mine owners, we put the fear of God into their carcass, and they said "Hide me" too. Don't you see you have got them, if you will only be wise. I have seen those fellows tremble. I have been in strikes, and I didn't come in yesterday. I worked in the mines, but I didn't dig coal, but I did help to load it. I went in on the morning on the day shift, before daylight, and I went in on the night shift, with these poor slaves. I found the children perishing and the wives dying, there was nothing in the house, the company had stopped everything. They have brought the same thing in here. They have brought on war. The organization was a baby then, and they worked long hours and got poor pay, they didn't get enough to get a jag on when they worked full hours. We began to educate them. I went into the mines to put literature into the hands of those slaves. I was the first one who came over here and put literature into your hands in this class struggle. My friends, I have stuck to the job.

I have been maligned, and the women I was fighting for have turned their noses in the air, and have said, "Oh, that horrid old woman." And those women love the dogs better than they love humanity! They decorate themselves in new costumes made of the blood of your children and your wives, and now when you kill a handful of guards they raise a great howl. You are to blame because you didn't clean them up. (Loud applause.) When you go at it again, do business. I don't know whether you are an operator or not, but if you are take your medicine. (Loud applause.)

One of these cats came down on the train from Cabin Creek the other day. She said, "You are Mother Jones, are you?" I said, "Yes, what about it?" She said, "What are they doing on Paint Creek?" I said, "Go up and find out." She was one of the corporation cats.

Now, then, we are here, my friends, in protest against a system of peonage such as the world has not dealt with in all its ages. You are building jails, you are paying millions and billions of dollars to take care of the criminals you have made. You operators rob the workers, and your wives live in luxury, they turn their skirts away from the workers. One poor slave said to me — he was sitting down on the steps of a church — he said, "Mother, I have worked ever since I was a boy, and they have got it all. This is all that is left, this old worn out frame." Just then he saw an operator, his family and wife in a carriage, and he said, "I have got to run, I will be discharged if they see me talking to you." Down in Harrison County, West Virginia, I held a meeting. The operators sent me word," If you come down to our mining camps, we will have you shot." I said, "Is that so?" "Yes," they said, "the mine owners said, they will have you shot." When I got off the train, I said, "All right. I will go." I said, "If you are a lap dog for a mine owner, you can be one for me. You go down and tell the operator I am going down to rouse his slaves, and he can shoot me and be damned." Did he shoot me? Not on your life. I told him to come to the meeting. That is the way I pray.

I told Judge Jackson how I prayed. When the time comes in the history of this struggle that a mine owner or Baldwin guard will intimidate me I want to die that hour.

In the old chattel slavery days the old black mammy took up the battle and dug through the earth, and said to the young slaves, "Come and dig with me." They made a tunnel to get away. Do you black fellows do that today? No, you don't. There are a few of you would do it. But the most of you won't do it. What did your mammy do? What did your fathers do two generations ago? They rose up and defied law, property rights, courts, and everything. He said, "Bring your blood-hounds, but we are human, we will be free." And they did free themselves. Why? Because the nation rallied to them, the nation saw you were determined to free yourselves.

When you men will rise and say this is our fight, it will be done. We asked the courts and they wouldn't do it; we asked the Governor and he wouldn't do it; we asked the sheriff and he wouldn't do it; we asked the officers of the law, and they wouldn't do it. They said they would do it, and you see how they have been doing it.

The Governor was able to do something when the operators wanted him. The sheriff said, "Oh, God, we are up against it." The mine owners said, "Ha, Ha, we will get the troops in." They telegraphed to Pennsylvania [where the West Virginia National Guard was on joint maneuvers] to accommodate the operators, the Governor and the sheriff telegraphed immediately for them to come back. Can you deny it? No, you can't deny it. I have got the goods on you.

I want to say, men, if you organize to a man — Don't the churches have a right to go up Cabin Creek and talk about Jesus? Have you? If the ministers have a right to go and talk about Jesus, I have got the right to go and talk about what Jesus did (laughter), where you have got guards to beat our brains out.

Let me say to you, my friends, let me say to the Governor, let me say to the sheriffs and Judges in the State of West Virginia, this fight will not stop until the last guard is disarmed. (Loud applause.)

Forty thousand men, forty thousand braves, said to me, "We are ready for battle, Mother, if they don't do business." So we are, my friends, and the day of human slavery has got to end. Talk about a few guards who got a bullet in their skulls! The whole of them ought to have got bullets in their skulls. How many miners do you murder within the walls of your wealth-producing institutions! How many miners get their death in the mines!

A fellow said to an operator, "Why don't you prop the mines?" "Oh," he said, "Dagoes are cheaper than props." Every miner is a Dago in their estimation, every miner that they can rob.

You go into the mines and work ten or twelve hours, ten years ago. We made a fight and brought it down to nine. Up New River you work ten and twelve, and when you get your statement there is nothing on it. You look at it and scratch your head, and say, "Bookkeeper, I dug more coal than this." He will say, "Get to hell out of here." Then you shrug your shoulders and off you go, instead of taking the bookkeeper by the back of the neck and knocking his head against the wall. Oh, that is terrible, I know. I know the *Gazette* and the *Mail* say, "Oh, she is horrible." Yes, but I am dealing with a horrible condition. When you take the conditions from these fields we will be as tame and polite as your wife when she hammers hell out of you. (Applause.)

Some of you fellows with only one arm — some of you traitors to your class, with one arm on you — they had taken one off to beat you with — went in and cheered for that gang yesterday. You cheered for McKell.

Let me tell you about McKell. The old man McKell was a pretty decent man. I will give everybody credit whether against me or for me. When you had that strike in 1902 I went up to Glen Jean. The Baldwin guards were at Thurmond.

I said to the Baldwin guards, "Don't you come up, I am going up to see McKell to do business with him tonight, don't you come on the train," and the conductor said, "If you do I will tell Bill Baldwin and you will lose your jobs."

I went up to his home. I know your ears are cocked. I know your ears are cocked, to tell him, but tell him to come here and I will tell him. He started a tirade of insult and abuse of the miners. I told him I didn't come there—it was his house—I didn't come there to quarrel, I camed to negotiate a settlement. I said, "If we can't discuss this matter in a peaceful, intelligent way, I will go."

I keep a tab on those fellows. I am not like you, take a glass of whisky and say, "Oh, hell, it is all right." (Laughter and applause.)

Then they call themselves independent Republicans! Independent monkey-chasers! (Laughter and applause.) They say they will take off the guards and call the Legislature in extra session. They need not call the Legislature. They know it, but they think you don't know it. All they need is to tell the sheriff to disarm the guards.

I want to call your attention to another fellow. When _____ was beat up by the Baldwin guards, _____ [the stenographer who recorded the speech omitted the names], who was nominated for sheriff yesterday, had the information right in his hands. Then the miners of the country had to pension him owing to the fact of the brutal assassination of the guards. This man Malone knew it. It was right at his door. I keep an eye on those crooked politicians. He says we will have to do away with the Baldwin guards. He runs a detective agency with Dan Cunningham, who went up to murder the miners at Stanaford Mountain. They went with labels on their breasts. It is enough to make anybody disgusted. No wonder these mine owners beat your wives, no wonder your children will rise up and curse you. It is time for you to stop it. You are not dealing with a rotten politics, you are dealing with a system that is old and strong.

Let me say to you it needs men of America, men of a great state, it matters not to me whether you are a judge or whether you are a merchant, you are still a citizen of this state. Let me say to you, my friends, there is a feeling abroad in the land, I have traveled over it, and I know the pulse of the workers. I know the pulse of the intelligent people.

I want to say to you here, my friends—you needn't go so near God Almighty to take a picture, come here to take it (this was spoken to a young man who went up on top of the grand stand to take a photograph of the crowd)—There is a spirit abroad in the land, there is an undercurrent going on, and unless the wise men of the nation get together and save her I want to say to you, my friends, a cry in the night from the hungry mob is an awful teacher, you need but a sword for a judge and a preacher.

Oh, men of America, I want to say to you, we are dealing too much with the intellect. A nation that does not deal with the heart of man will perish. In fifty years you have produced more wealth than it took five hundred years in Babylon, Greece and Rome to travel the same road you are traveling today. They didn't take warning. What happened?

I went to a place in New York. A lawyer of Wall Street said, "Mother Jones, I would like to show you a picture. Will you go?" I said, "I am twenty-one years old, I will take care of myself." There is a place there if you turn your nose inside of it it will be snapped off. The government knows it but you guys don't know anything about it. I went in. It cost $2.50 for hanging your cloak up. I sat down at the table. My cloak wasn't worth $2.50, so I kept it on. We ordered supper. Now this place is where the opera houses and theaters are built and opened. It is supported by the blood-sucking tribe of Wall Street gamblers. There came in a woman between two fellows. The lawyer said to me, "Mother Jones, do you know how much the cloak on that woman cost?" "I don't know," said I, "It looks like Russian sable. If it is, it cost twenty thousand dollars." "That cloak," said he, "cost $50,000.00. Those fellows paid for it and they never worked a day in their lives." I said, "They never paid for it." I said, "My boys paid for it." (Applause.) Then they sat down and feasted like Belshazzar did long ago.

Then came along another gang. They sat down at a table, and got so full and debauched they upset a table and smashed everything on it. When they did there was a check written out instantly for a thousand dollars. $1.50 will pay for what is on your table. Put that down (to the reporter). Oh, you bloodsuckers, well know it. So them blood-suckers up in New York well know it.

My friends, you are exploited, you are robbed, you are plundered. You have submitted to it, you haven't protested. You grunt but you don't fight as you ought to do. You don't have to kill the guards, all you have to do is to go to the ballot box and vote them out of business. (Applause.)

Now, my friends, after I left you, before, when I was in Utah a poor creature came to me one morning. Her husband was among the revolters. He was carried off to the jail with one hundred and twenty-five or thirty others. The wife came to me, she held in her arms a babe, and said, "Mother Jones, do you see my Johnnie?" I said, "Yes, I see your Johnnie," and the tears streamed down her breast. She said, "Oh, Mother, you know my Johnnie isn't strong, I was afraid he would get hurt or killed in the mines. We got a lot from the company and I took in boarders, I was trying to pay for a shelter, so if anything happened to John I would have a shelter for the children. Do you see my Johnnie, he was born at 11 o'clock at night, and I got up at half past four in the morning and cooked breakfast for eleven men to go into the mines. Now, they have got my John, my home, my health." She says, "Mother, tell me, my God, what am I going to do?"

I want to say to this audience, I knew at five o'clock in the evening those blood-hounds were coming in to arrest those men next morning. I said to the boys, "Go up in the mountain and bury your guns." I didn't want a clash. "Bury your guns." They said, "No, Mother we will need them." I said, "No, boys, go and bury them." At half past four in the morning I heard the footsteps. I went to the window. The first I saw was the Mormon sheriff. I said, "What is the trouble?" He said, "We have come to get these dogs." I said, "What have they done?" He said, "They don't go to work." "No, they won't," said I. They arrested those men, that were in tents at the foot of the range, and drove them up the road without a particle of clothing on them.

Put that down (to the reporter). And they know it is true. They hit them with their guns, and their ribs shook like aspen leaves. They begged to put on their clothes. "Oh, no," they said, "Go to work." And the profane language that was used was horrifying—they were church members. The ministers can say "hell-fire" and "damnation," but if you are not a church member you mustn't use it.

Those wretches were taken into court and tried, and that woman perished with her babe and four children. They don't murder, do they? They don't murder, do they?

With the bleached bones of these people you build your churches, your Y.M.C.A.'s, and your institutions. You have robbed and plundered these people, and they will build it into churches, and they will be churches, too, and the love of God will be there—or will it be the love of capitalism or the operators. Look into the churches, and see the big fellow at the front singing "All for Jesus." They murder for Jesus, they rob for Jesus, and own the government for Jesus, and scare hell out of the sheriff for Jesus. (Loud applause and laughter.) Get behind those fellows. They say, "Our Father in Heaven." You can hear them forty miles, crying to heaven, "Give us today, Oh, Lord, give thy son his daily bread," and "Oh, Lord Jesus, fix it so I can get three or four fellows' bread." (Laughter.)

Now, my friends, you can't blame those people after all, coming down to it. They couldn't change the system if they wanted to. We, the people, have got to do it.

I will give you an illustration. I want to ask any man here, is this government today the same kind of government it was sixty years ago, when the immortal Lincoln was in Washington?

(Cries from the crowd: "No, No, No, No.")

Well, it wouldn't fit in. The government of forty or fifty or sixty years ago wouldn't fit in.

Government changes as the field of production changes. It has done that all down human history. It had to change with the field of production. Literature changed and the newspapers are more vicious today than they were fifty or sixty years ago. Public opinion is moulded from what you read in the papers and magazines and what you hear in the pulpits. And your religion is not what it was fifty or sixty years ago. Then the Catholic bishops did not visit Washington and wine and dine with the Presidents. They do it now.

It is essential, because they have got the power and the people have multiplied. Religion changes without changing the order of production.

I want you to bear that in mind, my friends. Your judges are owned and controlled by the ruling class. You need not expect any justice in the courts; I don't. I don't look for justice.

Did you have a Salvation Army sixty years ago? No, you didn't. Why? They weren't needed. Capitalism hadn't developed. Did you have the Holy Jumpers fifty years ago? No, you didn't. Did you have the Holy Rollers? No. Did you have the Sanctified Saints? No. They weren't needed. Why weren't they needed? Because capitalism hadn't developed. It was when they reached in for the private ownership of the industries that the master class added those auxiliaries to their bulwark.

I have made a great study of those things, my friends, and I will prove it to you. I happened to be in El Paso after a strike. One hundred and fifty of our men were murdered. I was going through Arizona at that time. One hundred and fifty men were murdered. They hung others upon the trees. I went to El Paso. I said to the boys, "I will go down and cross the line from El Paso. I will get the information I want." I went into Mexico, and as I was going I met three miners coming over the bridge. The boys said to me, "Mother, for God's sake, where did you come from?" I said, "I thought they had you murdered." They said, "No, we have been in the range three days and nights, we haven't had anything to eat." I said, "I will give you some money, go up and make yourselves at home. I am going to hold a meeting on the corner tonight." So, I went up, and the boys met me. We got $18.50 collection. I gave them $5.00 apiece, and said, "Now we will go and eat, and while we are eating we will talk things over." So while we were going down the street there was a mob howling and yelling at each other, calling each other liars. I thought the whole town of El Paso was going to be torn to pieces. So I stuck my head in. Directly I caught on to the game. I said to a policeman, "What is it? Why are they fighting?" He said, "I know what the fighting is about, it is about Jesus." He said, "The Salvation Army occupies this corner, the Holy Rollers that corner. There is only two corners. These fellows get all the money. They want to swap corners, and let the Salvation Army take that." I said, "Isn't the money for Jesus? What difference does it make?" He said, "Don't you think Jesus ever sees that money."

I don't know whether you ever watched women when they get religion the first time. They get up to heaven without being sent for. I went in and watched it. It was funny for me. Those things have a wonderful philosophy for me. The Holy Rollers were over there rolling for Jesus, and the Holy Jumpers were over there jumping for Jesus. The money belonged to Jesus. I gathered up all I could, I kept watching. I went to the policeman and said, "I have got a lot of Jesus' money, what shall I do with it?" He said, "You will keep it." I said, "Well, that is what I thought I ought to do." While those people in their hearts meant well, they didn't understand that they were the machine of capitalism hoodwinking the people while the chains of slavery were woven around them.

I know a lot of you will go off and condemn me, but you condemned Christ, you condemned every man and woman that ever dared to raise their voice in behalf of truth and justice, and you will do the same with me. But I don't care what your comments are. There will be a judgment day, and YOU WILL PAY THE PENALTY. (Applause.)

I want to tell you that.

I want to say, my friends, it is a fine illustration; every avenue is commercialized today by the ruling class of the age in which we live. We write slander we rob each other and say it is right; we rent each other out to the ruling class to beat us.

(A voice: "That is what we do.")

I want to say, my friends, it is time to stop it. Say, brave boys, say, the star that rose in Bethlehem has crossed the world, it has risen here; see it slowly breaking through the clouds. The Star of Bethlehem will usher in the new day and new time and new philosophy—and if you are only true you will be free—if you are only men—if you only go home and leave the saloons alone. Mother knows how often you need a drink—

(Cheers from the audience and clapping of hands, particularly noticeable of one woman.)

You needn't clap your hands. It is to your disgrace. You needn't do it. If you understood the philosophy you would keep your hands down, and use your head to the best interests of the race. If you knew their aching backs, their swimming heads, if you knew the empty stomachs, if you knew the food that goes into their mouths you wouldn't clap your brutal hands like a thug, you wouldn't do it, my sister woman, you wouldn't clap your hands at these poor boys. They often need a drink. Many times they are often worn and exhausted. Like the big brewers in Milwaukee, when I went there to reach out a helping hand to three hundred girls they had enslaved. One of the brewers said to me, "Mother Jones, I saw a terrible picture in Massachusetts, you don't see it here." He said, "I saw a woman on the side walk and the little boys and girls were throwing pebbles at her and bullying her. You don't see it here." I said, "There is a cause for that. Don't you know there is an underlying cause for that? Don't you know that Massachusetts has been a manufacturing state for some generations. Wisconsin is an agricultural state," said I. "Don't you know that the grandfather of this woman went into those slave pens of capitalism and in her infancy she was ground into profit, she never had a square meal, never had anything to develop her nerves. All the brutes gave her was to develop the muscle and bones for profit. Don't you know the mother and father of this creature also went into that slave pen? Don't you know we have made a fight to bring the hours down from sixteen to ten, from ten to eight?" "We have made a fight to give them a little more food to develop them. Don't you know your class have robbed them, and when this woman came into the world she was starved and a nervous wreck? Your own girls here you are robbing and their children will be the same."

If this woman could stay in her home and plant love there, and girls' instinct, they wouldn't throw stones at this object of pity.

This woman was a nervous wreck. If she didn't get a drink of liquor she would have been in the insane asylum, and us paying six million dollars a year for the support of them!

Look at the class pirates that sail the high seas and don't need the riches. We will stop drinking when you give us what belongs to us. When you take us out of your shacks and give us what belongs to us, we don't need anybody to howl for us.

Often I have had to give my boys a drink, they had to have it. A fellow met me on the street one day, he had asked half a dozen people for a drink. He said, "Give me ten cents, I want to get a drink." I said, "Here is fifty cents, go and get a bed and supper." The man looked at me, and shook hands. Eight years afterwards that man came up to me on the train and said, "I believe your name is Mother Jones." I said, "Yes, sir, it is; what about it?" He said, "I want to grasp your hand, I would have died one night but for you." I was blank. "What about it?" said I. He went on to tell me. "Now," said he," if there is anything on earth I can do for you, I am in business, I am worth over seven hundred thousand dollars today," said he, and he handed me money for the Mexican refugees. If I had let that man go that night he would have stolen, because he had to have that drink. The police would have clubbed him and put him in jail and degraded him.

Let us know the cause of the suffering race. Let us put less feathers on the outside of the skull and a little more intelligence on the inside. (Applause.)

Away back in Palestine they were robbing and plundering them. There was a humble carpenter that came. It was not the leaders that came to him, it was not a member of the church that came to him, it was not a society woman, she would shun him then as she would now, if he came to her. It was that woman crushed by economic wrongs that came to wash his feet with her tears and wipe them with her hair — then he gave her the hope, the light of the future economic age. It was she in gratitude that fell at his feet and paid tribute to him — it was on her sacred head he placed his hands.

It has ever been the humble that have done the world's enlightening. It has been those that have been pointed to with scorn that have had to bear the brunt.

I have had to measure steel in the dead of night with the blood-hounds of the ruling class. I have measured steel with them in the lonely hours of the night. It is the society women that dragged me out of bed in the night, when fighting for you, and with the bayonets in the hands of seven of them, put me out of the state and told me never to come back. If women were true they wouldn't raise men to do such acts.

(Cries from the crowd: "You are right, You are right.")

No, they wouldn't, my friends.

It was Miss Helen Gould, the great philanthropist, that hired blood-hounds to come in in the morning. She took them out of the penitentiary, they came in at 4 o'clock where I was locked up. I never undressed myself for eighteen nights. He planted his gun under my nose and said: "Tell me where I will get three thousand dollars of the miners' money, or I will blow your brains out." I said, "They wouldn't be any use to you after you got them out." I was alone at four o'clock in the morning. He was a big ruffian. Helen Gould took him out of the penitentiary, like these guards up here, to shoot me if I dared to interfere with profit.

He said, "Where is the money?" I said, "Up in Indianapolis." I said, "Write to them, they are good fellows, they will send it to you." He said, "Haven't you got any money here? How do you pay these bills? Haven't you got any money?" I said, "Yes, I have some money." He said, "Out with it or I will blow your brains out." I pulled it out — I am generous — out I came with the money. I took 50 cents out, and, says I, "That is what I have got, but I am not going to give it to you." He said, "Is that all? How are you going to get the money which is in Indianapolis when you get out?" I said, "I will telegraph for it when I need it." He said, "If you don't shell it up I will kill you." I said, "I am not going to shell it up." He said, "Why?" I said, "I have got Helen Gould's small-pox, and when I get out of there I will need the money to get a jag on to roast them off."

I suppose if you were there you would clap your hands and say, "Shoot her." None of your chatter, blackguards, we don't need it. We will open up without anybody to tell us, when these blood-sucking pirates give you what belongs to you. Now, boys, we are facing the day when human liberty will be yours. I don't care how much martial law the Governor of West Virginia proclaims, I have had martial law proclaimed where I was more than once, but I didn't stop fighting. When he pulled off his martial law I began it again, and he had to bring them back. Do you see how you can do the business? If they proclaim martial law, bury your guns. You can tell him that if you see him. If the Governor proclaims martial law, bury your guns. I have been up against it. They hauled me into court.

Stand by the militia, stand by the boys. Don't allow no guards to attack them. (Cries of: "That is right, That is right.") Stand shoulder to shoulder with them.

I want to say here in behalf of General Elliott. I know him well. I have had some experience with his manhood. I want to say to you he will never hurt the workers. He will only do what he is forced to do. But don't you force him to do anything. He won't do it if he can help himself. It was General Elliott who arrested me in Clarksburg when he was United States Marshal, by the order of Judge Jackson. General Elliott did not undertake to send me to jail, nor did he send a deputy with me. There was nine of us. He sent a young man, who is now on the *Evening Mail* in Charleston. When we got off in Parkersburg, the young man and I were going one way, and four or five deputies and eight boys were going another way. I said, "The boys are going the wrong way." "No," he said, "they are going to jail." He said, "We engaged a room for you at the hotel." I said, "I would rather go board with Uncle Sam, I have better company than at the hotel." (Laughter and applause.) I said, "My colleagues and I have fought this battle for years, and when they are jailed, I will be jailed, and when they are hung, I will be hung." So I went to jail. Major Elliott gave the jailer orders, and I was treated courteously. His wife and daughter came down to the trial, and went out with me; they offered their home for me to rest. I shall always remember Major Elliott, I don't care what position he holds he won't hurt you, and he will tell the Governor.

Be true to the boys. We will capture the militia some of these days. We will join the militia and say to the blood-sucking fellows, "Get off your perch." (Laughter and applause.)

I know some very good operators, but they are dictated to by the syndicates, the oligarchy in Washington, so they can't help themselves.

You are to blame, and no one else. You have stood for it. You don't stand in your union. If you would, when you were organized up New River, you wouldn't have this condition today. Don't blame the Governor. I blame him for violation of the law, that is what I blame the Governor for. (Applause.)

I am going to be with you, I am going to stay with you, I don't care what the papers say, they can jump on me, but they never weaken me. I am just as strong as ever. One corporation lap dog on Paint Creek, one of the C. & O. agents, I will clean him up when I get to Huntington. I won't say anything about his generosity. When you give those fellows a little bit of office — What are you looking at that watch? — That will watch you devils well, my boys.

I was in court when the judge condemned a man and said, "You are a bad fellow." The fellow said, "I am not half as bad, not half as mean, nor half as wicked as the judge" — then he stopped, and the judge got furious. The fellow continued — "as he thinks I am." The judge said, "Connect your sentence."

Now, my boys, we are facing a new day. I am one of those who believe as the immortal Hugo did. I read Hugo's works when I was young. Hugo was my idol, he was inspiring. He said so many grand things. I felt that he had the agony of the race in his body.

So, my boys, I said, we are in the early dawn of the world's greatest century, when crime, brutality and wrong will disappear, and man will rise in grander height, and every woman shall sit in her own front yard and sing a lullaby to the happy days of happy childhood, noble manhood of a great nation that is coming. She will look at her mansion and every room will be light and there will be peace and justice.

I see that vision today as I talk to you. Oh, God Almighty grant — Oh, God almighty grant — God grant that the woman who suffers for you suffers not for a coward but for a man. God grant that. He will send us another Lincoln, another Patrick Henry. God grant, my brothers, that you will be men, and the woman who bore you will see her God and say, "I raised a man."

(Cries from the audience: "Right, Right, Right," and applause.)

[George Wallace Papers, West Virginia Collection, West Virginia University.]

Speech at a public meeting
on the steps of the capitol
Charleston, West Virginia

In the second week of August Mother Jones performed a feat which she often boasted of in later years, and which lost no drama in the telling. For some eight years Cabin Creek, the next valley over from Paint Creek, had been unorganized, and armed guards dominated the unincorporated company towns with machine guns placed at strategic points. No organizers were allowed beyond the entrance to the valley. However, the town of Eskdale was incorporated and, in two forays there, Mother Jones managed to convince the unorganized miners to join the strike begun at Paint Creek. On one occasion she faced down fifty guards at a machine gun emplacement. When the men struck the guards began evictions from the company houses, and many of the miners' families moved into the tent colony set up by the UMWA at Holly Grove.

With both Paint Creek and Cabin Creek now solidly behind the strike Mother Jones called a mass meeting for 15 August in Charleston, where she presented a series of resolutions amounting to an ultimatum to Governor William E. Glasscock to end the guard system. At the time, the militia had moved into the strike area to preserve order, but martial law had not yet been declared. Governor Glasscock's response to the ultimatum was to declare martial law in the strike zone. The militia began, with only partial success, to confiscate the arms of guards and miners, collecting six machine guns and over eighteen hundred rifles in the next several weeks. Later events proved that many of the miners followed Mother Jones's advice to bury their guns.

This speech illustrates Mother Jones's particular brand of socialism, in which she broadly sketches the roles of different groups in American society, using familiar names. The exploiters—Marcus Alonzo Hanna, Helen Gould, Andrew Carnegie, the Guggenheims—control the national economy. Presidents like Grover Cleveland and Theodore Roosevelt support their interests, as do Senators Nathan B. Scott and Stephen B. Elkins of West Virginia and Senator Charles W. F. Dick of Ohio. Governors such as William E. Glasscock of West Virginia and James H. Peabody of Colorado are weak henchmen of the capitalists, unable or unwilling to support the interests of the public. Some governors—John Peter Altgeld of Illinois and Davis H. Waite of Colorado are alluded to, though not by name—have risen as advocates of the ordinary citizen. The capitalists create or manipulate institutions like the Civic Federation, churches, and the YMCA to mislead the people regarding their true interests, and they find in the Pinkerton and Baldwin-Felts detective agencies the instruments to carry out their inhumane policies. The people have the right to defend their homes and persons and to enjoy free speech and freedom of assembly. They have the right to bargain collectively, and, as they come to understand their rights and their power at the ballot box, they will eventually overthrow the oligarchy and take over the control of the means of production. In the present circumstances they are exercising their rights of assembly and petition, but if the governor will not act, they will have to maintain their rights themselves.

§   §   §

This, my friends, marks, in my estimation, the most remarkable move ever made in the State of West Virginia. It is a day that will mark history in the long ages to come. What is it? It is an uprising of the oppressed against the master class.

From this day on, my friends, Virginia—West Virginia—shall march in the front of the nation's states. To me, I think, the proper thing to do is to read the purpose of our meeting here today—why these men have laid down their tools, why these men have come to the State House.

To His Excellency, William E. Glasscock, Governor of the State of West Virginia:

It is respectfully represented unto your Excellency that the owners of the various coal mines doing business along the valley of Cabin Creek, Kanawha County, West Virginia, are maintaining and have at present in their employ a large force of armed guards, armed with Winchesters, a dangerous and deadly weapon; also having in their possession three Gatling guns, which they have stationed at commanding positions overlooking the Cabin Creek Valley, which said weapons said guards use for the purpose of brow-beating, intimidating and menacing the lives of all the citizens who live in said valley, and whose business calls them into said valley, who are not in accord with the management of the coal companies, which guards are cruel and their conduct toward the citizens is such that it would be impossible to give a detailed account of.

Therefore, suffice it to say, however, that they beat, abuse, maim and hold up citizens without process of law, deny freedom of speech, a provision guaranteed by the Constitution, deny the citizens to assemble in a peaceable manner for the purpose of discussing questions in which they are concerned. Said guards also hold up a vast body of laboring men who live at the mines, and so conduct themselves that a great number of men, women and children live in a state of constant fear, unrest and dread.

89

We hold that the stationing of said guards along the public highways, and public places is a menace to the general welfare of the state. That such action on the part of the companies in maintaining such guards is detrimental to the best interests of society and an outrage against the honor and dignity of the State of West Virginia. (Loud applause.)

As citizens interested in the public weal and general welfare, and believing that law and order, and peace, should ever abide, that the spirit of brotherly love and justice and freedom should everywhere exist, we must tender our petition that you would bring to bear all the powers of your office as Chief Executive of this State, for the purpose of disarming said guards and restoring to the citizens of said valley all the rights guaranteed by the Constitution of the United States and said State.

In duty bound, in behalf of the miners of the State of West Virginia.

I want to say with all due respect to the Governor—I want to say to you that the Governor will not, cannot do anything, for this reason: The Governor was placed in this building by Scott and Elkins and he don't dare oppose them. (Loud applause.) Therefore, you are asking the Governor of the State to do something that he cannot do without betraying the class he belongs to. (Loud applause.)

I remember the Governor in a state, when Grover Cleveland was perched in the White House—Grover Cleveland said he would send the Federal troops out, and the Governor of that state [John Peter Altgeld of Illinois] said, "Will you? If you do I will meet your Federal troops with the state troops, and we will have it out." Old Grover never sent the troops—he took back water. (Applause, and cries of: "Yes, he did.")

You see, my friends, how quickly the Governor sent his militia when the coal operators got scared to death. (Applause.)

I have no objection to the militia. I would always prefer the militia, but there was no need in this county for the militia, none whatsoever. They were law-abiding people, and the women and children. They were held up on the highways, caught in their homes and pulled out like rats and beaten up—some of them. I said, "If there is no one else in the State of West Virginia to protest, I will protest." (Loud applause, and cries of: "Yes, she will; Mother will.")

The womanhood of this State shall not be oppressed and beaten and abused by a lot of contemptible, damnable blood-hounds, hired by the operators. They wouldn't keep their dogs where they keep you fellows. You know that. They have a good place for their dogs and a slave to take care of them. The mine owners' wives will take the dogs up, and say, "I love you, dea-h" (trying to imitate by tone of voice).

Now, my friends, the day for petting dogs is done; the day for raising children to a nobler manhood and better womanhood is here. (Applause and cries of: "Amen! Amen!")

You have suffered, I know how you have suffered. I was with you nearly three years in this state. I went to jail, went to the Federal courts, but I never took any back water. I still unfurl the red flag of industrial freedom, no tyrant's face shall you know, and I call you today into that freedom, long perched on the bosom (Interrupted by applause).

I am back again to find you, my friends, in a state of industrial peonage—after ten years absence I find you in a state of industrial peonage.

The Superintendent at Acme—I went up there, and they said we were unlawful—we had an unlawful mob along. Well, I will tell you the truth, we took a couple of guns, because we knew we were going to meet some thugs, and by jimminy (interrupted by applause).

We will prepare for the job, just like Lincoln and Washington did. We took lessons from them, and we are here to prepare for the job.

Well, when I came out on the public road the Superintendent—you know the poor salary slave—he came out and told me that there were Notary Publics there and a squire—one had a peg leg, and the balance had pegs in their skulls. (Applause.)

They forbid me speaking on the highway, and said that if I didn't discontinue I would be arrested. Well, I want to tell you one thing, I don't run to jail, but when the blood-hounds undertake to put me in jail I will go there. I have gone there. I would have had the little peg-leg Squire arrest me only I knew this meeting was going to be pulled off today to let the world know what was going on in West Virginia. When I get through with them, by the Eternal God they will be glad to let me alone.

I am not afraid of jails. We build the jails, and when we get ready we will put *them* behind the bars. That may happen very soon—things happen overnight.

Now, brothers, not in all the history of the labor movement have I got such an inspiration as I have got from you here today. Your banners are history, they will go down to the future ages, to the children unborn, to tell them the slave has risen, children must be free.

The labor movement was not originated by man. The labor movement, my friends, was a command from God Almighty. He commanded the prophets thousands of years ago to go down and redeem the Israelites that were in bondage, and he organized the men into a union and went to work. And they said, "The masters have made us gather straw, they have been more cruel than they were before. What are we going to do?" The prophet said, "A voice from heaven has come to get you together." They got together and the prophet led them out of the land of bondage and robbery and plunder into the land of freedom. And when the army of the pirates followed them the Dead Sea opened and swallowed them up, and for the first time the workers were free.

And so it is. That can well be applied to the State of West Virginia.

When I left Cabin Creek ten years ago to go to another terrific battle field, every man on Cabin Creek was organized — every single miner. The mine owners and the miners were getting along harmoniously, they had an understanding and were carrying it out. But they had some traitors who made a deal with the mine owners and the organization was driven out of Cabin Creek. There were no better miners in the whole State of West Virginia than on Cabin Creek, no better operators, in those days. You got along together. They were trying to make it happy and comfortable for you but the demon came and tore the organization to pieces, and you are at war today.

I hope, my friends, that you and the mine owners will put aside the breach and get together before I leave the State. But I want to say make no settlement until they sign up that every bloody murderer of a guard has got to go. (Loud applause.)

This is done, my friends, beneath the flag our fathers fought and bled for, and we don't intend to surrender our liberty. (Applause.)

I have a document issued eighteen years ago, telling how they must handle the labor movement — pat them on the back, make them believe that they were your devoted friends. I hold the document, taken from their statement in Washington. It plainly states, "We have got to crucify them but we have got to do it cunningly." And they have been doing it cunningly. But I want to say in answer to your statements, that you are dealing with a different class of workers today than eighteen years ago. We have begun education, we have educated the workers, and you can't enslave them. They will come again, and you will either take to the ocean and get out of the nation and leave us alone, or you will settle right with us. (Loud applause.)

It is different now, my friends. It was Mark Hanna who said some years ago — the shrewdest politician America ever had — he said, "I want to tell you that before 1912 the Republican and Democratic parties will be about to get their death blow."

Never in the history of the United States was there such an upheaval as there is today. The politicians are cutting each other's throats, eating each other up, they are for the offices. Teddy, the monkey-chaser, had a meeting in Chicago, he was blowing his skull off his carcass about race suicide. God Almighty, bring him down the C. & O. and he will never say another word about race suicide. The whole population seems to be made up of kids. Every woman has three babies in her arms and nine on the floor. So you will see there is no danger of race suicide. When he sees this he will keep his mouth shut on that.

See the condition we are in today. There is a revolution. There is an editorial in one of the papers in your own state showing how little they have done for the workers, that the workers are awakening. The literature is being circulated among them. I myself have circulated millions and millions of pieces of literature in this country and awakened the workers. On the trains they say, "Oh, Mother, you gave me a book and that woke me up." As long as you woke up right it is all right. He says, "I have woke up right." Then if you woke up right, you are my children.

Oh, you men of wealth, oh you preachers, you are going over to China and sending money over there for Jesus. For God's sake keep it at home, we need it. Let me tell you, them fellows are owned body and soul by the ruling class, and they would rather take a year in hell with Elkins than ninety-nine in heaven. (Loud applause.) Do you find a minister preaching against the guards?

(Cries from the audience: "They are traitors, moral cowards.")

He will preach about Jesus, but not about the guards.

When we were crossing the bridge at Washington, the blood-hounds were at the company store. These blood-hounds might have thrown me into the river, and I wouldn't have known it. The men were hollering "Police! Police!" I said, "What is the matter with you?" They said, "Oh, God, murder! murder!" Another one came out and his feet never touched the side walk.

My boys came running to me and said, "Oh, Mother, they are killing the boys." The traction car turned the corner. I said, "Call them boys here." Then they went, they thought I had an army with me. Then I picked up a boy streaming with blood where the hounds had beat him.

You are to blame, you have voted for the whole gang of commercial pirates every time you get a chance to free yourselves.

It is time to clean them up.

(Cries of: "She is right, she is right.")

If this nation is to march onward and upward the day of change is here.

I have been reading of the *Titanic* when she went down. Did you read of her? The big guns wanted to save themselves, and the fellows that were guiding below took up a club and said we will save our people. And then the papers came out and said those millionaires tried to save the women. Oh, Lord, why don't they give up their millions if they want to save the women and children? Why do they rob them of home, why do they rob millions of women to fill the hell-holes of capitalism.

I realize, I remember what they did to me, the Guggenheims, I remember what the Guggenheim blood-hounds did to me, one night in Colorado. They went to the hotel after we had organized the slaves. I took the four o'clock train for the southern fields, and the blood-hounds, the chief of police, and the whole gang of commercial blood-hounds came up to the hotel and went to the register to find my room, and the hotel keeper said that I had left at four o'clock. We had a meeting that night. They took a fellow and drove him down the street barefooted and put him on the train and told him to never come back. And we are very civilized! They don't do that in Russia, it is in America.

They took me and put me in jail—I had the smallpox, I had the Helen Gould smallpox covering me all over. And at four o'clock in the morning they came and the blood-hounds—Helen Gould's blood-hounds—and they bound four hundred miners in Colorado, for gold, and threw their widows and orphans out on the highways in the snow. When I was fighting the battle with those wretches they put me into a pen which you built, a pest house, it was burned down before morning, it wasn't worth fifty cents. We went down by a store and the storekeeper said, "God Almighty, put us down in the cellar and they won't know us, put the dirty clothes on us"—when them dirty clothes found out that there was such a lot of rotten carcasses under them, the dirty clothes turned over. (Applause and laughter.)

If your sheriff had done his duty as a citizen of this state and according to his oath, he would have disarmed the guards and then there would have been no more trouble.

(Cries of: "That is right, that is right.")

Just make me Governor for one month. I won't ask for a sheriff or policeman, and I will do business, and there won't a guard stay in the State of West Virginia. (Applause.) The mine owners won't take sixty-nine thousand pounds of coal in dockage off of you fellows. Sixty-nine thousand pounds of coal they docked you for, and a few pounds of slate, and they give to Jesus on Sunday.

They give your missionary women a couple of hundred dollars and rot you under pretense of giving to Jesus. Jesus never sees a penny of it, and never heard of it. They use it for the women to get a jag on and then go and hollow for Jesus.

I wish I was God Almighty, I would throw down something some night from heaven, and get rid of the whole blood-sucking bunch. (Laughter and applause.)

I want to show you here that the average wages you fellows get in this country is $500.00 a year. Before you get a thing to eat there is $20.00 taken out a month, which leaves about $24.00 a month.

Then you go the the "Pluck-me" stores and want to get something to eat for your wife, and you are off that day, and the child comes back and says, "Papa, I can't get anything." "Why," he says, "There is four dollars coming to me," and the child goes back crying, without a mouthful of anything to eat. The father goes to the "Pluck-me" store and says to the manager, "There is four dollars coming to me," and the manager says, "Oh, no, we have kept that for rent!" "You charge six dollars a month, and there are only three days gone." "Well," he says, "it is a rule that two-thirds of the rent is to be kept if there is only a day."

That is honesty! Do you wonder these women starve? Do you wonder at this uprising? And you fellows have stood it entirely too long. It is time now to put a stop to it. *We will give the Governor until tomorrow night to take them guards out of Cabin Creek.* (Very loud applause, and cries of: "And no longer.")

HERE ON THE STEPS OF THE CAPITOL OF WEST VIRGINIA, I SAY THAT IF THE GOVERNOR WON'T MAKE THEM GO THEN WE WILL MAKE THEM GO.

(Loud applause, and cries of: "That we will." "Only one more day." "The guards have got to go.")

We have come to the chief executive, we have asked him and he couldn't do anything. (Laughter.)

The prosecuting attorney is of the same type — another fellow belonging to the ruling class. (Applause, and murmurings in the crowd.)

Hush up, there, hush up, hush up.

I want to tell you that the Governor will get until tomorrow night, Friday night, to get rid of his blood-hounds, and if they are not gone we will get rid of them. (Loud applause.)

Aye, men! Aye, men, inside of this building, Aye, women! Come with me and see the horrible pictures, see the horrible condition the ruling class has put these women in. Aye, they destroy women. Look at those little children, the rising generation; yes, look at the little ones; yes, look at the women assaulted. Some one said that that place ought to be drained up there. The mine owner's home is drained; the superintendent's home is drained. But I want to ask you, when a man works ten or eleven hours in the foul gas of the mine day after day if he is in condition to come out and drain.

(Cries of: "Not on your life, No.")

I have worked, boys, I have worked with you for years. I have seen the suffering children, and in order to be convinced I went into the mines on the night shift and the day shift and helped the poor wretches to load coal at times. We lay down at noon and we took our lunches, and we talked our wrongs over, we gathered together at night and asked "How will we remedy things?" We organized secretly, and after a while held public meetings. We got our people together in those organized states. Today the mine owners and the miners come together. They meet each other and shake hands and have no more war in those states, and the working men are becoming more intelligent. And I am one of those, my friends, I don't care about your woman suffrage and the temperance brigade or any other of your class associations, I want women of the coming day to discuss and find out the cause of child crucifixion, that is what I want to find out. I have worked in the factories of Georgia and Alabama, and these blood-hounds were tearing the hands off of children and working them fourteen hours a day until I fought for them. They made them put up every Saturday morning for missionary work in China. I know what I am talking about. I am not talking at haphazard, I have the goods. Go down, men of today, who rob and exploit, go down into hell and look at the ruins you have put there, look at the jails. We pay six million dollars a year to chain men like demons in a bastille — and we call ourselves civilized! Six million dollars a year we pay for jails, and nothing for education.

I have been in jail more than once, and I expect to go again. If you are too cowardly to fight, I will fight. You ought to be ashamed of yourselves, actually to the Lord you ought, just to see one old woman who is not afraid of all the blood-hounds. How scared those villains are when one woman eighty years old, with her head gray, can come in and scare hell out of the whole bunch. (Laughter.) We didn't scare them? The mine owners run down the street like a mad dog today. They ask who started this thing? I started it, I did it, and I am not afraid to tell you if you are here, and I will start more before I leave West Virginia. I started this mass-meeting today. I had these banners written, and don't accuse anybody else of the job. (Loud applause.)

It is freedom or death, and your children will be free. We are not going to leave a slave class to the coming generation, and I want to say to you that the next generation will not charge us for what we have done, they will charge and condemn us for what we have left undone. (Cries of: "That is right.")

You have got your bastille. Yes, we have no fears of them at all. I was put out at twelve o'clock at night, and landed with five cents in my pocket, by seven bayonets in the State of Colorado. The Governor [James H. Peabody] told me — he is a corporation rat, you know, he told me never to come back. A man is a fool, if he is a governor, to tell a woman not to do a thing. (Loud applause, and cries of: "Tell them again," "Tell them about it.")

I went back next day and I have been back since the fight, and he hasn't bothered me. He has learned it won't do to tamper with women of the right metal. You have a few cats (mocking) — they are not women, they are what you call ladies. There is a difference between women and ladies. The modern parasites made ladies, but God Almighty made women.

(Applause and cries of: "Tell us one more.")

Now, my boys, you are mine, we have fought together, we have hungered together, we have marched together, but I can see victory in the heavens for you. I can see the hand above you guiding and inspiring you to move onward and upward. No white flag — we cannot raise it, we must not raise it. We must redeem the world.

Go into our factories, see how the conditions are there, see how women are ground up for the merciless money pirates, see how many of the poor wretches go to work with crippled bodies. I talked with a mother who had her small children working. She said to me, "Mother, they are not of age, but I had to say they were, I had to tell them they were of age, so they would get a chance to help me get something to eat." She said after they were there a little while, "I have saved forty dollars, the first I ever saw. I put that into a cow and we had some milk for the little ones." In all the years her husband had put in the earth digging out wealth, he never got a glimpse of forty dollars until he had to take his infant boys, that ought to go to school, and sacrifice them.

If there was no other reason, that should stimulate every man and woman to fight this damnable system of commercial pirates. (Cries of: "Right, right.") That alone should do it, my friends.

Is there a committee here? I want to take a committee of the well fed fellows and well dressed fellows, I want to present this to the Governor. Be very polite. Don't get on your knees. Get off your knees and stand up. None of these fellows are better than you, they are only flesh and blood — that is the truth.

(Committee formed around Mother and started into the Capitol building.)

These fellows all want to go and see the king. (Laughter.)

I will give the press a copy of this resolution and this petition, that was given to the Governor.

Now, my boys, guard rule and tyranny will have to go, there must be an end. I am going up Cabin Creek. I am going to hold meetings there. I am going to claim the right of an American citizen. I was on this earth before these operators were. I was in this country before these operators. I have been seventy-four years under this flag, I have got the right to talk. I have seen its onward march. I have seen the growth of oppression. And I want to say to you, my friends, I am going to claim my right as a citizen of this nation. I won't violate law, I will not kill anybody or starve anybody, but I will talk unsparingly of all the corporation blood-hounds we can bring to jail. (Laughter.)

I have no apologies to offer. I have seen your children murdered, I have seen you blown to death in the mines and there was no redress. A fellow in Colorado says, "Why don't you prop the mines?" The operator said, "Oh, hell, Dagoes are cheaper than props." Every miner is a Dago with the blood-sucking pirates, and they are cheaper than props. Because if they kill a hundred of you, well it was your fault. There must be a mine inspector kept there.

The night before the little Johnston boys were killed, the mine inspector — John Laing is a mine owner, he wouldn't inspect them — the mine inspector went there and said the mines are propped securely. The next morning the little Johnston children went to work, and when they were found their hands were clasped in their dinner buckets with two biscuits.

You work for Laing day after day. He is mine inspector. But he wouldn't be if I had anything to say about it. He would take a back seat.

Boys, I want to say to you, obey the law. Let me say to the Governor, and let me say to the mine owners, let me say to all people, that I will guarantee there will be no destruction of property.

In the first place, that is our property. It is inside where our jobs are. We have every reason to protect it. In the mines is where our jobs are. We are not out to destroy property. We are out to preserve and protect property, and I will tell you why. We are going to get more wages, and we are going to stop the docking system. Put that down. Your day for docking is done. Stop it. If they don't stop it we will. (Cries of: "Good, good.")

We'll take care of the property. There will be no property destroyed. (Cries of: "Not a bit.")

Not a bit, and if you want your property protected these miners will protect it for you, and they won't need a gun.

(Cries of: "It is our interest to do so.")

We will protect it, at the risk of our lives. I know the miners, I have marched with ten thousand, twenty thousand, and destroyed no property. We had twenty thousand miners in Pennsylvania, but destroyed no property.

They used to do that years ago, but after we have educated them they saw that violence was not the idea. We stopped it. We organized. We brought them to school once again. I will tell you why we are not going to destroy your property, Mr. Governor. Because one of these days we are going to take over the mines. (Loud applause.)

That is what we are going to do. We are going to take over those mines.

The government has a mine in North Dakota. It works eight hours, not a minute more. There are no guards, no police, no militia. The men make a hundred and twenty-five dollars a month, and there is never any trouble at that mine. Uncle Sam is running the job, and he is a pretty good mine inspector.

(Cries of: "Tell it, mamma, I can't.")

There used to be, when I was in Illinois before, a bunch of these black brutes down at Arbuckle, and we had them organize. There was a fellow whose name was Sy. We have them in the miners' union, as well as in the mines. I asked them whether they were grafting in the union—they got ten dollars apiece each month, twenty dollars in all. I went down and when they came up reading the financial statement and all those ten dollars were read, I said, "What is the ten dollars going for?" They told me. I said, "Get out of camp, I have no use for grafters."

We have them in the union. They have learned the lesson from the mine owners. There was a good old darkey there, and said, "Oh," said Sy, "I done talked to the Lord for a week, and the Lord jest come and whispered in my ear last night, and said, 'Sy, Sy, Sy, I have done had a talk with Mother about that graft. Come down tomorrow night.'" Sy said, "O, Lord Jesus, don't fail to let Mother come," and I went. He said Jesus didn't lie. Jesus said, "Mother come here for sure, she take care of that money, and wouldn't let them fellows get it for nothing." At once the fellows said Amen.

So we put a stop to the graft. We have a lot of grafters too. It is a disease. We have learned the game from the fellows above.

I want you to listen a moment. I want the business men to listen. You business men are up against it. There is a great revolution going on in the industrial world. The Standard Oil Company owns eighty-six great department stores in this country. The small business man is beginning to be eliminated. He has got to get down, he can't get up. It is like Carnegie said before the Tariff Commissioner in Washington: "Gentlemen, I am not bothered about tariff on steel rails," he says, "what concerns me and my class is the right to organize."

The day for the small man is gone, and the day to rise is now here. We want the right to organize. Carnegie said that in a few years — he went into the business with five thousand — he took seven thousand five hundred. He said he knew the time was ripe for steel bridges, and they went into it. He closed out his interest for three hundred million dollars.

Do you wonder that the steel workers are robbed? When one thief alone can take three hundred million dollars and give to a library — to educate your skulls because you didn't get a chance to educate them yourselves.

A fellow said, "I don't think we ought to take those libraries." Yes, take them, and let him build libraries in every town in the country. It is your money. Yet he comes and constructs those libraries as living monuments reddened with the blood of men, women and children that he robbed.

How did he make three hundred million dollars? Come with me to Homestead, and I will show you the graves reddened with the blood of men, women and children. That is where we fixed the Pinkertons, and they have never rose from that day to this. And we will fix the Baldwins in West Virginia.

The Pinkertons were little poodle dogs for the operators. We will fix the Baldwins just the same.

Some fellow said, "You are talking on the porch of the State House." That is the very place I want to talk, where what I say will not be perverted.

Senator Dick said, when I met him, "I am delighted to see you, Mother Jones." I said, "I am not delighted to see you." He said, "What is the matter?" I said, "You have passed the Dick military bill to shoot my class down, that is why I wouldn't shake hands with you." That is the way to do business with those fellows. All the papers in the country wrote it up, and he was knocked down off his perch. I will knock a few of these Senators down before I die.

(Cries of: "Tell it Mother, I heard it.")

I will tell you. I want you all to be good.

(A voice: "Yes, I will. We are always good.")

They say you are not, but I know you better than the balance do.

Be good. Don't drink, only a glass of beer. The parasite blood-suckers will tell you not to drink beer, because they want to drink it all, you know. They are not afraid to tell you to drink, for fear there will not be enough for their carcass.

(Cries of: "The Governor takes champagne.")

He needs it. He gets it from you fellows. He ought to drink it. You pay for it, and as long as he can get it for nothing any fellow would be a fool not to drink it.

But I want you to be good. We are going to give the Governor until tomorrow night. He will not do anything. He could if he would, but the fellows who put him in won't let him.

(Cries of: "Take him out.")

I don't want him out, because I would have to carry him around. (Applause.)

I want you to keep the peace until I tell you to move, and when I want you every one will come. (Loud applause.)

Now, be good. I don't tell you to go and work for Jesus. Work for yourselves, work for bread. That is the fight we have got. Work for bread. They own our bread.

This fight that you are in is the great industrial revolution that is permeating the heart of men over the world. They see behind the clouds the Star that rose in Bethlehem nineteen hundred years ago, that is bringing the message of a better and nobler civilization. We are facing the hour. We are in it, men, the new day, we are here facing that Star that will free men, and give to the nation a nobler, grander, higher, truer, purer, better manhood. We are standing on the eve of that mighty hour when the motherhood of the nation will rise, and instead of clubs or picture shows or excursions she will devote her life to the training of the human mind, giving to the nation great men and women.

I see that hour. I see the Star breaking your chains; your chains will be broken, men. You will have to suffer more and more, but it won't be long. There is an awakening among all the nations of the earth.

I want to say, my friends, as Kipling said. He was a military colonel or general in the British army, and he said:

100

We have fed you all for thousands of years,
And you hail us yet unfed.
There is not a dollar of your stolen wealth
But what marks the graves of workers dead.
We have given our best to give you rest;
You lie on your silken fold.
Oh, God, if that be the price of your stolen wealth,
We have paid it o'er and o'er.
There is never a mine blown skyward now,
But our boys are burned to death for gold;
There is never a wreck on the ocean
But what we are its ghastly crew.
Go count your dead by the forges rail
Of the factories where your children lie,
Oh, God, if that be the price of your stolen wealth,
We pay it a thousand fold.

We have fed you all for thousands of years;
That was our doom, you know.
Since the days they chained us on the field,
Till the fight that is now on over the world.
Aye, you have beaten our lives, our babies and wives,
In chains you naked lie.
Oh, God, if that be the price we pay for your stolen wealth,
We have paid it o'er and o'er.

We are going to stop payment. I want you to quit electing such judges as you have been. This old judge you had here, he used to be your lawyer. When this fight was on he was owned by the corporations. When you wanted him he went off fishing, and got a pain in his back. Elect judges and governors from your own ranks.

A doctor said to me in Cincinnati, "Did you ever graduate from a college, Mother Jones?" I said, "I did." He said, "Would you mind telling me?" "No," I said, "I graduated from the college of hard knocks. That is my college, I graduated from that college — hunger, persecution and suffering. And I wouldn't exchange that college for all the university dudes on the face of God's earth." (Loud applause.)

I know of the wrongs of humanity; I know your aching backs; I know your swimming heads; I know your little children suffer; I know your wives, when I have gone in and found her dead and found a babe nursing at the dead breast, and found the little girl eleven years old taking care of three children. She said, "Mother, will you wake up, baby is hungry and crying?" When I laid my hand on mamma she breathed her last. And the child of eleven had to become a mother to the children.

Oh, men, have you any hearts? Oh, men, do you feel? Oh, men, do you see the judgement day on the throne above, when you will be asked, "Where did you get your gold?" You stole it from these wretches. You murdered, you assassinated, you starved, you burned them to death, that you and your wives might have palaces, and that your wives might go to the sea-shore. Oh, God, men, when I see the horrible picture, when I see the children with their hands off, when I took an army of babies and walked a hundred and thirty miles with a petition to the President of the United States [Theodore Roosevelt], to pass a bill in Congress to keep these children from being murdered for profit. He had a secret service then all the way to the palace. And now they want to make a president of that man! What is the American nation coming to?

Manhood, womanhood, can you stand for it? They put reforms in their platforms, but they will get no reform. He promised everything to labor. When we had the strike in Colorado he sent two hundred guns to blow our brains out. I don't forget. You do, but I don't. And our women were kicked out like dogs, at the point of the bayonet. That is America. They don't do it in Russia. Some women get up with five dollars worth of paint on their cheeks, and have tooth brushes for their dogs, and say, "Oh, them horrible miners. Oh, that horrible old Mother Jones, that horrible old woman."

I am horrible, I admit, and I want to be to you blood-sucking pirates.

I want you, my boys, to buckle on your armor. This is the fighting age. This is not the age for cowards, put them out of the way.

(At this point Mother stopped suddenly and said to some one in the crowd: "Say, are you an operator, with that cigar in your grub?")

Take your medicine, because we are going to get after you, no doubt about it.

(Cries from the crowd: "Give it to them.")

Yes, I will. (Cries again: "Give it to them.")

I want you to be good. Give the Governor time until tomorrow night, and if he don't act then it is up to you. We have all day Saturday, all day Sunday, all day Monday, and Tuesday and Wednesday, if we need it.

We are used to living on little, we can take a crust of bread in our hands and go.

When they started that Civic Federation in New York, they got women attached to the Morgan and Rockefeller joint, they wanted to revolutionize the mechanics in Washington. One day I went to their dinner. An Irishman, a machinist, rolled up his sleeves, and ran into a restaurant and got a piece of bologna as long as my arm — you know it is black. He got some bread. He put a chunk of the bologna into his mouth, and put some bread in his mouth, and went out eating. One of these women came along and said, "Oh, my man, don't eat that it will ruin your stomach, it will give you indigestion." He said, "Oh, hell, the trouble with my stomach is that I never get enough to digest."

That is the trouble with half our stomachs. We don't get enough to digest, and when we do get something we are afraid to put it in lest it won't digest.

Go to the "Pluck-me" store and get all you can eat. Then you say to Mirandy—You say, Oh, God, I have a pain in my stomach. You wash yourself, and she holds the water. The mine owner's wife don't hold the water. "Oh, Mirandy, bring the linen to take the corporation hump off my back."

I can't get up to you. I would like to be there, I would give you a hump on your back.

Boys, stay quiet until tomorrow night. I think it would be a good thing to work tomorrow, because the mine owners will need it. The mine commissioner will get a pain in his skull tonight, and his wife will give him some dope. The mine owner's wife is away at the sea-shore. When she finds no more money coming, she will say, "Is there any more money coming?" He will say, "Most of the miners are not working." She will say, "Take the guards and shoot them back into the mines, those horrible fellows."

The Governor says, if you don't go to work, said he, in the mines or on the railroads, I am going to call the militia, and I will shoot you. So we went. I said we can get ready, too. What militia can you get to fight us? Those boys on Paint Creek wouldn't fight us if all the governors in the country wanted you to. I was going yesterday to take dinner with them, but I had something else to do. I am going some day to take dinner with them, and I will convert the whole bunch to my philosophy. I will get them all my way.

Now, be good, boys. Pass the hat around, some of these poor devils want a glass of beer. Get the hat. The mine owner robs them. Get a hat, you fellows of the band.

I want to tell you another thing. These little two by four clerks in the company stores, they sell you five beans for a nickel, sometimes three beans for a nickel. I want to tell you, be civil to those. Don't say anything.

Another thing I want you to do. I want you to go in regular parade, three or four together. The moving picture man wants to get your picture to send over the country.

(Some one in the crowd asks what the collection is being taken for.)

The hat is for the miners who came up here broke, and they want to get a glass of beer. (Loud applause.)

And to pay their way back—and to get a glass of beer. I will give you five dollars. Get a move on and get something in it.

Speeches

This day marks the forward march of the workers in the state of West Virginia. Slavery and oppression will gradualiy die. The national government will get a record of this meeting. They will see men of intelligence, that they are not out to destroy but to build. And instead of the horrible homes you have got, we will build on their ruins homes for you and your children to live in, and we will build them on the ruins of the dog kennels which they wouldn't keep their mules in. That will bring forth better ideas than the world has had. The day of oppression will be gone. I will be with you whether true or false. I will be with you at midnight or when the battle rages, when the last bullet ceases, but I will be in my joy, as an old saint said:

> Oh, God of the mighty clan,
> God grant that the woman who suffered for you,
> Suffered not for a coward, but Oh, for a man.
> God grant that the woman who suffered for you,
> Suffered not for a coward, but Oh, for a *fighting* man.

(Loud applause.)

Bring the hat in, is that all you got? (As the hat was handed to her.) That is all I got.

Go out and get some more, that is not enough to go on a strike.

Any of you big fellows got any money in your pockets? If you have, shell it out, or we will take it out.

(A man coming up out of the crowd: "Here is ten dollars, I will go and borrow more. Shake hand with me, an old union miner. My children are able to take care of themselves, and I will take care of myself.")

Fight. ("Fight, right. I have a good rifle, and I will get more money. If I don't have enough to pay my railroad fare, I will walk. I don't care if this was the last cent I had, I will give it to Mother, and go and get some more.")

Maybe the Governor will give something.

(Cries of: "Call him out." "Governor, governor governor.")

The Governor is sick. He can't come out. (Applause.)

(Cries of: "Better stay sick.")

Hand in the money (From some one: "The Governor is sick?")

Mother: Yes. He has got a pain in his stomach. Go over and form a parade, the motion picture man wants to take a picture. Go ahead and arrange the parade—Get out, and get them in a line.

(Cries of: "Governor Glasscock.")

Hush up, the poor fellow is sick.

(Cries for: "Houston, Houston.")

(Cries of: "Gone to the hospital.")

Now let us go home. Be good boys. I am coming down to the camps to see you.

(The crowd did not disperse, but waited until some one got up on the box. The writer learned that his name was Walter Deal, who made a speech. At this point Mother Jones came out and got upon the box and began to speak.)

My object in coming back to you is this: That this meeting stand adjourned until we hear from the Governor. We are going to have a committee. There is always a lot of hot air orators that like to blow off hot air on occasions like this. There is nothing in what they say. We want brain work, not hands, but brains. There is no more speaking here, this meeting stands adjourned until we hear from the Governor. I told you to organize and march along here.

We will let you know. Go home to your camps. The Governor ain't going to come, he is occupied. This meeting stands adjourned, no more hot air here.

You have heard the motion to adjourn, ready to vote. As many as are in favor of adjourning, hold up your hands.

(Very few held up their hands.)

Now you have got to go.

(Calls for the contrary vote.)

Mother don't permit the contrary.

We can't forget that we are men. We have been tendered courteously the ground. It is nothing but right, but if the chief executive wanted to protest he could have done so. He has given us the ground. You have talked the causes of the grievances. Wait until you hear from them. Leave the Capitol alone.

(The meeting adjourned.)

Go home, boys, when we need you again I will call on you. I will be down tomorrow, and if I am not down the telegraph will be going.

[George Wallace Papers, West Virginia Collection, West Virginia University.]

Speech at a public meeting
in the courthouse square
Charleston, West Virginia

In the three weeks following her speech on the steps of the capitol, Mother Jones continued to speak in the strike zone, closely watched by the militia. The tent colony at Holly Grove grew as evictions forced more miners from their homes. Incidents of violence continued, but the military courts were relatively evenhanded in their application of justice, and an uneasy quiet settled on the strike area. Although she portrayed Governor William E. Glasscock as ineffectual, he showed some sympathy for the miners. He had first tried to bring the miners and the operators together in a joint conference, proposed a board of arbitration, and then offered himself as a mediator between the parties; all these possible courses were accepted by union leaders and rejected by the operators. Glasscock finally appointed a commission headed by Patrick J. Donahue, Catholic bishop of Wheeling, to investigate conditions and report to him.

The following speech was made to an audience of miners whom Mother Jones had led on a march to the capital. In it she continued her aggressive promulgation of the rights of the miners, but mixed with it a measure of conciliation, urging the miners to act peacefully, to cooperate with the militia, to remain sober, and to protect property. The burden of her protest was that no representatives of labor sat on the governor's commission.

§ § §

This great gathering that is here tonight signals there is a disease in the State that must be wiped out. The people have suffered from that disease patiently; they have borne insults, oppression, outrages; they appealed to their chief executive, they appealed to the courts, they appealed to the attorney general, and in every case they were turned down. They were ignored. The people must not be listened to, the corporations must get a hearing.

When we were on the Capitol grounds the last time you came here, you had a petition to the Governor for a peaceful remedy and solution of this condition. The mine owners, the bankers, the plunderers of the State went in on the side door and got a hearing, and you didn't. (Loud applause.)

Now, then, they offer to get a commission, suggested by the mine owners. The miners submitted a list of names to be selected from, and the mine owners said, "We will have no commission." Then when they found out that Congress, the Federal Government was going to come down and examine your damnable peonage system, then they were ready for the commission. (Applause.)

Then they got together — the cunning brains of the operators got together. What kind of a commission have they got? A bishop, a sky pilot working for Jesus; a lawyer, and a member of the State Militia, from Fayette City. In the name of God, what do any of those men know about your troubles up on Cabin Creek, and Paint Creek? Do you see the direct insult offered by your officials to your intelligence? They look upon you as a lot of enemies instead of those who do the work. If they wanted to be fair they would have selected three miners, three operators and two citizens. (Cries of: "Right, right.") And would have said, "Now, go to work and bring in an impartial decision." But they went up on Cabin Creek — I wouldn't have made those fellows walk in the water, but they made me. Because they knew I have something to tell you, and all Hell and all the governors on the earth couldn't keep me from telling it. (Loud applause.)

I want to put it up to the citizens, up to every honest man in this audience — let me ask you here, have your public officials any thought for the citizens of this State, or their condition?

(Cries of: "No, no, no.")

Now, then, go with me up those creeks, and see the blood-hounds of the mine owners, approved of by your public officials. See them insulting women, see them coming up the track. I went up there and they followed me like hounds. But some day I will follow them. When I see them go to Hell, I will get the coal and pile it up on them. (Loud applause.)

I look at the little children born under such a horrible condition. I look at the little children that were thrown out here.

(At this moment an automobile came down Kanawha Street and turned around and went back, but in turning made considerable noise which attracted some attention and interrupted the speaker, who said, "Don't bother about that automobile.")

Now then, let me ask you. When the miners — a miner that they have robbed him of one leg in the mines and never paid him a penny for it — when he entered a protest, they went into his house not quite a week ago, and threw out his whole earthly belongings, and he and his wife and six children slept on the roadside all night. Now, you can't contradict that. Suppose we had taken a mine owner and his wife and children and threw them out on the road and made them sleep all night, the papers would be howling "anarchy."

(Cries of: "Right," and loud applause.)

When you held a meeting the other day down here at Cedar Grove,

107

the *Mail* said that evening that you were drunk. I want to say to the *Mail,* it was a lie of the blackest dye. (Loud applause.) There was never in the State of West Virginia a more orderly, well-behaved body of men than those miners were that assembled at Cedar Grove. The militia were there to see that we were sober, and we were before they came, and we were sober when they went away. The *Mail* never told you, when the mine owners and their gang of corporation pirates met at the Hotel Ruffner and filled their rotten stomachs with champagne and made you pay the bills. (Loud applause.)

Now, then, the State of West Virginia is the only state in the union — I have spoken in every state in this union, and in every city, I have spoken. When I got on the train at Charleston last Sunday morning to go up to _____ (The speaker tried to remember the name of the place but could not) that has been clamoring for me since I came into the field — the militia at Pratt got instructions to jump on the train and go to Deepwater and find instructions there. They got on the train and went up and got instructions, and followed me up. They got an Irish _____, [omitted by the stenographer], when I was taking coffee, to watch me, for fear that I would slip away from them. The rat that stood there wasn't worth noticing, because a man won't do those things.

Well, when I got off the train at Lively, I understood those men had to walk fourteen miles in the hot sun to keep me from talking. I want to tell you something. The mine owners nor Glasscock, haven't got enough militia in the State of West Virginia to keep me from talking. (Loud applause.)

When I found those men I looked them over. I found out they were working men. If they had been some of the big guns, you bet your life I would make them walk. I would make the fat get off their rotten carcasses. But when I surveyed those boys I said, "Boys, I want to tell you, this is a fourteen miles walk, it is a bad rough road, and to keep you from walking that distance in the baking hot sun I will refrain from going." They said the boys can go, the men can go, but an old woman with her head white eighty years old can scare hell out of the whole state, and she can't go. (Loud applause.)

Shame on your manhood! If these operators were true, and if they were not thieves, they would not be afraid of anybody. (Cries of: "No.")

But when they plunder from these miners, these children, my fellow citizens, countrymen, thrown out on the highways and mothers insulted — do you think that they will be good citizens when they grow up? I don't. The revenge and resentment will be buried there if they grow into manhood, it will develop, they will kill, they will murder to get even with those who robbed them. I want you to stop that. I don't want it to go on. Your Governor may, but I don't. I want the children to have the best of influence, I want the children to have good schooling, I want women to know nothing but what is good, I want to leave to this nation a nobler manhood and greater womanhood. Can I do it? No, I can't, boys, with the administration you have got, I can't do it.

(Cries of: "We'll change that.")

I can do it if you men and women will stand together, find out the seat of the disease and pull it up by the roots.

(Cries of: "Yes, yes, yes.")

Take possession of that state house, that ground is yours. (Some one interrupted, and the speaker said: "Shut your mouth.")

You built that state house, didn't you? You pay the public officials, don't you? You paid for that ground, didn't you? (Cries of: Yes, yes.")

Then, who does it belong to? Then why did the militia chase you off? You have been hypnotized. The trouble has been that they wanted the slave system to continue. They have had a glass for you and your wives and children to look into. They have you hypnotized. They want the ministers to tell you when you die you will have a bed in heaven. The blamed chambermaids might be on a strike and we wouldn't get a chance to get a bed. (Loud applause.)

Now, then, I will go to the tents and when those poor women — I have seen those little children — my heart bled for them — and I thought, "Oh, how brutish the corporations must be!" God Almighty, go down and look at those conditions! Go see those miners! They tell you about how much — they have a list of questions up here, "How much do the unions do to train the miners to clean the yards." Did you ever know of such a damned, silly insulting question? (Loud applause.)

I want to ask those fellows that put that down, "How do you suppose, when we have to fight you, we have got any time about yards?" You have got the yards. We clean them for you and you don't thank us for it. Your wife lives in style. Look down at those houses there on the river front. She dresses with the blood of children. She buys a dog and calls it "Dear little poodle, I love you." And you stand for it! And you stand for it! And you are a lot of dirty cowards, I want to tell you the truth about it. You are a lot of cowards and you haven't got enough marrow in your backbone to grease two black cats' tails. If you were men with a bit of revolutionary blood in you, you wouldn't stand for the Baldwin guards, would you?

(Cries of: "No, no, no.")

No, you wouldn't. Or Glasscock either. When they saw you were going to clean up the guards they got the militia down and they don't allow President Cairns, of the Miners, to go up Cabin Creek. They don't allow Mr. Diamond to go up. But I want to ask you if the militia does allow the mine owners to take transportation up there? They do?

(Cries of: "No transportation.")

You know as much about it as a dog does about his daddy. (Loud applause.)

I have been under martial law before, I have been in states where martial law was, but it was never carried to that extreme. We were at least allowed to go and visit our people. Here in West Virginia you can't go. You can't hold a meeting. I want to say to you that the right of free speech will be carried on if they hire all the militia in the state to murder us. We won't surrender that right. We will hold meetings. We will hold peaceful, law-abiding meetings. We will hold them all along. I have here a book, if I had the light to read it, one of the most damnable documents that those mine owners are sending out for the miners to sign.

I have got letters here from the slaves on the Norfolk and Western, "For God's sake, Mother, come up and do something for us." I have got letters from the Fairmont region, "Oh, Mother, for God's sake, come and do something for us." I have them from New River, "For God's sake, come and do something for us, and help us."

Isn't there something wrong? Say, boys, stop it. For ages and ages and ages they have kept the lash on you. I could see it the day I went to Kaymoor. The poor devils were scared to death. I had to tell them to come with me. They were afraid of the blood-hounds. And while I talked the blood-hounds sat there. They made me wade the creek.

Now, every citizen will admit that when you rent a house the landlord has a right to give you a passageway to go to that house. You have a right to invite who you please to your table, haven't you? The blood-hounds came along and you have got to get out.

Now then, is that something that the State must boast of? Is that something that you citizens will endorse?

(Cries of: "No, no.")

Very good, then. They will come to you on election day. I will tell you when you can carry a bayonet and they can't meddle with you. You can carry a bayonet on November 5th, and you can go to the ballot box and put a bayonet in there and *stick it to their very heart*. (Loud applause.)

Then they can have no militia.

(Cries of: "Won't they steal the ballots?")

They will not steal it if you do your duty. I would like to see the corporation blood-hounds steal my ballot if I had one. I would clean them up. He would go to the machine shop for repairs and he wouldn't come out in a hurry when I got through with him. (Loud applause.)

You fellows with the corporation hump on your backs, I hope you will.

Now, I want to say this: Ten or twelve years ago when I came in here, you had to work eleven or twelve hours, didn't you?

(Cries of: "That is right.")

They made you load coal for any price they wanted. We brought on a fight and got twice that for loading coal. We reduced the hours to nine. Up there on Paint Creek and Cabin Creek you obeyed the laws at that time. You had a good union at that time, but you have done in industrial unions as they do elsewhere, you elect the man that wants the glory instead of the man that will work for you. I am going to put a stop to that. I want to tell you we are going to organize West Virginia. I am going to stay in here until you have good officers. And you will have no officer that will get a detective from the sheriff to go up Paint Creek with him. By the gods you won't.

I don't want an escort that murders my brothers on Piney and Stanaford Mountain. I don't want an escort to go with me. And you elect them to office, those contemptible murderous blood-hounds. I am protesting. I am speaking against the insults, I want to tell you that. I don't do anything behind anybody's back. What I do I will do openly, straight above board. I have knocked down your officers before, and I will knock them down again. They will play no double game when I am around. I have just as bitter feeling toward them as toward the Baldwin guards.

Another thing, when you elect a committee, elect men that can go to the superintendent and talk like men.

Another thing I want you to do, boys. You have got a contract with the Kanawha companies, and I am responsible for closing those mines these days. I want to say to you, Go back peacefully, law-abiding, leave drink alone. When we have won this battle we will all get a jag.

Go back to work. Those men have their contracts made outside and they are losing them. We have been upsetting their deal. I want to deal fair with every man. There are some good operators, some good men, but their hands are tied. We must not bust them up in business, as long as they are going to give us a hand and help us we will help them. Go back like men and go to work. One operator said, "Mother, I have had to throw away six contracts." I don't like that. I am not very fond of mine owners as a rule, but there is a sense of justice everywhere. I want you to help the men that have stood by us — stand by them.

I will be in here until the next officers are elected. I am going through the whole district and I will pick the men and I will openly advocate them. If they are not the fellows I want I will throw them down just the same as I would a Baldwin guard.

I am going to say to the police, the militia, the Adjutant General, and to every one in this audience, that we will carry on this fight, we will make war in the State until the Baldwins are removed.

(Loud applause, and cries of: "Right you are.")

Vote for Tincher for Sheriff, I say this to all of you.

Another thing I want to say, there is a rumor gone out that you miners tore up the C. & O. track. I know it is not right, but it has gone out that way. I know who tore the track up. But the papers all through the country put it on the miners—the whole gang of thieves, all the other papers in the country, outside of *The Labor Argus*. I want you to guard the C. & O. tracks and trains everywhere. The young men on the C. & O. are our men, and they are working to help us, and I want you to protect their lives. Don't meddle with the track, take care of it, and if you catch sight of a Baldwin blood-hound put a bullet through his rotten carcass.

(Loud applause.)

Now, I want to tell you, boys, we will not bother the C. & O. Road.

I want to say another thing. There is another man who travels the C. & O. Road, I asked him some time ago to go up to Huntington. He has been going to speakings. He went up. I was going down that evening, and all the coaches were full, and I was worn out. The express manager as well as this brother and I went into the Pullman car and took a seat and sat down and talked the whole way. No, he did not go watching me. I invited him, but I wouldn't invite the blood-hounds to go up to Kayford with me, or Eskdale. His name was Cochran.

The sheriff offered me an insult that I am going to resent.

(Cries of: "Tell him about it.")

I don't allow any of those blood-hounds to watch me as I travel.

He travels up there, and I have known him for twelve years. He is a pretty good fellow.

But the other blood-hound used to be up on the C. & O. and on New River trailing me like a dog. Somebody told me up on the creek who it was.

Boys, this fight is going on. I may have to call on you inside of two weeks again to make another move. Then I will get the police with me, and I will have them all educated by that time. (Loud applause.)

Now, I want to say, my friends, I have only one journey to go through this life; you have only one journey to go through this life; let us all do the best we can for humanity, for mankind, while we are here.

That is my mission, to do what I can to raise mankind to break his chains. The miners are close to me. The steel workers are. I go among them all. One time when I took up the Mexican question, I went to Congress to save some lives; I had never seen them in my life, but they appealed to me and said, "It is up to you, Mother, to save our lives." I went up to carry the matter to Congress. It came up before the big committee. They were Dalzell, Congressman, representing the Steel Trust—he was chairman of that big committee; Simth, representing the Southern Pacific Railroad, was a member of that committee; Champ Clark also was a member of that committee. Dalzell said to me, "Mother Jones, where do you live?" I said, "In the United States, sir." "What part of the United States?" said he. I said, "Wherever the workers are fighting the robbers, there am

112

I." (Loud applause.) "Sometimes I am in Arizona fighting the Southern Pacific blood-sucking pirates and thieves," said I. "Sometimes, I am up on the Steel Range, fighting those murderers and plunderers, sometimes I am in Pennsylvania fighting the robbers and murderers and blood-suckers there, and by the Eternal God we will clean you up and put you out of business."

Now, my brothers, don't violate the law. Let them see that you are law-abiding.

Now, the *Mail* said that I was going to speak tonight. Yes, I did. The *Mail* said it supposed I was going to ridicule the Governor, and the Salvation Army. I never ridicule. Never in my life. I never will. I criticize the Governor, but I do not ridicule him.

Another thing I do to my people, I show them how the Salvation Army came into existence. It was a necessity for capitalism. When it developed machinery, capitalism began to develop, an oligarchy of Wall Street began to reach out, and it had to have a Salvation Army to work on the workers' brains and keep them contented. I am a student of those things. I find out the cause that produces things. I am not fighting the Salvation Army. I do at times show how the Salvation Army, the church and every other institution becomes commercialized in the age in which we live. I do not ridicule them. They are in a way to do good work. I do not approve of them for I know they are capitalistic in their make-up.

When the *Mail* or any other paper says I ridicule them I want to state it is false. I always show up to the workers how they are hypnotized, and I don't care whether it is the Salvation Army or the church or the Bishop on this Commission [Patrick J. Donahue], or not.

The selection of this Commission was the three wings of capitalism. There is no wing of the workers on that Commission. From the questions they ask it is a plain truth that they understand nothing of your disease or trouble, and have never made it a study.

Now, then, my brothers, I am not going to be muzzled by the *Mail*. I have been assassinated by the slimy pig before, but it never made me retreat. I have measured steel in the middle of the night with the blood-hounds, but it never made me give up the red flag. I tell them we are in the fight to a finish.

Now, my brothers, I want you all to return home, peacefully, law-abiding. Go home. I don't mind you taking a drink, I know you need it. I don't belong to the temperance brigade at all. As long as liquor is manufactured it is going to be sold for profit. When you take the profit out of it, just as you have out of the postage stamps, then you don't need any temperance howlers. It will be made pure, and we will drink it pure. So the temperance brigade will keep it in the background. If we want a drink we will take it, and we are not going to offer any apology for it.

113

Be good. Mother is going to stay with you. I am going to Colorado. There was a sheriff in the county, and the mine owners asked for the troops, and the sheriff said, "You can send no troops, no militia, into the county I have charge of. The men elected me." He was the sheriff, and he did not allow the Governor to send the troops in there. There was no tyranny in that county. Once and awhile we licked a scab, we wanted to put brains in him, he had none. That sheriff is going to run for Secretary of State, and I am going out to sweep the state with him. I will put him into office, if it is the last thing I do. I want to put in all the officers, and we have got to put out the fellows who stand with the robbing class, and we have got to put them out of business, we have got to make an honest nation. You can't be honest today. A girl goes to school, to church, and prays to Jesus. On Monday she acts like the devil when she sells to you. The whole machinery of capitalism is rotten to the core. This meeting tonight indicates a milestone of progress of the miners and workers of the State of West Virginia. I will be with you, and the Baldwin guards will go. You will not be serfs, you will march, march, march on from milestone to milestone of human freedom, you will rise like men in the new day and slavery will get its death blow. It has got to die. Good night.

(Applause.)

[George Wallace Papers, West Virginia Collection, West Virginia University.]

Speech at a public meeting
on the lawn of the YMCA
Charleston, West Virginia

On 21 September 1912 Mother Jones led a march of miners' children through the streets of Charleston and made her last fully recorded speech in the Paint Creek strike, though her role in the strike was by no means played out. In the relative quiet that prevailed under martial law, and while Governor Glasscock's commission was conducting its investigation, she traveled and spoke in and out of the strike zone. Martial law was lifted on 15 October, but was reinvoked on 15 November for two more months. She traveled to the northern part of the state and to Ohio to elicit support for the strikers. In November she addressed a mass meeting in New York. Again in December she spoke at meetings in Cincinnati, Columbus, and Cleveland, went to New York for another rally, and returned to West Virginia for speeches at Eskdale and Holly Grove just before Christmas. On 5 January 1912 she spoke again at Wheeling, and on the tenth to a large crowd at the Armory in Washington, D.C. No copies of these speeches have been found.

A series of clashes between guards and miners at Mucklow in early February led Governor Glasscock to impose martial law a third time on 10 February. Two days later, as Mother Jones was leading a small delegation to the governor to protest against conditions in the strike area, she was arrested in Charleston and taken to the martial law zone where she remained imprisoned until 8 May. Since no official records were published, the precise charges against her and even the final sentence are not known; later, she said that her sentence was for five years in the penitentiary for stealing a machine gun. At any rate, from her place of imprisonment in a private house she was able surreptitiously to send out a number of appeals to Terence V. Powderly, William B. Wilson, Senator William E. Borah, Senator John W. Kern, and others. A resolution was introduced into the Senate to investigate conditions in the coal fields of West Virginia.

Meanwhile, a new governor, Henry D. Hatfield, had taken office in West Virginia and was determined to settle the year-long crisis. With the cooperation of John P. White of the UMWA, he imposed a settlement which granted some of the miners' demands, although not the end of the hated mine guard system. Court martial sentences were remitted; those who had already been committed to the penitentiary were paroled, and on 8 May 1913 Hatfield freed Mother Jones. She went to Ohio for a speech and then to Washington, where from the Senate gallery she listened to the debate on the Kern Resolution to investigate conditions in West Virginia and saw it passed.

During the latter part of May Mother Jones spoke in a number of cities, climaxed by a press conference and an address at Carnegie Hall on 28 May which has not been preserved. Two months later she traveled to northern Michigan to assist the Western Federation of Miners in their strike in the copper country.

§ § §

I want to say to those children, they will be free; they will not be serfs. We have entered West Virginia — I have — and a hundred thousand miners have pledged their support to me, "If you need us, Mother, we will be there." Five thousand men last Sunday night said, "We are ready, Mother, when you call on us."

The revolution is here. We can tie up every wheel, every railroad in the State, when we want to do it. Tyranny, robbery and oppression of the people must go. The children must be educated. The childhood will rise to grander woman and grander man in happy homes and happy families — then we will need no saloons. We will need no saloons, nor any of your prohibition. As long as you rob us, of course we drink. The poison food you give us needs some other narcotic to knock the poison out of it. They charge you $2.40 for a bushel of potatoes at the "pluck-me" store. Ten pounds of slate in 9700 pounds of coal and you are docked — then they go and "give for Jesus." "How charming Mr. _____ [Charles Cabell] is, he gives us $500.00."

Let us, my friends, stand up like men. I have worked for the best interests of the working people for seventy-five years. I don't need any one to protect me. I protect myself. I don't break the law. Nobody molests me, except John Laing. John is the only dog in West Virginia that attacks a woman. He is the only fellow that would do that. I am not afraid of John Laing. I would give him a punch in the stomach and knock him over the railroad. I don't know who punched him — he lost his pistol. I put my hand on him and told him to go home to his mother. I gave him a punch in the stomach, and he fell over the railroad track and lost his pistol. He didn't know he lost it until he reached home.

He said, "You are disturbing *my miners*." My slaves! Scabs! Dogs!

Boys, I want to say here, don't go near the saloon today. You need the money to buy bread. When we win this fight then we will make pure liquor. We will go to Washington — we will go to see Taft, because Wilson and the Bull Moose will be out of business. We will make Congress take over the liquor question, and make them make pure liquor. It will be like the postage stamps. We will need it for our stomachs. These fellows that are howling to make it "dry" — we will make it devilish wet — we are going to hand it all over to Uncle Sam. We won't put the brewers out of business, we will make Uncle Sam put them all to work, and reduce the hours of labor to six. The operators said, "God Almighty, what are you talking about? Six hours!" Then we will go home to the children, and nurse and feed them. We will take the children out in the sunshine — (Cries of: "We will own the land") — and bring happiness into our homes. And then you will not want to drink. We will have a violin and music in every home, and the children will dance. Shame! Forever shame! on the men and women in the State of West Virginia that stand for such a picture as we have here today — (Probably referring to the children that marched in the parade) — Shame! When the history is written, what will it be, my friends, when the history of this crime, starvation and murder of the innocents, so they can fill the operators' pockets, and build dog kennels for the workers. Is it right? Will it ever be right?

Now, I understand Mr. White is going to speak at the court house. He will have something to tell you.

This strike ain't going to end until we get a check-weighman on the tipple. That is the law. It is on the statute books — that your coal will be weighed.

The last legislature of Colorado passed a check-weighman law bill, to pay for the check-weighman. The check-weighman was selected by the miners. When I was in Nevada and Utah and in Idaho, I got letter after letter from those poor slaves. These letters would begin: "Mother, God Almighty, you ought to see how they are helping us. The first one had 900 pounds more in it than I ever got before." Another fellow said, "I had 1200 pounds more." Another said, "My car weighs almost twice as much as it ever had done." When the law went into effect, how their weight increased! Even now those fellows are begging me "When are you coming back, Mother? We are ready to strike the blow. They will never rob us again."

You miners here have stood for it, you have starved your children, starved yourselves, you have lived in dog-kennels — they wouldn't build one for their dogs as bad as yours. You have lived in them and permitted them to rob you, and then got the militia for the robbers. You can get all the militia in the state, we will fight it to the finish — if the men don't fight the women will. They won't stand for it.

Be good, boys, don't drink. Subscribe for the *Labor Argus*. If I was sentenced to sixteen months to jail, and these guys found it out I would be in jail longer. I don't worry about it. I am down at the Fleetwood when-

Speeches

ever they want to put me in jail for violation of the law, come along for me, come. There is coming a day when I will take the whole bunch of you and put you in jail. (Applause.)

[George Wallace Papers, West Virginia Collection, West Virginia University.]

Mother Jones speaks at an open-air meeting in Star City, West Virginia, 1918. (West Virginia University Regional Collection)

Advertisement of Mother Jones's speech at Carnegie Hall, *New York Call*, 27 May 1913.

Speech at a convention
of District 15, United Mine Workers of America
Trinidad, Colorado

In early September 1913, Mother Jones attended the convention of District 15, UMWA, in Trinidad, Colorado. Her first appearance before the delegates was a brief one to urge them to boycott products of the Pells Brewery, where the workers were on strike.

§ § §

I want to ask you to please remember while you are in town, that the Pells Brewery Workers are on strike. They did not strike without a cause I am sure. The Brewery Workers Executive Board are about as able men as we have in the labor movement and I am pretty sure they would not endorse a strike without a cause. Be sure you don't touch the Pells Brewery Beer; if you drink it you will be full of scabs, so I warn each and all if you do get beer get union beer, get beer that is made by men working under decent conditions, and don't patronize those places, if you get hold of any fellow who does, hammer him good. I am not going to hold the convention any longer and I don't want you to forget that beer question.

[Typed minutes, convention of District 15, UMWA, Western History Collection, Denver Public Library.]

Speech at a convention
of District 15, United Mine Workers of America
Trinidad, Colorado

This speech and the two that follow are the only complete speeches pre-served from the year-long strike in Colorado, from September 1913 to September 1914. During this time, Mother Jones was deported by the militia from Trinidad, Colorado, and was imprisoned by them twice: first for more than two months in relative comfort in Mt. San Rafael hospital, and again for twenty-three days in the Huerfano County Jail in Walsen-burg, where the conditions of her semibasement cell were appalling. When not in jail, she shuttled from Denver to both coasts, making speeches in Boston, New York, Washington, Seattle, and British Columbia. She made a hasty round trip to El Paso to try to prevent the importation of scabs from Mexico, three more journeys east for speeches in New York, with a side trip to Washington to testify before the House Committee on Mines and Mining, and speeches at a socialist camp meeting in Oklahoma. For a woman approaching eighty years of age, it was a record of almost in-credible activity, broken only by a week of relaxation as a guest in the Connecticut home of Caroline Lloyd, sister and biographer of Henry Demarest Lloyd.

Coal mining in Colorado had been marked by conflict and violence even before the turn of the century, and a crisis had come in 1903–04 when John Mitchell and the leaders of the UMWA had made a settlement that registered gains in the northern fields but left the more isolated and larger southern field around Trinidad unorganized. It was dominated by two producers, the Victor-American Company and the Colorado Fuel and Iron Company, part of the Rockefeller financial empire. In contrast to the northern field, most of the miners in the southern area were recent immigrants—Italians, Mexicans, Slavs, Greeks, and others—brought in after the troubles of 1903–04. As in West Virginia, the companies owned the coal camps and dominated the local communities politically and eco-nomically. After the settlement of 1904 Mother Jones had resigned her position as organizer for the UMWA, contending that the key to success in Colorado lay in organizing the southern field, however difficult that might prove.

In the intervening years, the UMWA conducted several organizing drives which were blocked by legal maneuvers and the anti-union policies in the

122

southern field. In April 1910 the miners in the northern field struck once again. Mother Jones had played a part in some of these events, and the union was now determined to bring the southern miners into the fold. The operators were similarly determined to maintain their position, strengthening their forces in some cases by employing Baldwin-Felts guards who had recently served in the West Virginia strike. When District 15 met in convention at Trinidad the delegates were to vote on a strike, and the choice of the meetingplace was a direct challenge to the Victor-American and Colorado Fuel and Iron companies. This time, Mother Jones assured the delegates, they would not be abandoned by the international union.

§   §   §

I want to say a few words regarding that telegram [rejecting the plea of the editor of the Pueblo *Star Journal* not to strike]. Insofar as the public has had some ten years to protest against the horrible conditions that exist here, they have failed to take up the question that arises today in the nation, that is, industrial democracy. Realizing that it fails to demand better conditions, strike I know is the last resort. I do not advocate strikes and have prevented many of them throughout the country. It has been ten years since you have awakened to the fact that outrageous insults are being heaped on humanity in Colorado.

What would the coal in the mines be worth if you did not work to take it out? The reporter for the Pittsburgh paper was speaking to the manager of the Colorado Fuel & Iron Company mines some time ago and asked why greater care was given the mules than the men, and the manager very humanely replied, "A miner is cheaper than a mule to a coal company." That is on record in the Pittsburgh *Survey* of Pittsburgh, Pennsylvania; it was from that I took it; he said they were only Dagoes. What a statement that is to be made by any human being. I want to say they are not Dagoes, because when a man comes to this country and the immigration commissioner passes him through, he is immediately an American citizen. He is no longer a Dago, nor a Scotchman nor an Irishman; he is immediately an American citizen, supposed to learn our laws and comply with them. It is strange anyone should be called a Dago in our day. They used to do that long ago when the boss would go to the Irishman and say, "Pat, give me $10.00; I heard those Welsh Rabbies say they would clean you up." Pat would say, "Sure I'll give you $10.00." Then he would go over to the Welshman and say, "Those Irish called you Welsh Rabbies, put up $15.00." And the Welshman would. Don't you see their plan was to divide the working class? History tells us of a man who lived two thousand years ago. He was a slave at that time and he was bought and brought to a strange land, then sold to someone else and ran away. When he was brought to court for what he had done, they said to him, "Who are you, stranger?" "I am a man. I am interested in anything that affects my class," was the reply of this slave. "I am devoted to my class." I wish to God I could permeate every worker in the State of Colorado with the same pride that filled this slave so many years ago. Whatever affected his people affected him, so, my boys, let it be with you. One brother said he got fair pay. I want to ask you what he calls a fair pay for the miners. You produce about $10.00 a day. You get one-tenth of it. The other fellow gets the balance of it. Do you call that a square deal? I want to assure you my friend it is not. We have suffered here too long. We tried before to demand our rights, but the miners were beaten up, so were other men who came to lend a hand. They were beaten on the trains; they had no protection whatever.

One morning about that time I had to leave for one of the other camps. I happened to sleep a little late and missed the train. I saw a boy beaten right here in Trinidad just as the train pulled out. There was no redress for it.

The time is ripe for you to stand like men. If the operators don't come to time, we will. This thing of standing for slavery in this country is going to come to an end. We are not going to raise the coming generation to be highwaymen. We are going to raise them to be intelligent, law-abiding citizens. We will take a hand in making the laws.

The governor can stop a strike any time. If I were governor I would stop a strike by simply saying, "These men have a grievance and demand redress from you. Come and discuss these questions with the miners on the fair soil of America like intelligent, law-abiding citizens. If you refuse I will close up your mines. I will have the state operate mines for the benefit of the nation." It is not right for public officials to bring scabs and gunmen into any state. I am directly opposed to it myself, but if it is a question of strike or you go into slavery, then I say strike until the last one of us drop into our graves.

I went into the city of Charleston, West Virginia. I knew those boys since they were little trapper boys. One night the minutemen forced them and their wives and little babes out of the camp. They marched twelve miles before they found shelter. This was on the fair soil of America. If it was Russia we would rise in arms against it.

I have been in strikes of one kind or another. I have seldom been out of a strike for years, therefore I knew what to expect and told the boys to stand loyally together and be true to each other. I then said those boys must be saved if it costs me my life, so without waiting to consult the advice of the miners' officials, I took the 8:30 o'clock train and went to Paint Creek. There I found men, women and children turned out of their homes by the Baldwin-Felts thugs. Then I said: "I will not leave the state until the Baldwin-Felts thugs leave." We appealed to the Marshal and other deputy officials, but they refused to give us any help. By this time I was thoroughly disgusted and said to some of the boys, "Tell the people I want them in Charleston Thursday afternoon. I will attend to their expenses, we are able to pay them. Charter trains if you have to." Three thousand of our men assembled in the city that day. We had our demands printed on banners and with them we marched to the State House grounds. They were ours, we had a right to take possession. I walked into the State House and asked for a platform. They brought it out and I got on it. We learned a lesson there with many others, that was, if the workers would only wake up to the fact that if they solidify their forces, they can get anything they want. I urged a petition to the Governor [William E. Glasscock] and told him we appealed to the Sheriff and other officers and being turned out everywhere we at last came to the Chief Executive of the State for redress. We told him we lived in America where our fathers fought for freedom. We lived in the Union, therefore, we had a right to unite our forces. We demanded that privilege. We asked the Governor to banish the Baldwin-Felts guards because I knew when we cleaned them out everything would come with it. I said, "We will give the Governor until 8:00 o'clock tomorrow night; if he does nothing by that time we will. I believe we have our rights as American citizens as much as the President or Governor has. We propose to observe those." The Governor and the state officials stood behind me. I appointed a committee and said, "Take this document to the Governor's office, present it to him yourselves and don't go on your knees; we have no kings in America. Stand erect on both feet with your head erect as citizens of this country and don't say 'Your honor' very few have honor. They don't know what it is." Returning, they said, "The Governor will do nothing for us; he will make no response to this document." They asked why and I said, "Because the political machine that nominated him have control of him." The Governor stood there with hat in hand and did not say a word. He had the opportunity of making himself the greatest man in the United States by saying, "Mother Jones is most unfair, the machine did not nominate me, the people did." But he did not say a word; he knew I was right. After the meeting the men saw they were to have no protection and declared they would protect themselves; so they bought every gun in Charleston. They did no underhand business there, they simply brought their guns and ammunition to their camps to fight back, and it did not let up until an extra session of the Legislature was called. I appealed to the people of the state to demand an extra session of the Legislature because there was a threatened revolution. The undercurrent was so great in this country they feared a great national outbreak of the people and consented to an extra session of the Legislature and discuss the questions. It was time to do something when women and children were beaten by guards. The man that will not protect himself against a Baldwin-Felts guard has no right on the soil of America. We have a right to protect our women and children.

The fight was still on when I went to Cabin Creek. There was a stone wall built there eight or nine years ago and no organizer dared go beyond that wall or he would come out on a stretcher or a cripple. Two young lads came to me and said, "Mother, will you do something for us?" They were trapper boys, the coming men with the spark of humanity in them. They said, "Mother, we are in a difficult position. Up in Cabin Creek no one dares to come near us or they will be shot. We have no organization, would you come?" "I certainly will," I replied. "But," he said, "If you go they might shoot you." "Let them shoot," said I, "I would rather be shot fighting for you than live in any palace in America. We will get past that wall."

We held a wonderful meeting that day. If there had been a Victor Hugo there with a pen he could have paralyzed the world with it. It never will be produced as it really was. The men came over the mountain with their toes out of their shoes and their stomachs empty. Fifteen hundred men of every description gathered there. Even the Baldwin-Felts thugs came. When I had talked to them one hour and a half I said they looked up as much as to say, "Ah! God, is there a grain of hope for us?" Others would look at the ground, very likely thinking, "All hope is dead." Ah! it was an historical meeting, boys. Oh! yes, it was historical and it will go down in history some say. When I was about to close that meeting I said, "Boys, let Mother tell you one thing. Freedom is not dead, she is only gently resting. She is sleeping quietly waiting only for you to call." The voices of those fifteen hundred men rang out with, "Ah! Mother, we will try to be true. Will you organize us into the United Mine Workers of America?" They lost all fear and humanity and came to the front. They arose as one man. When I organized them I said, "Put on your mining clothes tomorrow, don't say a word about this; don't speak of it in the mines. Take your pick and continue to dig out the wealth. Be good and don't make any noise about it." They were discharged, of course. The strike came and I had to go to them. On the way I met an armed gang of guards with the miners. I walked over to one who was the captain of these bloodhounds and put my hand on the muzzle of that gun. I stood there and addressed the miners with my hand on the gun. Never in all my history did I see anything like it. That fellow thirsted for man's blood; he actually thirsted to see the blood of those miners. "Don't you dare to let a bullet out of that," said I, "I don't have trouble where I am; I don't stand for it." The gang got afraid. At another time when I stopped on the road to address a meeting, a big Greek got behind a tree and said, "Come away or they will shoot you," but I stood up and held my meeting there. Soon an officer came to me and said, "Mother Jones, I can't let you talk there any more." I answered, "I am on the public highway. It belongs to me. I have a share of the stock there. I have a right to talk here." They stood there with their guns in their pockets. They did not shoot a bullet.

Don't be afraid, boys; fear is the greatest curse we have. I never was anywhere yet that I feared anybody. I do what I think is right and when I die I will render an account of it. These miners have suffered, but it will have to come to an end, my boys. If your operators do not give to you that which is fair, then I say strike, but let the strike be the very last move you make. Don't put it off either. The time is ripe now. If they don't come to time we will lay down the tools. We will go home. We will be quiet and good. We will tell the people, "Hands off; this is our strike. We are able to look after our own business." We have waited a long time, boys; I wanted to come here sooner, but I have been busy, and now I will tell the Baldwin-Felts guards I shall stay here and we will win just as we did in West Virginia. We drew the attention of the whole world. The whole civilized world centered her eyes on West Virginia and why? Because we attended to business. We didn't allow any weaklings among us. If I saw a drunken organizer in the camp I ordered him out immediately and I will do the same here. If they think more of their stomachs than they do of your cause, they must go. The boys know I get after them. But we have good men in our ranks, thank God; we have men at the head of the United Mine Workers of America that I am proud of. If I were to leave you tomorrow I would feel that I had left men at the helm that you need not be afraid of.

The operators of the northern coal fields will have to come to time and New Mexico operators will have to come to time. You would have won when you struck before, but when I went to Louisville and asked you not to call off the strike, you were like a lot of lapdogs, afraid. I told you then it was your fight and you had to win it. There is a man there who can prove to you that if you took my advice then there would be no strike in northern Colorado today. I know something about strikes. I didn't go into them yesterday. You have been trained by your masters to be dependent when there is a crisis on. Now you see we enter the bull pens, you fill the jails. I was carried eighty-four miles and landed in jail by a United States Marshal in the night because I was talking to a miners' meeting. The next morning I was brought to court and the judge said to me, "Did you read my injunction? Did you understand that the injunction told you not to look at the miners?" "As long as the Judge who is higher than you leaves me sight, I will look at anything I want to," said I. The old judge died soon after that and the injunction died with him. At another time when in the court room the judge said to me, "When you are addressing the court you must say 'Your Honor.'" "I don't know whether he has any or not," said I. He turned me loose on my good behavior in a short time.

Someone said to me, "You don't believe in charity work, Mother." No, I don't believe in charity; it is a vice. I wish there was never a charitable institution in the world. I would destroy them all if I had my way. We need the upbuilding of justice to mankind; we don't need your charity, all we need is an opportunity to live like men and women in this country.

Young men, let me say to you, keep away from the saloon, the pool room, the gambling den. There is nothing for you in them. Develop your brain and heart by serving humanity and reading human history. Be true to your fellow men and stand loyally to the cause of the worker. No power on earth can dissolve us and we will get what we want if we are loyal. If you go ahead and do right, victory is yours. The United Mine Workers of America will never leave the state of Colorado until the banner of industrial freedom floats over every mine in the state. It is up to you, my boys, to gain victory. I will be with you and your officers will be with you. I know these boys. I have worked with them. I have watched them. If they were not deserving of all I say, I would be the first one to condemn them. You need never distrust them.

Stand together and don't surrender this time. You will not be asked to do so by your officers. They will sell the coats on their backs first. I know them. I never knew them to quit. They did a lot for the fight in West Virginia. They have never yet told me what to do except they say, "Mother, why don't you take a rest?" My answer is, "When I organize Colorado and Alabama, then you can tell me to rest if you want to, but not until."

I want you to pledge yourselves in this convention to stand as one solid army against the foes of human labor. Think of the thousands who are killed every year and there is no redress for it. We will fight until the mines are made secure and human life valued more than props. Look things in the face. Don't fear a governor; don't fear anybody. You pay the governor; he has a right to protect you. You are the biggest part of the population in the state. You create its wealth, so I say, "Let the fight go on; if nobody else will keep on, I will."

[Typed minutes, convention of District 15, UMWA, Western History Collection, Denver Public Library.]

Speech at a convention
of District 14, United Mine Workers of America
Pittsburg, Kansas

The series of events in Colorado was almost a replay of the previous year's strike in West Virginia. The Colorado miners struck on 23 September 1913 and moved into tent colonies set up by the UMWA. The coal companies imported hundreds of guards and armed them with machine guns and armored cars; miners, too, purchased guns and ammunition. Mother Jones made speeches and traveled to the tent colonies to encourage the strikers. When Governor Elias M. Ammons visited Trinidad to examine the situation first hand, she led a march on the hotel where he was staying, but he refused to see her. She led another march of miners to the governor's office in Denver, complaining of the actions of the guards; he agreed to accept a formal report of complaints. In October, after numerous fatalities in clashes between miners and guards, Governor Ammons sent the state militia into the Trinidad area, and General John Chase deployed them across two counties with orders to disarm miners and guards, though with small success.

Meanwhile, Mother Jones left the strike zone to use her influence nationally on behalf of the strikers. Her first trip in November was to the east coast to make speeches in Boston and Washington, where she urged federal intervention. She returned to Denver in time to address the Colorado Federation of Labor on 19 December, and left almost immediately for a two-week visit to El Paso to try to stop the importation of scabs from Mexico. On 4 January 1914 she returned to Trinidad and was immediately deported to Denver. On the twelfth, she made good her vow to return to Trinidad, was seized by the militia, and was imprisoned in Mt. San Rafael hospital for two months. On 16 March her captors took her to Denver and released her. On 24 March she once again boarded a train for Trinidad, but was removed by the militia in Walsenburg, Colorado, and confined in the Huerfano County jail for twenty-three days before being taken again to Denver where she had an interview with the governor.

During the latter part of April she again spoke at rallies in Boston, New York, and Washington. On 23 April she testified before the House Committee on Mines and Mining on conditions in West Virginia, Michigan, and Colorado and recommended government ownership of the mines.

Speeches

While she was in Washington, the most horrifying of the many brutalities of the Colorado strike occurred: women and children were burned to death at Ludlow when the militia set fire to the strikers' tents. She left immediately for Denver and arrived in time to address a mass protest meeting on the capitol grounds on 26 April.

The following speech was delivered four days later at a convention of District 14, UMWA, in Pittsburg, Kansas. Mother Jones was on her way to another round of speeches in New York, but stopped off at the district meeting to urge the delegates to increase their financial contributions to the strike in Colorado. The UMWA treasury was rapidly becoming exhausted by the constant drain of sustaining the embattled strikers and by almost equally heavy expenses for the legal defense of union members who had been charged with various crimes or were being held in prison under martial law.

§ § §

Chairman [John P.] White: Now, this morning I know that I voice the sentiments of this convention when I say that we appreciate the presence here of our great old organizer, Mother Jones. (Applause.)

Yesterday I gave you a pretty strong bump about Colorado, and what you were going to do about the money that you had loaned the national organization, that I plead guilty to being responsible for, so God help you, for I put you in the hands of Mother Jones now. (Loud applause.)

A Delegate: I think the brothers ought to put up their pipes, put them in their pockets.

Mother Jones: You should join John D. Rockefeller, you are getting so nice. Now, I will say to you, as I did to the audience Sunday in Denver, in the capitol grounds, who did so much hand clapping, the trouble with the workers of this nation, and probably every nation of the world, has been that they have used their hands instead of their heads. Now, the time has come in history when we have got to use our heads instead of our hands so much.

One thing I want to make a statement to you before I go, is that I am not in quite the trim I wanted to be to go after you today, because I have been doing so much of it, you know, that I have to have a little time to think it over, and I have not had it when I came here, so the rocks may not strike quite as hard as I want them to.

About 200 years after the world's greatest agitator had left the world, left His Message behind to man, the Romans had not yet grasped the real import of that message, so they went way down into another nation and there they captured quite a number of agitators. They didn't call them agitators in that time, but amongst those that they captured was one, and when they brought them into Rome, if they didn't turn them over

130

as slaves, or keep them themselves, they sold them into slavery to someone else, and there was one who annoyed them very much, who disturbed the pleasant order of things, and they said to him, "What is your message here below? What are you doing? Why do you keep up this continual agitation?" And he said, "Being a member of the human family, whatever concerns my brothers in the struggle of life concerns me; I cannot rest until I explain to them why these conditions exist." And he said, "This is because I see the heartaches and the sufferings of my fellow beings, that is why I am an agitator"—he was a poet and painter. They said, "Then you will be sold into slavery," and he said, "I am already a slave; while one human wretch of the great industrial force is oppressed, I am oppressed."

I wish to God I could permeate every man in this audience, not only in the audience, but in the city; not only in the city, but in the state, with the same sentiment that permeated the breast of that pagan slave long ago in the ages of time.

You see, my brothers, the trouble with us all is we don't feel the pains of our fellow beings in the great struggle. I wonder if the nation felt the horror of that affair at Ludlow? Why, if that happened in Mexico we would go down to clean up Mexico, and it happened here at home and there is very little said about it, when every man should shoulder his gun and start to Colorado to stop the war there. (Applause.)

We are moral cowards, the whole of us are. We sit down chewing the rag about spending some little money and time. We want to let the world know how much we know, and the result is we know damned little. I happened to be in Washington to get a hearing before the Federal Commission when I heard of this, and it so shocked me that I could not hold myself. I wanted to take the train right away and go back, but the hearing before the Congressional Committee was for tomorrow, and I had to stay to get that hearing. As soon as it was over I started for Colorado again.

No time in modern history has there been anything so horrible as this trouble in Colorado. I know those men in Colorado pretty well. No state in the Union has truer, better fellows; they have made a great fight against the men in power. There is no question about it. The poor fellow that got killed, this Greek [Louis Tikas], when I went to Ludlow, when the battle first started, the tears came streaming down his face, and he said, "Mother, they jumped at me to go war, and I got away and let the capitalists fight their own battle. I am here now, and this is my battle, the battle of right for the class that I belong to." That summed up the whole philosophy of the labor movement. In other words, it was a battle for freedom for the class that he belonged to. And he said, "Mother, I need a gun." I said, "You will have one, Louie, if Mother has to take her hat off and sell it, you will get the gun." (Applause.)

Now, those brave men were the men brought over, most of them, after the last strike that we had in Colorado; Rockefeller sent his agents to Europe and brought those fellows over. He has been able to crush them, rob them, persecute them until he has made his millions out of their precious blood, and then he goes into church on Sunday and is hallowed by the people of this great nation.

Three women were roasted to death on the eve of bringing into the world another generation. There were six roasted, six murdered. Something that has never happened in Mexico, and then the dear Governor of Colorado [Elias M. Ammons] goes up to Washington and says we must have conservation of the trees, he says, in Washington, to the Senators, and to the nation, we must have conservation of the trees in Colorado. The corporations never thought of conserving the lives of the children in the state against the invisible government. Why, men, you have no grasp of this thing at all. The horrors of it cannot be depicted by human pen, or penned into the history to come. When these children were piled up, sixteen that we know of, don't know how many more were roasted, whose bodies were never found, and those bodies were piled up one after another and carried to their last resting place, how many people in the United States grasped the horror of that thing?

(Cries of "Not very many.")

I wondered when I stood before that committee and [they] asked me if I would approve of sending the Federal troops to Colorado, I said, "I am deadly opposed to the bayonet going anywhere in an industrial conflict. Gentlemen," I said, "it is not the bayonet we want; it is justice. We are opposed to the bayonet." I stood aghast when I took up the Sunday morning paper on the train going into Denver, and I saw where the women of the city of Denver had gone up to the Governor and asked for the Federal troops to be brought in. Imagine the women of a nation calling for the bayonet to settle a strike. It has never yet been settled by bayonets, and it never will. I said in an interview with the *Denver Times* there is the trouble with the nation. The woman raises her son to take up the bayonet and go out and murder in the interest of the employing classes. Not until that woman becomes educated to a more human conception of her duty to society will society take its place in the civilized world. The woman is the foundation of society, and that woman should know the cause of their troubles, and the trouble with you has been that you have never allowed your women to come into your meetings and take a share in discussing these great questions. When I looked at the gunmen that came up every night at 6 o'clock and brought their bayonets, sixty-five young men, some of them nice young men, and when I got to talking with them afterwards, and they watched me day and night with their bayonets, I said to one of them, "Did it ever occur to you," said I, "that nobody ever carried a bayonet to sit down and watch the old, black mammy in her days of slavery when she was incarcerated, and you boys sit down as citizens of the nation, the boys whose destiny the future of the nation lies in your hands, you come every night at 6 o'clock with a bayonet to watch the old woman that she don't dare breathe outside of the window for fear her breath would contaminate the crowd outside." And these young men stood aghast, and they said, "Mother, we never knew we had to meet this; we never knew we had to come out and fight the miners. As soon as this is over we will never again take up a gun for them. We will leave the state before we will do it," and that was true. There were many of those young men that were not found again, and some of them had to be put in jail in Denver before they would take up the gun. They put them in jail. There lies the disease. We have too many sentimental orators that are looking to see if they can see their picture in the paper. Mine gets in, but it is a damnable looking thing (applause), I assure you.

I happened to be down—I just want to show you the modern woman of today, not the miner's wife in Colorado and West Virginia, not her, but your modern parasite. I happened to be in San Francisco; I went up to hear an orator on the rostrum. He was rather dramatic. I sat there and listened to him, you know, and in my estimation he didn't say anything that touched the real class war, but when he got through along came a bunch of the cats, and one said, "Dear comrade, we are so charmed; I really thought when I was listening to you that it was almost Jesus that was speaking." (Laughter.)

Just imagine those women, the mothers of the nation, coming out with such rot in these terrific struggles of ours, when every woman should arise in her right and stand shoulder to shoulder as the woman of the old Romans did 2,000 years ago, when they marched barefooted through the desert to carry the message of hope to their sister women and their brothers. That is the type of woman that has seen the jail and the scaffold and has stood side by side with her brother, working on the battlefields, urging him to keep on in this desperate struggle until victory is ours. It is a wonderful battle. Three hundred miners—I have been receiving letters from the men in Washington asking me for God's sake, Mother, when are you coming to us. Some of them were appealing and pathetic. I could not reach them with a reply because the post offices are in the company's stores, and I know that all of these letters—I know because a railroad man once in Alabama put me on; he said, "Mother, there is scarcely a letter that goes through the mails that belongs to you people but what is criticised and read." The postmaster in one of the towns in West Virginia also told me of some things that were going to take place; that the mine owner had sent the mail out, and he said, "I warn you now," and for that reason I could not reply to these letters very well. But when these men—300 men—

were roasted to death while they were making wealth for their master there was not very much said about it. Their own children went to their bodies. The heads were blown off in that mine, and their own children went to look at the bodies and opened the shirts to see if they could recognize it as their father. That was the only way that they had to recognize that it was their own father, and when those bodies were brought out of the mines they were there making wealth for the Philip Dodge Copper Company. I said before a mass meeting of the Trades Council of New York, how many of you men went down to the office of the Philip Dodge gang of thieves on 99 John Street; how many of you laid down your tools and went down and told those bloodthirsty pirates, you stop murdering our men or we will take a hand in the game? Not one. They don't think of that. They can go and play pool and go on to the saloon and get a drink. I don't object to that if you get it, if you stop there, but when I want money to buy guns they have not got any, to defend the wives and children of these men; they have not got any. All honor to Wyoming, she sent us $15,000.00 right down. I didn't come here to talk to you. I came here to get after you; I want every infernal cent that you have in your treasury turned over to go to Colorado to make this fight. Don't you know, boys, that this fight is the greatest battle, industrial battle, ever fought in America? I know it is. Some of our boys, our leaders, said to me when the fight was first started out in Colorado, they said, "Mother, we have got them" — we were going out one day to meet the other side — "we have got them on the run," and I said, "Is that so?" And they said, "Yes," and I said, "Those fellows have not moved yet; Mother knows them. If this strike is settled next April," I said, "I will feel we are doing good work." That is just what I said. "Now don't get it into your heads," said I, "that this is going to be a Sunday school fight. Never in the history of America will we have to put up a greater fight if the miners' organization is going to stand." You are the revolutionary forces of the labor movement in America. You are the power they are afraid of. You are the power that the invisible government is after; the miners' organization is the real power of the labor movement of this country. Now, you are the fellows they are going to break, and I want to tell you that I learned from an officer of the militia — he didn't intend to tell me — but you have the secret service men in your organization raising rows and creating discontent. I got that from an officer of the militia; he didn't mean to tell me, but it came out in a conversation, and when these fellows are talking I generally take down everything they say. I put it inside of my skull, and when they are gone I put it down in black and white. Now, you have got your men that are trying to disrupt this organization. It is up to you, my boys, whether you go down in defeat or rise in this great nation like men ought to rise. It is up to you. I said to President Wilson last October — I went up with Senator Lane of Oregon to see him; there was a terrific crowd there that day, and I said, "Mr. President, I realize this is a very busy day with you." "Yes, it is, Mother," he said. I said, "My object in getting this interview with you today was to discuss the Colorado situation with you fully." "I am very interested in that," he said, "Mother Jones, and I am certainly interested in the conflict in Colorado."

I said, "Mr. President, it is very essential that it be looked into by the administration." Now, the trouble, I said, boys, is that we have traveled fifty years in history, we have created machinery and wealth, we have elected men to office, political. These men have no grasp of the great revolution that is going on. It is just like in Colorado and West Virginia and Michigan; they are dummies, they are not men that are looking after the welfare of the nation. They are time servers, I want office, I must have office, and they are elected and nominated like this fellow up in West Virginia—Hatfield—they held a meeting down in Kentucky to decide which one they would elect or nominate in the convention for Governor. The miners nor the workers were not at that caucus. It was the mine owners, the invisible government that was there, and he was selected, he was elected because he could serve them nicely. When they sent for me to go down to Ohio so that I could agitate there and I sent for the Attorney General, and I said to the Attorney General, "You can tell the Governor that he can chain me to that tree outside the door, or turn his dogs of war loose and riddle me with bullets, but I will never leave West Virginia until I get ready to." (Applause.)

International President White: And you didn't, neither.

Mother Jones: You bet your life I didn't. I have no boss; I don't recognize a boss. (Applause.)

When he sent for me in the United States Senate—perhaps you don't know how all this came about; it is a funny affair, and I will tell you the truth about it right here today. There was a fellow from Pittsburgh, a newspaper man on the *Leader,* and he came, and he had to come in the back way and he saw the people that the militia had rented that room from, and downstairs was a cellar, under the lounge, there was a carpenter they had, and we took two planks and loosened them, and any fellow I wanted to see could come up through there, and the militia was outside of the door. They are awful bright cusses, you know. So he came in the back door and up through the hole, and I said, "Bring him up," and we lifted the boards and he came up and spent the whole afternoon with me, and I gave him all of the inside of the affairs of West Virginia, and the next day he was coming along and he was with a boiler inspector of the government and he bowed, and I said to the boiler inspector, "Are you coming in to join the militia." "Oh, no," said he, "I am going over to the Houston mine to examine it," and this fellow was with him, and I said,

"How do you do"—I didn't let them know I knew him, and I said, "Are you a subsidized spotter?" And with that the militia came along and said, "You cannot talk to us," and they took him and they took the other fellow and put him in the bull pen and fixed his kodak—he had one on his shoulder—and kept him there for two hours, and he went into Pittsburgh and wrote up everything. He just slaughtered them, the Pittsburgh *Leader* did. Well, then, there was the wife [Cora Older] of the editor of the San Francisco *Bulletin,* he sent her there and she couldn't get an interview only when the militia was around, but she went away, and she went to *Collier's Weekly,* that was the only place that she could get into, and she wrote it up, and she saw a couple of Senators and it came up in the Senate. I saw in the Cincinnati *Post* where an article said that Wall Street had telephoned to Senator Kerns to withdraw his resolution and they would make it an object, and the party they used was a personal friend, an old-time friend, and the article said they didn't telegraph, they didn't wait to go; they used the most immediate means of reaching him, and I looked at that and I said, "My God," says I, "if this thing goes on unchallenged we are up against it," and I looked and I said, "There is none of these fellows in Charleston will think what an important thing this is," and I sat down to write a letter to Senator Kerns, and when I got half through I tore it up, and I walked up and down the floor, and it looked like Jesus or somebody near him had whispered to me, and I sat down and wrote a telegram to Senator Kerns from out of the military prison: "I send you the groans, and tears, and heartaches of the men, women and children as I have heard it, pleading with you to push the investigation, and the children will call you blessed." There was a telegram from the Governor [Henry D. Hatfield] stating that I was not a prisoner, but was detained in a very pleasant boarding house. The Governor stated in his telegram, "She is not a prisoner." He said we had peace and prosperity here in West Virginia until these agitators came in, and he said the grandmother of agitators is that old woman, Mother Jones. She is really the grandmother of all the agitators, and he said when she comes into a state she tears everything up, but a gentleman from South Carolina, he paid me quite a tribute, and he said there is no question about it, and when he read that telegram from the Governor, Senator Kerns got up and read the telegram I had sent him; he said, "I have another telegram from this very pleasant boarding house," and he read it. Now the Senator told me in fifty years nothing had ever struck the Senate as that did, in the United States Senate. Now, the great trouble with us is that we don't grasp these things, and don't know how to use the opportunity that presents itself for the working class of this country. Some men get into office in the industrial field the same as in politics, they are after the office, and they don't think of the terrible responsibility placed up their shoulders. They don't give that a thought, and you go to work and recommend men as organizers, and if they don't prove right and somebody reports it to the president, as we have done, I don't deny it, and I will do it every time if it was my own brother that was at fault. (Applause.) Then if he discharges them there is the whole rank and file up against the administration because he sent this fellow away. I wrote to the office in some of these cases myself. They were blowing it into their rotten stomachs, living in hotels and hiring another man to do the work outside, and charging the whole thing up to the organization. (Applause.) The same was true in West Virginia, and I don't hesitate to get up and say so, and for that reason they got the ax after me, but they have never got my head yet. When a man in this age wants to go out as an organizer, and your president or your vice-president don't know him very well, and he puts him out, and he doesn't prove right, he can remove him very readily, and if he does the whole of you are after him. Your district is insulted because your district president took a drunken bum off of the force. If he had not taken him off I would have gotten the police to have arrested him, because I ain't going to stand for it. How many of you fellows, when you pay your assessments, when you pay your dues — how many of you fellows after years have got enough money to buy your wife a dress — how many of you have?

(A Voice: "Not very many.")

Mother Jones: When the idle days, and everything, is taken into consideration, how many miners do I know through the country that put the last dollar they have into the organization so that it will bring relief for their children, and yet your organization goes out and blows it in. I want to appeal to you boys, for the honor of the organization, for the principle that we agitate, I want to appeal to you, don't have any favorites, don't have any pets; if you are going to recommend a man to organize be sure he is right. I have known them to go to locals before their time expired as board members; I have known them to go to locals and tell them what fine fellows they were, orators, and I have listened to those damned fellows and they didn't have oratory enough to start a cat fight. Boys, we are in a different age in the human history of the world. The history of the world never had an age like this, never. And I plead with you for the suffering of these men and children as I have seen it, you know. I plead with you to help your officers move the machinery of your organization onward and upward. You have got the secret service men of the big interests in your organization. You have got them, boys. Now, I want to state to you in the early days of the fight in West Virginia, long ago, there was a president of that district; a mine owner, who was very favorable to us, came and reported about him, and the board members and all, and I don't always take stock, I generally watch myself very carefully, and one day after I had got a line on things it was time to get rid of that thing. It was a crucial time in the history of the organization there, and I called the national officers into my room and talked and discussed the thing with them, and I couldn't get them to move until they had called a convention. I said, I am opposed to spending money on the railroads. I am opposed to giving it to the hotels, and I stated we have to get rid of this fellow. Just then a national board member came in, and he said one of the Baldwin guards was after our president, and he used to work for Jesus more than the organization, and he told about how bad he felt. I am not working for Jesus, He doesn't need me, He is able to look after himself, and I said, now is the time, and I asked where he was and they told me, and I went over in the rottenest hole in Montgomery—it certainly was—and when I walked in that brute, drawing his salary as an officer of the organization, lay there on an old, dirty, filthy mattress, the mattress was on the floor, and he had a bottle of whisky that long (indicating) beside him. (Laughter.) It is nothing to laugh at; this is a serious thing, and our organization was up against it at the time; we had to watch every angle, and I went in and said, "What is the matter?" "Oh, Mother," he said, said he, "the Baldwin guards are after me." I said, "That is too bad, but," I said, "what are they after you for?" And he said, "Because I have been too good to the miners." And I said, "You had better resign." And he said, "If you will tell me to, I will do it." And I said, "You are too favorable to us, but if you resign the Baldwin guards won't be after you." I went over and got $50.00, and I said, "You sign this resignation and I will tell them then that you are not an officer any more and they won't bother you." He signed the resignation and I paid him $50.00 down, and I don't know whether they have paid me the $50.00 or not.

President White: You can present your bill when we win the strike.

Mother Jones: I said, "Here is $50.00, and the Baldwin guards won't bother you, but if you are in town in fifteen minutes I will have you hung to a lamp post. I have 100 miners ready to do the job. He said, "Am I president no more?" And I said, "No, and you will never hold an office again while I am on earth," and a board member was just as beastly drunk all of the time and arrested for killing a woman, and this is what you have to contend with. I mention these things because I plead with you that we are up against it. If you don't use your brains and your manhood you will not save the labor movement of this country. The powers that be are afraid of you, and they have got their tools among you, and I ask you here to stand like a solid stone wall against the common enemy. When any fellow is beginning to disrupt the harmony of the organization, put him out. Don't bother with him. You have no time to waste with those fellows. The poor children that were roasted to death at Ludlow,

138

their voice is coming to you, and as I said, some day we will find that they did not die in vain. They died for a great cause, in a great battle, and they didn't give up their lives in vain, my boys. I believe if you are true there is no power in the world can conquer you. And the labor movement, and the children in factories, mills and mines, are sending their message here to you today. If you could see the letters I get from the girls in different factories: "Oh, God, Mother, we were afraid they would kill you. Mother, we want you; they are robbing us, they have destroyed our womanhood."

I have stood in Milwaukee, when the brewery workers came to me at that time, I was working for poor Mexicans that were going to be extradited and hung. The brewery workers said, "We want you to go to Milwaukee for us; we have so many hundred girls we cannot touch there, we can't organize them, and will you give us a hand?" "I don't know what I can do in there," I said, "but I will try it, anyhow." I went up there. Every time I would undertake to organize those girls the brewers would discharge them, and so I concluded I would go to Cincinnati and put it up to the board of brewery workers. I said, "I cannot do anything, and I don't want to take your money for hotel and railroad fares unless I bring you results," and I said, "There is only one way you can get those fellows; the miners are in convention; get them to boycott the beer." I showed where they were in jail for white slavery, and the brewers' wives rose and holloed, "She ought to be hung." Well, boys, one night at 11:30, in the city of Milwaukee, I was coming from away out of town where I had a notary public taking evidence from witnesses who were robbed in the breweries of Milwaukee for $2.50 and $3.00 a week, who worked in water up to their knees and were getting diseased. I had to change cars. While I was waiting for the transfer car I was so cold—it was very cold—and I didn't have any more clothes than the law allowed, I will tell you that, and I was backing up against a telegraph pole to keep the wind from my spine, and while I was there a young girl passed me. She didn't seem very well clad. It was late, and I wondered what emergency there was that put that girl on the street at that hour of the night, and just as she passed me a man came the other way. She threw her arms around the man, and she said, "Take me for a dollar." This was on the streets of Milwaukee. The man on his honor said, "My God, girl," he said, "why do you do this? What would I do if it was my daughter?" and the girl broke down in my hearing and said, "Mister, don't blame me; I work over here in a department store; I get $2.75 a week. My father is dead, and my mother is sick. I have two little brothers and a sister. I send $1.50 to my mother; I pay 75 cents for my room; I have 50 cents to spend and clothe myself," she said; and out of the blood and womanhood of that girl, and thousands like her, we build the machinery that builds the great palaces of the invisible government, and we say it is right. She was some man's loved one. He pressed her to his breast before he passed away. She was loved and caressed by some mother, but she is only a sample of the thousands and thousands of the working children who are driven to ruin, and we are responsible for it, my boys. It is a horror to be thought of, and when I looked, or picked up the paper and saw where these sentimental women in Chicago were going to Marshall Field's and to others of the leading classes, asking for an increase in wages, and telling how much the maximum wage ought to be, and how much they could live on, and these women never thought of making Marshall Field produce their books to see the profit they made out of the life and blood of these girls. They didn't think that far. They don't belong to the class who is crucified. They belong to the sentimental class, and they must not hurt the feelings of the blood-sucking pirates. And, my brothers, were I to relate all of the horrible instance I have seen it would paralyze this nation, and yet we sit idly by and grumble a little bit if we happen to appropriate a few dollars to those who are making this fight. Will you arise? Will you give us the money, and we will make the fight and free you in Colorado. (Applause.)

One of the Standard Oil agents, while the Governor was in Washington, goes to the Lieutenant-Governor and told him to send the militia down there. They had to take the militia out of the strike zone before they could turn me loose, and war began, and then they went back to the Governor and asked him to send the militia back. This Lieutenant-Governor was a Citizens' Alliance man during our last strike of ten years ago, and was ready to shoot and murder our people. Now you see what you are up against, boys. This is a horrible state of affairs. I want to show you another instance. Three or four days before I was turned loose there was a note slipped under my door, and the party knocked at the door and said, "Mother"; I said, "What is it?" He said, "Here is a note under the door," said he, "for you, and read it." And I took up the note and read it, and he signed his name. The name struck me, and I began thinking about the name before I read the note. I read the note, which said: "Mother, I am turned loose today, I have been in jail for so long"—two weeks, anyhow—"I am turned loose today and I want to do something for you, and I want you to tell me how I can start it." I slipped the note back under the door, and he said, "I am going out and I will start something for you to get you out of here." I looked at the note, and the name struck me at the time, and I began to think where had I seen that name or heard it before, and I began searching my brain, and I located the fellow over in West Virginia. I didn't see his face, it was the note struck me, and I sat down and replied: "If you are turned loose, you obey the law and attend to your own business, you don't need to do anything for me, I am attending to my affairs here, and you attend to your own affairs outside."

That very night that fellow went out to one of the camps and murdered a union miner, and he was brought back, and he is never going to be punished for it. He was a gunman in the service of the thugs in West Virginia, and I told the boys so when I came out. Afterwards, when I went back to the jail to get some things I had, this fellow came to the door. And he said, "Mother," said he, "do you know who I am?" And I said, "I think I do, you are one of the rats in West Virginia." He said, "I was secretary of the union at Levette and secretary of the Socialists." He was a gunman.

President White: He killed the secretary of our local.

Mother Jones: Yes, sir, that very night that he sent me that note asking me how he could start something, so you see you have to be on the alert. Our people out there thought he was a fine fellow. Why, I said, "He is one of the gunmen from West Virginia." The whole gang was rotten to the core and said I, "It was only through that that I was able to get the boys to awake to the fact."

Now, boys, you have to be on the alert. I hope I have not said anything to hurt your feelings, but I want to tell you the destinies of this organization is more sacred to me than my life, because the whole labor movement of the nation, and in fact, in Europe, depends on your manhood. (Applause.)

You know I didn't come in yesterday, and you know I never looked for an office. You know I have faced the guns and been duped by the enemies, because it is your children that are dear to me. No one knows the future for them better than I do, and for that reason I am pleading and appealing to your manhood. I am appealing to you because I may soon cross to the far shore, I am appealing to you — tomorrow I will have passed my eighty-second mile-stone in my life. A reporter said to me, of the Denver *News,* the day I was about to leave, "Mother," said he, "when did you enter the first battle?" "On the grand Trunk Railroad," said I, "when I was a girl." My father was working, and in those days there was no law to force them to pay you, and they used to hire the men and keep them two months without a penny of wages and then they would go away and never pay the men. And I happened to be one of the victims, as the child of my father who was not paid, and I knew where the fellow lived, out on the edge of town, in a very comfortable place, and I organized an army of girls and we went out there, and I made that fellow pay us the money that he owed us. (Applause.)

I said, "That was my first industrial battle." There were no laws then. They could rob you as they liked, and they rob us yet, only in a different way. They rob us for Jesus and for everybody. They took up the speech that I made in West Virginia and the investigation committee asked me, "Did you make that speech?" "Oh, yes," I said, "I did." I said, "I heard

Ingalls make a speech in the early '60s, and that speech was nothing compared with that." They asked me if I said they robbed miners to send Jesus to China, and I said I did. I told them they took money from the miners in weighing coal, etc., and you go to the women down in Kentucky and give them four or five hundred dollars to foreign missions as Cabell did to send Jesus to China, and they will say, he is just lovely, he is a Christian, he gave us so much money, and they know Jesus lives in that country, and you know that He couldn't stay there because they would murder Him if they got Him. I told them it was the modern system of hypocrisy, and among the women in particular. The women don't go into the economic fights; if they did, we could clean it up tomorrow. They go in for temperance. They don't want you to drink. We have nothing to do, we must drink. (Applause.) If we don't drink it, the other fellow does. (Applause.)

I say this is the age when the workers have got to stand together, we don't want to starve. I said, "The great trouble with you gentlemen is that most of you can sit here and smoke your fine cigars, and you know nothing of the aching backs and hearts of these wretches." Boys, I went to the Ludlow the first days of the strike. I will never forget it as long as I live. It was a picture I never saw in industrial history before. I passed twenty-eight wagons on the way coming down, twenty-eight wagons in fourteen miles. The women had their babies in their arms, some of them, and were walking in the mud. These are the women that fight the great industrial battles for liberty. They had their babes in their arms, the rain was coming down, and some of the little ones were sitting on the wagons. There was no man in America that would have given $20.00 for all those twenty-eight wagons. That was what they got from the Standard Oil for taking their lives in their hands and going down into the darkness of the earth and bringing out the coal that moves the world onward and upward, and you miners have got the thing in your own hands. The destinies of this nation lie with you. For instance, we have 750,000 miners. Suppose that we had 700,000 of them organized in this country.

Now, stop your gaping, you can go to sleep when you get home. (Laughter.)

Now, if you got 700,000 organized, you would be in the top of the great pinnacle in this country. In 1820 the first coal was discovered in the anthracite region. Now, you can remember when you had no organization — I can — when the poor fellow had to fight the battles. Now, in these years, in the last fifty years in the history of this nation, look and see what the miners, and the miners alone, have done. Look at the thousands and hundreds of thousands of miles of railroads that you have built. Look at the liners that are plying the oceans, connecting nation with nation. Look at the telegraph lines, look at the streets, the subways, the elevated ways —

who has built them—the miners. You move the nation. Stop your bickering and be men, and let capital know it. You can put your hand behind your back and say to the pirates in Washington and the Standard Oil trade, now, make laws for us; if you don't we will freeze you to death. Think of the millions of dollars they got in 1912, and they took it all from you, and the miners produced all that wealth, and you have not a voice in this, and Rockefeller can tell you that he won't settle with you. The commissioner said to me, "Mother Jones, if Rockefeller concedes everything else, will you waive the union?" "No," I said, "we will concede everything else, but I want the union." (Applause.) And he said, "Well, he don't want to recognize the union, he don't want to make a contract with them." I said, "Don't Mr. Rockefeller make contracts for the coal that these men dig?" And he said, "Yes, sir." "Have they not got a right to have a contract from him what they will sell their labor for? Don't he make a contract what he is going to sell the coal for and don't they have the same right to make a contract of what their labor is worth?" and they said, "Yes." Now, I will tell you what I did say, I didn't say it to them because I thought it was not wise, but I have said this, if I was President of the United States I would settle this strike very quickly. How? I would simply send to Rockefeller, the old man, who has 40 per cent of the stock in Colorado, because he is really the owner, he holds the balance of power, and the balance of the stock is divided among a large number of people, and they have not got the balance of power, but Rockefeller has. I said, I would send for Rockefeller, the real owner of those mines, and I would also send for Mr. White, the president of the miners who dig the coal, and I would tell both of them, "Do business before you leave here, both of you."

They said, "If you do that, they will close the mines." And I said, "If they do that, let the government take the mines and run them." I want this convention—I think there is a Congressman that has introduced a bill to take over the mines—I want everybody to write to that Congressman a letter—if he was a Congressman.

President White: I think Congressman Bryan.

Mother Jones: Write and tell him to go to it, now is the time, we are behind you, and when Rockefeller sees that power behind him, we can paralyze every industry, we can freeze their wives and daughters and their colleges if they don't do business with us, and you bet your life they will do business, and don't you worry about it.

Now, I will tell you what I came out here for. I didn't know the president was here until late last night. I don't know whether he would have let me come or not, but I would have come anyhow. Boys, I may never again appear before you. I may not be able to fight many more battles for you, but I stand here on behalf of the babies whose lives went out, I stand here on behalf of those great women who stood the storms of winter while you had shelter, I stand here on behalf of the women that heard the bullets whiz through the little tents that you had furnished them, I stand pleading with you in their behalf to send us the money, and I will tell you now there will not a dollar of that money go to waste. It will bring results. We will win the strike in Colorado, or every one of us will go to our graves in your defense in this great battle of the West. (Applause.)

There will be no backsliding. The brave women from the northern Colorado fields came to me Sunday. "Mother, they have four machine guns, but if you will come down we don't care for their bullets." "I will be down," said I, "and they can use their machine guns, they can slaughter us, but we will give our lives that the workers of America shall furl the flag of freedom." (Applause.) We are not going to surrender for no man, and there will be no compromise, and they can send all of the Federal troops, and all of the bullets of the Federal troops can go through us, but we will live in history as having made the American industrial body of workers free, and so, my brothers, that is why I am here today.

Now, the history of my incarceration was nothing. It was one of the things that take place in our industrial battles. It was horrible to look at, but no matter, but when they took me off of the train that morning and put me down in that cold place, the colonel [Edward Verdeckberg] who had charge there said, "Mother, this is the most repulsive position I have ever been placed in in my life. Won't you go back to Denver? This cellar," said he, "is not fit for a human being to be put in." I said, "Colonel, I appreciate your manhood and feelings fully, but it is a question of constitutional rights with me. I will not surrender them to any militia or political despot." I said, "I shall stay in this cellar until the Governor loosens my hands and tell me that I can go where I please." Several times he said — and I must say for him that he was as kind as they would let him be — and he did everything that he could. I was allowed to communicate with the outside some. Now, it was deplorable, and I don't like sympathy, sympathy never got me anything, and I have no use for it. We don't want sympathy, we want to stand out straight before the world that we are fighting the battle for our own cause. When I was to be turned loose they had to take the whole militia out before I could be turned loose. It had to be withdrawn from the strike zone, because they didn't want to go into the Supreme Court to reverse the Moyer decision. That was what I was fighting for. When I got out, after nine weeks without speaking to a human being, without reading that much of a paper, without getting a line or an envelope or a postal card, and had only talked with the lawyer for the miners [Horace Hawkins] three times, and when I got out of there, they kidnaped me out. There is no question about it, they came up, and I want to tell you boys it was the only time in all my life that I felt I was gone, when they brought the automobile and took me down the back stairway and put me into an automobile and went all around every dark street with that automobile, I really thought I was going to say good-bye to everyone. They didn't take me to the station of the Santa Fe, they didn't wait for the C. & S. to come in, they took me to a crossing, held up the train there, and the secret service men of the Santa Fe Company, who are also members of the militia, and United States deputy marshal and a member of the Santa Fe secret service got me on that train, and when I got onto the train I felt relieved, I thought I had not fought the last fight. (Applause.)

The colonel went into Denver with me, and the general met me at the depot. I didn't know he was the general, and I said to the colonel, "Who is that fellow you were talking to?" and he said, "That is General Chase," and I said, "General, if all I hear about you is true, I don't want to walk with you." They wanted to take me to the Elms Hotel, and I said, "No, I don't want to go there." They said that we would go to see the Governor at 9 o'clock, and I said I wanted to take Mr. Hawkins with me. They said that it wouldn't be necessary, and I said it was necessary with me, and I told them to make it 10 o'clock, and I told them I would not go until Mr. Hawkins came down, and we called over the 'phone and asked General Chase, he asked him what about Mother Jones, is she still a prisoner, and he said, "Oh, no, she is free." And within two hours the *habeas corpus* proceedings were going to the Supreme Court, and to block that was why they had turned me loose, and I said when I went back, I said, "This military despotism will have to stop." I said, "There is nothing unjust or unfair in fighting for liberty, and I said "I will go up and I will force them to either keep me a prisoner or let me go to the Supreme Court," and they had held me in this cellar for nine weeks, and just the day before the *habeas corpus* proceedings were to come up, the colonel came in the morning at 9 o'clock and said, "Mother Jones, I have good news for you," he said, "I don't know whether you will consider it good news or not," and I said, "I suppose the Governor has played his game, he has turned me loose," and he said, "Yes, you can go where you please." And he said, "The Governor told me to tell you that you can get transportation from him to any part of the state that you want to go." And I said, "You can tell the Governor for me that I have never in all my life accepted any favor from the enemy, and that he can keep his transportation, I transport myself." (Applause.)

"I realize that," he said, "if you did, you could never make the fight you have." And so the boys came down, the jailer telephoned for the boys and they came down and we went up to headquarters, and we all had a good time—doctors, lawyers and merchants—we all came in, and then I went on in to Denver. I telephoned to our attorney and said if he could force the thing, if he could get it to the Supreme Court, that I was willing, that I was ready to go back to the cellar. It was an awful place. Strong men died there. Last winter some strong men breathed their last in that cellar from the disease they got in it—but they can't disease me. I will give them a fight to the finish, and all we have to do is to quit being moral cowards, rise up like men and let the world know you are citizens of a great nation, and you are going to make it great. The great industrial war is on, and it is up to you to back us up, and I will guarantee that you will never shed a tear that you have backed my boys and girls in Colorado. Now, boys, don't be bothering about any money you have given us. You have not given us enough. I want more, I have got to have it, and if you don't give it to me I will loot Congress, I have to have it, any way, because that fight has to be won, and don't be bothered about what you have given or are going to give. Get a move on you, and let it go down in history that Kansas, the miners of Kansas entered their treasury and said, "Keep up the fight, we are behind you and for you to the end, and if you need us with guns, we will come out." (Loud applause.)

President White: I was sure that Mother Jones would put the quietus on the feeling as to our securing the money of Kansas for the Colorado miners last fall. Her address ought to relieve the mind of any man who was in doubt as to what I said yesterday, that I would exhaust every treasury in the United Mine Workers, regardless of any crooks or anybody else, that we were going to win that fight. (Applause.) No one could have told it better than her, because for more than four of the last six months of her life she has spent in the bastille for the principles she advocated here. What she said about the organization having crooks in its ranks is absolutely true. I told you that more than 280 so-called union men in your ranks are in the employ of the operators, and I have the goods to prove it, too. Now, I am requested to announce that Mother Jones will speak at Frontenac tomorrow afternoon at 1 o'clock at the school house park. So those of you who are in a position to attend that meeting are cordially invited.

Mother Jones: And bring your money, because I want money. I hope nobody grumbles at giving money. Don't you know we had a fight in West Virginia, and it took a lot of money to run that fight there? Don't you know that we had boys do heroic work, and they were the young fellows? They were the trapper boys when I was there a few years ago, and they are grown to men now. If history was written on that strike it would paralyze the nation. It has never been touched. Your chief officers don't understand it. I have talked to the crooks, boys. I will give you an illustration of it. When I was going up Battle Creek—

Delegate Busse: I have been in the labor movement in Germany and France, and the 1st of May is a holiday. Here, the first day in September is Labor day, and I insist that this convention—I make a motion that this convention will not be in session tomorrow, and we all celebrate the Labor day of all nations. Tomorrow is the Labor day of all nations. They call it the Socialist Labor day, but we don't care—

Mother Jones: You sit down, I have the floor. At 11 o'clock one night I was in Butte, Montana, and took up the paper and seen where the Paint Creek Coal Company would not pay their men, and I said, this means that the organization will be wiped out of West Virginia, and I will take a hand in the game. I went in. Two young boys came to me down in Montgomery, about 11 o'clock that night, and they said, "Mother, we were trapper boys eleven or twelve years ago," and they said, "Mother will you do something for us?" And I said, "Why, boys, you know anything in the world I can do I will do, what is it you want of me, going anywhere tonight?" and they said, "No, but for nine years nobody has been up Cabin Creek to us," and I said, "What is the matter, I left you organized and went away to Colorado?" But the boy said, "There is not an organizer come there," and he said, "You don't know the condition we are in." I said, "All right, boys, I will go." I said, "Is it an incorporated town," and they said, "Yes, there was," and I said, "Can we get there to hold a meeting?" and they said "Yes," and I said, "Is the meeting billed?" and they said "No," and I told them not to have anything to do with it, that I would get a couple of railroad men to circulate the bills, and about that time along came an official of the miners and said he was going with me tomorrow, and I said, "No, you are not," and he said, "Oh, yes, I am, I am an officer," and I said, "I don't care what the hell you are," and he said, "I want to go up there," and I said, "No, you are not going, for nine years you have not been there, that is a very dangerous place to go about, and I don't want to involve the organization, if anything happens, and I want to take the responsibility," and he kept insisting and insisting, and went away, and I went to the Governor and told them that I wanted the militia. I went out the next morning, I forgot about the officer going with me, I saw him at the creek, and his jugular vein was filled with whiskey, and his lips were burned, and I trembled because I knew the danger of that creek, and the organization was more sacred to me than anything else. I went in and laid down back of the store where the family lived. Directly two or three of the boys came in and said, "Mother, do you know you have a detective with you?" and I said, "No, I did not, but I supposed they were here, though," and they said, "Yes, there is a detective with you," and I said, "What does he look like?" And they said, "He has a red necktie," and the fellow came up on the train with me. I had not seen him for ten or eleven years, and I said to him, "Is your name Cochran?" And he said, "Yes." And I said, "You are the fellow that the C. & O. paid for two years to watch me." He said, "I have changed, I don't do that now." "A rat never changes," said I, "Once a rat always a rat." Now, that meeting was the most pathetic thing in history that day. It went off all right, and when I closed I told the men that freedom was not dead, it was only gently sleeping. Those men, some of them there with their toes out of their shoes, came down not knowing what was going to happen, and I said to those boys, I said, "Boys, freedom is not dead, she never dies, she is gently sleeping, and when you call her, she will waken," and that crowd hollered. "Oh, God, Mother, call her now." There was never in the history of the labor movement anything so pathetic as that was, and they said, "Mother Jones, will you organize us?" and I said, "Yes, I will, into the United Mine Workers." With all the spotters around they stood facing the guns, and I said, "Yes, I will," and I went there and this officer said, "We have not got the ritual." I said, "You have nothing to do with this," and I had them hold up their hand and I said, "Swear to God Almighty that the very minute you desert this organization you hope you will drop dead, and your children and wives with you," and they did, and I said, "When you put on your clothes in the morning, you go to work and say nothing about the meeting," and when they started to work they were discharged in the morning, and some of those men came ten to twelve miles over the mountains with nothing to eat, and what change I had I gave to the poor fellows. I gave them some money to get a few cigarettes with. (Laughter.)

President White: Or to get a cold one.

Mother Jones: They told me they would never again pick up a gun against us, and I said, you are good boys, and had good mothers, and good homes, and those boys gave me lots of information after that. Every Saturday night I used to distribute to my boys 25-cent pieces — I lost five dollars in the game one night. (Applause.)

[Delegate O'Bryan made a motion to send $10,000 to District 15.]

Mother Jones: Come up here and shake hands with me.

[An amendment and a substitute motion were debated briefly.]

Mother Jones: Boys, I don't believe that you have got a man in the miner's organization, if they knew this thing as I do, but what would give the last dollar that they had, or the last dollar that they can earn for the cause, and don't discuss the matter, just say the treasury is at the disposal of the national president for use in Colorado if he needs it. (Applause.)

[Debate continued on the proper method of authorizing the contribution, and whether the rank and file should be consulted. President J. P. White also spoke at some length.]

Mother Jones: I am going away, and I want to say to the convention I have received letters from the D. & R. G. railroad organization that said, "Mother, we will need you soon, but we will help you now. Anything that you want for the United Mine Workers in Colorado you can have." The railroad men of Colorado are standing with us. God Almighty, stop this discussion over a few dollars and cents and tell John D. Rockefeller we are going the whole route. (Applause.)

[*Proceedings of the Fifteenth Consecutive and First Biennial Convention. District No. 14, United Mine Workers of America, April 27 to May 5, 1914. Held at Pittsburg, Kansas. Together with The Evidence in the Case of Prairie Creek Coal Mining Company, Mammoth Vein Coal Company, Kali-Inla Coal Company and Coronado Coal Company vs. Charles S. Keith. Also the Report of Ex-President Alex Howat.* Copy in the Kansas Collection, Pittsburg State University, pp. 201–23.]

Speech at a special convention
of District 15, United Mine Workers of America
Trinidad, Colorado

The Ludlow Massacre marked a turning point in the Colorado strike. Armed miners attacked the guards and destroyed tipples in retaliation, and the militia abandoned Trinidad for fear of being overwhelmed. On 29 April 1914 the first detachments of federal troops arrived in Denver at the order of President Woodrow Wilson. Gradually, they replaced the Colorado militia, and the threatened civil war was arrested. At the president's behest, the Department of Labor sent mediators into the field, and various plans for ending the strike were explored. Wilson proposed that he should appoint a three-man presidential commission to oversee a wide-ranging settlement that amounted to a three-year truce in the Colorado mining industry. Meanwhile, federal troops maintained order in the affected areas. The UMWA international officers, aware of their depleted treasury, were eager to accept the president's proposal, but left the final decision to the miners of District 15.

During the six months that followed her speech in Kansas, Mother Jones was seldom in Colorado. In May she met a series of engagements in New York, taking a brief rest at the end of the month with her friend, Caroline Lloyd, in Connecticut. In early June she left for Seattle, and crossed into Canada to participate in a strike of coal miners in British Columbia. She returned to New York for a series of speeches in June and July, followed by a quick tour through the midwest. Her schedule of speeches was interrupted from time to time as she lobbied in Washington for strong federal action in Colorado; her basic solution was for the federal government to take over the mines, a course that was debated in cabinet meetings. Just a year after she had urged the Colorado miners to strike, Mother Jones came back to Trinidad to advise them to accept President Wilson's proposals.

The delegates voted to accept the settlement, but the strike dragged on for three more months. The coal mine operators would not agree to all the provisions of the president's plan. Finally, without their agreement, President Wilson announced the appointment of his special commission, largely a face-saving gesture, and the UMWA declared the strike over in December. Although the strike was lost, conditions in Colorado improved markedly over the next three years. The Victor American Company signed a contract with the UMWA in 1917, and John D. Rockefeller, Jr., initiated new labor policies at the Colorado Fuel and Iron Company.

§   §   §

Now, boys, many things have happened in the last year. One year ago today I talked to you about industrial freedom. We are living in a great nation. Industrial despotism will have to die and you, my boys, must use your brains, you must study and think. The sword will have to disappear and the pen will have to take its place. We are the bulwark of the nation.

Thank God that we have another great man, another Lincoln, in Washington today in our President. (Applause.) He does not rush into things but weighs everything carefully in the scale.

If there are any representatives of the Colorado Fuel & Iron Company here, I want to tell you to keep out. You cannot vote in this Convention, for none but bona fide working men will have a vote here. If you are here, I will find you, I can spot you immediately, for I can smell you four miles away. (Applause.)

I want to say to the delegates that they need not worry about any more scabs coming to America for they are shooting them all to pieces in Europe.

Now, boys, come, let us reason together. It is not star oratory we want today, it is logic. The delegate from LaFayette said I had no voice in this convention because I was not a delegate. There is not a miner's union in the United States but what I am a delegate to and have been for years.

There is one thing I want to tell you about. A fellow in New York said to me, "Mother, I have a great invention, I have been working on it for a long time." "What is it going to do," said I, "dig coal?" "O hell, no," said he. If he was going to do that I was going to block his scheme. "I have been listening a great many years," he said, "and I went to work to invent something that was needed and I thought a skull scraper was the finest invention and when you need it let me know."

I happened to be in both the Anthracite strikes. The fact of the matter was I was in Maryland and the National officers sent for me to come from Maryland to Hazelton, Pa., as they expected to call out the 170,000 miners in that section. There were not 6,000 of them in the organization. Delegates came to that convention, only a few, and they said, "What on God's earth can we do?" They said, "Mother, there are only a few of us, what are we going to do?" I told them to wait until we heard the matter discussed in convention. I got the key to the situation as I had not been in the Anthracite field for a good many years. Now don't get it into your heads that I did not understand the inside working of a mine. I went on the night shift and the day shift with the boys of Pennsylvania. I have gone into their homes, and took their babes in my arms and laid down on a pallet of straw. I have nursed their dying wives, and I know what a miner has to contend with. They worked sixteen and seventeen hours per day.

The State administration was against them and a few of us did the job just as Christ did long ago in Palestine. A few of us got together and we said we must move. We did, we organized so that today they have very fair conditions. I have met the militia in Pennsylvania in the dead hour of the night, I have walked the mountains of West Virginia nine miles at night after holding a meeting with the slaves of the caves because we did not dare go into a miner's home for shelter, for if we did they would be thrown out in the morning.

The Anthracite miners struck, but that strike cost the organization practically nothing. I spent the money myself and I only spent $450.00 in that strike altogether. I visited the homes of the miners and the people said, "No, we will not take it because it has come from other miners."

We boast a great deal of our bravery, but we have none. Not a blamed bit, and I have not any because it took seven military men to pull me out of a room and put me out of the State. That fight went on right here in Trinidad and not a man was lost in the whole battle, so you see we are great people here, and the militia had sabres, and the old woman did not even have a pair of scissors, still she scared hell out of the whole State administration.

In Pennsylvania we had a strike under the Erie company. They owned everything. We went in there and we kept that strike up for nine months and no support came from the National but $500 in the nine months. I went out to the farmers and gathered up provisions and the company had us nearly licked. I went to a meeting one night where there was a lot of young fellows and we discussed the revolution. The men were going to work the next day and I put it up to these men and said, "What are you going to do?" The chairman suggested that they take a vote on whether they would go to work the next day or not. I said, "No, this meeting is adjourned, and we will meet here tomorrow at nine o'clock." The next morning I put it up to them and they said, "By the eternal Gods, we will have freedom." We won that strike, but we did not get everything we wanted. We were sensible enough to take what we could get out of the greedy employers, and said to the boys, "We will come back at the wolves again."

When we fought that strike in the Anthracite, there was no money, only about $9,000 in the whole treasury of the United Mine Workers. We had a very small organization, practically speaking, and when that strike was ended after six months we had one million dollars in the treasury. The strike went on for six long months. The promises were not made to them by President Roosevelt that are made to you today. I know the whole inside of that strike perhaps as well as any one in the country.

You can say what you please but I have nothing to do with political parties. What I have to do is organizing, educating and getting what I can for my brothers. In no strike in the history of this nation, whether a railroad, a machinists or any other strike, and I know for I have been in most of them, at no time did any chief executive of a nation come to the front as President Wilson has. I am not of Wilson's politics and I care not what politics a man has if he come out and tries to break one chain for my class, I say God speed, and I want to say to you, boys, I have not deserted you, I never will.

At the time of the strike in West Virginia, I cancelled engagements in San Francisco and went to West Virginia. I went to Charleston and took the Cabin Creek train and went up there. A little boy came to me and he said, "Mother, have you come to stay with us?" "Yes, I have come to stay with you," and the tears trickled down his cheeks as he told me how they had beaten his mother and his baby brother and driven his father away and he said: "If I live to be a man I will kill twenty of them."

They were not United States bayonets. They were corporation bayonets, and corporation bayonets are in the hands of sewer rats and the others are in the hands of men. While in West Virginia, I was a guest of the State, I was arrested and placed in the bull pen. But they didn't keep me quiet there for I was raising hell more than if I had been out. Now these boys didn't get what they wanted in that settlement in West Virginia. They came to me and asked my advice and I said: "Take what you can get out of the pirates." The newspaper men asked: "What do you think of the settlement?" and I told them it was alright, it wasn't what we wanted, but what we could get. The mine owners of West Virginia have begun to realize what that settlement means to them. You were never in the condition here that they were in West Virginia. I was not followed here by the Baldwin-Felts thugs in the dead of night or horseback as I was in West Virginia. In a battle we had there seven of my brothers were murdered in cold blood and twenty-one were wounded.

When we appeal to the President to open the bars for us, you must remember that we have in Washington today a type of statesman we have not had since the days of the immortal Jefferson and Lincoln.

One big Senator in Washington said to me, "Mother, if they ever arrest you again I will leave my seat in the Senate and come out and defend you."

They held a meeting in New York, not gotten up by the labor leaders but by representative men of New York. Senator Martine came down from Washington to speak at that meeting and to that audience he said, "I have been advocating the government ownership of mines for forty years and I am going to continue it."

That is the type of men we have in Washington today, different entirely to what they were.

The whole human race is up in arms and when this war is ended in Europe there will be no rotten royalty to bring on the wars. We have got to have common sense. Oratory never won a battle in human history. The President of the United States, when he found you could not settle your difficulties, sent the Federal troops here to defend you, and now if you don't accept this proposition what more can he do. He has to withdraw the troops. The constitution gives him so long to keep them here and I don't know but what he has already overstepped that authority now.

Another thing, you have allowed here in this strike is to let everybody get a hand in it. Now this fight is ours, we have got the United States with us and we are fighting the greatest moneyed power in the world. John D. Rockefeller controls the whole of New York City and New York with its millions of population has to submit to him. He owns the mines, the industries and the railroads clear through the nation, but one man arises against that power and says to the miners of Colorado, I will be with you if you are fair. He faces the greatest moneyed power in the world and says these miners shall at least have a showing.

One time when some of our boys were being tried in Ohio a young man came into court, and sat and listened, then said, "Boys, will you give me your case?" The boys told him they could not because they had no money. "I did not speak of money," said the young man, "I spoke of your case in court." The boys consented that he should take their cases but told him they had no money. They were held over until the next term of court and every man except three was acquitted and three got sentences of thirty days. Nine months afterwards the Knights of Labor, of which I was a member, raised $900 and carried it to the home of that attorney and they gave it to him, but he told them he could not accept it. He said, "I agreed to take their cases without money and I have been well paid," but they said: "If you don't take the money we will be accused of being grafters, so please accept the $900. He accepted it and gave the man a receipt for it and said: "Give that money to the wives and children of the men who were in prison to get clothes and a good meal with." Do you know who that man was? That was the man who afterward became President of the United States, President McKinley. A man is a man to me, I don't care what position he holds, if he breaks one link in the chain that binds me to industrial bondage.

I stand facing the far east, sounding the voices of the babes of Ludlow, I stand here bringing their tears, their wasted hopes to you, the heartaches of the mothers, the screams and the agonies of those who gave up their lives there; but they did not die in vain. They stirred the nation from end to end and you never again will see such a condition of slavery in Colorado.

Ohio is on strike and they have written to me asking me to come. They are trying to negotiate a wage agreement.

Now, boys, you know I have no interests outside of the welfare of the children yet to come. I have carried your case to Congress, to the President, and I feel that we ought to pay that tribute of respect to the head of the nation in accepting this proposition. It is not all we want but Christ did not get all he wanted. So, boys, take my advice, I beg of you in the name of the women and children of Ludlow to pay that tribute of respect to the President of the nation, saying that we appreciate the move he has made and I believe you will get more.

Now, don't say Mother Jones is playing politics. I never played politics in my life. I have been a Socialist for twenty-nine years and I would hammer a Socialist if he is a crazy lunatic just the same as any one else. I am not living for nothing, I hold no office only that of disturbing. Before I leave the world, I have a contract with God Almighty to stay here eighty-two years more, there will be no bayonets and no guns, we will all be great citizens, and the bayonets of the future will be the pen, which is mightier than the sword. The next thing the public officers will do at Washington will be to take over the mines. We want the mines and we want the oil fields and we are going to have them. I stand here today as one pleading with you, I ask you to accept the President's proposition. Let the nation know that the United Mine Workers are not what they are represented to be by General Chase and his staff of pirates. I want the people to know that you miners are men and law-abiding citizens.

[*Proceedings of the Special Convention to Consider President Wilson's Proposition for Settlement of Colorado Coal Strike. District 15, U. M. W. of A. Held at Trinidad, Colorado, September 15, 16, 1914.* Copy in Western Historical Collection, Denver Public Library, pp. 19–22.]

Speech at a public meeting in the Labor Temple
Pittsburg, Kansas

After Mother Jones's speech in Trinidad which advised members of District 15 to accept President Wilson's settlement, the Colorado strike continued to dominate Mother Jones's activities over most of the next year, though her part was played on several levels. She visited Wilson at the White House in October 1914 and urged him to keep federal troops in the area, solicited funds from other unions to bring relief to the strikers whose support from the UMWA strike fund would soon run out, and returned to Trinidad at Christmas to deliver relief funds and encourage the miners and their families in their distress.

In January 1915, she journeyed to Washington for more lobbying, and then to New York for speeches and attendance at the hearings of the Commission on Industrial Relations, where she heard testimony from Ida M. Tarbell and John D. Rockefeller, Jr. Rockefeller introduced himself to her at the hearings and invited her to visit him at his office at 29 Broadway, where she and Frank Hayes, vice-president of the UMWA, talked to Rockefeller for several hours. She urged Rockefeller or his father to go to Colorado and see for himself the conditions in the coal fields controlled by his companies. She herself soon was back in Colorado, and there met with W. L. Mackenzie King, Rockefeller's labor advisor, on two occasions. Although King's developing plans called for company unions rather than representation by the UMWA, he agreed with her that a visit by Rockefeller would be desirable; meanwhile, he was working with the local managers to modify some of their former policies even before he presented his full-fledged plan to Rockefeller.

In April, Mother Jones went back east and prepared for her testimony at hearings of the Commission on Industrial Relations on May 13–14, and continued to follow the operation of that body in Chicago in June. She spoke in Butte, Montana, in July, and conducted a series of organizing rallies for the UMWA in Missouri.

The following speech, delivered at Pittsburg, Kansas, between engagements in Missouri, represents another facet of Mother Jones's career, her activities in many causes célèbres. She had held or participated in many public meetings for Moyer, Pettibone, and Haywood, officers of the Western Federation of Miners, whose arrest and trial in Idaho had attracted much attention as a perversion of justice; for the Mexican revolu-

tionaries in the United States before the overthrow of Porfirio Diaz; for Pouren and Rudowitz, radical Russian emigrés whose extradition was sought by the czarist government; and for other people caught in legal or bureaucratic toils.

In this particular case, Mathew Schmidt and David Kaplan were implicated in the bombing of the Los Angeles Times *in 1910. The evidence on which they were tried and convicted was regarded by many as tainted and inadequate, and a long legal battle began that was to occupy Mathew Schmidt's sister Katherine for many years. Mother Jones corresponded with Katherine Schmidt and usually stayed with her when she visited California. On this occasion she contributed her own unique brand of oratory to the general protest of the meeting against the trial of Schmidt and Kaplan.*

§   §   §

Now, I realize the hour is late and I think you have got a pretty good share of instructions tonight if you are going to make use of them. The great trouble lies though that you don't make any use of it; after you get out of the hall, you forget to pay attention to it, but you have got to realize this: That we are facing a conflict in this country such as the nations of the world have never known before. We are going through an economical crisis and whether the people will be able to meet that crisis or not is the question.

I feel tonight much as that toiler away back in the ages did, two hundred years after the world's greatest agitator was driven off the earth for creating a disturbance about the existing conditions. There arose in Carthage a terrific agitation; it disturbed the Roman Empire and they thought it was time to put a stop to it, so they went down to Carthage and arrested a large number. Those they did take, they either held them in slavery or drove them into slavery, and among those was a youth, and they asked this youth, "What is your occupation? Who are you?" "I am a man," he says, "A member of the human family; I belong to a class who have been robbed, and exploited, persecuted and murdered along the centuries of time. I want to educate that class as best I can to throw off their yoke." He was not a Christian in the modern definition of the word. He was a pagan slave, but he understood the wrongs of his fellow beings. He knew nothing about churches nor charity bazaars, or temperance brigades; he knew nothing of social settlements; he knew and felt their ways enough to do a human act, on that account he took up the battles of his class.

I wish that I could permeate every man and woman in this audience with the same spirit that possessed this pagan slave so many centuries ago. If I could, we would very soon change this condition.

The fight with the steel workers is only just a part of the great industrial conflict. The fight is everywhere going on. Here is the fight down in New Jersey. They were not organized men; they could scarcely speak the language, but they knew they had been fooled. They knew they were robbed. They brought the gunmen from New York down there. Some of the men they had indicted, and they brought them down to fight those battles against those wretches. This, my friends, was the mighty conflict. They murdered some of them, but even though they couldn't speak the language, they felt the pressure that was being placed upon them, and they revolted against it. It was just a part of the conflict in Colorado and in West Virginia, in Calumet, and all over the country.

The electric manufacturers in Chicago have an army of slaves. They went to give them a picnic. They had to go to that picnic, if they did not, they would lose their jobs, and so they went. They had to pay thirty-five cents apiece in the coffers of the high-priced burglars for getting murdered — thirty-five cents apiece they had to pay for the privilege of being murdered in cold blood. Do you think that such a thing could exist in a nation of people if they had one vestige of Christianity? They have a whole lot of hypocrites, but not a damned bit of Christianity.

When we were discussing the iron workers fight, it is the same everywhere. It don't make any difference whether you are an iron worker or a longshoreman or a railroad man. It don't make a bit of difference. The other fellow has got the gun and the gunman, and you have nothing, and you don't want anything because you don't know how to use it. Over in West Virginia they murdered the children before they were born; they hired gunmen and they kicked the babies to death before they were born — the gunmen did.

In Colorado they burned them to death in the holes into which they ran to save themselves. They threw oil on them to be sure that they were murdered; babies were murdered; women, when their sides were burned off, and their arms, they were carried to the morgue, and gave birth to the coming generation when they were dead two days. They are a civilized nation, aren't they? Highly civilized! No doubt about it! And I want to tell you something: I blame our women for the murder of all those children. If our women were women of a nation awake to their duties, then no captain or his burglars would dare roast our children to death.

We go to Sunday School, and we work for Jesus. Jesus don't need us; he can take care of himself. We work for temperance. What are you going to do with brewery workers — three million of men — starve them to death? We will become temperate when you give us what belongs to us, and we get enough to use and what we want to eat, and go on yowling like a lot of cats about something you don't know nothing about.

You sent to Europe a bunch of women on a peace commission. They went to Europe on a junketing tour, you might call it. They have had a peace commission out for twelve years junketing over the nations of the world, eating and drinking with the murderers and high class burglars of the nations of the world. We have had the bloodiest war in modern times going on, and then you sent over a commission of women, and one of them collapsed when she got to London. Oh, me, it's horrible! And off she goes in a nervous collapse, but she took mighty good care that you didn't send a peace commission to 26 Broadway of those women to tell the murderer, John D. Rockefeller, "You hold up your murdering of the people, or by God, we will do business." No, no; they were getting the money from John D. They were getting the money, and it wouldn't do to offend His Majesty, and why should they? The President of the United States sent Congressman Foster down to 26 Broadway to tell him to come and talk the coal conditions over. He turned the President down, and over one million of people never opened their mouths; never said a word. It wasn't the President that 26 Broadway insulted, it was one hundred million people. One hundred million people took this dope from the insulting rat, and you are the moral cowards, that is what you are!

It took three hundred of you fellows with a belt of bullets around your stomachs and bayonets on your sides, and it took three hundred of you fellows to put one old woman eighty-three years old in the pen.

Coming down from Des Moines the other day, I was telling a professor—it is hardly credible such a thing should happen in this country— why, there is no crime on the face of God's earth but what is committed in this country, and the people stand for it, and say, "Amen," and every judge on the bench is put there by the economic despots that he has served; he is put on the bench; he ate and drank and wined with them; he is educated by them, and his associates have been out of that school, and his duty, his business is to put workers in prison for life, and tear them away from their families, and you sit down and howl here, "Hurrah!" and go on, and when you get out you don't do a thing. You have no red blood in your veins!

When you come to look at it, one of them fellows who took me off of the train one morning after my fare was paid, fifty miles beyond where I wanted to go—he had a strutting coat on him, and belt of bullets around his stomach, and this fellow had a strap to tell you he was a step above the other fellow, a captain. "Where are you going to put me?" says I. "Well," he says, "We are going to put you in the cellar under the court house." "Well is there a chimney there?" says I. "Well, I don't know; why, do you want a fire?" says he. "I am not particular about the fire as I am about the chimney." "What do you want the chimney for if you don't want a fire?" "Because I have got a trained pigeon, and he is to go to Washington and back and bring me a message." "How does he bring it?" "There is a new invention, and the message is put on a band around his foot, and he drops it down in the chimney, and then he squeaks and I know it is the pigeon." "And was that fellow coming to Trinidad when you was there?" "Yes, he came every week." "And they never found out?" "No." "And they don't block up that chimney?" "No." Just imagine a woman raising a sewer rat like that; imagine the state government putting a belt of bullets around that fellow's stomach; imagine such a thing in the twentieth century; just think of it! What a horrible indictment against our civilization those things are!

I put in twenty-six days and nights in that hole; I had the rats down there in the hole, the cellar rats, to fight, and the only thing on earth that I had to fight with was a quart beer bottle, and there wasn't a God blessed thing inside of it, and I was scared to death for fear I would break it, and as soon as I got one fellow there was another that kept running across. I had to throw that bottle those twenty-six nights. I had to fight that fellow, and when the General sent me word I was free, I could go now where I pleased and he would pay me, I could have transportation anywhere I wanted, I said, "You tell that fellow in there that I have never in my life taken any favor from the enemy of my class, and I won't take anything from him; I will transport myself where I want to go."

And that is the trouble with us; we get on our knees to those fellows. We think they are great. They are only great because we think so; there is not greatness in them. A newspaper man sat on a platform with me in New York not long ago, and says, "You have got to realize you are dealing with great brains." I had to follow him. I want to take issue with the former speaker. You are not dealing with great brains; you are dealing with wolf brains; with snake brains; with rat brains. *Great* brains never stoop to those things. Great brains are interested in a nobler manhood, and a grander womanhood, and a higher, nobler work. Great brains never sell themselves for a smile to the pirates of nations. We are cowards and because we are cowards they make us build jails and penitentiaries, and pay wardens and guards, and they put us in them. We build palaces and put them into them, and we are awful wise! We put rags on our women, and we decorate their women with all the finery of the nation, and we are wise. There is no question about it, we are very wise at all!

I just want to call your attention to something, because I know it is getting late and you want to go. A whole lot of you here have got to go slaving in the morning, and if you ain't on time you will be docked. Listen to this indictment:

I personally helped to take from one of the death cellars the destroyed and mutilated bodies of eleven little children and two women, although I had been deported by those in command. The laws and the byps [*sic*] of blood in uniform ventured under the protection of the law. The hellish death cell was cheated of two bodies. Mrs. Mary and myself. We got out through a storm of bullets. One left three children and the other left two in that ghastly hole. (At this point she began reading from the pamphlet, which I did not take.)

The machine gun was transported from West Virginia across the state and landed in Colorado. Let me ask this of you. Is there a railroad company in America which would haul that machine gun to the miners for them to defend their wives and children? Well, then, don't you see you have got a government of 26 Broadway? Don't you see you have got no rights under this government? Don't you see the railroad men haul these murderous machine guns to murder their brothers in Colorado, and they haul the gunmen, and when the working class wake up there will be no railroad men haul any machine guns to murder my class. We know our duty; we needn't blame those fellows. They don't do anything but what we let them do, not a single thing. Every move they make they know we will stand for.

I want to show you where they get their money from when they are working for Jesus. If a man wants—I heard a fellow tell this in a convention—if a man wants a good room to live in, the laboring man, he has to pay the pittance price, from 25 to 50 cents a day, for getting even the privilege to work. Anyone who refuses to pay the boss, or refuses to buy him drinks, has to give his room to someone else; he can't work there. Everyone who goes to work in any mine which belongs to Rockefeller, has to pay from ten to fifteen dollars to the boss, and he has to buy him drinks on pay day for getting the privilege to work under the earth to bring out the minerals that Nature placed there. Then they have the saloons. The ground probably cost $50.00, and the saloon keeper's charge $1,500.00 for the privilege of running the saloon. Every man is taxed from forty to fifty cents; every miner must pay. If there are three thousand miners who work in and around that mining camp, you see the money that goes. Then you see how it goes on Sunday morning.

Then on Sunday morning John the Baptist goes up to church and he gives so much to Jesus, and he tells the minister, "Now, send him to Hell, so he don't get on to the job"; and the ministers stand for it, and one minister from Chicago went to Cleveland the other day, last Sunday, a week ago today, and he preached a sermon, and John was sitting there— "Oily John" was sitting there in front of him—and he said that "Oily John" was the greatest man the nation had ever produced; that he did more good than any other man in the nation; there is no doubt but what he is the greatest murderer the nation had ever produced; no question about it, the greatest thief; there is no queston on earth about that. But when it comes to the good, he can't be equaled in crime; he has murdered, shot, starved, sent to an untimely grave men, women and children by the thousands that I know, and if that is your modern version of Christianity, my God

Almighty save me from getting any of it into my system. Such philosophy is outrageous to preach in this age of modern machinery. To let ten men in this nation dictate what we will eat and drink and wear, and where we will live; they own the nation; they dictate the policy to the President, and no one dare go beyond the dictates of that pretense, and I want to make a statement here. You are rapidly marching into benevolent absolutism. That is what the American nation is coming to.

I agree with Mr. Darrow that the ballot will not bring us anything. I have watched the reform movement for the last fifty years. I have come to the final conclusion that there is only one thing will bring us relief, and that is for us to stand on both feet. When they murder our children, tie up every industry and for every working man they kill, you kill one of them. Put that down as anarchy if you wish. Put it down for every working man. After this for every man they send to the penitentiary, let us send one of them over the road, and it will soon stop. You bet your life!

Ah, but some fellow will say when he goes home: "Oh, hell, that was too radical." Christ said ten thousand things more radical than I only preaching Christianity, and that is modern Christianity. I want to tell you men and you women, too, you have no blood in you. You run around preaching foreign missions and temperance. You don't know any more about it than the blankest pagan. Get out in the fight! Organize; stop talking!

You have got a street car system. Are you president of it? They have not got it organized. Every time you take a ride on it, you go to work and back on a scab car, and a scab crew, and you don't do anything. I don't ride on the street car line in Kansas City unless I have to; I ride everywhere in Chicago because those boys know what is what. You bet your life that the Chicago fellows know. They know how to tell them to get off their perch. I used to, forty-five years ago, go away over on the West Side and meet with those boys in the night alone. We didn't have any salaries in those days, not a bit; we had to go and carry our messages to each other. We went to work there once and a Catholic priest got after us hot and heavy, and we went right down to his parish and when we elected a member to the city council right out of his parish, and one of them to the legislature, he shut his mouth after he saw what we could do. He didn't say anything more to us. We elected four men to the city council, three to the legislature. We have changed since that; we aren't doing business as we used to do.

I want to make a statement here that no minister can dictate to me my economics; he can tell me about Heaven, that is a long way off, but I am dealing with things here; I am dealing with things that confront me now; I am dealing with the bread and butter question. I don't know whether they have bread and butter on the other side or not, and I don't care much if I can get it here. A Sky Pilot once when I was down in Texas came to a poor little woman who had a lot of little children, and he said, "Sister, I want Brother John to donate to me a bale of cotton when it is ready, when it is picked for the Lord," and she says, "Oh, brother, I have been sick all summer and we owe the doctor and the druggist and my little ones have no shoes or clothes." "Well, the Lord will send it to you, and you give the bale of cotton," he says. "I don't think we can, brother," she says. And he turned to me and he says, "Won't you donate to the Lord, sister?" "What Lord?" says I. "The Lord Jesus." I says, "Why he was a carpenter, he knows how to build his own house." So he says, "Well, the Lord will take care of you." "He has enough to do to take care of himself," says I. It just shows you the rotten superstitious stuff that they pour down our throats and we swallow, and we don't protest, and we go in rags. When you see those wretches of children in the city of New York stamped to death; when you see women with their hands smeared with the blood of children.

When I was speaking to young John D., I portrayed an incident that happened down in Utah where they had us all hemmed in. They locked me up for smallpox, and they took all of those men that were there at the foot of the range and dragged them out of their tents in the morning, beat them with their guns; they howled like demons as they went up the road. These poor wretches begged to be permitted to put their clothes on; they were shaking with cold, and all the response they got was a hammer of the gun. When they had gone a poor woman came with a babe in her arms. She said, "Mother Jones, you see my John?" "Yes," I says, "I do." "Well, let me tell you, Mother Jones, he was born at eleven o'clock at night, and I got up in the morning and cooked breakfast for eleven men to go back into the mines." I said, "What did you do that for?" "Oh, Mother, wait until I tell you. My John was not strong; I had four or five little ones; I wanted to give them a chance in life if I could. I rented a piece of ground from the company, and I thought I would put a little shack on it and keep boarders. I took in boarders to pay for the house so that I could send the little ones to school." "Now," she says, "Mother, they have got my John; they have my house; they have got my health. What will I do with my children?" And the quivering heart and aching breast and swimming head of this woman—thousands like her that I know are suffering today.

Helen Gould and her class carry on their philanthropy, and state and President say she is a great woman, and with the bonds of these people they built that mansion there. They build their Y.M.C.A.'s, and they will give you anything; they will give you a pass to go up beyond, but don't come back; you will get everything, but don't kick, don't protest; you are a good citizen, and you cowardly fellows in the trade unions—I wouldn't give ten cents for the whole bunch of you. Just imagine what an army we are; just imagine one old woman with her head gray, she didn't even have a pencil in her hand, and she scared hell out of the state administration; one old woman can do you, and you fellows sit down here and not a word do we get out of you, not a word. You are moral cowards.

Over there in West Virginia one day, they were walking up and down there with their thumbs in their mouths. "Did you ever shoot any rabbits?" says I. "Yes," says they. "What did you shoot them with?" "We have a gun, Mother," says they. "Have you got the gun yet?" "Yes, Mother." I wonder if the reporters are here. You can have this for the morning if you want it, and then you can tell about it, and I heard those fellows say, "Those fellows are threatening to come down here and clean our wives and children up." "I will tell you what to do," says I. "You go get that gun and either go up that mountain and clean them fellows up, or go and throw your rotten carcass into the river and the fish will chase you out. The fish won't leave you in. Now, you do one thing or the other; go up that mountain or jump in the river." And they did, and that was the last fight we had. You bet your life. Buy guns, yes. And I will borrow money or steal it to buy guns for my boys, and I will not only do that, but I will make them use them, and I will tell you why.

Now you can tell the editor to clean me up tomorrow if you want to. I will tell you why. These fellows robbed my class; he hires murderers; he pays them with the money I ought to feed my children with; he buys guns for them; he pays their transportation; he pays them wages. Then if he can do that, I can pay for the guns for my own class and use them.

Now, boys, the fight is on. I am glad the editors are here. Sure the editor is a slave. What the matter with the editor is, if he don't do the work he will have to go; they will get another editor. That is what is the matter with him. Don't you say a word to the editor. These are pencil slaves and we are pick slaves. That is the only difference. I always take the newspaper boys' part; whenever I can help them I do it all over the country. I give them all the information I can so they can do the best they can. Some of them don't get any more than $10 a week.

We have stayed here long enough for tonight for I know you are tired. I will come back and I have got to go away tomorrow to tend to some other business.

Now I want to tell you something. Here at last we are organizing the Joplin district. For twenty-five years we have been working on them. Twenty-five years ago I went down there. It was an utter impossibility to get those fellows together, but we are getting them together now. I had a tremendous meeting in Joplin Friday night. I promised to come back to go to Webb City, to Carthage and Richmond, and other places, and we are getting those boys together. Joplin furnished all the scabs for the whole Western part whenever they were needed. One time we had a strike in Bisbee, Ariz. I was on the train going out. The conductor told me that there was fifty of them in the next train; I thought I would go in and look them over. So I went in to their smoker and I sat down. We didn't have anything to drink but they had a lot of scab tobacco to smoke, and I got to talking. The company paid their fares from Joplin, fed them, took care of them until they got to Bisbee, and when we got to Bisbee I had forty-seven of them all the company had was three. I made union men out of forty-seven of them. I sent some of them down to Mexico to work there, to sow the seed of unionism among them, and so, boys, we must stand together. The time is here. They are going to clean us up if we don't clean them up. Now, we have got the power; we have got the numbers; they know we have the power, but they also know that they have kept us from realizing our power. Now we have got the power and we will have to do our work. Johannsen said if they would just stop for one day — Joe, I don't want the workers to stop for one day. All I want them to do is to stop at noon, and not move a step, not move a shovel or a pick or a railroad until the next morning, and they will get off of their perch. Don't you worry, you can make them move.

Young John D. Rockefeller came to me and he said, "Would it be safe for Mr. Rockefeller to go to Colorado?" "Well," I says, "Mr. Rockefeller had a lot of murderers out in Colorado; he has hundreds of them there, and I am an old woman with my head gray, and if I am not afraid to face his murderers, why should he be afraid to face his own murderers?" And I said, "There is nothing to fear. Go out; change the conditions and the people of the nation will be with you, but they are not going to do it." Had I been President of the United States I wouldn't have waited for the people to holler, I would have sent a subpoena to 26 Broadway and two officers, and I would have put the handcuffs on that fellow, and I would have brought him down to Washington handcuffed, and I would have done so. Now you will have to do business, or by the eternal, the government will put you out of business; but you have not the blood, or the stamina in you. You will go off, coming home with a hump in your back so tired you can't walk, disgruntled with yourself and the world.

I will show you how easy this can be done. Over there in Washington the telephone company wanted to extend its lines, and they sent their representatives over to Virginia, and they went in a piece of ground. They began digging the holes for the poles and the farmer came down and said, "What are you doing?" "We are digging holes for poles, the telephone company wants to extend its lines." He said, "But this is my ground." "It don't make any difference," they said. "I paid for it," said the farmer. The old fellow says, "I have got the deed, it don't belong to you; you can't dig any holes here." "Oh, but we can, the company says we have to," and the old fellow went in and brought his gun, and he says, "Get out now; get over the fence, and don't you come back." He kept the gun cocked then and they went away, and in a couple of days they come back and they went away, down again to dig the holes and the old farmer came down and said, "Didn't I tell you to get out?" "Yes, but the telephone company sent us back." "But you can't come," said the farmer. "Oh, yes we can," said they, "We brought an order of the court." "An order of the court?" "Well, read the order of the court," said the old fellow. And so they read the order of the court and the old fellow he shuffled around and put up his shotgun, and he had a bull in the barn and he walked out to the barn and opened it and he had the fellow tied because he was a vicious animal, and he was ready to play the game, and he had some blood in him, and he opened his barn door and said, "Sic em," and the bull made a dive for them and they got off the fence and they said, "Say, Mister, won't you take that bull in?" The old farmer said, "I have got nothing to do with the bull; you have got the order of the court." "Take him in, we want to work," says they. "Hell," says he, "Why don't you read the order of the court to the bull."

(At this point two telegrams were sent to the President of the United States on the unanimous vote of those present in which a protest was made against the Caplan-Schmidt trial.)

[Printed copy in the Western History Collection, Denver Public Library.]

Speech at a convention
of the United Mine Workers of America
Indianapolis, Indiana

Mother Jones came to the 1916 convention of the UMWA at Indianapolis fresh from several weeks of activity among the striking steel workers of the Youngstown, Ohio, area, where she had gone after her UMWA organizing in Missouri. The miners were still licking their wounds from the fight in Colorado, and the leaders of the union were concerned that there might be a grass-roots rebellion. They had spent over four million dollars on the Colorado strike, exhausting the treasury, and had had to borrow substantial sums. Although the strike was over, the UMWA had assumed responsibility for legal expenses in Colorado for the more than four hundred felony indictments of union members.

Duncan McDonald and Adolph Germer, two delegates from District 12, introduced a resolution for a three-man committee to be appointed to investigate the financial management of the union. President John P. White and his associates resisted the motion, contending that the committee which examined the report of Secretary-Treasurer William Green had all the information needed at their disposal and that no special investigation was needed. In the ensuing debate, old quarrels were revived and old wounds reopened, and personal charges began to fly.

Into this situation stepped Mother Jones, who, uninvited, was permitted to take the platform. She scolded the delegates for wasting time, for allowing themselves to be divided. Without denying that there were legitimate differences and criticisms, she reminded them that the past four years had seen the organization through its most difficult years—the Paint Creek strike in West Virginia and the year-long Colorado strike just concluded, as well as other problems. In a dramatic gesture, she called on McDonald and Germer to come forward and shake hands with White, Hayes, and Green, and they complied.

For the next fifteen minutes, she regaled the delegates with funny stories, some drawn from her own experience, others mere comic relief. When she stepped down, Vice-President Frank Hayes, who was presiding, called for a vote. The report of the committee was accepted, and the McDonald-Germer resolution was defeated; the rebellion had been quelled.

§   §   §

Speeches

Vice-President Hayes: The delegates will take their seats. Here is a delegate without credentials. I suppose she needs no introduction to this convention—Mother Jones. You can't stop her from talking.

Mother Jones: I want to tell you, boys, you never saw a woman you could stop. When we had the convention in Colorado to call off the battle, there was a certain delegate there—the corporations had their tools there to prevent us from accepting the President's proposition, and I could see the game played, and I got up to nail some of them, because I can smell them four miles away—and this fellow says, "Mother Jones is not a delegate to this convention, and she cannot talk." "I want to serve notice on you," said I, "that I am a delegate to every labor convention in the United States."

Now, you have had a lot of talk to and fro, accusing each other. There is no question but what mistakes have been made, and if you want to find the fellow in office that don't make mistakes, go out to the graveyard and you won't find him there either. You have nearly four hundred and fifty thousand men. You can't expect all these men to take the same view or survey of things. We are not brought in contact with each other. Some of us are brought up in the mountains; some of us down in the hollows; some of us in the valleys; some of us in the canyons, and we cannot survey these things in the same way, and this thing of tearing each other up will have to stop. I want to say to you, Duncan McDonald, you haven't got one dollar in your treasury that belongs to Illinois. It belongs to the miners of this country; every dollar of it belongs to the working men, whether they are miners, steel workers or train men. That money belongs to us, the working class, and we are going to use it to clean hell out of the robbing class. Now, you were talking about expenditures yesterday— the terrible expenditures! God Almighty, you spend more money here blowing off hot air than would keep us for a year traveling around like Rockefeller. Boys, put a stop to it.

President White made some remark—I did not exactly catch it—about the attacks they made on me in Colorado. I want to tell you, President White, don't ever lose any sleep about the attacks they make on me.

President White: I know it.

Mother Jones: I fought and made the whole administration in West Virginia lay down. I put them up against the bar of the nation, on trial for their crookedness, and you did not hire any lawyer for me, and I would not hire one either, because a lawyer is the damndest crookedest thing outside of a strike-breaker that there is. They came down there to the bull-pen and they wanted to defend me. I said, "You can't meddle with my affairs. I want to be here with the boys." The same thing was tried in Colorado. I spent three months there and five weeks in the bull-pen of West Virginia. I was picked up on the streets, where I went to keep the peace.

I brought a committee up to the Governor [William E. Glasscock], paid their way myself, for the poor boys had no money, in order to keep peace; and the tools that had sold their honor and their manhood to the corporations threw me into an automobile, took me twenty-five miles away, and although the civil courts were open, handed me over to the military, and I was kept there three months. Every now and then the old sewer rats would come down and try to get me to go to Ohio. "Oh, no," said I, "West Virginia suits me." I want to show you something. I want to put you on to it. After our men were arrested, kept in the bull-pen, taken into the military court, my colleagues and myself, five days and five nights we refused to recognize the right of that court to try us. We don't know yet whether that pill-peddler of a Governor [Henry D. Hatfield] had us sentenced for life or not, and I don't care.

Now, I will give you another history. I may not see you again. I am going out tonight, but I will be back again to watch you. The general [Charles D. Elliott] who kept my brothers in the bull-pen, arrested them, held them there with their bayonets, wanted to go to Congress. One night when I sat at the dinner table in a restaurant in Washington the bellboy came in and he said: "There is a man in the office who wants to see you, Mother Jones." I went in and I said: "Are you the person that wants to see me?" He said: "Yes, General Elliott sent me to see you." That was the general of the militia—of the sewer rats in West Virginia—the uniformed sewer rats—and he said: "He wants to get a letter from you so he can read it; he wants to go to Congress." I said: "The General is entitled to the letter. I will give it to him; certainly I will. There is no doubt but what he ought to have it, but I want you just to convey the knowledge to that gentleman that I have not forgotten the time he kept my brothers and myself in the bull-pen to accommodate the mine owners when we were fighting for liberty. I have not forgotten when that gentleman heard the babies crying to have their fathers kiss them before they went away, and they never saw them again. You tell the General for me he will get a letter from me, but I will remind him that he went to Charleston, and contrary to the constitution, kicked the labor measures to pieces. I will give him a letter to send him to hell," said I.

I want to tell you something. We have had awful times, boys. Some of you that are here have no idea of what this administration has been up against. I know it is an impossibility for us not to have hard feelings sometimes. I have had it sometimes—no question about it; but you have got to understand that very often men are sent out that have no grasp of this thing. You are not dealing with the situation today you were ten years ago, and no organizer should be put on the staff that is not able to reach out and grasp the enemies of the other class. It is a pie-counter; each and everybody is reaching out for the pie-counter without knowing how to digest it. That is the trouble with our administration today—a lot of you blowing off hot air today are a little jealous. You did not get a job, or another fellow wants the job you have got, and so it goes. I can tell you, you can have my job any time, but you cannot muzzle me. I will fight for my class until the last chain is broken. I do not ask any favors of Mr. Green, or Mr. White, or Mr. Hayes. I will hammer them just as quick as I will you—no question about it—if things don't go right.

Boys, I want to tell you these past four years have been the most strenuous years that this organization has ever gone through. Now you can rent halls and come here to the convention. I remember the time when we had to send to the saloons to get you in to vote on something. We don't do that now. You have traveled beyond that. You are here on the job, blowing off hot air. We don't have to send for you to get you to vote on a thing; you are here to do it. I remember a time in the city of Chicago when we went out into the hills to meet, forty-five or fifty years ago. The boys came to me one night and they said, "Mother the weather is getting cold and we have got a place to meet inside." I said, "Where? We have no money." They said, "No, we haven't, but a saloonkeeper told us he would give us a room back of his saloon. Would you mind coming?" I said, "No, I would not. I will go back of a saloon any time to help you boys. Where is the saloon?" He told me. I said, "Let's go," and we met there every Thursday night. We had three meetings, when the saloonkeeper came into the hall and said, "You get to hell out of here! You don't drink enough beer to pay for the gas!" Today you can pay for the gas and the beer both.

Now, boys, let Mother talk to you, and let's put a stop to this thing. Let's take a vote on the whole thing and squash it. Let Duncan McDonald and Adolph Germer come up here on the platform and shake hands and bury the hatchet with President White. The corporations have got their paid tools here. I don't mean to say these newspaper men are the ones. I believe they are good fellows, these fellows; but I mean to say that right amongst you are the paid hirelings of the big interests. There is not a single move you make in this convention that is not registered to the big interests as soon as it is made. Now, then, put a stop to it and shake hands and say, "Here, there is no power of the high-class burglars will ever separate us, the miners of this country. We are linked together for the final fight, and we must and we will stand before the world and show that we have got common sense and judgment and no spite at each other." Duncan McDonald, you come up here and shake hands with President White, and you, Adolph Germer.

(Delegates McDonald and Germer complied with Mother Jones's request and came to the stage and shook hands with President White, Vice-President Hayes and Secretary Green.)

Mother Jones: In Chicago, some time ago when I was there, a man came to me and he said — but first and foremost, a bunch of little boys came and they said, "Mother, they are arresting the little boys that have no homes and they are taking them into court and taking their fingerprints and putting them in the Rogues' Gallery. Will you come with us and see if you can stop it?" I said, "Yes, I will," and we went to call on the Mayor, but the Mayor would not see us. He belonged to the temperance brigade, and we did not; I guess that is the reason. We went from there to Judge Olson. I had trained the little boys to make their speech to the judge, and they talked, and I want to say to you here, if those boys grow up to be men, they will be a tremendous asset to this nation in the days to come. I sat there listening to these little fellows as they talked to the judge. The judge got carried away with them, and he said, "Well, boys, I am going to stop that. I am interested in you." We went away, and the boys came back and said, "Mother, will you come some day and talk for us at our club?" and I said, "Yes, I will, on Saturday," but on Saturday I walked about six miles with about seven thousand girls, showing up the parasites, showing how they get the life blood out of these girls that had to work from 5:20 in the morning until 7:30 at night, making $1.80, and when they complain, the boss tells them, "If you don't like it, get to hell or out on the sidewalk and make a living." That is the reply of the boss.

I was worn out; I had to speak to about three thousand people after I got back to the hall, and so I did not go on Saturday night, but I went on Sunday, and I talked to those boys. Before I left Chicago, Sunday, a man came to me and said, "Mother Jones, I want to tell you the history of a little boy." I said, "All right." He said, "His mother died when he was a baby; he was put in an orphan asylum; from there he was sent to the Reform School; from the Reform School he was sent to a farmer. He went into the house ten minutes before noon one day to get a piece of bread," because these farmers eat their breakfast early, like you fellows do, "and the woman undertook to beat him. He ran to open the door and she took the broom and beat the little fellow away and locked the door. He went under the table, and this woman began beating him." No doubt the poor woman was worked to death. "After she got through beating him the boy ran out and got a shotgun and shot her. He was not thirteen years old. He was put in the penitentiary for life, no friends to defend him."

Now, the laws of Illinois prohibit the incarceration of a boy of that age for life in the penitentiary. Notwithstanding that, there was no one in the State of Illinois that took up the battle of this homeless child. Society made a criminal out of him. Now, I am going to Chicago. A party told me, "If you will take the matter into court, I will pay the expenses of a lawyer." I told Mr. White, and he said, "Mother, you go and you do that. Any assistance you need you can call on this organization and

I will give it to you," and he says, "I will go further, Mother; I will give that boy a home until he grows to manhood and educate him."

Now, boys, I am going to Chicago to take that matter up with attorneys. I am going down to the prison. I am going to see that boy. I am going to get the records of the court. I am going to the Governor, and if the Governor won't do business, I am going to get Mr. Green, Mr. Hayes, Mr. McDonald and Mr. Germer — because they live in Illinois — to go and see that Governor, and if they can't bring him to time, I am going to take it into court and fight it to a finish. That is why I am going away tonight, and I would have gone away last night but you were snarling at each other here.

Now, I want to tell you something before I go. There is a corporation up here in Washington. They wanted to extend their telephone lines, and when the men were digging the holes for their poles the farmer who owned the land came down and said to them, "What are you doing?" They said, "Digging holes for the telephone poles." He said, "What the hell is the matter with you? This ground is mine!" They said, "That don't make any difference, the telephone company can plant their poles in any ground they want to." He said, "You get out of here." They said, "Oh, no." He walked up to the house and got a shotgun, and he said again, "You get out of here," and over the fence they went, and up to Washington, and the old fellow put his gun up. A couple of days later they came again, and they were going to dig the holes again, and the fellow came down with the shotgun and said, "Didn't I run you away from here once?" They said, "Yes, you did, but you can't do it now." He said, "What's the reason?" They said, "Because we have got an order of the court." He said, "Well, read the order of the court," and so the telephone representatives read the order of the court, and the old fellow went in and put his shotgun up. He went out the back door and went down to the barn and opened it up. There was a thing in the barn, a pretty ferocious thing, and he unchained it. These fellows were laughing to themselves about how they had licked the old farmer — how the telephone company had licked the farmer with the wonderful court order. Just then the old fellow says, "Now, sic 'em Bull," and Bull went after them. He shook his head at them and they went over the fence. The fellow came out on his front porch and sat down and began smoking, and these fellows came up and said, "Say, Mr. Farmer, we have got to plant these poles. Won't you call your bull off?" The farmer said, "Why don't your read the order of the court to him?"

Then I will tell you another story. Teddy Roosevelt was out West after we had our strike in 1904. Well, Teddy went out to Colorado hunting wolves, but he could not get as many as he wanted. He heard that a ranchman out there had a splendid dog for hunting wolves, and he sent some of his lap dogs up there to get this wolf dog. The farmer said he would not either rent nor sell that dog, and they went back and reported, and Teddy sent them back again, but he still said no. So Teddy himself went and the man said, "No, you can't have my dog; you can't rent it or buy it." Teddy said, "Do you know who I am?" The man said, "No, and I don't care who you are." Teddy said, "I am Theodore Roosevelt, President of these United States." The man said, "I don't care a damn if you were Booker T. Washington, you could not have my dog."

Vice-President Hayes: There is only one Mother Jones!

[*UMWA Proceedings* (Indianapolis: Bookwalter-Ball Printing Co., 1916), pp. 311-18.]

Speech at a convention
of the United Mine Workers of America
Indianapolis, Indiana

Although the resolution to investigate the administration of the finances of the union had been defeated, many of the delegates remained critical of John P. White and the other international officers. During what was to be a routine session, White gave up the chair of the convention and went to have some publicity photographs taken with Mother Jones and Terence V. Powderly when news came that Ed Doyle, the secretary of the Colorado UMWA, had launched into a tirade against the leadership. White abandoned the photographic session and hastened back to the floor of the convention, though he left the gavel in the capable hands of a youthful John L. Lewis. They managed to put down the threatened rebellion, and the delegates voted to expunge Doyle's remarks from the record. Later, White and the executive board declared District 15 no longer able to support itself and sent in more amenable officers to take over from Doyle and John Lawson, who had been elected president of the district. John L. Lewis, as he rose to mastery of the UMWA in the early twenties, repeatedly used the same technique by sending his own officers to take over from locally elected officials, first in Kansas and Nova Scotia, and then in other districts.

Once again, on 29 January 1916, Mother Jones addressed the convention, reminiscing about the history of the organization and her own experiences. She stressed that only by standing like men and standing together had they won victories in the past, and she urged them to stand behind their present leaders. If they proved false to the miners, she asserted that she would be the first to expose them. The answers to the problems of the miners could be solved only by unity and aggressive unionism.

Besides giving the members her usual blend of humor and pathos, she went to some lengths to defend the officers, White, Hayes, and Green, for their management not only of the Colorado strike but of other problems from Pennsylvania to British Columbia. She even had a good word for the Woodrow Wilson administration, particularly the role of the Secretary of Labor, William B. Wilson. With a combination of reminiscence, scolding, and cajolery, she tried to turn the attention of the audience to the future and the need for more organizing. She announced her own plans to take on the hardest jobs, to bring into the UMWA fold all

the most recalcitrant areas: southern Colorado, West Virginia, and Ala-
bama. In the long view, the UMWA was making progress, and she pre-
dicted that with unity and determination they would make more.

§   §   §

Boys, I have looked over this convention from the platform, and I want
to give expression to the feeling that in this gathering are men of the most
highly developed brains this country can produce. You have come from
the picks, but you are developing, and I want to say to you to keep on.

Now I want to call your attention to a few things. Away back in the
old Roman age, two hundred years after the world's greatest agitator was
murdered by the ruling class, there arose in Carthage a tremendous agitation among the oppressed, the exploited, those who had borne the burden for ages. The Romans began to be disturbed and thought they would
go down to Carthage and capture those who were responsible for the agitation. They went down. All they captured in those days they retained
as slaves or sold into slavery. Among the group that was captured was
a youth. The Roman judge asked, "Who are you?" The youth said, "I
am a member of the human family." "Why do you agitate?" asked the
judge. "Because I belong to that class that has been crushed, robbed,
murdered and maligned in all the ages, and I want to break the chains
of my class."

I wish I could convey that spirit to everybody in this audience today.
If I could we would have another story to tell when we come here for
the next convention. That is the spirit that should possess us all — that we
belong to the class that has borne the burdens of the nations, that has
been starved intellectually, physically, and otherwise. But we are breaking the chains. Everywhere I go I see the sentiment growing.

I was in Youngstown, Ohio, two months ago. I spoke in Niles and other
places. I am going back next week. They have asked me to come. When
I saw the horrible condition of those slaves in the steel mills, when I saw
the shacks they lived in, when I saw them up against those furnaces for
twelve hours a day, when I saw them going home weary and broken, I
thought, "Some day, not in the far distant future there will come another
John Brown and he will tear this nation from end to end if this thing does
not stop." Those men were worn and weary and tired. The first thing they
did after coming out of the mills was to go to a saloon and get a drink
to brace them up to go home.

But I am glad to say we are making progress. When those men struck
I was not at all surprised. Here is what one of the officers says: "Just what
caused it I have been unable to determine, but from what I have been
told I fear it has been caused by the armed guards on the bridge. Had
these guards been kept within the limit of the mill property I doubt if

175

there would have been any trouble with the workers. Witnesses told me the guards on the bridge fired the first shots, that aroused the fury of the mob and there was no holding them in check. I do not look for any further outbreak unless an attempt is made to operate the mills with strike breakers."

It is the gunmen that start the trouble. They started the trouble in West Virginia, in Calumet, and they started it in Idaho, Colorado, and everywhere. If this government does not take steps to protect the people then the people will have to protect themselves against gunmen. In Colorado the strike was not on a month when they began. I was in Aguilar and got a telephone call to go to Ludlow. Lawson happened to be there. I hunted him up and said: "There is some trouble in Ludlow; let us go there." We got into an automobile and I told the driver to move as fast as the roads would allow. When we got to Ludlow we found the men there without weapons, they were bewildered, they were not able to defend themselves. The gunmen were there on the track shooting at the tents where the women were. There were about half a dozen guns in the camp and Lawson started to take them away. I said, "Lawson, you leave those guns with the boys so they can protect themselves. If the law does not protect us we must protect ourselves."

There was a law and order crowd out there, there was a law and order crowd in West Virginia and in the Calumet region. Now let me make this statement to you newspaper men. Down all the pages of human history law and order has destroyed every nation that has gone down never to rise again, because law and order were in the hands of the fellows who violated every law of right and justice. I have been in strikes for many years, I was in strikes before many of you were born, and I know what they are. We are always the victims of the brutality of the other class.

In my experience Colorado was no worse than West Virginia. They did not make me wade the creek in Colorado, but in West Virginia the gunmen made me wade a creek up to my hips to keep me from going to a meeting. The corporation dogs were on the track. The representative of the Baltimore *Sun* was with me. He started to go on the track and the dogs said, "She cannot come with you." The newspaper man said it was an outrage to make me wade the creek. Then one of them said, "I don't care a damn! Only for her there wouldn't be any trouble here." I am going to tell you right here—and you newspaper man with the white head put it down—that as long as there is an industrial slave in America and I am alive I am going to raise a row.

They didn't do half as bad in Colorado as they did in West Virginia, and I am here to prove it. In West Virginia they ran the death special up the creek, shot the men and women and the crowd on board said, "Run the train back until we give them another bout." Yes, they roasted the

176

babies in Calumet on Christmas eve, they roasted a few in Ludlow. They roasted seventy-five in Calumet on Christmas eve. They shot seven working men in the streets. They shot them in West Virginia. Now I am going to tell you that if you men had any blood in you, if you would have stopped fighting each other, mustered your forces and organized they would not have dared to shoot anybody. As long as you come here to the convention and blow off steam that has been gathering for two years, instead of coming here to do business for the future you will not gain much.

There is a fellow up in New York; I saw him one day and he said, "I am inventing something, a wonderful thing. I am sure you will take stock in it." "Sure I will," I said, "if it amounts to anything. What is it?" He said, "It is a skull scraping machine," and I don't know of anything more useful than that. If we could get our skulls scraped until they were clean we would come here and do business.

In West Virginia I went up Cabin Creek. There were thirty men on the track. We were going to a meeting. The gunmen were huddled together and the machine gun was turned on the boys. The boys did not have a pistol, they did not have a stick to defend themselves with. These gunmen were thirsting for the blood of men who had not injured them. I jumped out of the buggy I was in. The boys said, "For God's sake, Mother, don't go up there! They will kill you!" I said, "I couldn't die a more glorious death than defending your rights." I went up and put my hand on the machine gun and said to those corporation bloodhounds, "You can't shoot a bullet out of that," and one fellow who was thirsting for human blood said, "Take your hand off that gun." I said, "No sir. My class makes those guns and I have a right to put my hand on this one. You have got mothers, wives and daughters. I don't want to hear their groans and see their tears. My boys, too have mothers, wives and children; I don't want to hear their groans or see their tears. They are not fighting you, they are fighting the class that is robbing them. Don't you want to give this nation a better citizenship, morally, physically and intellectually?"

One man stood behind a tree with a gun. I said, "You come out in the open." I went down and took him from behind the tree. He had his finger on the trigger of the gun. I took him by the back of the neck and said, "You come here." After that I went up and held my meeting. The supe came along and said, "Mother Jones, you cannot talk." I said, "For God's sake, did you ever see a woman that couldn't talk." I talked for an hour. The supe didn't want to stop me, but the fellow who owned him was on the track and he wanted it done. I didn't want to be too hard on the supe and I said, "I am here on the road and have a share in it. I have been told I could walk on the road." He said, "You are a little bit on the company's property." For about an hour and a half I talked and fooled the poor supe. I don't know whether he lost his job or not.

Some of you who came here don't know what we have to do who are in the trenches. We are trying to fight our battle peacefully, but it is a question if we can. The past has never been peaceful, it is a question if the future is going to be; but we are moving on, we are using brains instead of weapons, we are organizing, we are getting together. The children in Calumet, the children in Colorado, the men in West Virginia, did not die in vain. When I was going to Washington to try to get Congress to make an investigation in Colorado I got a telegram from Dawson, N. M., saying, "Come down, Mother; we want to join the boys in Colorado." Time and again I got that message, but I concluded it was best to bring peace if we could, but the very night I was leaving for Washington I was told that 285 men were blown into eternity in the Dawson mine. The mine belonged to the Philip Dodge crowd that are now fighting the miners in Morenci. Those boys in that mine and those babies in Colorado, Calumet and West Virginia did not die in vain; they gave up their lives on the altar of human freedom and in the future men will stop and ponder and wonder at these sad days of old when we roasted babies on the altar of God-cursed gold.

It was not the Rockefellers that did it, it was not the Shaws, it was the working men of the nation; they are responsible for the death of those children. If you were not cowards you would be organized, you would pay your dues, you would carry on the campaign of education that would bring peace to the nation. If an assessment is put on some of you say, "I don't want to pay it; I pay my dues but I am not going to pay any more." Why you poor, measly, half-starved wretch, do you know what the men and women did who tramped the highways and byways to make it possible for you to have the means to pay the assessment with? I know if you don't.

Now some guy down the road will say, "What does Mother Jones know about mining, anyway?" Don't I know about mining? Don't I? I worked on the night shift and the day shift in Pennsylvania from Pittsburgh to Brownsville. There isn't a mine that was open in those days that I didn't go on the night shift and the day shift, and I know what you have to go through. Then some fellow says, "I don't think we ought to have a woman on the payroll." What do you think of that, Secretary Green? The man who asked that never read a thing in his life, he never even did a bit of thinking. The most valuable person on the staff of President Lincoln was a woman. She gathered more correct information from him and delivered it than all the men he had, and I want to make the statement here that if you had twenty women in Europe they could stop that war. Twenty women with a consciousness of what war means to the children yet to come could stop that war. Don't you think they have as much sense in Europe as you have? They are all grown fellows who are fighting each other, and if they think it is better to go out and fight for the king than for humanity, for civilization, why, let the guys do it and let us fight at home to preserve this country.

If I were President of the United States I would put a pipe line along the Atlantic seacoast; I would take one thousand trained men and put them there and say, "Now you do business." And you don't need an army to pay from twelve to twenty thousand dollars a year to the fellow with straps on his shoulders who goes strutting along like a peacock. You are the fellows who pay all the bills. Why, you ought to see those fellows who were in Colorado and West Virginia. And then the President is talking about preparedness — with a gang of sewer rats like that! Why, they couldn't prepare to clean the hall here, that gang couldn't.

One morning they took me off the train at Walsenburg. I had my fare paid to Trinidad, forty-five miles beyond. One fellow said, "You will have to get up." "What is the matter," said I, "are we in Trinidad?" "No, we are getting near Walsenburg." "I have a ticket to Trinidad." "It don't make any difference, you have got to get off the train, we are the militia." I got off the train and there were the guns. I asked where they were going to take me and they said to the basement of the court house. I asked if there was a chimney there. They said, "Why? Do you want a fireplace?" The fellow who said that had a strap on his shoulder and a belt of bullets around his stomach. I said I wasn't particular about a fire but I wanted a chimney. "What do you want a chimney for?" "Because I have a trained pigeon and he goes to Washington every week and comes back and brings me all the news." "Did he come every week you were in Trinidad?" "Yes, every night." "And they never found it out?" "No," said I.

Just imagine a nation putting a belt of bullets around the stomach of a thing like that. He had a gun hanging by his side, a couple of pistols, and he was sent out to shoot working men. Now just imagine what you are up against when you meet a thing like that! Another fellow in Trinidad told me: "My mother is in the insane asylum in Pueblo, and they fined me thirty dollars because I slept ten minutes too long and did not get out here on duty to watch you." "Why didn't you sleep all night, you fool?" said I. That is the type of man that is in the army, the navy and the militia.

I have been arrested five times by the militia and you have never had to hire a lawyer to defend me; I defended myself every time and I made them turn me loose. Neither Secretary Green, Secretary Perry nor Secretary Wilson ever received a bill from me for my services. I have sent in expense accounts, but I have never yet sent a bill for services to the labor movement. The Secretary sends it to me, but I don't know yet what he pays, I am not financier enough. As I told Rockefeller, "If you gave me your institution, I would wreck it tomorrow; it would not last a month after I was in. All I want money for is to use it to lick the other fellow."

I am not going to take any money to the grave; I didn't bring any here, and I don't want to go up to God Almighty as a high-class burglar.

There have been some tragic things taking place. Belk is acquitted in Colorado and Zancanelli is kept in jail. Ulich was in jail ten months. I was there three months. I presume I would still be in jail in West Virginia if Senator Kern had not taken the matter up. I want to say to you here that every working man in the nation owes a debt to Senator Kern. It was he who brought my case on the floor of the Senate when Goff—the corporation tool—said, "We had peace until they came in there, these foreigners." Well, we are not foreigners when we are creating the wealth and allowing them to rob us, we are good American citizens then; but when we protest against their robbery we are foreigners immediately. Goff said the biggest agitator in the country, the grandmother of all agitators, was old Mother Jones. Thank God I have lived to be a grandmother in agitation! I hope I will live to be a great-grandmother in agitation!

You have made more progress in government, boys, in the last three years than you had made in 125 years prior to that. We have got more recognition in the last three years than in all that time. The Secretary of Labor [William B. Wilson], who is a member of the President's cabinet, was in Pennsylvania when the strike at Arnot took place. That was before the anthracite strike. I was sent for and went there. The men were going to work next morning. I addressed a meeting that afternoon. Nobody went to work next morning, but I was thrown out of the hotel at eleven o'clock at night—I was an undesirable citizen. I went up the mountain. I saw a light and kept crawling up until I got there. When I got to the house a man there said, "Did they put you out of the hotel?" I said, "Yes, but I will put them out before I get through with them."

The president of District No. 2 worked day and night and gave all he had to that strike. One night I sat in W. B. Wilson's house. He was there with his feet bare. About eleven o'clock at night we were talking about a move I was going to make when a knock came on the door. Wilson opened it. I left the room. Three men came in, sat down and discussed the strike. One of them said, "Say, Wilson, we can make it twenty or twenty-five thousand dollars if you go away and let this fight fall to pieces. You can take the old woman with you." Wilson never told that, but I heard it. He got up with his voice quivering and said, "Gentlemen, if you have come here to accept the hospitality of my home it is yours, every inch of it; if you have come here to get me to betray my fellow men and my own family, there is the door." Next morning we had black coffee and bread for breakfast but we made the fight and won. If they have had a fight since I never heard of it. Now, that man is the Secretary of Labor, and you knife him and say everything about him, yet he went barefoot, tired and weary and he did not get a Taft stomach on him when he was out organizing.

You stood here and attacked this man — President White. Now I want to make this statement before I close. I have worked under all your administrations. There is Flyzik back there. He comes here from the State of Washington. He was a kid when he walked fifteen miles over the mountains with me in Pennsylvania to meet the militia. The officers of the organization were sleeping in Hazleton when that army of women with Flyzik and a bunch of the other boys met on Track 13 in the middle of the night and brought out 5,000 men. You gave a ten-thousand-dollar house to the chief executive, but you never gave a dollar to those women, and they didn't own a shingle on the houses they lived in.

This administration has had more fights on its hands, more to go up against than any administration you have had since you were organized. The officers have had to stand more abuse — and I know the whole of them but I am not under obligations to any of them — than the officers of any previous administration. I am not under obligations to any of them. I don't allow one of them to pay for a meal for me. Do you know why? Because I want my hands clean, and if they don't fill the bill I want to go after them with clean hands and tell you all about it. We have got to be true to each other.

I made many trips from Colorado to see President White. I made many trips from West Virginia that nobody knew anything in the world about, because I wanted him to be familiar with everything that was going on. A man who has had Nova Scotia, Westmoreland, the Southwest, Vancouver, West Virginia, Colorado and Ohio on his hands has not had much peace — I want to tell you that! I have watched these strikes with a great deal of care and I know how the people in this administration have acted. I am not in the habit of defending people who do not deserve it.

Here is a headline in a paper: "Forty armored strike-breaking cars gift of steel magnate to the State." The gasoline castles, Gary and the rest of them have donated forty armored autos in answer to these warnings, so that the gunmen can go in safety and attack you in your strikes. And you had better line up because I don't care what political party you have in Washington, you must have an organized economic army on the industrial field. If you have that you can make Washington, Indiana, and every other State come to time. Get into your unions, pay your dues like men and don't be grunting and saying, "By God, here is another assessment!" The other fellows sit back and laugh when you do that; they say, "We have them going now, we have got them divided."

Years ago I went to the coke ovens in Pennsylvania where they worked the men twelve and fourteen hours a day. I walked eighteen miles to get into the cotton mills and expose the infamies of your charity brigade, your foreign missions and other hypocritical movements of the capitalists who were murdering the children in the mills. A lawyer sent me five dollars.

He sent it by one of the boys for the work I did in the mills. They were taking the hands of those children in the mills with their machinery. I took eighty of them to Philadelphia with me and showed them to the ministers and every one else in order to stir up the nation to the crime it was committing. We walked all the way to Oyster Bay from Philadelphia to see the man who was President of the United States at that time [Theodore Roosevelt] to try to get Congress to pass a bill to stop that slaughter of the children in the mills, mines and factories, and he would not see us. He is a brave guy when he wants to take a gun and go out and fight other grown people, but when those children went to him he could not see them. But we did not stop, and out of that fight we made has come this child labor bill that is before Congress. One paper called me a horrible woman for taking the children out. Why the kids had the time of their lives. Everybody fed them. We got into the Oriental Hotel where the Wall Street people eat, and there was steak and quail on toast — the first time I ever ate quail on toast. We had the finest feast we ever struck. The young ones all went back strong and well, but they had to go into the mills again. However, Pennsylvania has passed a law that keeps them out.

I never in my life asked President White for a favor. I wouldn't take it from him if he wanted to give it to me. I want to say to you here that you have the hardest-worked President, Vice-President and Secretary you have ever had in your history. You talk a great deal about young John D. Young John D. is not to blame; you are to blame. They couldn't keep you from organizing in Colorado if you were men enough. I had a conversation of two hours and twenty minutes with John D. I found him one of the most unassuming men. Young John D. never said "I cawn't," and "I shawn't"; he talked simple like we do, and that is more than some people in the labor movement do. If you line up and demand your rights in a logical way Colorado will be the best organized State in the Union, and John D. Rockefeller will help you to organize it.

I am going to Youngstown. I didn't ask Mr. White whether or not I could go — I am going anyhow. I went to the garment workers in Chicago. Somebody said afterwards, "Did Mr. White tell you to get away?" I said, "No, sir, he didn't; and if he had I would not have done it." Nobody owns me. When it comes to a fight for my class I don't care if they are revolters or not I am going to be with them when they are fighting the common enemy; then when the fight with the other fellow is over I will fight to make them come back into their bona fide organization. Girls worked in Chicago for eight cents an hour. In the strike the police got ten dollars for every girl they beat up. We are going to stop that.

I will be 85 years old next May, and I am as well able to fight as I was forty years ago. Don't bother about politics; keep close to the economic struggle; don't allow politicians to interfere with your business and we will attend to ours. Don't let the ministers bother you, we know the Lord Jesus Christ as well as they do. They don't let us go into their church conferences and they have no right to come into ours. I said to a man in New York, "Keep your hands off; this is our fight. I don't want any freedom that comes from the other class; I want the freedom I have fought for and bought myself and then I will keep it."

Our men in West Virginia were beaten up, and when I was in Washington and they asked me if I told the miners to buy guns I said, "Yes, I did; I told them to buy guns because an armed people have never yet been conquered." When the Governor of West Virginia [William E. Glasscock] sent to Boomer to get the guns he sent a doctor [Lawrence C. Montgomery] — a political lickspittle. They let him bill the meeting and pay for the hall rent. I went down and took possession of it and said, "Boys, have you got any guns?" "Yes, Mother, sure." "Did you pay for them?" "Sure, we paid for them." "Then the guns are yours. Don't you give those guns to Dr. Montgomery, to the Governor, to anybody else who comes after them. Keep them at home and if any gunmen come there to invade your homes do business." That is the way to do business, isn't it, Mr. Newspaper Man? Lawson gave the guns to the military when they came in. You bet your life I wouldn't have given them up!

I am going into the Fairmount region to organize the miners there; I am going up the Norfolk and Western, and I am going to take big, long Tom Haggerty along. And I want the very best organizers there are in the United States, the very best men you have, and I am going to pick them myself. We are going to turn over West Virginia thoroughly organized, and then, if I am spared I am going down to Alabama. If I am not alive I will be up with God Almighty and I am going to tell him to fix me up so that I can go down and raise hell with them anyway. An old mine owner in West Virginia said, "Why don't you die?" I said, "God Almighty wants me to live long enough to raise hell with you and make a man out of you instead of a thief."

Now, boys, be good. Stand by your officers and when the day comes they are not worthy of your confidence and support I will be the first to come to the front and tell you. Go home with a new heart, with new resolutions, with the hope of a new day for the children who will come after you. John Brown committed murder in his day; the courts of the country condemned him and he was hung. He was a criminal in the eyes of the court and in the eyes of many of the Nation; but he was a hero in the eyes of God. He started the war on chattel slavery. We have got to carry on the war on industrial slavery.

Boys, look back the stairway of years, look back over our fights. I remember our fights in Chicago when we hadn't a penny, when no organizer was paid, when we had to tramp six miles to attend a meeting and we did it cheerfully. I look back on those grand days when the men who fought so well paved the way for the movement you have today. Many of those men are in their graves. Martin Irons is one of those who was persecuted. I went to see his grave after he had been dead nineteen years. It was in Brownsville, Texas. When I got off the train I asked the agent if Martin Irons was buried there. He said he was. I got a butcher named Williams to go to the grave with me.

Martin Irons was a hero, but he was maligned, vilified and persecuted. He gave up his life that you might be here today. His grave was by a fence, overgrown with weeds and neglected. It was marked by a broken shovel. When he was Master Workman of the Iron Mountain Division he was called from Kansas City to St. Louis. The strike call was written up. When he was being shown to his room by the bell boy they said, "Come this way to this room." He went back with them to a room they had rented, they put a pistol to his head and said, "You sign this strike call or we will kill you." He signed the strike call. The secretary and treasurer were Pinkertons.

When Martin Irons left Kansas City I had five dollars. I wanted to give him three. He wouldn't take it. He said, "Mother, they have taken my home, killed my wife, they have ruined me, they have taken everything!" I said, "No, Martin, they have left you your manhood, and that is worth all the wealth in the world." So that day when I knelt at his grave in Brownsville I remembered these things. Humanity had forgotten him, but there was a mocking bird singing over his grave. I wrote the matter up. The boys in Mount Olive, Illinois, said they would give me a grave for him. I intended to raise his body and bring him up with the martyred dead in Mount Olive, but the State Federation of Missouri took the matter in hand and sent a tombstone there. If I live long enough I will bring Martin Irons' body and that tombstone to Mount Olive and bury him with his co-workers. When he was on the rock pile in Memphis, Powderly sent him fifteen dollars to pay his fine. You boys have no idea of what we went through in those days. I look back over the long struggle, the dark hours, the suffering, and I know it was not in vain. I see the sun breaking through the clouds.

When I come back from Youngstown I will go to Colorado. The gunmen are there but they won't touch me. I am not a bit afraid of them. I am going into all the mining camps, Mr. White, whether you agree with me or not, that belong to John D. Rockefeller and I am going to organize the men into the United Mine Workers of America, no matter who is with it or against it.

[*UMWA Proceedings* (Indianapolis: Bookwalter-Ball Printing Co., 1916), pp. 956–68.]

Speech at a convention
of the United Mine Workers of America
Indianapolis, Indiana

*The year 1916 was a busy one for Mother Jones, who traveled across the
country and back twice in the year. Her usual organizing and participating
in strikes went on, but she also devoted time to political campaigning and
to an attempt to secure the release of a group of union men who had been
sentenced to federal prisons.*

*Mother Jones had engaged in political campaigning before, but always
for Socialist candidates, as in her support of Eugene V. Debs for President. In 1916, however, she lent her oratory to the causes of Democratic
Governor George W. P. Hunt of Arizona and to John Worth Kern, the
Democratic senator from Indiana whose resolution for an investigation
of the conditions in the coal fields of West Virginia had probably brought
about her release from imprisonment in 1913. In correspondence and
speeches she made it clear that she had not changed her politics, but that
she felt personal obligations to both men, and that she felt that working
men generally owed Hunt and Kern their support for their strong prolabor stands. Unfortunately, none of her campaign speeches has been preserved. Both candidates were defeated.*

*She also met defeat in her attempt to gain pardons for Frank M. Ryan,
president, Eugene A. Clancy, executive board member, and other officers
of the International Association of Bridge and Structural Iron Workers
who were convicted in Indianapolis in 1912 of abetting the bombing of
the* Los Angeles Times *building in 1910. Mother Jones visited the convicted dynamiters in state and federal prisons in California, Kansas, and
Georgia, organized a concerted group of applications, and presented them
in person to President Woodrow Wilson. However, the attorney general
had already recommended, on the basis of previous applications, that no
pardons should be granted.*

*Besides these special efforts, Mother Jones pursued her usual course,
speaking widely throughout the country, participating in a garment workers' strike in New York in February, streetcar men's strikes in El Paso and
New York, and an organizing tour for the UMWA in West Virginia in
the autumn.*

*In contrast, in 1917 she traveled very little, spending the greater part
of the year in West Virginia. From her headquarters in Charleston, she*

made strenuous efforts to organize the New River field to the east. The wartime labor policies of the Wilson administration, which called for no strikes and a ban on opposition to unionizing, opened up to some extent the nonunion areas for a drive by the UMWA. With the aid of Lawrence "Peggy" Dwyer, a one-legged veteran miner who had formerly worked at Cabin Creek, she held meetings and agitated among the miners through the length of the valley.

When she came to the international convention of the UMWA in 1918, she could report progress on the organizing drive in West Virginia, though much remained to be done. Once again, she urged the miners to support their president, Frank Hayes, who took office when John P. White accepted a position on the War Labor Board from President Wilson. Hayes had chosen as his vice-president the former statistician at UMWA headquarters, John L. Lewis, who took over many of the duties of the international presidency because of Hayes's weaknesses. Despite her dislike of John L. Lewis, Mother Jones endorsed the leadership of the union and called on the members to support Woodrow Wilson as their wartime leader. Strength and unity gained during the war would produce victories for the workers later.

§   §   §

I want to say, boys, that I am glad I have lived to see this gathering of the miners in this country in this hall today. Years ago no one ever dreamt that this great mass of producers would meet in the capital of a great state. I am not going to throw any bouquets at you — I am not given to that at all. I did not expect to speak in this convention. I came here more to look it over until the officers of West Virginia came back. For the first time in the history of West Virginia we have good officers; that is, we have honest, clean, sober men. They don't make any crooked deals with the high class burglars — and if I catch one of them doing it I will see that he is hung so he will not make another.

I want to call your attention, as I have often done, to a few illustrations of what is taking place the world over today. History tells us that away back in the days of the Roman Empire they were gathering in the blood of men who produced the wealth, just as they have been doing up to this time. Back in that time the Roman lords said, "Let us go down to Carthage and stop the agitation there." They went down and all they arrested at that time they sold into slavery or held them. They do pretty much the same today, for the courts put you in jail, which is worse than any slavery. The Roman courts said to one young man, "Why do you carry on this agitation? Don't you know it is dangerous?" The young man said, "No, I didn't know it was dangerous, but I will tell you why I carry it on. I belong to a class that has been robbed, plundered, murdered, maligned, vilified, jailed, persecuted all down the ages, and because I belong to that class I feel it is my duty to awaken that class to their condition. The earth was not made for a few, but for all God's people." I wish I could imbue every man in this hall today with the same spirit that had possession of that pagan slave. Mind you, he was not a modern Christian, he was a pagan slave, but he was teaching Christ's doctrine to his brothers.

We are in a war today, the nation is facing a crisis and you must not look at it with indifference. Never in the history of the American nation has the government assumed such a responsibility as it has on its shoulders now. Don't think this war will end tomorrow, not at all. And if we are going to have freedom for the workers we have got to stand behind the nation in this fight to the last man. There may be those who want peace. I don't want peace on any terms. I am not willing to take it or concede it. Perhaps I was as much opposed to war as anyone in the nation, but when we get into a fight I am one of those who intend to clean hell out of the other fellow, and we have got to clean the kaiser up. Now, mind, you, I don't mean the German people, I mean the kaiser, the dictator; I mean the grafter, the burglar, the thief, the murderer—the men of that type will have to be cleaned up.

I heard you talking about the responsibility for the shortage of coal. There is no shortage of coal. The miners of this country are willing to dig coal day and night if the nation needs it. But there is a shortage of common sense in making the other fellow give up the cars. The miners are willing to dig Sunday, Monday, or any other day, but they can't get the cars. Without anybody knowing anything about it I took a trip from Charleston to Cincinnati. I got an old sunbonnet, put it on and went into every yard. I looked over the yards and saw cars by the hundreds laid away instead of being given to the miners. The miners in Cabin Creek worked only six hours in one week, and in Paint Creek not an hour. And then somebody will come forward and blame the miners! Let me tell you the miner is the best citizen there is in America. The miners in the Fairmont region haven't had cars, and the shortage of coal cannot be blamed on them. I counted sixty cars of coal this morning as I came along and they were all sidetracked. Why are the engines not taken from other roads and attached to those cars to take them where they are needed? You cannot do business up in Washington, you have got to do it out through the country. Sitting down blowing off steam in Washington won't settle the question; you have got to have some people out to do the work. Not the fellow working for a dollar a year. That kind of gentleman won't know anything about it. Pick men from among the coal miners who understand the situation and they will furnish the coal. The President has taken over the railroads. Well, then, let us have cars. But cut out the watered stock, because if we own the railroads we are not going to stand for watered stock. They have been robbing us long enough and we will attend to that later on—we are not going to bother with it now.

Every miner in West Virginia is perfectly willing to work day and night if the government needs him. The miners cannot produce the coal if you don't give them the cars to dump it into. The trouble lies with the railroads. What we must do is to settle down to one thing—no more strikes in the mines, not a single strike. Let us keep at one strike, a strike to strike the kaiser off the throne. Let us settle little grievances without conflicts, because the nation is in no condition to deal with those things today. Never in our history has a President had such things to contend with. Not Washington, not Lincoln, not a President who ever sat in the presidential chair has gone up against it like the man who is there today. I am not in the habit of paying tribute to public officials as a rule, but I will say that the first time in your history you have been recognized as good citizens of the United States has been by the present chief executive of the nation. When he wrote to you he at least recognized that you are the bone and sinew of this nation, for without you the nation would perish. So I say I pay my respects to President Wilson. He took a stand that no President ever did before. He offered a proposition for the settlement of the Colorado strike when it looked very dangerous for the nation. I don't believe even President Wilson realized how dangerous it was, but he sent out a proposition and the miners accepted it. You have been a little free from strikes since, but not from internal agitation and conflict. Now, boys, I want to tell you we have got to stop and bury all internal bickering and rise like men to meet the danger to our nation. This is not time to fight to see who will be officers. You know when there is wrong there is no one in your ranks who will fight it more openly than I will, but I feel this is a time to give an example to workers all over the world.

I congratulate you on this magnificent convention. Talking to a mine owner today we discussed a few questions. He said, "I want to show you what organization does. In 1902 we had a convention of miners in West Virginia. In 1918 we had another. I stood in that convention and surveyed the men who were there representing some 30,000 members. As I looked at them I saw the change that had come about. The men in the convention this year got down to business, discussed vital questions; there was no conflict, each brought out his views, he got a hearing and then all agreed finally. That is the outcome of organization, education and agitation. They were not drinking; they were attending to business.

I was in that convention and we didn't have any temperance cats howling around there; we didn't need them. The men had learned self-respect since they got shorter hours, did away with the pluck-me stores and got their pay in Uncle Sam's money instead of corporation scrip. They did not have to buy Armour's rotten beef from the company store. At one time I was staying at a miner's home after holding a meeting in 1901 with the enslaved army that was in the mines at that time. The mother got up in the morning and opened a can of Armour's choice roast beef. She started to put it in the buckets of the boys and found three fingers in the can under a layer of beef. Farther down she found part of a hand. I got it and took it away with me. We were going to have a meeting in the opera house in Montgomery the next day. I showed the men what they had to pay for in the pluck-me store, It was Armour's choice roast beef, mind you, and three fingers of the worker had been chopped off. They don't have to do that now. If they got a can of that sort of stuff they would hit the pencil pusher over the head with it, but in 1901 they had to take it or they were blacklisted. They are not blacklisted now, they have an organization behind them.

Another thing they have now is schools for the children. That convention in Charleston last week taught me one great lesson. There were men there from along the Kanawha River that were in bondage fifteen years ago. Often I had to go around in those days to hold a meeting with them in the dead of night. Now I can go in the daytime in all but a few places. We cannot do that in the Pocahontas field yet, but we are going in there one of these days, and I tell you when we do there'll be hell let loose. We want them to understand we are going out. America is fighting for democracy abroad and we are going to fight at home, so that when we lick the fellows abroad we will have here at home a nation with laws that will not be set aside by the Supreme Court. When that day comes the Supreme Court will not be telling you you are criminals. The Supreme Court doesn't know what it is to suffer. In Washington, where four or five of them were discussing the great issues of the day, an old fossilized fellow who had been dead forty years before he was born said, "You know that the miners and the workers spend their money in saloons." I let him shoot off his hot air a while and said, "How much of your money did they ever spend? How much of their money did you spend? You spend a lot of it, because you have a stomach four miles long and two miles wide. If the miners do take a drink once in a while they need it. They have to go into the mines and work in water day after day and watch the roof for fear it will come down on them, watch for poisonous gases, and in West Virginia in some places they have to spend fourteen hours a day, or did some years ago. You know nothing about these things. You have been living off the life blood of your fellow-man and you have no conception of what he has to contend with."

To go back to the war. We will stay with Uncle Sam. He is the best uncle you ever struck. There is no other uncle in the world like Uncle Sam, and the convention must express its deep appreciation of President Wilson, who is the first President that ever sat in the executive chair of the nation who recognized this body of workers. It isn't anything but what he should have done, but he is the first one that did it, and for that reason I want to pay my respects to him. If we are going to have any difficulties let us go to the national government and put our case before them before any strike is called. Let us dig the coal and let us demand that we get cars to fill with the coal. You know there is a game being played because Uncle Sam has taken over the roads. The pirates are onto the game and they are trying to embarrass the government. I will tell you what we will do. We will line up an army in West Virginia, capture the cars, get the engineers and firemen to run them down to the mines, load them and run them to Washington and New York.

You have a young president here; he is very young yet, but I want to tell you something. I want you to stand behind President Hayes and help him, and don't harass him any more than you can help. Let us stand together as one man behind him. There never was an hour in the history of organized labor when it was so essential for us to bury the hatchet, stand together and fight this battle of the nation to a finish as now. And when we have won, if they don't give us a square deal we will fight then. I want you to stand behind your president and do everything you can. He is young now, but before he gets through he will grow old. You have got a secretary [William Green] who is one of the most able men in America in the industries. I have been watching him carefully. I watch them all and I know them all from A to Z.

I was traveling all night and I was fussing all day yesterday. A fellow asked me if I didn't think it was time for me to die, and I said, "No, I have a contract to clean hell out of you fellows and I cannot go up until I have helped civilize you." Now, be good boys and let us make one grand body of men in America that stands loyally for the flag. You must understand that the men who watered the clay for seven long years with their blood, with blistered feet, weary backs and throbbing heads, they did it in order to hand down to you the noblest emblem ever handed down during all the generations of men as an evidence of their belief in social justice and industrial freedom. I happened to be one of those who walked over the clay those men watered with their blood to give me a vision of freedom. Their memory is dear to me. Every star in that flag was bought with the blood of men who believed in freedom, industrial freedom, particularly. Now it is up to us to carry on the work. Organize, organize, organize.

There is a system of industrial feudalism in the State of West Virginia but before another year ends the backbone of that damnable system will be broken and men will rise beneath those stars and stripes as they should rise, free for the first time. We propose to put the infamous gunmen there out of business. We will make them find other occupations.

You are robbed and plundered to pay these gunmen that are hired to keep you in industrial slavery. If it takes every man of the 500,000 miners in this country to march into West Virginia we propose to drive out that feudal system that survives there. It is an outrage and an insult to that flag. They may as well prepare for business for we are going to do it. The president of the Winding Gulf gang said in Washington, "Don't you know that Mother Jones swears?" I was asked, "Do you swear, Mother Jones?" I said, "You don't think I'm hypocrite enough to pray when I'm talking to those thieves!"

Now line up and stand with the government. No matter who says no, you fellows, every man of you, stand together, and when the fight is over across the water, if we have any kaisers at home we will line up. We will have the guns and our boys will be drilled. We will do business then and we will not ask to borrow money to buy guns. We will have the guns Uncle Sam paid for and we will use them on the pirates and put a stop to slavery. We will give the children of the future a chance to grow. We will teach the people of all the world what that flag stand for and we will not be betrayed by the workers. Let us pledge ourselves in this convention to stand beside the President until the battle is won. I would advise every one to join the Home Guards. Some one would ask why I recommend that. I recommend it because when they call out their army to crush the workers and destroy the future of the nation we will have the guns and we will turn them on the common enemy, not the workers. You have a chance today that has never come in the history of this country before and I want you to take advantage of it.

I had an appeal made to me that touched me more than anything has in years. A company of boys were going abroad from Bentley, West Virginia. The mother of one of the boys fainted. Her boy, with tears in his eyes, gazed at her. In spite of that the last thing he said was, "Mother, keep up the union until we come back and then we will all be one." There never was a grander appeal made by men who had been in slavery and bondage and had just accepted their chance. When they made that appeal I got a new light. I saw those boys going over the ocean to fight the battle for freedom, and they said, "Keep the boys together until we return and then we will all be one." So I say to you, boys, keep up the education and the agitation.

I know there may be some who will find a little fault with what I am going to say, but let me make this appeal to you: Instead of going to poolrooms and playing poker with mine owners or with anyone else, get a book and read and study and prepare yourselves for the future. When you have an idle time, when you feel your brain is rested, get food out of some economic work by some master mind. When you play poker with a mine owner and you win some money from him it is a bribe and he gives it to you for that purpose. I know some of you will condemn me, but I am onto the game. Stay at home and bring up your children to be good citizens. Your wives and children are the best companions and home is the best place in the world.

I want to say to you, President Hayes, if you send any organizers into the field where I am and they play poker games, if you don't take them out I will lick them and put them out. I complained about one and you took him out. The fellow lost $35 playing poker one night and I lodged a complaint against him. He wouldn't lose that money, it would go in on the pay roll and you would pay it. Now, I am warning you, and I want to tell you, Mr. Hayes, if you send any leeches and bloodsuckers into West Virginia we will send them out. We won't put up with them. We have got good men; there is no organization in the country that has as good men as the miners have, but they seldom get on the pay roll. Those men have got to work if they come into the field where I am or I will put them out.

(A motion was made to print the speech made by Mother Jones.)

President Hayes: That will be done without a motion. I have known Mother Jones for a number of years. I have worked with her in various fields, and she has always had the respect of the international organization. For seven years she worked under my direction as an organizer and the only orders I ever gave her was to go where she pleased. She always did that and she always said what she pleased. She is a free lance in this movement and I think the "young president" will profit by her suggestion.

So far as the organizing staff is concerned, it compares favorably with any other organizing staff in the country. I don't think Mother Jones intended to reflect upon the many good men on the organizing staff. If there is any man among the organizers who is not honest and who does not perform his duties, he goes off that staff. In the case she referred to the man went off the staff immediately when she reported to me. I want to make that clear so that there will be no misunderstanding in the minds of the delegates to this convention as to where I stand upon the question she brought to your attention. I appreciate the splendid work Mother Jones has performed in the interest of this movement. She has rendered valiant service and in behalf of the delegates I desire to thank her for her address this afternoon.

Mother Jones: I worked under President White from the time he became president until he resigned and never at any time did he tell me what to do or where to go. There was only one time in the whole history when he said to me, "Mother, would you go into West Virginia and see if you can straighten out the boys?" I went in, but that is the only time he ever said a word to me in all the years I worked under him. I want now to express my appreciation for the kindly and courteous manner in

192

which he treated me. If other presidents who preceded him had done the same the miners would not have been required to spend the amount of money they did in organizing some of the States and fewer lives would have been lost. We have harmony in West Virginia and we are certainly indebted to President White for that.

[*UMWA Proceedings* (Indianapolis: Bookwalter-Ball Printing Co., 1918), pp. 359–67.]

Speech at a public meeting, "Mooney Day"
Peoria, Illinois

On 6 April 1919, Mother Jones took time out from a strenuous speaking tour for the striking steelworkers to attend a Mooney Day meeting in Peoria, Illinois. Of all the causes célèbres *which she espoused, the case of Thomas J. Mooney lasted longest.*

Mother Jones's first acquaintance with Mooney came in 1915 when Mooney appealed for her help in gathering funds for his defense against charges in California courts of having been involved in dynamiting property of the Pacific Gas and Electric Company. Although acquitted of those charges, he was again arrested in July 1916 and charged with murder resulting from the explosion of a bomb during the Preparedness Day parade in San Francisco. He was convicted and sentenced to death, but public outcry against the suspected use of perjured testimony led the governor of California to commute his sentence to life. In prison, Mooney began the twenty-three-year fight to clear his name that brought him release in 1939. Mother Jones lent her voice at various rallies in support of him, including this one in Peoria. Whenever a new governor came into office in California, she visited him with a personal appeal for justice for Mooney. Her last letter to Mooney was written from her sickbed in suburban Washington eight months before she died, thanking him and some of his fellow prisoners for the roses they had sent her.

On this occasion, the military intelligence agents who monitored possible subversive gatherings filed a copy of the printed proceedings of the meeting. They had had Mother Jones under intermittent surveillance during the war, and continued it for at least another year.

§   §   §

Friends, fellow workers, we are living today in the greatest age the world has ever passed through in human history. The whole world is ablaze with revolt. The uprising among the unfortunate workers is suppressed in the daily press. I took a clipping while in New York the other day, out of the New York *World,* which said that the human race has never in human history passed through an age like this. There was once back in Greece, a young man, two hundred years after the world's greatest agitator was marred, crucified, hung, maligned, vilified, by the powers there. There arose in Carthage an agitation and the courts became uneasy. They sent down to Carthage in those days a force that arrested all those who were in the agitation movement which was eighteen hundred years ago. We have not changed the program very much since. We have talked a lot about Christianity, but we have never seen any Christianity yet. There has never been any Christianity on the earth and there is not going to be any for a while yet! They held them in slavery or sold them, if they did not need them, and so, they brought them into court. Among those was a young man and the judge said to him "Who are you?" He said, "I am a man," a member of the human family. The judge asked, "Why do you carry on this agitation?" The boy replied, "Because I belong to a class that in human history have always been crucified, robbed, murdered, jailed, maligned, vilified, starved and because I belong to that class, I feel it is my duty to awaken that class to their power and their duty." He was sentenced, of course. I wish I could convey that spirit that this pagan slave, eighteen hundred years ago, possessed. He was not a Christian in the modern cave. He was a Christian to Christ's philosophy. He felt the wrong to fight fellow workers. My friends, we have worked down eighteen hundred years and never in human history did we pass through such a treacherous, insidious, brutal age as this. It is in a different form, but it is the most insidious age that human history has ever passed through. Capitalism sits in the saddle and she is riding it to a finish.

Now I want to show you something. I just came in from Pennsylvania; I went in there from West Virginia. I went up to an old battle ground and I got an inspiration that woke me up; I thought that the cyclone was coming. We must get ready for it. There was twelve thousand men marching up there, where the great steel robbers who robbed the people and murdered them, then tried to cover their hypocrisy by giving a thousand dollars to Billy Sunday. As they marched along, among them were almost three thousand uniformed soldiers. The war has not been in vain. It has taught our boys to come home. This march, my friends, was the most remarkable scene that I have witnessed in many years. It was a terrible cold day, but these boys, cold, ragged, and some of them hungry, marched on. The mayor said we could not have any speaking, we could march, but no speaking. "What are we going to do, Mother?" "We will talk," I said. "He will put us in jail." "What if he does," said I. "We have been in jail before and when we get sense enough we will put the other fellow in jail. So I am going to talk, he can put us in jail; there never was a man made that could stop a woman from talking." As we passed by the cement walls of the steel works, the American Steel Works, I took notice of the walls. There were holes where one could shoot the bullets out from the inside of the barricade. We sent our boys abroad under the impression that they were going to war for democracy. Their mothers wet the clay with tears; they gave them up generously, believing it was going to bring a better civilization to their children yet to come. Their bones are weathering on the soils of France. Today you are walking over their flesh. We have not achieved democracy yet. Our workers are being picked up, taken before a capitalist judge, sentenced to ten or twenty years in the penitentiary. Ninety-five working men were sentenced in Chicago by the judge for five to ten years in the penitentiary. I want to ask the audience what was the matter with that judge's head! If he could take twenty-nine or thirty dollars as a fine, he would have set them free. He imposed upon the workers because they went by the name of the Industrial Workers of the World. My friends, in every great movement that humanity has ever had, there has been advanced ideas, people have taken their lives in their hands, gone out to carry those ideas, though we do not put on airs, and cast them into jail. I went into that jail, I was coming from the west, I saw large bodies of men, many of those men have talked with me on the great industrial battle. No better men are to be found. I gave them money in front of the court the day I left. Let me analyze this thing for a moment, here is a judge who has never worked a day in his life, just sits upon the bench. Here is a prosecuting attorney, here is a jury — with poisoned mind — none of these have any conception of law or justice. They are no better than high class burglars. The judge renders the sentence on these ninety-five American citizens that develop the industries and go out into the lumber yards. He sentenced these men to go to jail, they who have wives and children. There is no one to provide for them. The little girl works in the department or dime store, she comes home, finds the mother lying on the bed, sick; the little baby crying for papa. She is hungry. Their papa was taken away from them. The little girl sells that which is most sacred to woman, to get bread for mother, and then she must wear a label on her back — the Fallen Woman. You should rise to grander womanhood and put a stop to this damnable thing. If they had a little humanity in them they would not think of rendering those decisions. My friends, I look at this thing, for I have had experience in the horrors of this awful system! In New York I went to see a senator, I've been all through the west and I got next to Congress to introduce a bill to repeal this espionage act and let those men be turned out of jail. What working man who lived in America would ever dream of throwing the bomb to murder his own class? Don't I see the horrors? The rottenness of the whole thing! I went myself to see the governor; I don't pay very much attention going to see those people because I realize that every governor and public official is elected by the big business. I did not expect to get anything from the governor but I went down more for the agitation, more for the honor of our courts, more for the preservation of our institutions that are revolutionized. Mooney is only one man but the court represents the nation. When the court can be prostituted in the interest of dollars, what is there for the interest of people? The court is a bulwark of American institutions and when the American working man loses confidence in those courts, where are we going? That is the question to be asked. That is what I went to California for. You working men, I place the responsibility on you, not on the judge, you are the powers. The judge, the president, the governor, the legislature is not the majority. We, the people, are.

Some of the governors ought to be electrocuted, but I don't mean Governor Lowden, because that fellow has got some humanity in him. I know that governor of Colorado is a member of the Steel Trust. The women had the ballot there three years and they burned up their children. Their sons, their husbands, burned the children alive and the women had the ballot and they put those governors in. Colorado bid fair to be one of the revolutionized states in the union and the women got the ballot and since then it is reactionary. I want every symbol of justice given to the woman but I want to tell you that the worst of all the brutal attacks made upon me has come from the women. I am going to be honest with you because the woman has the power to change the nation in one year if she wants to do it. But she won't do it; she belongs to too many clubs, neglects her home, and is not educating the coming generation. My friends in uniform, I want to talk to the women because I know the power of women — if they will stop being little Sunday School parasites. Now, there is that woman who lost her three children. She went out to get protection and lost her senses. Children were burned up. Five persons were murdered there. The jails were filled. The courts were busy.

I myself have spent over three months and twenty-six days and nights on a cement floor under the court house. When the fool sheriff took me off the train, "Where are you going to put me?" I asked. "In the basement under the court house," said he. "Do you want a fire?" "Not particular about it, I want the chimney," said I. "What do you want the chimney for if you don't want the fire?" "I have a trained pigeon that brings me messages from Congress and I send messages back." And he believed it. Think of a woman raising an idiotic thing like that, putting a bayonet in his hand and telling him to go out and shoot the workers and their children. Don't you think civilization has gone mad? I want to wake you up. He will let loose and the other fellow will do something. Yes, it is a tragedy. I went to New York to see some parties there before I came into Pennsylvania. There are one hundred fifty women that they are going to deport. Our prejudice comes down to the citizens of a nation in a great age. These people are to be deported because they said something that did not suit the interests. The children of these women must go into the mines to work. These women, whose husbands rebelled, were thrown out on the mountains. The children of the coming generations came into the world with only the stars for a shelter, the clay for a pillow, their fathers dead, and their people in subjection. I will give you the history as I gave it the government. Because I have known for years what these rascals have done to make their money for destroying the nation. In West Virginia they took the roofs off the houses, stole the food that they had, and now people blame the mothers there if they say they don't like America. Now they are going to be deported for that. They don't deport the rascals that deceive and rob them. That is what you are up against, men. The governor said I must not go down to the courts and talk to those fellows. When they get into an office they think they own the whole nation.

I would have all the officials know that my fathers fought for several long years and waded through their blood and it's a proof for what they stood for and fought for. They lead me to stars and stripes and it is not going to perish, for we will fight as patriots should to take care of that flag. We have other nations that we have to fight. If you starve these men and women for dollars what are you going to do? I looked out and saw the children coming out of the school room doors. Many of those children will never again cross the school room door, they will have to go out and fight for bread. They may wind up in a penitentiary or an asylum. The parents are robbed for Liberty Bonds, for Y. M. C. A. funds, for the War Saving Stamps, for Red Cross, for Knights of Columbus, and for the Salvation Army. Those that were not able to buy the food to give them vitality, they are still paying those Liberty Bonds. Now while these people are held in subjection, still they talk about democracy. It takes four hundred million dollars a year to pay the police bills and the workers are robbed to pay that. At the time of the civil war, that was the greatest industrial battle ever fought in America.

When I was in Washington, I heard the word Bolsheviki and I wondered what it meant, so I went to the library to find out and I found that Bolsheviki stood for the majority taking over the industry. The industry belongs to us. We run them. They don't belong to the other fellow. He stole them. He is a high class burglar. If that is the definition, then I am a Bolsheviki, rule by majority. One of these days, Mr. Judge, it is coming when you will never sit on the bench to decide the destinies of the working man until you have worked ten years as a working man. Today, my friends, change is coming! Our boys are coming home in their uniforms. We sent them abroad to shoot the Kaiser. Let me tell you, we are going to get some Kaisers here at home.

I don't care about political parties. I went down to the Greenback parties, to the Populist party, in fact I went through them all. I found some of the parties most powerful weapons, but money interest prostitutes them all. Nowhere have you elected a man in this last election that represents your interest. I do not care what political party you put in power because we are of the economical power. We have the power to do and we will

198

do it! They are not going to fool us there. It was not the political party that gained the eight hour day for the railroad man. They had met in New York, both sides, spent thousands of dollars. They came down to Washington, sat in the cabinet office, president at the head, discussed the matter, didn't come to any agreement, the railroad magnates wouldn't concede anything, declared it unconstitutional, went to the higher courts, was held up by the supreme court and was passed at midnight and the supreme court is not afraid of its job. I don't care who is in the White House, they have a life job.

Look at this watch of mine. Two hands there, nice looking, but let me take the hands out and it will be no good. It would be useless too, and your two hands are like unto the hands of the watch. You are the tools that move the nation. The Salvation Army, the Y. M. C. A., we build their institutions, pay for them, feed the people and everything. We are going to change that. The page is turned. The world is a moving magnet; a new civilization is coming; the pendulum is swinging as it has never swung before. It behooves us to do our duty.

Men leaders, call your organization together, get a fellow to lead you to hell or to heaven. Let us call your employers together and you lead them. You will get the inspiration out of their school after a while. You will get sense. The nation can't do without you. You are the ones that moved the industry. The ones that freed all wealth. It is our duty to take a day off and stand together. I want Mooney pardoned and we must get him a new trial and that is what I am after. I want the courts of our nation vindicated! They might put me in jail for saying this but they can do so for all I care, for they will have to feed me then. Mooney is a man that would not hurt a child! There is not a more loyal citizen in America than Mooney! And now, Mr. Judge, you might as well take a night off the day before you sentence Mooney again, for you will soon be the working man.

[*Mooney Day Held at Coliseum, Peoria, Ill., April 6, 1919,* RG 165, MID 10110/G4, National Archives.]

Speech at a convention
of the United Mine Workers of America
Indianapolis, Indiana

With the end of the First World War, President Woodrow Wilson's first priority was the peace conference at Versailles, and after that his unsuccessful campaign for ratification of the treaty, but his administration also began a rapid dismantling of the machinery of war. Would the nationalized railroads and communications system be returned to their former owners, and, if so, under what conditions? Militant labor, made more confident by its wartime role, was anxious to have a part in these and other major decisions, and 1919 was not only the year of Versailles, but also a year of strikes: a general strike in Seattle, a police strike in Boston, and two major national strikes toward the end of the year in the steel and coal industries.

The UMWA, the largest American union with membership approaching the 500,000 mark, was determined to assert its increasing strength, but was plagued with problems of leadership. John P. White, the last elected president, had resigned to serve on the War Labor Board, elevating to the presidency his vice-president, Frank P. Hayes. Hayes, in turn, had proved ineffectual, leaving the way open for his appointed vice-president, John L. Lewis, to move in and position himself for confirmation as leader in the presidential election scheduled for 1920. Other possible candidates included John H. Walker, who maintained that he had been counted out by White's administration in the last election, Frank Farrington of Illinois, Alexander Howat of Kansas, and Robert Harlin of Washington. Hayes finally resigned, and John L. Lewis became acting president in name as well as reality, but before he left office Hayes had presided over a conference of leaders of the union that had set an ambitious agenda: a sixty percent wage increase, a six-hour day, a five-day week, and nationalization of the coal industry.

The large wage demand was not without some justification. In October 1917, the union's leaders had agreed to a Fuel Administration maximum wage of roughly five dollars a day, to be in effect until the end of the war was declared. Meanwhile, inflation had soared, the peace treaty had not been signed, and a declaration of the end of the war was not in sight, yet they were still bound by the now obsolete technicality. Tales of war profiteering made the continuing inflation less bearable while domestic de-

mand for coal remained high and the demand in Europe, much of whose coal industry had been devastated by war, insured a good market for some time to come. The miners' union was determined to redress what it considered the injustice of the current situation. The new acting president responded by leading them to a national settlement which he could claim as a victory, although his rivals criticized it as inadequate.

Although the stated demands of the Hayes conference in the spring of 1919 were perhaps designed to bring about the downfall of the acting president, John L. Lewis did not flinch. He called a special convention to meet in September, and when the delegates authorized the officers to call a strike he did so on 1 November, despite pleas from the Wilson administration and injunctions issued by federal Judge Albert B. Anderson. On Armistice Day, 1919, he indicated that he was willing to negotiate with coal industry leaders. When those negotiations in Buffalo and Philadelphia came to an impasse, he and the union held out. Finally, in an hours-long session with the invalid President Wilson, a settlement was reached that would depend on the arbitration of a presidentially appointed board. The final decisions were far from the original demands of the miners, but the UMWA had made its strength felt in its first nationwide strike.

Whether by choice, happenstance, or the manipulation of John L. Lewis, Mother Jones's participation in the coal strike was limited to the two following speeches delivered at the special convention in Cleveland, Ohio. Instead, during much of the year, she was deeply involved in the steel organizing drive and the unsuccessful strike that followed simultaneously with the coal strike.

For her, organizing steel workers and participating in their strikes was nothing new. Wages, hours, and conditions of work in the steel mills made the industry, in the eyes of labor leaders, one of the most backward sectors of the economy. Like the miners, the steelworkers had proved themselves during the war, achieving prodigies of production, but not sharing, as they thought, in the profits of the companies. As part of the postwar assertiveness of labor, in 1919 the American Federation of Labor set up a steel organizing committee under the direction of John Fitzpatrick, president of the Chicago Federation of Labor. The operations in the steel center of Pittsburgh were directed by William Z. Foster. In her autobiography, Mother Jones asserted that, when in Seattle, she decided to join the battle, but in a letter to John H. Walker dated 5 February 1919, she indicated that John L. Lewis asked her to go to Pittsburgh as a contribution of the miners to the steel organizing drive. Once committed, she threw herself into the work directed by Foster, holding meetings throughout the Pittsburgh area, and speaking widely in New York, Ohio, Indiana, and Illinois during the drive. She continued to use her talents to the bitter end of the unsuccessful strike in 1920. Thus, she was removed from the great

201

battle of the miners in 1919, except for a flying visit to the convention in Cleveland. Whether he diverted her or not, it was certainly to the advantage of John L. Lewis to have her otherwise occupied as he planned and led the coal strike. She had never accepted easily the orders of elected presidents of the union; his tenure was too uncertain to have to contend with any dissent from her. As far as his running for the presidency in 1920 was concerned, he probably knew that she had no use for him, and would prefer any of his rivals to him. It is not known that she ever played politics in earlier presidential elections, but the rank and file held her in affection, and John L. Lewis's chances of election would be better if she was busy elsewhere and not exerting whatever influence she might have against him. In this convention the need for solidarity outweighed her dislike of Lewis, and her final plea to them was for the delegates to bury the hatchet and support their president.

§ § §

I didn't come into the convention this afternoon to speak, but they took me by surprise—like the police did. I am not going to take up much of your time. There has been too much time spent in oratory. For the last four weeks I have been with the steel workers. If you want to see brutal autocracy, come with me to the steel centers and I will show it to you. The world does not dream of the conditions that exist there. Eighteen years ago I talked to the men of Youngstown and they said to me: "What are we going to do, Mother?" "I don't know what you are going to do unless you get together," I told them. The steel company, with its usual methods of bribery, gave them stock at eighty dollars a share. In a few months it dropped to thirty dollars, although they could not strike. They had them by the throat. A few of them struck, but they had to go back beaten. If there is any body of men in the United States that require your thought and consideration it is the steel workers. I was in Monessen last Sunday and 18,000 men came to a meeting. Some of them were worn out, some had hopes for another day. Some had their backs bent with the burden of years and the whip of the master, but they all came believing there was a new message for them.

One chap said to them, "You know we are going to have a strike. Now you must be peaceful, we must have peace." Imagine what a statement to make to men who were going to strike. I wonder if Washington was peaceful when he was cleaning hell out of King George's men. I wonder if Lincoln was peaceful. I wonder if President Wilson was. And then this gentleman gets up and tells us we must be peaceful. When he sat down I said: "I want to take issue with you"—an old fossilized thing that hadn't worked for twenty years, but he drew his salary—"I want to tell you we're not going to have peace, we're going to have hell. Strikes are not peace. We are striking for bread, for justice, for what belongs to us."

The speaker who preceded me referred to Mr. Gary. The boys wrote and asked Mr. Gary to give them a hearing. He refused. Then the President of the United States wrote and asked him for a hearing and he refused again.

Mr. Chairman, I would like to be President of the United States for one month. If I had been President and Mr. Gary had said, "Nothing doing," I would have sent two United States marshals up with a pair of handcuffs, have him brought to Washington and said: "Now, there is something doing." Going on your knees to a bunch of robbers and begging will do no good. When any pirate insults the President of the United States he insults the whole nation.

The men of Monessen were told by the mayor on the first of April that they could not speak, but we talked anyhow. When I addressed the meeting I said: "Mr. Mayor, I will give you a lesson it may be well for you to follow. When I was a rather young woman, down on the Mississippi River, where there were no railroads to carry passengers in that direction, they used to go on the steamers. The freight was carried in those steamers and the ones that got in first got the most freight. One particular steamer was making an effort to get in first. A lot of steam was coming out of the steamer and the captain thought he would lose the race. He told a darkey to sit on the valve. He did. After a while he said, 'Massa, this thing's getting too hot.' 'Never mind, keep your seat.' After a while the darkey said, 'This is getting too hot, sure.' 'No matter, I want to get into port.' The darkey stayed a while longer and said, 'Massa, if you don't let that steam out it will blow hell out of all of us.' What happened? In a few minutes the steam blew the captain and all of them into the Mississippi River. Mr. Mayor, let them blow off their steam. You are a great deal safer if they do that, and so is the nation." These men in public office who want to stop free speech are creating more Bolshevism and I. W. W.-ism than any other institutions you have got.

I said to the 18,000 men in that meeting: "How many of you are going to come into this strike?" They all put up their hands and gave three cheers for Uncle Sam. The Sunday before we went to Duquesne. The secretary of the steel workers was arrested. Another man got up to speak and he was pulled off. And then, of course, I had to step in—it wouldn't go unless I said something. I got up and all I got a chance to say was: "Men, stand like the men of '76," when two big, burly policemen got me by the shoulders. "What's the matter?" said I. "Come and we will show you." "All right," said I. I went along. I have been in bull pens and locked up before, but this was the first time I was ever behind iron bars.

Then the lap dogs of the Gary crowd came there and one of them said: "Now, Mother Jones, I want to tell you something." I had my nose between the bars looking at him. He said: "With your experience you ought to do a wonderful lot of good; you should not be agitating." "Why?" I asked. "Because," he said, "you could do better work." "I thought this was a very good work." "Oh, no," he said. "Stop a minute," I said. "Right here in and around Pittsburgh today a million people went on their knees and paid a tribute to the man who agitated nineteen hundred years ago in Palestine; and not only that, but they arose and sang songs of gratitude to him."

Another lap dog of the steel trust said: "Oh, but He wasn't an agitator." "Why the hell did you hang him for then?" said I. He had no reply to make to that. Then he said that the people there were all foreigners. "That is the very reason we want to organize them," I told him. "We want them to understand what American institutions stand for, and if they do not understand the language they cannot understand the institutions."

"But they are all contented," he told me. "Then they are very dangerous citizens," said I, "because an American citizen is never contented; he sees a civilization beyond, and beyond that he is going to aim at and go after. We are going to organize them all anyhow, and you can jail us all you want. We build the jails. Now when we get brains enough we will put you in jail."

In Homestead the labor men were allowed to speak for the first time in 28 years. We were arrested the first day. When I got up to speak I was taken. Eight or ten thousand labor men followed me to the jail. They all marched there. When we went into the jail they remained outside. One fellow began to cry and said: "What for you take Mudder Jones?" and they took him by the neck and shoved him behind the bars. That is all he did or said. We put up a bond of $15 each. We were to come for trial the next day, but the burgess didn't appear. They postponed the trial on account of the mob that appeared outside. When they got me in jail the police themselves got scared to death. One of our men said: "Mother can handle those men." He was told, "No, nobody can handle them." "Yes, she can; let her get out." I went out and said: "Boys, we live in America. Let us give three cheers for Uncle Sam and go home and let the companies go to hell." And they did. Everybody went home, but they went down the street cheering. There was no trouble, nobody was hurt — they were law-abiding. They blew off steam and went home.

In Duquesne they took forty men. One man came out of a restaurant and asked what the trouble was. They got him by the back of the neck and put him behind the iron bars. He was kept from two o'clock Monday afternoon until ten o'clock Sunday morning without a bite to eat or even a drink of water. That was the only crime the man had committed. Is there

204

any kaiser who is more vicious than that? Do you think it is time for us to line up, man to man, and clean out those kaisers at home?

The steel workers have taken a strike vote and decided to strike. You men must stand behind them. Never mind what anybody says, that strike will come off next Monday. The miners and all the other working men of the nation must stand with them in that strike, because it is the crucial test of the labor movement of America. You are the basic industry. They didn't win the war with generals, and the President didn't win the war. They could have sent all the soldiers abroad, but if you hadn't dug the coal to furnish the materials to fight with, what could they have done? You miners at home won the war digging coal. You have been able to clean up the kaisers abroad, now join with us and clean up the kaisers at home.

Gary gave a banquet to the newspaper men in New York. I happened to be in New York at that time. During the dinner they discussed the labor movement, and some newspaper man said: "Well, you know there is a great deal of discontent." Gary said: "I will tell you what we can do — we can give them a cup of rice and that will quiet them." I want to tell Judge Gary to be careful or he may have to eat the rice himself before this thing is over. That is what was said to the people of France before the revolution, when they were starving, and the people didn't take rice; they did away with the divine right of kings, and we are going to do away with the divine right of these rulers who rob and plunder the people.

A woman was murdered in Pennsylvania the other day (Mrs. Fanny Sellens). You fellows didn't amount to a row of pins. You ought to have lined up fifty thousand men and women and gone there and cleaned up that gang that murdered that woman in cold blood. You haven't got any manhood in you. You want Congress to investigate. How very thoughtful you are. They got Congress to investigate for you. Not on your life. Why didn't you do as we did in West Virginia? We do business down there.

A Delegate: Our officers have told us to keep out of politics. I advise them to go into politics.

Mother Jones: Oh, shut up with your rotten politics. We have got things more serious than politics.

I went up Stanford Mountain and talked to a boy up there. He said: "Mother, when you find us you will find us always together." That very night up went the mine owners' gunmen and shot that man while he slept. One man lay dead over there, another over here—two as loyal men as ever lived—and the blood streamed down on each side. Even in death they were together. The shacks were riddled and those people had been murdered while they slept. Ten days afterward I went up the mountain again, and out in the field I saw a mother with her baby kneeling over the grave of one of those men. When she saw me the baby said: "Oh, Mother Jones, won't you bring my daddy back? Won't you bring him back, and let me kiss him?" When the history of these struggles is written by those who saw them at first hand it will not be a eulogy of officers, it will be a history of the crimes the workers have stood for, and hundreds in the days to come will stand aghast as they read.

I want you to stand by the steel workers. The call has gone out and I don't think it will come back. I know what I am talking about. I don't live in the parlor, I am not a Sunday School teacher, I am right down in the trenches and I see the horrors. I remember one awful night when that man came to see me (pointing to President Keeney, of District 17) at one o'clock in the morning. It was in 1912. He came to me with tears in his eyes and said nobody would come to them. He asked if I would come.

I was thinking it was time to break in there anyhow, so I said I would go. He said, "But they might kill you." I said I was not afraid, that I could meet no more glorious death than fighting those thieves and robbers. We went up that morning with a company of militia. Of course, the governor always have to send the bayonets when labor is going to pull anything off. In the face of a whole gang of operators those men asked me if I would organize them. I asked if I organized them would they stay in the organization. They all said "Yes." Then old "Peggy" Dwyer, who has only one leg, wheeled around on that and said: "Yes, we will stay," and they made good.

In West Virginia you have over 50,000 miners organized, and before another year you will have over 80,000. If you send a fellow in there that don't suit us, Mr. Lewis, we will ship him out. That is the way we do business. I put up many a scheme to get rid of the leeches, and there are a few more of them I will get after before I get through. I remember when that boy there (President Keeney) was a little fellow. I gave him a book one Sunday and said to him and a few more: "Go up under the trees and read. Leave the pool room alone. Read and study and find out how to help your fellow miners." And he did it.

I will probably go back to the steel strike tomorrow. I told the boys I would be back for a big meeting Thursday night. Yesterday I wrote the Attorney General [A. Mitchell Palmer] in Washington and told him: "This thing won't go and it is the duty of the government to stop it. The people will not submit to this tyranny and oppression." I also sent an article to the Washington *Times,* because that is at the seat of government, it is where the Congressmen and Senators are. I called attention to these cheap office holders, these pie counter politicians who have no interest in the nation. We have. Your children will be the future population of the country, and it is your duty to stand together in this great battle that is coming. And when we get through America will be here for the Americans and not for the cheap, rotten royalty of Europe. We are Americans.

When President Keeney had the army up on New River the governor telegraphed to General Wood for the United States troops. That is the first thing they ask for when you are concerned; but they didn't ask for the United States troops to bring Gary down to Washington. Oh, no, that is another thing. Did you ever see one of those fellows beat up by a policeman? You bet your life you didn't. Did you ever see one of those fellows build a jail or make a club to use on you? No, you build the jails and make the clubs and they use them on you. It is only the working man that gets clubbed. He finds the stuff to make the guns and the clubs, he hires the policemen — the other fellow does — puts the club and the gun in his hands and he goes out and gets you. Did you ever see a man with five million dollars in the penitentiary? No, of course not. Then why don't you build a jail and have a court that will put them in and put you out?

[*UMWA Proceedings* (Indianapolis: Bookwalter-Ball Printing Co., 1919), pp. 537-43.]

Speech at a convention
of the United Mine Workers of America
Indianapolis, Indiana

The next day, just before departing for Pittsburgh, Mother Jones made another appeal to the delegates to bury the hatchet and support their officers in the forthcoming coal strike.

§ § §

Now, boys, I have got to go; I am called away. I don't know whether it will ever be my privilege to attend another of your conventions. The battle of ages is on; we have got to fight it and it has got to be won. In an hour or so I will leave for the steel strike in Pittsburgh. I have no doubt the bonds of those poor steel workers will be broken before we end. It has been a long struggle, but it is going to come to an end.

Now, I am going to say a few words to you, and I want you to pay attention to what I say. Don't forget the men and women who gave up their lives for this movement in Utah, Colorado, West Virginia and tramped the weary pathway at night, often hungry and cold, to carry the message of a better day to you. Some of you remember the awful day at McCray's School House, when you walked forty miles, hungry and worn out, to attend that meeting. The fact of your meeting here today is due to the work of those men who are in their graves.

I remember one terrific strike on the Iron Mountain. There was no American Federation of Labor in those days. The organization wasn't very strong and men had very little money. When they were about to call the strike I said to one of the men: "I don't know whether it is safe or not; I question whether some of those aristocratic organizations will respond." He [Martin Irons] was called by telegraph from Kansas City to St. Louis. When he registered at the hotel he was being taken to his room when two men said: "Come this way." He went. They locked him in a room, put the strike call in his hand, and with two pistols at his head told him to sign it. He had to do it. The men were the secretary and treasurer of that organization, both detectives.

The strike went on, and of course it was lost. However, I think no strike is ever completely lost. We give the other fellows a fight and let them know we can come back. I met Martin Irons when he was going away with a little parcel under his arm. I asked him where he was going and he said:

"God knows! I don't. They have taken my wife, my home, my health — they have broken my heart. They have taken all I have — I don't know where I am going." "No, they haven't," I said, "They have left you the greatest gift God ever gave to man, they have left you an honest name and that beats all the wealth of the world."

I never saw Martin Irons again, but one day I got off the train at Bruce-ville, Texas, and asked the agent to take me to the cemetery where Martin Irons was buried. He took me to the grave of that warrior who paved the way for you. His only tombstone was the half of a broken shovel. I said: "This has ever been the fate of the heroes of the world." In Memphis he was arrested as a vagrant. T. V. Powderly sent fifteen dollars to pay his fine and got him off. I wrote the matter up and showed how he was deserted by those he tried to save. You have done that all the way down through history. He did more than any man I know. He was maligned and persecuted. I wrote about his neglected grave and the State Federation of Missouri put a monument over his grave. I made arrangements with the miners of Illinois to give him a grave and raise money for a monument. I may do that before I die, for I don't like to have him down there alone.

There are men lying in their graves today that marched through blinding snow storms, they slept in section houses, they got something to eat from the section men. They went barefooted to pave the way for you to meet here today, and, boys, I know that every insidious method is going to be used to wreck the organization they founded. You made mistakes, we all do. We were born hungry, the brain was starved. We had to work and let the other fellow live off us. Now I beg of you for the sake of your children, for the sake of the revolution that is going on, I beg of you for the sake of the heroes that are going to break into the war Monday for a better civilization, to bury the hatchet and come together, regardless of what may happen. Let the enemy see that we are a solidified army and ready for the war if they want it.

I have got sore myself at times, but you all know you haven't an officer I will not get after if I am convinced he is a traitor, and if he is I will get him down or die. There is more than one of them I got down. Now I am asking you to come together. Mr. Lewis, get those boys up here and make them shake hands, and you shake hands with them. Be friends.

Acting President Lewis: They are all friends of mine, Mother.

Mother Jones: Help your president to win the battle. Illinois was one State the powers that be were afraid of. Are you going to betray the boys that gave up their lives at Virden for this organization? No, I know you won't. Bury the hatchet. Your conventions are getting too big and cost too much money. The money comes out of your pockets and when you need it, instead of giving it to hotels, the railroads, and the pool rooms, save that money and raise hell with the powers that are on our backs. We need every dollar we can get to clean the other fellow up, because we are on the war path now. I have a picture here that was taken in New York. It is of Gary and Schwab, the two gentlemen that dictate to the government. We are going to move, and we are going to dictate to those two high class burglars.

Now, bury the hatchet, every one of you. Shake hands with your president and secretary and say that you will be friends from now on. I wouldn't have your job for a million dollars, Mr. Lewis. I learned ten months ago that a tremendous fund has been raised to destroy the United Mine Workers from within. They cannot succeed from the outside, but they are playing the game from within. I want you to get up and tell those pirates that they cannot destroy this organization, for it is founded on too solid a foundation and it is going on until we win.

[*UMWA Proceedings* (Indianapolis: Bookwalter-Ball Printing Co., 1919), pp. 616–18.]

Speech at a public meeting
Williamson, West Virginia

Exhausted by the constant travel and speaking engagements of the steel strike, Mother Jones went to California to recuperate, first in Los Angeles and then in San Francisco, where she visited friends in prison. But by April 1920, she was back in West Virginia to begin the assault on the last bastion of nonunion coal mining in the state, the southern counties of Logan, Mingo, and McDowell. Through her efforts, and those of others, in 1902 and 1912, the Kanawha field had been largely, if not completely, unionized. Between 1917 and 1920, much of the New River field had been brought into the fold and a new district, Number 29, was now an independent entity in the international union. A whirlwind campaign in the northern Fairmont field from June through August, 1918, had added another twenty thousand miners from that area to the union ranks; and, in contrast to her imprisonment eighteen years before, Mother Jones was allowed to speak publicly all through the field. Now, two years later, the UMWA was focusing its organizing on the far southern region to complete the conquest of the state for the UMWA. It proved to be the bloodiest battle of all.

Despite the gains of recent years, Mother Jones had fears for the future of the union under the leadership of John L. Lewis, whose election to the presidency in the fall she accepted as imminent. For unions generally, the prospect seemed bleak as strike after strike failed and the tide of the red scare continued to flow. Most of all, poor health was a cause of concern to Mother Jones's friends, and of complaints by her to them. By her own account she was ninety years old, and yet she had trouble coming to terms with the lack of energy she felt. Nevertheless, she threw herself into the fight in southern West Virginia. This speech was delivered in the very heart of one of the militantly nonunion areas, at the courthouse in Williamson, Mingo County, just across the Tug River from Kentucky. It was taken down, though imperfectly, by a military intelligence agent.

§ § §

(Note by reporter: Mother Jones spoke from an automobile in the public square in front of the court house, the reporter being seated at an upstairs window. There was great confusion in the street at all times during the address, and the greater portion of the time the speaker had her back toward the reporter. For this reason it was practically impossible to report the address and the report is necessarily very incomplete and disconnected. However, the following is a transcript of such notes as were taken.)

. . . The old condition is passing away. The new dawn of another civilized nation is breaking into the lives of the human race.

Away back, eighteen hundred years ago, two hundred years after the world's savior was hung there arose an agitation. The Roman lords got uneasy about it, and they said, "We have got to stop this agitation and this education. If we don't they will get the best of us. That won't do." They sent down and brought up all those they could get together to come in a hurry to Rome. They either sold them into slavery or held them, and among those that was brought in was a young man. When he came into the Roman court to get his decision the Judge said, "Who are you?"

"I am a man, and a member of the human family."

"Then why do you carry on this agitation?"

"Because I belong to a class that all down the ages have been robbed, murdered, maligned, crucified, deluded, and because I belong to that class I think it is my duty to be with that class and to put a stop to these crimes."

I wish I could convey that same spirit that possessed this pagan slave eighteen hundred years ago to every working man in my hearing today. If he possessed that spirit of manhood the other fellow would come and ask us for the right to eat instead of asking him for the right to eat. But we haven't come to that spirit yet, because all down the ages the system has been going on to enslave us. This pagan slave was not a Christian. By no means. He was a pagan in those days, but he was teaching real Christianity. He was teaching Christ's Christianity, that an injury to one working man is an injury to all. But they called him a pagan.

It don't make much difference what we are called, it is what we do that tells. It is how much we use the brain that nature gave us. Today you have closed the war in Europe, so they say, and remember this war was a psychological movement of the system. There is no getting away from that. It was not brought on by the Kaiser; it was not brought on by President Wilson, nor by Lloyd George, or any of that crew. It was conditions. Revolution forced it, because men don't think. Now, this war, you were told, was a war for democracy. You went abroad to clean up the Kaiser. You made twenty-four multi-millionaires during that war besides those you had before, and for every millionaire, every high-class burglar that you made, you killed three Americans. Their bones are bleaching on the soil of Flanders. Now, then, the boys have come home, and they are trying to hypnotize them. But you can't do it. (Applause and laughter.) You can't do it. You must remember the pendulum is changing, my friends.

The force of the human mind has taken on a change entirely. That is the cause of the unrest. The servile working class issues in a servile political class in the nation and the world.

Today you can see the unrest, not in America, not in Mexico; it is all over the world. You don't get it because your papers are not permitted to convey it to you. What is the cause of this unrest? That is the question. What caused the uprising in Seattle? What caused the uprising of the railroad men all at once? What caused the uprising of the miners when the court issued the injunction? For a month they didn't go to work and dig any coal. But what was the cause? Because there is a new conception of human rights entering the brain of man. The Mayor may not see it; the Governor may not see it. Their thoughts are in another channel. But the man who sits on the tower knows before the thunder clap comes there must be a clash of clouds, and he sees the clouds clashing and gathering and he warns that the storm will break. So it is with us, my friends. The terrible Bolsheviki or I.W.W.'s or Reds can't stop it. (Applause.) Deportation won't stop it. It is the new era, the new manhood and womanhood coming to life, my friends. Has it stopped the agitation, deporting them over to Russia? Not at all. It has not stopped it. Now, here the other day over in England they were loading up a lot of ammunition on a ship to go over to Poland, and after a while the fellows found out that stuff was going over to Poland to fight the Bolsheviks. They took everything off the ship. They said, "Go to Hell; we are not going to furnish that." (Applause.) You don't get that in the papers. That wouldn't do for the American working man to get that in his skull. O, no; that is dangerous. The miners said, "We are not going to dig any coal; they can't run the ship without coal." So they didn't dig any, and they didn't get the stuff. Do you see the game?

Over there in Portugal they all went on a strike against the methods of Parliament over there. They are striking everywhere. They are striking over there in Ireland, and the Irish are raising Hell in America, too. (Laughter and applause.)

You see, it is a new fever, my friends, that is brought on. Men have come home to America from the war, and they have been told, "Now let's clean up the Kaiser in Germany and we will have democracy." Well, they came home. They didn't find any democracy but an increased autocracy at home. They came back, and therefore they have lined up and they are giving us the signals, the railroad men, the miners and all around. Now we are after the robbers, the Kaisers at home. There is the whole of it all in a nut-shell. All industrial Kaiserism has seen its day. They know it. You read after Schwab, the great steel magnate, what he says. *Them fellers* are beginning to take notice. They know their day is doomed. But they are going to give us a fight, and if they want to we are going to give them a fight, and we know how to raise Hell as well as they do. (Applause.)

(Here the speaker made reference to being in Pennsylvania and of her experiences there, but due to indistinctness it was impossible to report her remarks.)

I said to the boys, "They will put us in jail. They own the judges, but bye and bye we will be the judges, and we will put them on the scrap pile."

The boys got up in the automobile. They went with me. I said, "There is not doubt but what they will put us in jail, so let's get ready for the jail." They said, "Mother, you can't go to jail." I said, "All right; I will go; let's go." We went into Homestead.

For twenty-eight years the voice of labor was not raised in Homestead. They would not dare. They were shocked. America will be America. We went in and one of the boys got up to talk in an automobile. The Chief of Police came along. "Under arrest, sir." The next fellow got up. He says, "Under arrest, sir." Well, I thought it was time for me to speak. (Laughter.) I got up. The Chief of Police said: "You can't talk here, madam."

I said, "What is the matter with you? You have been dead twenty years. Don't you know God Almighty never made a woman that couldn't talk?" (Great applause.)

Well, they didn't think anybody dared to talk to the Chief of Police. I said to the Chief of Police: "I want to tell you something. Before I would be a lap-dog for those steel robbers . . . I would stand like an American under the flag as the revolutionist did before . . . (here the speaker's remarks were indistinguishable.)

All right; we went to jail. A thousand steel workers gathered around that jail inside of ten minutes — I want to show you your power — and the burghers run away. They got a pain in the stomach and went out the back door and went home. (Laughter and applause.)

The Chief of Police says, "If you will put up fifteen dollars bond we will let you out," and the boys came to the rescue all right. I didn't know there was eight thousand steel workers outside of that jail, and when we put up the bond the Chief of Police says, "You can't go out. It is dangerous to go out." I says, "Why?" He says, "There is a thousand men out there. We don't know what they are going to do." I said, "Can't you manage them?" He says, "Oh, God, no, you can't manage that bunch." (Applause.)

One time the fear of God got to their corporation heart. I am not referring to your officers here in Williamson. . . .

I slipped out of the door and I got up in the automobile and I said, "Three cheers for Uncle Sam!" and the whole sky trembled. "Three cheers for America! The greatest country in the world!" and they just yelled. I says, "Look here! We are going to take Pennsylvania away from the steel robbers and we are going to hand it over to Uncle Sam," and that crowd went wild with cheers. They realized who they were. Cowards! I got into the automobile and eight thousand men followed us down. I got out and I said, "Boys, everybody clear the streets and go home."

"Are you going to Pittsburgh, Mother?"

"Yes, I will be back tomorrow night."

In thirty minutes that whole town was cleared, nobody on the streets. There is a sample of the order of the workers, that if you leave them alone they are all right. But I want to tell you something. We could have spoke. The burgher was still sick. Ten thousand gathered around the jail tomorrow night, and we were to go again the following Monday. I left Pittsburgh and went up to Washington. I went into the Department of Justice. I saw the Attorney-General [A. Mitchell Palmer]. I went to the Attorney-General and said, "I have come here for the safety of the nation. The pulse of the nation is beating at fever heat. It is the duty of every man and woman, regardless of what position they occupy, to do their part to bring that pulse down as near normal as possible."

"I agree with you, madam," he said.

"Now," I said, "It is not the Bolsheviks; it is not the Reds; it is not the I.W.'s that America has got to fear. There is no danger from them. But the real enemy of the nation is the politicians that serve the interests before they do the honor of the nation."

I related the whole thing. He said, "Did they arrest you?" I said, "Why, I am used to that. I get lonesome when I am not arrested. (Laughter.) Certainly, I don't care for that."

I went away. The thing was stopped. We established an office there. They had an alley; we termed it "Rotten Alley"—the rottenest place in the country. We kept up the agitation until they cleaned the alley and put sanitary houses there for the people. Don't you think we did something.

I want to say here there wasn't a Y.M.C.A., there wasn't a minister, there wasn't a social settlement worker that took a hand to make conditions better for those workers. I am talking the truth. Why don't you ministers go out and preach as Christ did? You are afraid of the high-class burglars, and there are many. (Applause.) You are gambling in Christ's philosophy; but you are not carrying out Christ's doctrine, and I defy you to tell me so. How many of your ministers came with us in Cabin Creek when we cleaned out the professional murderers? There wasn't one of them. Not one of them. But one went up to Washington and asked the Immigration Commissioner to take down the bars so "I can bring in southern Italians." What do you think of that? He was working for Jesus — and if Jesus had ever let the bars down there would have been Hell. (Laughter.)

My friends, we are in the turning tide, and it is time for all to turn around, and you fellows here, I want to tell you twenty years ago I was here on this Norfolk and Western. I was at Pocahontas. We held a meeting. We were making a move. Now don't blame the Governor; don't blame the State officials; don't be forever charging up the government with the State officials. You yourselves are men of honor, high-principled men, and have stood and seen yourselves robbed of every ton of coal so much was taken out and professional murderers were hired to keep you in subjection, and you stood for it. Damn you, you are not fit to live under the flag. You took the food from off the table of the child. You paid professional murderers with that money you were robbed of, and then you never said a word. Not a single word out of you. You stood there like a lot of cowards going along chewing some scab tobacco (applause), and you have let yourselves be robbed by the mine owners. And why shouldn't he rob you? He has the right to do it if you let him do it. He is not in business for fun. He doesn't go into the mining business for fun. He goes in there to make all he can out of it, and no matter how he makes it he is going to do all he can. And you let him do it, and then you go about shaking your rotten head, not a thing inside. You call yourselves Americans. Let me tell you America need not feel proud of you.

We cleaned them up in the Kanawha, didn't we? When I went into the Kanawha River in 1900 these miners worked fourteen hours a day. They got forty cents for every ton of coal. That is all they got. Now, then, the children were in the mines; they saw no school; they never entered the school. They came out, threw themselves behind the stoves and there they lay until their mother picked them up to wash them.

Now we have changed that. We have taken the children out of the mines, out of the Hell holes; we have put them in the school rooms; we have made better citizens. They were able to go abroad and fight. They bought over seven million nine hundred thousand dollars in war bonds, the miners did. We did the same in Pennsylvania. We went in. "Do you go to school?"

"No, I never saw the school."

"How old are you?"

"I am just ten."

"How long have you been working here?"

"Oh, I have been here two years."

"Never went to school?"

"No, I never went to school."

"How long has Mikey been here?"

"Oh, Mikey, he is just seven. He came here eight months ago, I believe."

"Never went to school?"

"No, never went to school at all. And Joey fell down the chute and got killed."

"How old was Joey?"

"He was just eight."

Old Mother Jones was a frightful character! Good Lord, she is a horrible thing! What do you think of her? Oh, Old Mother Jones fought. I lined up four thousand women one night, took five thousand men out that no man could get near, from the crack team of Pennsylvania at two o'clock in the morning, with bayonets, and we didn't have a stick. All we had was a mop and a broom, and we mopped them up. (Applause.)

We brought the ten thousand men out and organized them. We brought out the striking men and organized them, and from that day to this these men have been getting along. I tell you, my friend, you have to remember, men, you have to remember, women, that America was not bought by dollars; that this great nation was bought by the blood of men who for seven long years marched the highways and byways. They bought it with their blood, and they left you and I the grandest emblem ever handed down the stairway of nations: the Stars and Stripes; and the first stripe in that flag is red, to guarantee that your liberty was fought for by blood and not by dollars; and they drove rotten royalty off. Today you are turning this great nation over to get hold of dollar thieves, and you will be worse than the slaves of ancient Rome if you don't wake up. Men, this is the time that calls on men. Lincoln said, "It is the time that tries men's souls." It is the time that tries men's hearts and brains. They who love the nation's honor, love her future and love the children that are yet to come know that the workers must be waked from their sleep.

I went to a meeting and the secretary of the steel workers went with me. He got up to speak. They took him. The next fellow got up; they took him. I got up. They arrested me. I wouldn't walk. They had to ride me. A big old Irish buck of a policeman said, "You will have to walk." "No, I can't." "Can you walk?" "No, I can't." "We will take you down to jail and lock you up behind the bars."

After a few minutes the chief came along.

"Mother Jones?"

"Yes, sir."

"There is some of the steel managers here want to speak to you."

"All right, let the gentlemen come in. I am sorry gentlemen, I haven't got chairs to give you." (Laughter.)

One good fellow says, "Now, Mother Jones, this agitation is dangerous. You know these are foreigners, mostly."

"Well, that is the reason I want to talk to them. I want to organize them into the United States as a Union so as to show them what the institution stands for."

"They don't understand English," he says.

I said, "I want to teach them English. We want them into the Union so they will understand."

"But you can't do that. This agitation won't do. Your radicalism has got to go."

I said, "Wait a minute, sir. You are one of the managers of the steel industry here?"

"Yes."

"Wasn't the first emigrant that landed on our shore an agitator?"

"Who was he?"

"Columbus. Didn't he agitate to get the money from the people of Spain? Didn't he agitate to get the crew, and crossed the ocean and discovered America for you and I?

"Wasn't Washington an agitator? Didn't the Mayflower bring over a shipful of agitators? Didn't we build a monument to them down there in Massachusetts. I want to ask you a question. Right today in and around the City of Pittsburgh I believe there has assembled as many as three hundred thousand people . . ." (At this point the words of the speaker were drowned by the starting of an automobile.) [Note: From other versions of this anecdote it seems likely that she referred to hundreds of thousands of people bowing the knee to Jesus—this was the Easter season.] "Jesus was an agitator, Mr. Manager. What in hell did you hang him for if he didn't hurt your pockets?" He never made a reply. He went away.

He was the manager of the steel works; he was the banker; he was the mayor; he was the judge; he was the chairman of the city council. Just think of that in America—and he had a stomach on him four miles long and two miles wide. (Laughter.) And when you looked at that fellow and compared him with people of toil it nauseated you.

We went into Pittsburgh.

"How old are you, Mother Jones?"

"I will be ninety the first day of May, 1920."

"Where do you live?"

"In the United States of America."

"What part?"

"Wherever there is a fight for justice and freedom against the wrong, and particularly right now against the steel men."

"Did you get permission to make a speech there?"

"Sure."

"Who did you get that permit from?"

"I got it a hundred and forty-three years ago from Patrick Henry, and Jefferson, and Adams, and Washington. That was before God Almighty ever thought of sending you here, and I have been using it for sixty or seventy years, and am going to use it as long as I am here."

I didn't have any lawyer; I didn't pay a penny to the court, nor a fine. I didn't pay any lawyer to hold me up. I had the goods on them.

I went to California. I went to San Francisco. I said to one of the wardens of the penitentiary, "It is very sad to see the faces of so many young people."

"Yes, it is." And he said, "We have 1850 more. Mother Jones, do you see that door? Every man that has crossed that door in the last year has been a young man."

I want young men to pay attention to that, and I want you women to pay attention to it, because a man is the reflex of the mother. Now, there is an indictment against us. There is an indictment against us, men, that every one that entered that door was a young man. There is something wrong in our social make-up, when we make criminals out of the youths, put them in jail, hire wardens and guards and pay them to take care of them and tax the people. Your whole system, my friends, is wrong. You have 120,000 lawyers in this country; you have got 133,000 in the penitentiary. I am not speaking of the local jails; I am speaking of the State and Federal prisons.

Do you ever stop to think why that is? You take the paper and see the murders and robberies. Don't you see, my friends, that there is something wrong in the social structure that must be removed to save the nation?

There is another phase to this that I want to call your attention to. The mother today is away from the home; she is out with a club. The child is raising itself. You go on the cars today, or go anywhere else, you let a lot of young boys and girls swing you aside. I saw a couple the other day knock down a man with crutches. They are not developed because the woman is out playing parlor politics instead of raising the children of the nation. I see this thing from all over. I have been down in Mexico, and have had talks with Madero and Huerta and with others, and have studied the thing, and there is a danger our nation is facing.

You talk of the woman's ballot. Let me say to you, my friends, I have got no confidence, and I will tell you why. I have been in Utah, where women and babies were turned out on the highways; I have been in Colorado, when two hundred men were bridled like dogs, put onto box cars, sent out of the State, and landed in the desert, walked twenty miles without a drink of water. I have seen it all. I am one myself that landed out there in the dead of night with five cents in my pocket — those human monsters. And never until the heart of woman changes can you get that human development in the hearts of men and women.

I have in my home the pictures of fifteen coffins filled with innocent babies murdered in Ludlow, and the women had had the ballot twenty-eight years. I have got some story. I don't belong to the women's club nor your social settlement gang. I belong to the fighting army of the working class that is going to break those chains, and, by God, we have got to do it. (Applause.)

Now, if you had the brains of a little boy out in Chicago you would be all right. A fellow came along one morning and asked a boy, "How far is it to the B. & O. Station, do you know?"

"Oh, yes, I know, sir. Go down to that corner, look up that way, you see a tower with a clock on it. It is the B. & O. Station."

"Thank you, my boy. Let me give you a ticket to a lecture tomorrow night. You are a fine boy. Let me give you a ticket to a lecture. I am going to lecture. I will show you the way to heaven."

The boy said, "How in Hell can you show me the way to heaven if you don't know the way to the B. & O. Station?" (Laughter.)

The boy used the gray matter in his head. He knew nobody could show him the way to heaven, and he had some sense and wisdom.

Nobody can show you the way to freedom, and I wouldn't free you tomorrow if I could. You would go begging. My patriotism is for this country to give to the nation in the day to come highly developed human citizens, men and women. We have the greatest nation in the world; but we have got a lot to do. You fellows have stood here; you have had gun men; you make the guns; they take them and they shoot you. You bring out the stuff to make the guns and go into the shops and make them, and when you get them made the other fellow takes them and hires professional murderers to keep you subdued. That is modern Christianity! I am one of those that believes in a different system. It is coming. In the coal regions we have sent the children to school and made better citizens of them. We have given the nation better citizens. But here you are with gunmen, robbed. I don't believe in asking the Governor for anything. He has got enough to do. The fight is yours and not the Governor's, and nobody has any respect for a beggar. You say, "We will see what the Governor can do," and the poor fellow can't sleep at nights. Damn you, why don't you Americans put a stop to this thing, clean up your rotten gunmen, put them out of business; let them go over to the Kaiser, or King George the Third, or some of those people that need them? We don't need them in America.

Another game they are playing. I read one of your papers yesterday morning, about the miners. I went through the mines in Pennsylvania, from Pittsburgh to Brownsville along the Monongahela River. I helped to organize them in the early days. We made no discrimination between the colored man and the white man. The colored man is not responsible for having a black skin. He didn't make that skin himself. Nature did it, and if you were born where the colored man's ancestors were born you would be black, too. He is not at fault. And let me say to you I have found more of the human in the black man than we give them credit for. I have had my experience in the civil war. In the New River when they were thrown out in the rain there wasn't a white man offered shelter. I walked twelve miles with a baby on my back, the mother with another in her arms, a little boy who hadn't seen eleven years, and had two years in the mines. We counted the ties for twelve miles in the rain with those babies, and a black mammy gave us shelter. I want to make a statement here. There is no race in the world that has made the progress the black race has made in the last fifty years. (Applause.) I know it. I have been to their colleges; I visit their homes. And I want to say, my friends, the newspaper man, this is not the time to sow poison. This is the time to sow harmony. If you are an American don't sow poison today in your press. Don't take the traitor's whip and use it to poison these workers against each other. I want to say to you newspaper men, "Arise like a man. Don't bother about the dollars the companies give you. If you can't make a living out of the paper, go out and work. Carry to your grave a sense of honor."

I understand there is a superintendent here has some goods on me. I want to tell the superintendent—I don't know who you are and I don't care (applause)—you are not the first I got wind of. I have walked over my ninetieth milestone. I have met every President of the United States since President Lincoln down. I have had talks with them with regard to conditions in certain places. I meet cabinet officers. I meet the Attorney-General. I meet them all. I have been in jail. I have been in bull pens, and my only crime was trying to get a better citizen for the nation in the days to come, to feed the child and send the child to school, so that he would be intellectually, physically and morally developed. I want to say to the superintendent here that it was not the type of a woman who mothered you who would get up and slander an old gray headed woman. I am used to that slander. You don't make me take back water. I am not of that type. I am a fighting American. (Applause.) You can't make me take back water. I don't know whether you are here or not. I don't care. You have got to realize this, that every man is a duplicate of his mother. If he has had a filthy rotten mother, he can't be anything else but the same. (Laughter.)

I go back to Palestine. I didn't see a welfare worker; I didn't see a church paper; I didn't see a club woman or a Sunday School teacher kneeling at the feet of Christ in Palestine. Not one. It was that woman cursed by economic wrong, when he gave her the right to a grander civilization and better economic age, it was she who knelt at His sacred feet and wiped them with her hair. It was on the hand of that woman Christ placed his hand. It was she who went to the tomb in early dawn. Mr. Superintendent, I am not afraid of your slimy tongue or slimy hand. Go to it. You can't bother Mother Jones. She is one of the type of American of the Revolution. I don't belong to the modern capitalists. I belong to the revolutionary age where men and women stood and fought. I belong to that type of woman who stood in Boston when they said: "If you don't stop working for the emancipation of slavery we will shoot you dead." The woman said, "Shoot now. We don't believe in actual slavery." And I say to you Mr. Superintendent, throw out your slime now. I don't live in industrial slavery, and by the God that reigns above I will fight you and every damned robber in America. (Great applause.) I am not afraid of God when I go up there, and if I am not afraid of Him I am not afraid of your slimy tongue.

(At this point the speaker read a newspaper article narrating treatment that had been given to strikers in Pennsylvania by the State Constabulary, but her remarks were so indistinct that they were unreportable.)

Now, men, I ask you to get together for the protection of the nation. I ask the mine owners for the safety of their industry, to let these men organize. You don't take a dollar of your money with you. Let your men organize. Discuss the affairs with them. I know and you know and we all know we don't agree all at once. You must remember you have crushed them. Let's make West Virginia the greatest state of the Union. Let's do away with the gunmen, professional murderers, and let the officers enforce the law, and not do as you have been doing. Use the force of law and let us make a great state and put a stop to this thing. I want to tell you men here, don't you let one of them professional murderers stay in this country. Get them out.

In Logan County during the war you were paying for twenty-five deputy sheriffs to keep Mother Jones out, and you said to the Government's representatives that the only way she could get in was over that hill, she could cut the wires and get in before you knew it. I want to say to the robbers of Logan that Mother Jones is going in, and she is not going to cut the wires, but she will cut hell out of you. (Applause.) We are going to clean up West Virginia. We are going to put her on the map in Washington as the leading state of civilization and Americanism, and we are going to take the flag that was bought by blood away from the blood-sucking robbers and murderers and we are going to raise it and live under the flag. We are going to take something out of your damned skulls and put something inside. We are going to fight for the Nation and State. Get out here in the fight. This is where the fight is. Not in politics. I don't care who you elect in Washington or in the State. We will civilize the people and we will get more money for you, and we will get shorter hours for you, and we will get better homes, and there will be no fellows coming to throw you out of houses, I will tell you that now.

Now, I want to pay my respects to your officers here. I want to say to the lawyers, "Get a move on you. There is 120,000 of you in this country and you put 133,000 in the jails and penitentiaries. Pretty good for you." (Laughter.)

There are four or five or six hundred men here. You are going to organize. Don't be afraid of anybody. Get a move on you. I am not going out of West Virginia, now, until I organize every working man in it. I am going to stay with you, and then when I get you all organized we are going to have a general dinner and we are going to invite the general manager to eat with us. Be good boys. Then we will go into Pennsylvania to the steel robbers. I am going back to this Norfolk and Western, and I am going into Logan. I am not going to take any guns. I am going in there with the America flag; that is my banner, and no rotten robber or gunman can meddle with me, because I will just raise Hell with him. (Applause.)

[Army Intelligence Records, RG 165, 10634/793/11, National Archives.]

Speech at a public meeting
Princeton, West Virginia

Seventy-five miles east of Williamson, West Virginia, through the coal valleys served by the Norfolk and Western Railroad, lies Princeton, West Virginia, where two months after her appearance in Williamson another of Mother Jones's speeches was recorded by a military intelligence agent. Only a few miles from Princeton stood the headquarters of the Baldwin-Felts Detective Agency, often the target of her attacks. In the heart of Baldwin-Felts country, with many of their detectives in the audience, she did not moderate her rhetoric. The length of the report, however, does not match the length of time of the speech, one and a half hours, as she described it in a letter to John H. Walker, 17 August 1920. By her reckoning, there were six to seven thousand people and "seven wagon-loads of Baldwin thugs."

§ § §

My friends, in all the ages of man the human race has trod, it has looked forward to that mighty power where men could enjoy the right to live as nature intended that they should.

We have not made millionaires, but we have made billionaires on both sides of the house. We have built up the greatest oligarchy that the world has ever known in history.

On the other side, we have the greatest slaves the world has ever known. There is no getting away from that.

I am not going to abuse the operators nor the bosses for their system. The mine owners and the steel robbers are all a product of the system of industry. It is just like an ulcer, and we have got to clean the ulcer.

(Hissing from the audience.)

God — they make me sick. They are worse than an old bunch of cats yelling for their mother.

Today, the world has turned over. The average man don't see it. The ministers don't see it and they don't see what is wrong. They cannot see it. But the man who sits in the tower and his fortune of clouds clash, knows there is a cause for those clouds clashing before the clap of thunder comes. All over the world is the clashing of clouds. In the office, the doctor don't pay attention to it. The man who watches the clouds don't understand it. People want to watch the battle.

I cannot understand why the student don't understand it. But he takes his life in his hands and goes out and operates it, but he don't own one product of it, and then the men say when there is an invention, "Why don't I get a fair share of this invention?" Well, it belongs to all the world to make the world happy, but you know the hog who is always grabbing the dollar. You have got to clean house on that person. You can do without dollars, but not without men and women to produce the wealth of the nation.

I am here today, and I may be criticized, but that don't worry me. The hired newspapers don't worry me. I am still Old Mother Jones, raising hell with the agitators. I don't go to sleep. I am not a suffragette, for I have been suffering all my life.

I am busy getting this working man to understand what belongs to him, and his power to take possession of it, and then we will use the ballot.

Get this into you! I don't bother about politics. I don't care. What I want is to get you solidified. If we don't give the bosses what they want, they will raise hell. The politicians know this very well. The question lies here in the ownership of my bread, and I cannot eat until I ask that brute for the right to eat. Now I have got to work or steal.

If you ever saw a policeman with a club in his hand, I want to ask you, did you ever see that policeman club a millionaire? But it is "Get out of here, damn you, go on to jail, damn you," if it is a working man.

You go to hear a minister, and the sky-pilots will yell "Hurrah for Jesus." They have a system.

Now, men, I want to tell you there is a rotten system. We have got to do away with it. I came into this State 21 years ago, when Mr. Houston referred me to Mr. Watson, and I went into his work. I met his men. The men who came to meet me were beat up by the guards that night, and why I wasn't beat up, I never have known. But they beat those men up and would have murdered them had I not been there. Twenty-five years ago, those men were under the rule of gunmen, crushed and robbed, and their children were being brought up that way. Two years ago, we went in and organized those fields, and no one was hurt. Schwab and Watson were the only ones hurt.

We are not fools or cowards, and we must demand the same rights in industry.

We had a fight in Colorado and I went from here. I left our men at Cabin Creek organized when I went away. When I came back there wasn't an organized man in it. I went up one morning facing the militia and the Baldwin-Felts gunmen and the mine owners, and I organized those men and we are organized today.

Their children are getting educated, and are going to better schools, and the miners get their money every two weeks. They are not paid in scrip, and can buy where they please.

I want you to understand that when I went up New River 20 years ago, I had to walk 19 miles of the night and count the railroad ties. I could go up there everywhere now and stay in a miner's house, and nobody comes to bother me.

We had some men murdered in Mingo. It is very sad. I do not like it. We had enough murder during the war.

To the millionaires that were made during the war, 25 or 26 for every millionaire that was made during the war, the bones of American youths are bleaching on the other side. They went over to destroy Kaisers, and they have come home to find more Kaisers than they ever found in Germany. Poor old Kaiser.

We have got it at home. They own the press, the pulpits and every avenue. You know that. You know that! (pointing to a gentleman in the audience) You know I am telling the truth. You have got on a white collar, and I know you are not a working man.

Our mission now is to clean up the monied Kaisers at home. You cannot do it by law, because they will declare the law unconstitutional.

I am out to do away with this, for it is a disgrace to the pages of American history. I am not a church worker or a Sunday School teacher, but I am one woman that will not stand to see the blood of babes lost.

By God, I am not afraid of the Baldwins. I licked hell out of them up Cabin Creek. They turned machine guns on us, but they didn't shoot me, damn them, by Jesus Christ.

I want you to see this. (Exhibiting a photograph.) Do you see it? It is a rapid firing gun, a machine gun. This went across seven states of this nation. The Baldwin-Felts—I am going to talk plain. I know that in a few miles from here is their headquarters. I know they are in this audience, but I don't take water when they are here; regardless of the Supreme Court, I am going to defend the honor of this nation.

Here is another one. (Exhibiting another picture.) They crossed seven states. There is the funeral of the fifteen babes that they murdered in Ludlow, Colorado. I have the pictures. Here are some more of the dead that were murdered by those machine guns. Here is some more of them.

(In a low, pathetic tone.) These were noble characters. They never violated laws. They were just asking for more bread to feed their children.

Here, I want to show you. Here is Baldwin-Felts men that left West Virginia and went to Colorado and put the State uniform on them.

Now, men, I don't care whether you are an operator, or who you are. Is that to the honor of the American nation in the days to come? When future generations read it, what will they think?

They took two machine guns across seven states. They sent the Baldwin-Felts thugs to murder babes in Colorado. The Baldwin-Felts are a product of a brutal system—the brute force development.

226

Now I am going to talk, men. I have come up against those things, perhaps, more than any other one person. I was up in Raleigh, and these Baldwin-Felts turned two machine guns on me—two here, and one here (pointing to each side of her head and her forehead). It was on Sunday and they put their guns against my head, but I took no back water, and they didn't shoot them. They didn't pull the trigger.

These Baldwin-Felts men, when they had that machine gun up there in Cabin Creek, turned that machine gun to murder thirty-six men that didn't even have a pen-knife, and were coming down to meet me. The men screamed, and I jumped out of the buggy and went up and put my hands on the guns and told them not to shoot a bullet. They told me to take my hands off and I told them I had a right to examine them. They made me wade a creek the next day up to here (pointing), but I came back and organized the men.

I am not like you, a pack of damn measly cowards. Damn you. They are so afraid of the operators—so afraid of the managers.

Did you ever watch a mule in a mine. If a mule turns his head around and the boss goes on, the mule takes to his hind legs and says "Get the Hell out of here."

Here is the thing. We are after this. This paper said today that I came in here and there is always trouble. Well, we are not after trouble. We are not looking for trouble. We are going to do this. The newspaper men are organized. The mine owners are organized and have their Union. The lawyers are in their Union. The sky-pilots are in their Union. The judiciary are in their Union. The merchants are in their Union. Don't you think we have the same rights they have? Now if you don't think so, we are going to show you, and we are not going to offer you or your press apology for doing it.

It is so sickening and nauseating to hear men talking today. We are moving.

I was along the Coast and after I had gone, the men sent for me to come back. Everywhere there is that unrest. Now, what is the cause of this unrest? It is injustice.

You cannot stop this thing with police. You cannot stop it with deportation, nor with the assassination of the press. It is the awakening. The night bell of the worker is ringing in the dawn of that new day. Hanging, deporting and shooting them is not going to stop it. There is nothing that will stop it but industrial and social justice.

That is the cause of the unrest. See what the miners are getting. They say, "You ought to see the fine homes they have." We don't howl at the fine homes they have got. They robbed us. We paid for their homes and we pay for our own.

They threw them out here at Matewan. Threw the children out—these

Baldwin-Felts. Suppose somebody would go to throw them out, they would have all of Baldwin-Felts taking care of them. These children, whose fathers created the wealth, are thrown out on the highways. A Baldwin-Felts —

(Here the speaker was interrupted.)

You muzzle that damn mug of yours up — if you don't, I will. I am not afraid of 9900 of you. I would clean you up just like a sewer rat.

The time is here. Don't beg the masters. Don't be afraid of them. If you want the organization you have got that right, and assert that right. Don't fear their bullets. How many Baldwin guards have they. I could take an army and clean the whole bunch out. Yes, I could. I could do it so quick you would be asleep while in the game.

The question lies here. The year is here. It is time to line up in our Union, to show no fear of no man. There is nobody that can come in to save you, unless you want to be saved. What would the black man do in slavery? Why is the Union so dangerous today? If it was safe in the days of Lincoln, who took the chattel slavery off your back, why shouldn't you, the industrial slave, take a lesson? He didn't shirk. That old black slave went like a man over to the Union.

When I got in town today, you were afraid to look at me. You bunch of damn cowards.

Look at that (showing another picture). This is the blood of the babes that stained the mountain. These babes struck for industrial freedom, for better homes, for better schools, for better manhood, for better womanhood, and you took their blood.

They put $60,000,000.00 into it. How long does it take to make $1,000,000.00? It takes 548 years to make one million dollars, working every day, seven days a week, and off the 4th of July every 25 years, at $5.00 per day.

These fellows put sixty million dollars in it, and they never worked a day in their lives. Where did they get it? They stole it out of the blood of the men they starved and shot.

I was put out of the State in the dead of night. They put me out of the State with five cents in my pocket. In the middle of the night. I got a document from the Governor [James H. Peabody] not to come back in the State. I asked the conductor on the Santa Fe train to take me and he said he would. I told him that I didn't have any money, and he said that didn't make any difference. The next morning I didn't wait to eat my breakfast. I sat down and wrote a letter. I said, "Mr. Governor: You notified your Gods of War by their bayonets to put me out of the state. You sent me a document not to return to the State. I want to notify you that you don't own this State. If I break the law, the civil courts that Washington and Jefferson established will deal with me. But you have no authority. After eight hours, I am right back in four blocks of your office. What in the hell are you going to do about it?"

He is dead now, and I don't know whether he went up or down, and I don't care a damn which.

They call us agitators. If it wasn't for us, we would be in the stone ages. It is the fearless convictions of honest men and women that fear no slander of the press.

I want to say to you in the crucial hour of a trying day, America stands with her arms open to her children. Where will you go? Come with me to old America. Will you come back to the days of Patrick Henry, Jefferson, Lincoln, or will you stay with Schwab and Rockefeller? Which are you going to take? That freedom was not purchased by dollars. It was purchased by the blood of men who believed in justice, and for which seven long years they fought. They did get discouraged sometimes, but they said they would go back. They drove them from the American shore, and it is up to you to say whether you are going to bring back the old America, and not let Baldwin-Felts run it.

I have gone in the factories. I have walked in cotton factories with little children that hadn't seen their sixth year, working 14 hours a day and eating corn bread. I worked in there until I got the information that appointed the Child Labor Law. I fought it alone. I took children out of the factories in Philadelphia and marched them through to New Jersey. I had to bear the slimy burden of the corporation wrecks. But I succeeded. When I came here, little boys worked in the mines, and went home broke at night.

You build jails and penitentiaries. You have today in the Federal and State penitentiaries and jails, 133,000. I want to ask you men, regardless of what position you hold, if there isn't something wrong in our nation when young men are filling the jails and penitentiaries.

I am going to say to Baldwin-Felts. You had just as well get a move on you in your damnable business, because we are not going to give up West Virginia until it is all organized.

I am going to pay McDowell County a visit. They can put me in jail if they want to, but I don't care, as I can always command more respect when I am in jail.

I knew young Al Baldwin 20 years ago. There were two Baldwins that I knew well, and if anything went wrong, they would come and tell me. One time when I went to Pocahontas the woman didn't want to give me a room in the hotel, and young Baldwin said, "Yes, you will, give her my room." I shall always appreciate those two men, but I want to tell you, since you became murderers—since these men are being robbed out of the coal they dig, so that we and our children have been deprived of the necessaries of life, and out of the money of which you are robbed, these

Baldwin-Felts men are paid. That wasn't done in the slavery days. The black slaves were fed and protected, and if they were sick, they were taken care of.

When you have as much American blood in you as the mule has, then you will be a man. I am ashamed of you. You miserable cowards. When you — you miserly un-American fellows making your living this way. You are staying where your brothers were murdered. You have to be a man to protect your brothers.

By God, I am not afraid of the Baldwin-Felts thugs. I would tell Uncle Sam straight that if he doesn't clean them up, we will.

In 28 years the voice from labor was never raised. I said to the boys, we have got to go in, and they told me they would put me in jail, and I told them that we built the jails and we had a perfect right to be put in them. Three of us went in to the steel workers. One fellow got up and told us that we were under arrest and told us to get out. I said, "Don't you know that God Almighty never made a man that knew how to coop a woman up." They didn't know that anyone in the world would dare talk to the Chief of Police like that.

We were taken up to jail and 8,000 steel workers gathered around the jail in about eight hours. There were 8,000 men there. I told them to hell with old Carnegie and all the robbers of the country. I went up to headquarters at Boston and told them not to fear the Bolsheviks, the Reds or the I. W. W. because the trouble was that the police were serving the capitalists.

But I don't bother with them fellows. I talk to Uncle Sam.

It is up to you men not to be afraid of the newspaper men. Stand up like Americans. Join the union. Do you belong to the United Mine Workers? Say, "Yes, I do." Put on your hat like an American.

(Pointing to a reporter.) He can write this in his paper tomorrow morning, that from the hair of my head down to my toes, I am a Bolshevik, and I want the world to know it. Tell the Senate and the Congress about it. The White House already knows it.

Yes, I took a whole lot of Bolshevik stuff and sold it, and the money I got out of it, I sent to the men in jail. Uncle Sam knows everything I do. No secret service man had a damn thing to tell on me, because I got ahead of him. He is playing the lap-dog, while I am playing American Womanhood.

The Chief of Police sent nine of his men, and they decided to let us talk, because they were afraid I would go to Washington, and I told him I understood he was there. I told him to take down every statement I made, and send it to the Supreme Court tonight so they could get it in the morning.

I am American enough to fight for my countrymen. You are fighting for the interest of the steel robbers. That is what you are doing, Mr. Chief of Police. I am an American from my head to my toe, and if Bolshevism come to America, then I am a Bolshevik.

The money you are robbed of to pay the Baldwin-Felts men must come back to your pockets. It must nourish and feed your child. I want to say to you, my friends, that we will stay with you. Some day this question will come up and it will be settled. In that grand array to come, a man who will stand up in these brutal days, when these murdered babes from the altar of your Gods, is in that great age to come, that we are so near now, which is breaking in the sunlight, you will get your reward. The voice of freedom is coming across the world's waters. The dawn is breaking.

The paper made a grand mistake. I walked over my 90th milestone on the 1st day of May. I spent seven months in a military prison. I was arrested and locked up behind iron bars in Duquesne. The warden told me that some manager of the steel workers was to see me, and one fellow said, "Mother Jones, if you could just speak, the good you could do, but the agitation is dangerous." That is the way of you today. The man that discovered America was an agitator. Did it do any harm? He was an agitator, and a pretty rapid one too. Washington and Jefferson were agitators, and Lincoln too.

They have no answer to give. The bosses have no answer to give when you stand up and say that you are an American, and you are not going to enslave me. Join the Union and don't be afraid of anybody. This is our fight; we have got to fight them. We have got to save them and we have got to educate them.

I am going to McDowell County, and they can put me in jail, but you know a woman 90 years old in jail will scare the hell out of them.

During the steel strike, I got a telegram from the miners in Europe, and they said, "We send you greetings. You are not asking for near as much as we now have, even though you live in America." That is in England. When they went to load a steamer to take ammunition and stuff over to Poland, the men found out that it was to fight the Bolsheviks, and they took it off, and the men said, "We don't steer your ship."

[Army Intelligence Report, 15 August 1920, RG 165, 10634/793/11, National Archives.]

Speech at a meeting
of the Pan-American Federation of Labor
Mexico City

Early in January 1921, Mother Jones left West Virginia to travel to Mexico City where she was to be the guest of the Mexican government during the meeting of the Pan American Federation of Labor. It was the high point of recognition of her role in the labor movement. As she approached the capital, delegations of workers brought flowers to her special train, and on her arrival the authorities conducted her to her apartment and placed a car and chauffeur at her disposal. She was a principal speaker at one of the meetings of the federation, and participated in various official functions, such as receptions at the presidential palace and the American embassy for the visiting labor leaders.

Since October 1911, when she had talked with President Francisco Madero in the early days of the revolution, Mexico had endured the devastation of civil war as various factions contended for the control of the government. By 1921 a new president, Alvaro Obregón, was beginning to bring about stability and to carry out the goals of the Constitution of 1917. Article 123 of that document embodied many of the ideals that had been advocated by the revolutionaries whose cause Mother Jones had taken up in 1906–11: the eight-hour day, the right to organize and bargain collectively, a guaranteed minimum wage, equal pay for equal work regardless of nationality or sex, social security, and public health and welfare programs. Obregón's minister of agriculture was Antonio I. Villarreal, one of the leaders of the Partido Liberal who had been imprisoned in the United States in 1907 and for whose defense Mother Jones had fought so long. It was probably he who arranged the invitation to Mother Jones to be the guest of the nation.

The Pan American Federation of Labor was one of many manifestations of hemispheric unity in the early twentieth century. Prompted by John Murray of California and Santiago Iglesias of Puerto Rico, Samuel Gompers of the American Federation of Labor created the framework for the organization, which held its founding convention in Laredo, Texas, in November 1918. Gompers had originally envisioned it as a counterpoise for the expansion of American business and industrial interests in Latin America. He and other labor leaders found it a useful vehicle for exerting influence on Woodrow Wilson's policies toward the area, espe-

cially Mexico. Theirs may have been the decisive voices in causing the United States to recognize the Obregón government, whose strongest institutional support was the Confederación Regional Obrera Mexicana. It was natural that the CROM should be the host organization and Mexico City the site for the third convention of the international body.

In her address, Mother Jones hailed the triumphant march of labor to greater heights in the two nations, in the hemisphere, and across the world. She saw the recently concluded world war as a tragic means of educating workers everywhere to realize and assert their power.

§ § §

Mr. Chairman and fellow workers: The speaker said he was presenting Mother Jones, of the Mine Workers. It is true I have given most of my time to the miners' organization, but I don't belong to any individual organization or creed; I belong to the workers wherever they are in slavery, regardless of what their trade or craft may be. I want to say this is something I did not expect was coming to my life while here below—the privilege of speaking and attending a congress where all the elements representing the opportunities of the Western Hemisphere are here to discuss in this meeting the breaking of the chains and bringing in the light that would never darken the world again. We are today passing through a crisis. Many people say it was the war, but let me say to you, my friends, while the war was tragic, it has done a most wonderful work for the world. Bear this in mind, it has awakened the workers in every corner of the earth. From every corner today forces are moving and touching the human heart to all the shores of the world waters, my friends, and if you only read the news and take up the papers, you can see the pulse beating.

It is a great age; it is a great time to live in. Some people call us Bolsheviks, some call us I.W.W.'s, some call us Reds. Well, what of it! If we are Red, then Jefferson was Red, and a whole lot of those people that have turned the world upside down were Red. Do you know that? What is the distinction? What is socialism? What is Bolshevism? What is I.W.W? Why, my friends, it is the soul of the unrest that is back of all these movements. Who can satisfy a hungry stomach with a small bite of food? You have got to have the food before the stomach gets satisfied. You can't satisfy the people today with what they had two or four years ago. They are thinking. Professors wonder what is the matter. Newspapers wonder what is the matter. The churches wonder what is the matter. They are all coming to save us, every one coming along. They have got a dose of medicine for us. Don't you understand what is the matter today? The man up in the tower, watching the clouds rumbling all over, knows that before there is a crash of thunder there are clouds everywhere, and so it is today, my friends. There is unrest everywhere, and it is not only in the United

States, but all over the Western Continent—it has reached everywhere. The reason is because the world's workers have produced the enormous wealth of the world, and others have taken it; therefore, when the war was over, soldiers began to ask what was this war for, and why did we give up our wives and join the army. There is discontent everywhere, no matter where you go.

The truth is reaching the hearts of the workers the world over, and we are in that age; we are in that day; as the shepherds were back in Jerusalem, when they were guiding the sheep along to care for them and see that they were fed. We are doing the same, we are developing the brain and heart of the workers and we are feeding them, my friends, on a logical line; we are not feeding them with stars rotating up in the sky, but with logic of today, and you have got to realize one thing—that we are never going back to the conditions we have left behind. We are in a new age when new conditions face us, and all these things we have got, we are going to keep. Now let me say to you, I know what is your inheritance. I have made a study of all those things.

One time I thought this thing was going too slow for me, and again it was going too fast. I have seen children murdered on the altar of gold. I used to get discontented. We licked the high-class burglars, and the boys wanted to give me something, and I asked them to give me a horse and buggy and a good harness and I would go out and circulate the literature among the farmers, and the boys got a horse, an old blind horse. They got him very cheap and I got my horse harnessed, loaded up with food and got a friend to go with me, and we went through the country and circulated literature, and I thought we were going to save the world overnight. Then we moved in another way, and so I got my crowd with me. We realize this, my friends, that you have got to educate the workers in the economic field.

Let me say this to you: There is no army of churches, no foreign home missions; there are no welfare workers; Y.M.C.A.'s; no Salvation Armies, that have done the Christian teaching for the betterment of the nations and of humanity that the trade union movement has done. It has made the enemies of capitalism on every side, but it has moved on regardless. It has faced the jails, it has been subjected to calumny and slander, but it has moved onward and upward and forward. Do not divide your forces. Bring in new blood and get together. Get together on the economic field. Now we have courts in America that put us in jail, but we get out again and they can't muzzle us, and we keep on talking and go on educating. We are not afraid of courts. The courts are what we make them, and when we get advanced enough we will tell Mr. Judge to take a back seat. But we haven't got that far yet, and this delegation is having a mighty mission to fulfill. We have got to bear this in mind. Why, all the world is centered on this congress, from all over the world they are looking at us here today.

Now, why am I in Mexico? I have perhaps to explain to you I was here when President Madero was elected and a very prominent Mexican in New York who had to leave his country came to talk matters over with me for two hours. He said, "I wish you would go to Mexico." I took it up with the President of the Miners, I got one of the metal miners and one of the coal miners to come with me, and we came down here. We spent some time at the Palace. We spent a couple of hours with President Madero, and I want to make a statement here; I never in all my life came in contact with a more noble human character than I consider President Madero to have been. I sat over two long hours with him, and he said to me, "Mother: Come down to Mexico; organize the miners, put them in the miners' union." But I said: "Mr. President, if I come down and do what I can at Cananea, the big American interests in all those mines will arrest me and put me in jail." President Madero said: "If they do I will come down and make them take you out."

Now this is the situation today, my friends, and you are marching on. No man living would ever have thought four years ago that you in Mexico would be where you are today. You are beginning to pave the way for a stable government of the people, and I want to ask you to do all you can to render all the faithful assistance you can to the noble men you have got in office now. I have studied them all, my friends, and there will not be an invasion. I want to tell you that now there will be no invasion, that Mexico will be yours. This congress will stop that invasion, if it does nothing else, and the oil trust nor none of these will come to capture this nation. I know that; I know what I am talking about, so it is up to you to stand like men; go on with the message from this congress to your people. I want to tell you something: Stop this thing of throwing stones at each other; it is a horrible disease today in the labor movement. The capitalists are doing their noble work, as they look at it. They are poisoning one against the other. Now the world was not made in a day. Mr. Tobin, Mr. Gompers nor Mr. Nobody else has not got the making of this thing. It is the workers themselves, and when the workers solidify the world will rise, my friends. As long as you permit the capitalists to keep you divided, calling each other names and poisoning each other, you are going to make no progress. Cut out this nonsense; get down to business and move along with the army. Now we have got a state over in West Virginia, the most remarkable state in the union, that does some remarkable fighting. We use the force of law wherever we can, but if we are forced to use the law of force, if the other fellow makes us, we do; we don't offer any apologies for doing it. We all have a gun, and we know how to use it; we don't do anything with it unless we are called on to do so. We are moving on, and we have better homes for our children, better playgrounds and we have time to educate and agitate.

We are united against a common enemy. Now we must stop all this ramble, every day going along, every day battling wherever we are as we go along. We are moving, my friends, and are going to keep that battle on and we can say to you miners of Mexico and the miners of the United States: "Unite." I speak so much about the miners, because mining is the basic industry and the miners are the federated army in the labor movement in America. I have learned them, and for that reason I remain with them. Again I am going to tell you, no good is coming from uplift. It is not coming from the top, it is coming from here, coming from below. It is doing this all over the world, and so you got this start two years ago. It has been traveling slowly around the world, and now it has reached the Western Hemisphere. It is the cause of human freedom, and we are prepared to enter the gate when that gate opens and the sun shines in that day that is coming.

There are many ideas brought in by capitalism to fool the workers. Capitalism knows the game thoroughly, for it has the time and the means to build the machine, and we don't. Now, I have gone over the country, I have been down here in Mexico and up in Canada and over in Europe and as for taking back water, the guns of capitalism can't make me do it. I fight for your children, and your women are to blame for lots of wrongs. I am going to be honest with you. If you raise the child properly we would have no murders and we would not have to resent war, because nobody would go to war. There would be more time in the home to develop the coming generations, plant the human feeling in their breast and show them their duty. If they spend their time in clubs, suffragette and welfare work, we will be our own welfare workers. We want the right of happy homes. We want a noble mankind, a great womankind; that is what we are after.

The American Federation of Labor can do more to advance the nations, to plant Christianity in the bosom of mankind than all the churches and all your institutions. I have had some experience, men and women; I don't think there is anyone else that has had to go through more than I have. I know that this institution of the American Federation of Labor is the one institution that is leading the nations upward and onward to the final goal. This may be my last visit to Mexico. My days are closing in. I want to say to you, young men, there is a mighty task to perform. The world never before had such a mission for you as it has now. It has granted that opening for you to enter a new civilization that will make the millions and thousands happier. I stand here pleading with you as one of you to stand together on the solid ground for industrial freedom for yourself. You are here for a purpose. You are here to make your home better. And in the days to come when you have departed the loved ones left behind will come over your grave and with the birds above they will sing that beautiful song: "He did well; he did his work for us; because of what he did we are here to kiss the ground he is in." Oh, men, the stories I could tell you and this convention gives me new life. There is sitting behind me a young man (Fred Mooney, of West Virginia) who was nothing but a child when I first saw him. He spent fourteen years in the subterranean caverns of earth for twenty-five cents from his master for fourteen hours a day in the darkness. He dug the wealth and he sent it out. Today he is the secretary of nearly 70,000 miners. I schooled them; I educated them; I used to give them Bolshevist literature long ago; yes, I used to give them Bolshevist literature. We didn't call it that then, I didn't name it for you.

My friends, you are here to unlock the doors to the coming age. I knew that poor man sitting there before me when he went barefoot in West Virginia many years ago. I have known Mr. Tobin many long years. I have known this man here (James Lord) with the red head, since he was a kid. I have hammered him often. I know them all, but I want to say to you here that you could not get better, truer men than they are. I want you to shake hands and when you adjourn this mighty convention, the greatest event in history, I don't think in all the ages of time there ever was a gathering as important as this is. It will go down in the ages of history. Unite your forces, stand shoulder to shoulder. Come up here and shake hands with Mr. Gompers. Shake hands with the boys. We are going on; we are going on for a better world; we are going to carry the message to Central and South America. We are going to carry the message that will conquer the common foe of humanity. We are going to take over the industry. We are going to take the money from the robbers that have robbed; yes, we are going to do business. I am trying to speak clearly. We have got the greatest, finest organization, but the robbers are trying to get the wealth, and we want to help you stand together. Some men have been thinking that my days are counted. I have more fight in me than ten years ago. You, South Americans, particularly, stand together now solidly. I am coming down to South America some day. Keep your heads level and build your organizations. Stand together, let nothing divide you, and make every part of this hemisphere a fit place for men and women and children to live in.

[*Proceedings of the Third Congress of the Pan American Federation of Labor* (Washington, 1921), pp. 72–76.]

Speech at a convention
of the United Mine Workers of America
Indianapolis, Indiana

After her Pan American Federation of Labor speech, Mother Jones's hosts urged her to stay on in Mexico, but she made a flying trip back to West Virginia before again occupying the residence they had reserved for her. From April to July 1921 she made her headquarters in Mexico City, speaking at Orizaba and visiting with her friend, Felipe Carillo Puerto, the governor of Yucatan. Her health, however, was not good, a fact which she attributed to the altitude in Mexico City. By the end of July she was back in Charleston, West Virginia, where the campaign to organize the southern counties was approaching a bloody climax.

For twenty years Mother Jones had worked intermittently in West Virginia and had seen the number of union men grow past sixty thousand; only in the far southern counties were there no unionized mines. Yet the timing of the UMWA drive for assaulting this last stronghold of the enemy was unfortunate. The nation had been through a sharp postwar economic crisis and the European market for coal was fast disappearing. The operators of nonunion mines in the southern counties were literally ready to fight to retain their economic advantage of nonunion labor in pursuit of the dwindling market. In Sheriff Don Chafin, the political boss of Logan County, they had a willing ally who deputized hundreds of men to keep out all agitators. During the organizing drive of the past eighteen months, many violent incidents had occurred between miners and armed guards, but the pitched battle of Blair Mountain between several thousand men on both sides brought about intervention by federal troops under Brigadier General Harry Bandholtz, with air support under the direction of Brigadier General William Mitchell.

The spark which set off the mass violence was the murder of Sid Hatfield, the prounion chief of police in Matewan, Mingo County, by armed guards in retaliation for his part in the killing of seven Baldwin-Felts guards in a street fight in Matewan. Hatfield's murder on 1 August, shortly after Mother Jones's return from Mexico, brought feelings to a fever pitch, which she encouraged by an emotional speech on the capitol grounds in Charleston on 7 August. On 20 August miners by the thousands began to assemble at Lens Creek and to organize an army, complete with a supporting medical unit, to march into Logan County, free the numerous union prisoners in Sheriff Don Chafin's jail, and retaliate for Hatfield's murder.

Governor Ephraim F. Morgan sent frantic calls to Washington for assistance. Since the national guard had been called into service during the war, he had no troops at his command. He called for volunteer companies to be set up, but he despaired of restoring order unless he had federal assistance. General Bandholtz was sent without troops from Washington to assess the situation.

On 24 August Mother Jones went to Marmet, where the army had halted. The next day she, General Bandholtz, and President Frank Keeney of District 17 tried to stop the forward movement of the army. In her speech to the miners, she read a telegram, later proved spurious, from President Warren G. Harding promising to use his good offices to end the armed guard system. District 17 officers continued with some success over the next two days to persuade many of the armed miners to return to their homes, but some refused to disband. Both General Bandholtz and Mother Jones left for Washington, assuming that the crisis was over. Sheriff Chafin precipitated a new crisis by sending police to arrest some union men; when shots were exchanged the disbanding army quickly reassembled and resumed its march toward Logan County. Two days of heavy fighting at Blair Mountain involved thousands of men on both sides, many of them former servicemen; the total casualties are unknown. Only when General Bandholtz brought in federal troops were the contending forces disarmed. Some five hundred union men were later indicted for various crimes, including murder and treason.

When she addressed the 1921 convention of the UMWA, Mother Jones could not have known, though she may have suspected, that her twenty-year-old dream of organizing West Virginia was over. She spoke hopefully of further progress, but UMWA membership had peaked in the state. The economic trends already in motion, the unfavorable climate of opinion created by the recent violence, the indictments of the district officers, the policies of the international union under the leadership of John L. Lewis—all these were working to undo the past years of planning and work. By the end of the decade, there would be less than a thousand UMWA members in the entire state.

§   §   §

Mr. Chairman and Delegates: I have been watching you from a distance, and you have been wasting a whole lot of time and money. I want you to stop it.

All along the ages, away back in the dusty past, the miners started their revolt. It didn't come in this century, it came along in the cradle of the race when they were ground by superstition and wrong. Out of that they

239

have moved onward and upward all the ages against all the courts, against all the guns, in every nation they have moved onward and upward to where they are today, and their effort has always been to get better homes for their children and for those who were to follow them.

I have just come up from West Virginia. I left Williamson last Friday and came into Charleston. I was doing a little business around there looking after things. We have never gotten down to the core of the trouble that exists there today. Newspapers have flashed it, magazines have contained articles, but they were by people who did not understand the background of the great struggle.

In 1900 I was sent into West Virginia; I went there and worked for a while, taking a survey of the situation. At that time men were working fourteen hours a day and they did not get their coal weighed. They weighed a ton of coal with an aching back, dug it, loaded it and didn't know how much was in it. However, we have moved onward and today they get their checkweighman, they get paid in cash instead of in company money as they used to; but that wasn't brought around in an easy manner, it wasn't brought around arguing on the floor.

I walked nine miles one night with John H. Walker in the New River field after we had organized an army of slaves who were afraid to call their souls their own. We didn't dare sleep in a miner's house; if we did the family would be thrown out in the morning and would have no place to go. We walked nine miles before we got shelter. When we began to organize we had to pay the men's dues, they had no money.

At one time some of the organizers came down from Charleston, went up to New Hope and held a meeting. They had about fourteen people at the meeting. The next morning the conductor on the train told me the organizers went up on a train to Charleston. I told Walker to bill a meeting at New Hope for the next night and I would come up myself. He said we could not bill meetings unless the national told us to. I said: "I am the national now and I tell you to bill that meeting." He did.

When we got to the meeting there was a handful of miners there and the general manager, clerks and all the pencil pushers they could get. I don't know but there were a few organizers for Jesus there, too. We talked but said nothing about organizing. Later that night a knock came on the door where I was staying and a bunch of the boys were outside. They asked if I would organize them. I said I would. They told me they hadn't any money. Walker said the national was not in favor of organizing, they wanted us only to agitate. I said: "John, I am running the business here, not the national; they are up in Indianapolis and I am in New Hope. I am going to organize those fellows and if the national finds any fault with you, put it on me — I can fight the national as well as I can the company if they are not doing right."

240

Thirteen of them came into the house. John was there. I said: "Boys, each one of you make yourself an organizer, go at night and get your brothers together." I went away and two weeks later I was coming to Glen Jean to get the train and the boys met me. They said they could pay for their charter then because they had organized and over a thousand had come into the union. We went up the mountains again. I requested the national organizer go up there and bill a meeting for me, Walker had gone home. The organizer came down and I asked him if he had billed the meeting. He said he had not. I asked him: "What's the matter?" He said: "The superintendent chased me down." "Why didn't you chase him up?" I asked. "Well," he said, "I didn't come over here to get killed." "Then why did you take the miners' money if you won't face the guns?"

I took a couple of young fellows and went up there. I don't care for these old fellows because they are worn out. I went up to Thayer on Saturday night and stayed there. The next morning I lined up ten or twelve trapper boys and we went up the mountain. We walked six miles. I sent the boys down to the town to tell the men to come up to the meeting. I told him to ask the general manager and the superintendent to come up, that we wanted to see them, and they came. The men sat down and talked. The company sent up one of their lap dogs, a colored fellow, and he rode a horse. The boys tipped me off to who he was. I told him to come over too, and he did.

I made him sit down at my feet and said to him: "Now I want to put everything in your skull the superintendent wants and you take it home to him." He wanted to get away but I held him by the hair. We organized every single man there that afternoon and from that day on they remained organized. A couple of years ago I went up there and the superintendent asked me to come into his office and sit down. I think they go along nicely together. You have got to use judgment and diplomacy today. This is a diplomatic age politically, religiously and industrially. You must use common sense and judgment.

I had to go again to one of Paddy Rend's mines. He lived in Danville, Ill. We had the place organized but the boss told me the fellows wouldn't take the jobs he gave them. There were four of them getting $10 a week. I went down one night and waited until the secretary made his report. I asked what the $10 was for. He said those fellows were on strike. I said: "But the mine is open; everybody can get work. They can get work and are not going to get ten cents. You fellows can not rob the miners while I am around. You fellows go to work or I'll clean hell out of you!" We stopped that swindling and holdup, and those who didn't go to work got out.

When we began organizing in 1903 the battle royal began. The companies began to enlist gunmen. I went up the Stanaford Mountain and held a meeting with the men. There wasn't a more law-abiding body of men in America than those men were. While they were on strike the court issued an injunction forbidding them to go near the mines. They didn't. I held a meeting that night, went away and next morning a deputy sheriff went up to arrest those men. He had a warrant for them. The boys said: "We have broken no law; we have violated no rules; you can not arrest us." They notified him to get out of town and he went away. They sent for me and I went up. I asked why they didn't let him arrest the men. They said they hadn't done anything and I told them that was the reason they should have surrendered to the law.

That very night in 1903, the 25th day of February, those boys went to bed in their peaceful mining town. They had built their own school house and were sending their children to school. They were law-abiding citizens. While they slept in their peaceful homes bullets went through the walls and several of them were murdered in their beds. I went up next morning on an early train. The agent said they had trouble on Stanaford Mountain, that he heard going over the wires news that some people were hurt. I turned in my ticket, went out and called a couple of the boys. We went up the mountain on the next train and found those men dead in their homes, lying on mattresses wet with their blood and the bullet holes through the walls.

I want to clear this thing up, for it has never been cleared up. I saw there a picture that will forever be a disgrace to American institutions. There were men who had been working fourteen hours a day, who had broken no law, murdered in their peaceful homes. Nobody was punished for those murders.

We then went into the Fairmont Field. One night while holding a meeting in New England I paid a fellow to go and circulate bills. We held a meeting on the sand lot. The United States marshal and the deputy marshal were there. When the meeting closed I went away. A little boy told me to get into a buggy and he would drive me to the interurban. When I was going over a dark bridge there were six or eight fellows at the company's store. One fellow asked me where I was going. I said I was going into Fairmont and asked him to take care of the slaves because if he didn't I would have to hunt a job for him next day.

Barney Rice, Joe Poggiani and another fellow from Indiana were there. I was hoping the boys would come, because those fellows could throw me into the river and say I committed suicide. Barney Rice came out calling: "Police! Police!" I asked what was the matter and he said they were killing Joe, that he was alone in the dark bridge and he had broken no law. The interurban turned the corner and I told those fellows to hurry. I ran into the bridge and the fellows who had attacked Joe had run away. He had a deep cut in his head. I dragged Joe out and bound his head up with a piece of my underskirt. I asked the interurban men to hurry him into Fairmont and they did.

Next day the boys came down to see Joe. There wasn't a detective or a gunman that didn't run out of the city that night. Every one of the cowards left. I had about 150 men at the hotel, and the general manager asked: "Mother, what can I do for the boys?" I said: "Send up a couple of drinks for the boys, because they need it." There wasn't a gunman stayed in town that night. Even the United States marshal got scared, but nobody was hurt except Joe.

That was the start of this thing. Later on I went into Wise County. Old Dad Haddow of Iowa was with me. The colored people gave us their church for the meeting. The gunmen told us we couldn't hold a meeting there and we went out and held it at the corner of two roads. I said: "Dad, have you a pistol?" He said he had and I told him he had better show it. I told him the law said if the pistol was exposed, even a little bit, he would be safe, but if he had it concealed he might be arrested. Those hounds got around Dad and nearly tore him to pieces. They took him to the office and those fellows came, the general manager with them, and said: "Mother Jones, what is the matter? I am astonished, really astonished! The idea of you going into the house of God with a pistol!" "Don't you know," I said, "that I know God never comes around a place like this — he stays a damned long way from a place like this."

The gunmen were there and I was arrested. The old man was nearly scared to death. They fined him $25. He didn't want to pay it, he wanted to appeal, but I said we would pay it. I paid the $25. That evening one of the men who had been in the crowd came to me and said: "Mother Jones, I want to pay my respects to you for paying that $25 as quick as you did. The scheme was to lock you up and burn you in the coke ovens." And you women raised those brutes! It is horrible to think of.

We battled on and here and there we organized and got better conditions for the men. In 1902 a board member and your President, John L. Lewis, went up Kelly Creek. They chased him out. I was determined to organize that Creek. I went to the town at Eastbrook and in the morning went across by ferry, then walked six miles. The company was paying two deputies to keep me out but we got into the mining camp. I told a merchant my business and he said we could use a hall over his building. I rented that for four months. I took the men down and organized them that night. The company suspected there was something wrong and the next day discharged forty of the men. Then the drivers got restless and came out. I was determined to finish the job and on Sunday went through the camp with the boys marching. I told them to ask every fellow they saw sitting on the steps of the houses to be an American and come down. They came.

We told Jack Roan, the manager, who had come over from Columbus that day, to come out. He didn't come out. In front of the hotel were two fellows and one said: "I would like to have a rope and hang that old woman to a tree." Another one said: "And I would like to pull the rope." After the meeting the boys pointed those men out. I stood with my back to a tree and said: "You said you would like to hang the old woman. Here is the old woman and the tree, where is your rope?" They ran away because there were more than a thousand men at the place. Since that day there has been no strike and no disturbance, but there is one thing we failed to do — we did not educate them thoroughly, because bringing them into the union was only the kindergarten; we should have educated them after they came in but we failed to do that.

Those men are isolated, they see very little of the outside world. The company controls everything. There is a company doctor, a company picture show, a company minister, a company teacher — for generally the teacher is the superintendent's sister and the chairman of the school board is the general manager's wife. Conditions are not like they are in Illinois or Pennsylvania. It is a peculiar state of affairs and very few organizers who go in there understand the psychology of the people.

Now I will come to the Cabin Creek strike. A statement was made before the Senatorial Commission in Washington that the International called that strike. I think Mr. White was President. The International did not call that strike and had nothing to do with it. I was in Butte, Mont., and saw that the Paint Creek Colliery Company was not going to recognize the union. I said I would go and give them a fight. The International office didn't know I was going there at the time. I went up Paint Creek and held a meeting. There was some military man there. Then I went around Kanawha and through the creeks there. On July 6 I went up Cabin Creek. At Montgomery the boys came for me at 6 o'clock in the morning and asked if I would go with them.

I left that Creek thoroughly organized in 1903 and went west. For nine years no organizer had gone up that Creek without coming out on a stretcher. Someone went to the Governor and told him I was going up there. That was a board member. He said a company of militia had better be sent there. The railroad men circulated the bills. When the miners came down they didn't know who was going to speak. They came over the mountains and their toes were out of their shoes. A man got up to speak and I landed him out of the wagon and told him I was running the job.

The militia, the mine manager, the general superintendent and the gunmen were all there that day. When I was half through my speech they asked if I would organize them into the United Mine Workers. I told them: "I did organize you once and you betrayed the organization." "Mother," they said, "We will swear that if you organize us now we will stick to the death." They didn't have a dollar to pay for their charter. I told them to go home and not mention the meeting to anyone, not even to their families, but put on their overalls in the morning and dig as many tons of coal as possible, and then the general manager [Charles Cabell] could go to Kentucky and take a few tons of what they dug and give it to the foreign mission cats to take Jesus to China so he won't get on to what they are doing here.

The gunmen were driven out of there and there has been peace ever since. They were driven out of Paint Creek, where they had sent a death special with thirty deputy sheriffs on board. When they wanted that special car equipped to send up the mountain the painters at Huntington said they wouldn't paint it. The machinists said they wouldn't equip it. Some other men were asked to do it and they said: "We will talk about it to-night and ask the Lord"—they were Holy Rollers. Well, the Lord must have told them to do it because in the morning they equipped the train and later that armored car fired into the tents of the strikers.

Here are the machine guns that were turned on us (exhibiting a picture). I went up to speak to the boys and the guns were turned on them. I didn't see them until I got on the track. There were twenty-five of those gunmen who turned on those law-abiding citizens. I put my hands on the guns. One fellow told me to take my hands off the gun. I said: "No, sir; my class go into the bowels of the earth to get the materials to make these guns and I have a right to examine them. What do you want?" He said: "We want to clean out those fellows, every damn one of them." I told him they were not doing anything wrong, that they were only trying to earn money for their wives and children. I told him if they shot one bullet out of that gun the creek would be red with blood and theirs would be the first to color it. They asked what I meant and I told them I had a lot of miners up above who were fully armed. There was nothing up the mountains but a few rabbits, but we scared hell out of them! We organized the men there. We have them solid to this day.

Those are the guns they sent across seven states to Colorado when the men there struck. The railroad men hauled them. Those are the guns that murdered the women and children at Ludlow, Colo. Here are the Baldwin thugs (showing several pictures). Here are some of the boys who were killed. Some young men joined the militia in Colorado, but when they found they were called out to turn their guns on the miners they went home. The mine owners said they would have to have an army. Here they are in this picture. They were not citizens of the state. The laws of Colorado said a man must be a citizen before he could put on the uniform, but these were the private armies of overlords and they kept committing crimes against the miners and their families until the horror of Ludlow shocked the country. Here is the picture of the children who were murdered.

After the horror took place at Ludlow Mr. Rockefeller asked me about it in New York. I said my suggestion would be for him to go out and look into conditions. He did and he was horrified at what he found out there. We drove those people out of Colorado — there are no Baldwin thugs there today.

When we had the Matewan fight they came down to throw the people out of their houses without any warrant of law. Two of those men who shot the people in Matewan had been in Colorado. Your women had the ballot in Colorado for twenty-eight years; there was one in the Senate of that state, but they never raised their voice against this infamy. What good is the ballot if they don't use it? They put the most infamous men in office, for they stood for the killing of those children. I put in twenty-six days in a cellar under the courthouse, where they had me locked up, and when a major came to me and said he would give me money to leave the state I told him he and the Governor could go to hell. The major got a fine place later for being so docile.

This war is going to go on until you bring it up to Congress. There would have been a great many more murders, Mr. White knows, if he hadn't stood behind me and helped me. He gave me money often to go places; he never turned me down and he knows I always got results. Senator Kern spoke about these things on the floor of the Senate and a committee was appointed to come down. No man ever stood on the floor of the Senate in Washington who did more for the working class than Senator Kern of Indiana, but the workers turned him down when the next election came.

A great deal more might have happened if Mr. White hadn't stood behind me in every move I made. Every one of our men was turned out and we never hired a lawyer. I don't believe in lawyers. I defy your bookkeepers to show one five-cent piece that was ever spent by me for a lawyer. I wouldn't allow it — I fight my own battles every time. If we weren't so ready to hire lawyers and sky pilots we would do a great deal better than we are doing.

You are not going to settle this question in West Virginia. It will grow and grow and reach into other states unless you demand of Congress to do away with private armies. That system is eating the vitals out of the honor of the nation. The father of the family is robbed; the money he honestly earns is paid out by the overlords to these gunmen, and the children are raised up under the influence of murderers and robbers and thugs. Your churches don't do anything about it; your welfare workers, your social settlement workers don't do anything about it. Your temperance workers say you can not have a drink. Well, we will have all the drinks we want and not say a word to you about it. You can introduce resolutions from now until doomsday; you can go begging to Congress — nobody has any respect for a beggar; you can go to Congress and tell the Congressmen you want this thing changed, that you want West Virginia put on the map of the United States.

The Governor can not do it because he belongs with the interest. The men in the state legislature can not do it because if they lose those jobs they can't get any others. You are to blame and nobody else. You have got the power to change it. Be men enough to arise and do it. West Virginia is coming back and things will be straightened out there. I see the court has put on another injunction.

President Lewis: Just applied for it.

Mother Jones: Well, didn't they put one on you before? In Washington the telephone company wanted to extend their lines and they sent their men over into old Virginia. The men began digging a hole one morning near a farmer's place. The farmer asked what they were digging a hole for. They said it was to plant telephone poles. The farmer said: "This is my ground; who told you to plant those poles?" They said the telephone company paid them to do it.

"But this is my ground," said the farmer. "That doesn't make any difference, the telephone company is a trust and can get the ground when they want it." The farmer said: "You get out of here." They wouldn't go and the old fellow got a gun and told them they had better leave. They jumped over the fence and left. He wanted them not to come back any more.

In two or three days the men came back. The old fellow looked them over and said: "Didn't I tell you not to come here?" "Yes," they said, "but this time we have got you. We have an order of the court and it gives us permission to plant these poles. You can not do anything about it. Read the order."

The farmer read the order, scratched his head for a minute, then went to the stable and unchained an animal he had in there. He led him out and said: "Sic 'em! sic 'em!" The bull went tearing down the road and over the fence went the telephone men. The old fellow went to his porch and began smoking. They asked him to chain the bull up. He said: "I haven't anything to do with the bull." They asked him again to call the bull off that they had an order of the court and they had read it to him. The old farmer said: "Yes, but why in hell don't you read it to the bull?"

The day is gone in American history when judges can assume the role of lords above us. The pulse of the world is beating, my friends, as it never beat in human history. Not alone in America is it throbbing but the world over. Editors don't know. They sit in the office using a pencil and stabbing us in the back sometimes. Ministers don't know; statesmen don't know; professors in the universities don't know what is going on; but the pulse of the world is throbbing for the civilization that was started back in Jerusalem two thousand years ago. You can not crush a man today; you may put him in jail; you may fill your jails, but the fight will go on. You are living in an electric age. The current is touching the human heart of man, and never again will the system of slavery that has prevailed in the past and that we are driving out now come into the world.

I want to warn that judge today that it is best to bring conciliation to bear than to drive us apart. America will live on, and we are going to march and we are going to bring back the old times of Patrick Henry and Jefferson and Lincoln. It is up to you to stop wasting time on technicalities and get down to business and save this money you are spending. You are going to need it. Put away your prejudice and let us fight. I spoke Labor Day in District 2. Then I went down into Mexico and New Mexico. I got a paper there in which I saw that President Brophy of District 2 was doing business. I wrote him a letter congratulating him. I am glad to know that District 2 has a good president, and, Brophy, I am with you. Whenever you want to raise hell with the other fellows, send for me!

I am going after this fellow (indicating Vice-President Murray) because he isn't doing business in Pittsburgh as he ought to. That used to be the old fighting ground. Vice-President Murray, you do business there.

And now I am going to say something to the women. The destiny of nations depends upon the women. No nation had ever grown beyond its women. Whatever corruption, whatever brutal, ugly instincts the man has he hasn't got from his mother. I have studied this for fifty years; I have studied every great man I have ever met and he has always had a great mother. Many times I walked fifteen miles to see a woman after I had met her son.

I want to say to John P. White before I close that I expressed appreciation of him for what he did for me when he was President. At no time did I go to him and explain to him what I wanted done but what he handed me money or endorsed what I had done, and we got results. I could have done a great deal more in West Virginia, but I think from all we can hear that we are going to go forward. Don't blame the Governor of West Virginia. Don't be so ready to knife him. There are things no statesman can override. This is a dangerous time. Presidents and Governors must move with care. There is no state in America that has better miners than West Virginia. Some of the noblest characters you have are there and you know it. They live up the creeks and the speakers who appear before them do not always use their language or appeal to them. You must know the life of those men. There isn't another state in the Union like West Virginia, and the organizers that go out, Mr. Lewis, don't understand the game. I have gone to Mr. White time and again and have told him to take them out because they didn't fit into the situation. I don't believe in giving the miners' money to anyone who doesn't bring results.

I asked Mr. Lewis to send a man into Mingo to handle the finance. He mentioned one or two and then said: "What do you think of Fowler?" "He is just the man," I said, and he gave him to me and we got results. I am interested in the children and in those poor fellows who can't be reached except by the capitalists' papers that go in. That is all they know. You must educate them, and I want to say, Mr. Editor of the Journal, that you ought to cut out that picture "How to Dress." We know how to dress when we get the money to dress with. What you want to tell us is how to pull that money out of the other fellow.

Up in Princeton the men were asking for years for organization. We sent a boy up to bill the meeting but didn't tell them who was going to speak. The boy had to run away the minute he circulated the bills or he would be killed. I went up with Mr. Houston, the attorney for the miners. We were told the meeting would be in the park three miles and a half away. I said we wouldn't hold it there, that we would start a riot out there, and then they would say: "Old Mother Jones went out in the park and started a riot." I said: "See if the city authorities won't give us a place in the town to meet." We got it and seven thousand men came there, largely railroad men, machinists and farmers. Seven cars of Baldwin-Felts thugs came down, loaded with whiskey and guns. There was no prohibition men there that day. Houston got up to speak and I saw that something was being plotted. I got up and spoke, but I hadn't talked more than ten minutes when they began to start the riot.

When I wound up my speech I said: "Mr. Baldwin-Felts guards, I am going to serve notice on you that I will take this thing up to Uncle Sam, explain the matter, and if Uncle Sam don't protect the children of the nation Old Mother Jones will. They won't be raised under the influence of murderers like you." The railroad men were afraid I would be killed and asked policemen to take me away. I told them I was not afraid of being killed, that I would rather die fighting than die in my bed. I want to say to you mothers to quit buying pistols for your children. Train them to something better than a pistol and a gun. Almost every child today has a toy pistol. You began training them to use a pistol while they were in the cradles and the welfare workers never raise their voices about it. The legislature should pass a law that no mother should buy a pistol for a child.

I am going back to West Virginia and I want to ask you, for God's sake, for the sake of the children, to stand up like men and work shoulder to shoulder. You are the basic industry of the world, you are the basic organization of labor. You and the railroad men get together. Meet with the railroad men and join hands, because the battle royal is ahead and you must get the railroad men with us so they will not haul scab coal, the gunmen, the militia and the guns to shoot us.

I had two guns put to my head on Sunday. I took the matter up in

Washington. The company telegraphed to New York for their lawyer to come down and watch me. I went to the War Department and from there to the Navy Department, then to the Fuel Department. The secretary there asked me what I would advise. I advised him to call both sides there and have him sit at the table. They came up. Dwyer, Ballantyne and myself sat in the room. The officials went to vaudeville that Sunday night although they were going to meet the Governor the next morning. You must discharge such men from office right away; you must do in the future as we have done in the past in West Virginia; we must act with the forces of law.

The miners' organization is the most law-abiding organization in the world. The miners are not law-breakers. They are honest, hard-working men. They break no law until the gunmen get after them. You must go to Congress and demand that the murderers and the gunmen who help rob, degrade and murder men, women and children be punished. I am going to take the matter up with the President and put the whole history before him. I will tell him this question is up to him and to get Congress to protect the miners of West Virginia.

Another thing I want to set right. The International office never called the Cabin Creek strike. That statement was made and it was never corrected. I went up the Creek and if anybody is responsible I am the one and not the International. I didn't ask the men to strike. The company discharged the men and then the strike was on. Now I want you to hold public meetings and wake the public to what is going on. Not one of the writers who went into Mingo, Logan or McDowell ever wrote the true story. That is why their scribbling has no effect on the public mind. If you show where the real evil lies and wake up the sleepy and indifferent public you will get those conditions changed.

[*UMWA Proceedings* (Indianapolis: Bookwalter-Ball-Greathouse Printing Co., 1921), pp. 727-41.]

Speech at a convention
of the United Mine Workers of America
Indianapolis, Indiana

Three days later, Mother Jones took the podium again to reiterate her intention of continuing the fight in West Virginia, and to urge the delegates to remain true to the long tradition of labor unity against the common enemy. She was speaking to a contentious group, where John L. Lewis, who had been elected president of the UMWA the preceding year, was using every stratagem at his command to retain control of the union. Disorder verging on anarchy marked many sessions of the fifteen-day meeting. Mother Jones's references to the expenses of the convention came out of the knowledge, which the delegates shared, that their treasury was virtually empty. Legal expenses alone for the past year had approached half a million dollars, and more such demands would arise out of the need to defend union members who were charged with crimes in West Virginia. Amid all the wrangling, Lewis and his rivals were maneuvering for political advantage.

§ § §

You know, boys, I cannot yell as loud as I used to. A group of men met in Louisville, Ky., and there were many of the Blues and the Grays. A short time before they had used the guns against each other. But they met and buried the guns and shook hands and said: "We have wiped out chattel slavery, but we are facing something darker, more dangerous, than chattel slavery. Now we must join together as one grand army to fight for industrial freedom and put a stop to slavery in the long years to come."

These men organized. That was before some of you were born. A few years before that they had been holding bayonets against each other, but they buried them, not to use them again. They organized and started out to carry the message of hope to their brothers. They had no money. In 1876, when the Union Pacific was bringing over Chinese to break the labor movement, the battle began there. They fought the battle, not with guns, but with intelligence. They made the government in Washington come out and put a stop to the Chinese coming in to invade the American labor movement.

I was all through those battles. I am now facing my closing hours of life. It hasn't been smooth sailing. There have been storms in the past for labor, and yet the real storm has not begun. I had a hand in that Chinese agitation; we kept it up and stopped the Chinese coming over. The Union Pacific had been bringing them over in hordes and using them to break the labor movement. This is not a yesterday's lesson with me.

I am now entering my ninety-third milestone. When you hold your next convention I may be moldering in the dust. Let me warn you now that the enemy is lined up and thoroughly prepared for battle. It must be with us as with the Blues and the Grays — we must shake hands and get together. I am going back to West Virginia. I am not going to give up the battle there, because I know it is the storm center of the labor movement. Let me warn you what is coming. There are stormy days ahead of you. There are going to be hungry days for your children. We have some good boys in West Virginia and some good fighters, but we have got some damn snakes, too. Look after the snakes.

Now the time is here for us to get together. Stop your foolishness. This isn't a mob gathering. The whole world is looking at this convention. There is a sane way of doing business; don't let the world think we are a mob gathered here in Indianapolis. I am not going to say goodby when I leave. I am going to be with you until death closes my eyes. Nobody can put me out. That has been tried, but I put out those who tried it before I got through with them.

The brave and true die only once; the cowards and traitors die often, and they have got some horrible deaths at that. Be true to your organization. The wires are set to break you up. I know what I am talking about. I am not looking for any office. What will the world think of us when the newspapers send out the poison ivy? You know the newspaper fellows have got to put in something to keep their jobs.

Do you know how much money you are spending here? It isn't your money; it is the money of the children and the women. You are giving the money to the capitalists, the hotels, street cars and pool rooms. You cannot give it to the beer rooms because you can't get a damn drop out of them. Now let us stop this foolishness that has been going on and go before the world as a sane people.

There are some fellows who don't want me to go back to West Virginia, but I am going anyway. One fellow said I couldn't do any more talking in West Virginia. Why, he's been dead for forty years and the world has run away from him! The world has been made for a long time, and the Lord has never yet made a man that has been able to stop a woman talking. The gunmen, the courts, the thugs and the militia have tried to keep me from talking, and they couldn't do it. My days are getting short, but as long as life remains I will stay with you.

You are the fighting army of the working class of America. I plead with you to do your business rapidly, get through here, go home and go to work to earn some money. We are going to win the battle in West Virginia. As long as I am able to crawl I will be around there.

Now, everybody bury the hatchet, do business like sensible men and go home.

[*UMWA Proceedings* (Indianapolis: Bookwalter-Ball-Greathouse Printing Co., 1921), pp. 874–76.]

Speech at a convention
of the United Mine Workers of America
Indianapolis, Indiana

In November 1921, Mother Jones fell seriously ill and was under a doctor's care for over a month at the home of John H. Walker in Springfield, Illinois. Her exertions in Mexico and West Virginia had taken their toll, but her letters indicate it was a sickness of the spirit as much as any physical illness that prostrated her. Her own protégés in the union leadership in West Virginia had exposed her "telegram from President Harding" as a fraud, and the drive to organize the southern counties had collapsed after the explosion of violence. The organization to which she had devoted much of her energy for a quarter of a century seemed determined to tear itself apart while the gains of the past dribbled away.

Inevitably, Mother Jones became involved in the power struggle as John L. Lewis bludgeoned his way to complete domination of the UMWA. After serving as acting president, he was elected president in 1920, though the legitimacy of the vote count was disputed. His rivals included Frank Farrington of Illinois, Alexander Howat of Kansas, John Walker of Illinois, and others. During the twenties he isolated and destroyed his rivals one by one. The first to fall was the president of District 14.

Alexander Howat, fighting against a compulsory arbitration law passed by the Kansas legislature, refused to order some of the miners of District 14 back to work when a dispute arose to which the law applied. John L. Lewis, seeing an opportunity to oust a rival, insisted that Howat had violated international rules and with the approval of the executive board instructed Howat to order the men back to work. When Howat rejected the instructions, he and his supporting officers were suspended. At the September convention, Lewis won a vote approving the action of the board, and in October 1921 he annulled the charter of District 14 and installed his own men to run the district. Farrington and Walker of Illinois, Robert Harlin of Washington, and others took the side of Howat. At the resumption of the convention in February 1922, the delegates spent most of their time arguing the Howat case rather than considering the forthcoming contract negotiations with the operators of the Central Competitive Field, the official business of meeting. In another riotous convention, Lewis announced a victory by the barest of majorities in the crucial vote on his actions regarding Howat. Opponents continued to fight for two more years to have the decision reversed, but Lewis maintained his control and moved on later to eliminate Farrington and then Walker.

Mother Jones had very little to do with these later battles, although her letters show her close attention to the course of events and her sympathy with the anti-Lewis forces. Somewhat recovered from her illness by February, she made one last appearance before delegates of the organization with which she had so long been associated. She deplored their internecine strife, but she left no doubt that she regarded Alex Howat as a fighter for the rights of labor who in the future would be honored, even though he was now being denied a place in the miner's union. It proved to be a farewell address. John L. Lewis did not reappoint her as an international organizer, and her official connection with the UMWA was over.

§   §   §

Boys, do you know that the whole world has got its eyes on this convention?

A Delegate: And on Howat, too.

Mother Jones: Everywhere the electric current touches it is notifying the world what you are doing here today. Don't you know your money is being wasted?

(A large number of delegates shouted, "Yes.")

Mother Jones: The children at home need the money to feed them. Have you no consideration for the men who laid the foundation of this great organization that the whole industrial world looks to you for a lesson? Do you know that you are able to assemble in this convention on the bones of the men who marched miles in the dead of night to get you together to bring more sunshine to your children and to the children of the nation? And then you are wasting time here.

A Delegate: It has been done by the officers.

Mother Jones: What can the officers do? Didn't you elect them? I want you to muzzle up now.

I came to this convention because of the headlines in the papers. I thought I would come here and look after you and see that you behave yourselves. You must realize, my friends, that we are facing a crisis in the industrial organizations of the world; you must realize that the enemy who has been fighting from the outside is now boring from within. You must wake up to the fact that all of us make mistakes at times, but there is a way for us to remedy those mistakes. Let us do it quietly, sanely and in a business-like way. You should not come to this convention to howl and hoot. Your officers deserve some consideration.

I don't endorse a wrong at any time. You haven't an officer in the country in any labor organization that I won't get up and raise hell with if he is not true to you. I don't get myself under obligations to any officer; I keep my hands clean and can fight any of them and do fight them and will fight them again if necessary. You came here to this convention to outline your coming contract and you are wasting all this time. You are putting a weapon right into the hands of the enemy to hit us with when the time for a settlement comes.

I was down in the state of Kansas recently. I was in Kansas twenty-five years ago. I drove through the coal fields with an old horse and wagon. That was the beginning of the organization in that state. I happened to be in Omaha when the boys came to me and said they would strike, but if they did they would be blacklisted. They asked me to come out there. I went out to Kansas and held a meeting that night in an old barn. The whole thing was closed up in the morning; there wasn't an engineer or anyone else working, and in five days we won the strike.

The boys wanted to give me some money but I told them I didn't want the money, but I wanted an old horse. The horse I had in mind was blind, but his two ears were open. So they got the horse and wagon for me and I piled the wagon with literature and went through Kansas and Missouri. There weren't many organized miners there at that time, but we got the men together and held meetings in the schoolrooms.

Now I have been in Kansas again. When I took this last trip to Kansas no individual asked me to go. The miners of Kansas telegraphed me to come to them if I was able to move. I want to make the statement now that whenever the miners call for me in any part of the country and I am able to go to them, God Almighty won't keep me from going. I studied the Kansas affair very carefully. In the first meeting I held I told them I came down principally to get Alex Howat out of jail. And I got him out, didn't I? You bet your life I did!

I have known Alex Howat for twenty years, and while I have not always agreed with Alex, I want to make this statement to the audience and to the world: That my desire is to have a million Alex Howats in the nation to fight the battles of the workers. He has fought for his men and he has fought that damnable law that the Governor of Kansas put on the statute books to enslave the workers. He fought it nobly and he was willing to go to death for it, and because he did he was put in jail and denounced. If Alex Howat never did anything else he called the attention of the nation to that slave law.

The New York *World,* in an editorial, denounced the Kansas Industrial Court Law. Men in the United States Senate said it wouldn't work. If the men of Pennsylvania had done the same thing that Alex Howat did in Kansas when the damnable Hessian law was brought over by Gruin of Philadelphia, and put on the statute books of Pennsylvania, we wouldn't have it now everywhere. At the first meeting I held in Kansas there were United States marshals, the sheriff and the mine inspectors. In that meet-

ing I made this statement: That whenever I went to Washington on the
B. & O. Railroad I got off at Harper's Ferry. I would ask the conductor
to wait three minutes and I would tell him what I wanted. The conductor
said he would always wait. My object in getting off was to pay my respects at the grave of a man from Kansas to whom a monument has been
erected in Harper's Ferry.

John Brown didn't come from Maine, he came from Kansas. It was
John Brown of Kansas that was fighting against chattel slavery. I have
never heard of a monument being built to the judge or the jury that condemned him to death; they are unknown; but there is a monument to John
Brown at Harper's Ferry and I never go to Washington on the B. & O.
Road that I do not get off and pay my respects to that monument. In the
years to come there will be another monument built to the memory of
a man from Kansas, and that will be built to the memory of Alex Howat.

I received a letter from one of those women in Kansas who took part
in that march. I want to read it to the delegates.

Ringo, Kansas, February 13, 1922

To the Delegates of the Convention:

Dear Fellow Workers: As a voice from the toilers, from the loyal
women of District 14, Kansas, we, the mothers, wives and daughters of loyal union men are depending upon you in the convention
as a body of experienced union working men to judge the wrong
that has been done us here in Kansas, a wrong which no court can
try to settle, but a wrong which can be justified by you when you
sit in the convention today. We depend upon you as friends, men
and judges to consider the future of Kansas, and in fact, in the whole
of the United Mine Workers.

We call to you, not for money, but for justice; not in behalf of
our district president, Alex Howat, and Vice-President August Dorchy, whom we in Kansas feel there were never two nobler men than
they are, who have stood for a principle such as the United Mine
Workers stand for. Men have fought for it, and while fighting for
that principle today in behalf of that principle, we, the women of
Kansas, ask your attention and ask you to try our case as a jury of
the United Mine Workers of America to decide upon a verdict that
will save our organization that is on the verge of being destroyed
by a few traitors within our organization.

Men, think well, as upon you depends much of the future of the
organization, even the lives of the women and children.

There is an appeal to every honest, thinking man, coming from the mothers of Kansas, and I want to say to you men here that those women will go down in history when the men who were guarded by guns in the scab hotel will be damned by the world.

I had a hand in laying the foundation of this organization in Kansas and I am not going to see it perish. It is going to stand as a monument to the workers of the nation. Now, boys, settle it, and stop this howling like a lot of fiends. Do business like men and then come here and meet your officers. Be good to them when they come, Mr. Lewis. Come to your board and to your own officers and settle this question. Now settle down to business today.

I didn't feel very well able to come here, but I wanted to talk to you. I wanted you to let the world see that you are thinking men, that your organization is dear to you, that the future of this country depends upon what you do in this convention. Stop all this noise. When we are through and we cannot get what we are entitled to we will go out and raise hell all over the nation. I don't feel very much like talking today, but here is one woman who, if I stand alone, I will stand behind Alex Howat for the fighting qualities he has and for the manhood he has shown.

When this gathering is over you fellows get together. Come before your board and do business there. Don't be giving those fellows (pointing to the newspaper reporters) a lot of stuff like they had when the Structural Iron Workers were in trouble. I am going to go before the board with you, and they have got to treat you right, because if they don't I will get after them. Now, be good boys. I left this convention yesterday almost broken-hearted. Four railroad men came to me on the street and said: "Mother, what is the matter with the miners? How could they take the vote they did against those Kansas men?" Don't you see that everybody is watching us? We haven't enough good fighters. I want to see more Alex Howats and I want to live long enough to develop them.

[*UMWA Proceedings* (Indianapolis: Bookwalter-Ball-Greathouse Printing Co., 1922), pp. 84–88.]

Afterword

In the years following 1922, Mother Jones continued to speak when her increasingly poor health permitted. She had several illnesses that required hospitalization, and she was constantly plagued with rheumatism that made it impossible for her to keep up the level of activity that she had previously known. She made her headquarters in Washington, where Terence V. Powderly, and later his widow Emma, kept a room for her in their house, but she frequently spent part of the year with friends in California. The only speech with any national significance she made at the Farmer-Labor convention in Chicago, 3 July 1923, where an unsuccessful attempt was made to found a national Farmer-Labor party. Her last known public address was in Alliance, Ohio, in 1926, when she was the guest of honor at a Labor Day celebration, but her remarks on these occasions have not been preserved.

Though often ill and restricted in her movement, she still continued to fight the battles of labor. The spring and summer of 1923 she devoted to writing her autobiography with the assistance of Mary Field Parton, and she hoped to devote any income from its sale to creating a fund to defend laboring men who were accused of crimes. Through personal appeals to governors whom she knew, such as Ephraim F. Morgan of West Virginia and Gifford Pinchot of Pennsylvania, she attempted to secure the pardon or parole of union men who were in prison. She carried a personal plea to each new governor of California for the release of Tom Mooney, and she participated in other such humanitarian quests for lesser-known men. When she was in Washington and her health permitted, she frequently visited the Department of Labor, and her correspondence with comrades in the labor movement, particularly John H. Walker, William Green, and John Fitzpatrick, shows that she followed labor affairs with a keen interest, even when she was bedridden.

Despite the kindness of friends and the concern and tributes of correspondents, she missed the excitement of the platforms where she had so often been the center of attention. She decided to cap her career with a hundredth birthday party to be held in Chicago on 1 May 1930, when she would celebrate with old comrades the passage of the years and the cause of labor. She would have one last hurrah and make one final speech.

The date of her birth had always been uncertain, resting on her own statements. The only written evidence available, a parish record in County Cork, Ireland, indicates that she was born in 1837. At different times over the years she laid claim to various years, ranging from 1830 to 1840, but on oath, on several occasions, she said that she was born in 1832. By 1920,

259

however, she had decided that her birth date was 1 May 1830, and that is the date she used in her autobiography. In 1929 she was living with friends, Walter and Lillie Mae Burgess, not far from Silver Spring, Maryland. As the hundredth anniversary approached, it became clear that a trip to Chicago was out of the question. Almost immobilized by rheumatism, on good days she could manage an automobile ride into the town or through the neighboring countryside. Reluctantly, she abandoned her plans for going to Chicago and planned instead to have the birthday at the Burgess home.

Although she had been confined to her bed for weeks, on 1 May she summoned up the energy to move from her upstairs bedroom to a rocking chair under an apple tree in the yard, where all day long she opened telegrams and letters, received visitors, reminisced with old friends, bantered with reporters, and presided over the cutting of the five-tiered birthday cake supplied by the bakers' union. Many labor leaders in their Washington headquarters had conspired to make the day a success and Paramount sent a crew to film the festivities. When she spoke into their microphones, she probably addressed more people than she had in years of street meetings and public addresses.

The *New York Times* report the next day contains the longest quotations from her birthday remarks:

> Out on the lawn she faced the talking picture cameras, took a deep breath and a drink of water, and began an impromptu speech which brought loud applause and sent the nearby circling crows wheeling back to the woods.
>
> A dog enjoying a nap in the May sunshine jumped to his feet as the white-haired labor leader said in a ringing voice:
>
> "America was not founded on dollars but on the blood of men who gave their lives for your benefit. Power lies in the hands of labor to retain American liberty, but labor has not yet learned how to use that power. A wonderful power is in the hands of women, too, but they don't know how to use it. Capitalists sidetrack the women into clubs and make ladies of them. Nobody wants a lady, they want women. Ladies are parlor parasites."

She added that she hoped to see the six-hour day and the five-day week and denounced prohibition. The camera crew finished their work and departed, but the celebration continued until evening. After supper, Mother Jones retired to her room, but continued to receive late visitors until about eleven.

Such was the last public appearance of Mother Jones. Her health improved a little during the summer, but as autumn approached it began to fail. She died in her room at the Burgess home on 30 November 1930. After a funeral service in St. Gabriel's church in Washington, she was buried on 7 December in the miners' cemetery at Mt. Olive, Illinois.

MOTHER JONES

The Avenging Nemesis of the Coal Miners

WILL SPEAK AT

Cooper
Union

Fourth Avenue and
8th Street

Monday
November
18th
AT 8 P. M.

MOTHER JONES.

Mother Jones has been in the Kanawha coal fields of West Virginia since the 1st of June, and will come to New York fresh from the scene of the most bitter industrial conflicts this country has had to endure.

Come and hear how men are kidnapped in New York, taken to West Virginia, and there made either to scab or be shot like dogs.

ADMISSION FREE   ADMISSION FREE

Under the
Auspices of the United Mine Workers of America

Typical advertisement for an appearance by Mother Jones, *New York Call*, 16 November 1912.

WRITINGS

Civilization in Southern Mills

The miners and railroad boys of Birmingham, Ala., entertained me one evening some months ago with a graphic description of the conditions among the slaves of the Southern cotton mills. While I imagined that these must be something of a modern Siberia, I concluded that the boys were overdrawing the picture and made up my mind to see for myself the conditions described. Accordingly I got a job and mingled with the workers in the mill and in their homes. I found that children of six and seven years of age were dragged out of bed at half-past 4 in the morning when the task-master's whistle blew. They eat their scanty meal of black coffee and corn bread mixed with cottonseed oil in place of butter, and then off trots the whole army of serfs, big and little. By 5:30 they are all behind the factory walls, where amid the whir of machinery they grind their young lives out for fourteen long hours each day. As one looks on this brood of helpless human souls one could almost hear their voices cry out, "Be still a moment, O you iron wheels of capitalistic greed, and let us hear each other's voices, and let us feel for a moment that this is not all of life."

We stopped at 12 for a scanty lunch and a half-hour's rest. At 12:30 we were at it again with never a stop until 7. Then a dreary march home, where we swallowed our scanty supper, talked for a few minutes of our misery and then dropped down upon a pallet of straw, to lie until the whistle should once more awaken us, summoning babes and all alike to another round of toil and misery.

I have seen mothers take their babes and slap cold water in their face to wake the poor little things. I have watched them all day long tending the dangerous machinery. I have seen their helpless limbs torn off, and then when they were disabled and of no more use to their master, thrown out to die. I must give the company credit for having hired a Sunday school teacher to tell the little things that "Jesus put it into the heart of Mr. _____ to build that factory so they would have work with which to earn a little money to enable them to put a nickel in the box for the poor little heathen Chinese babies."

THE ROPE FACTORY

I visited the factory in Tuscaloosa, Ala., at 10 o'clock at night. The superintendent, not knowing my mission, gave me the entire freedom of the factory and I made good use of it. Standing by a siding that contained

155 spindles were two little girls. I asked a man standing near if the children were his, and he replied that they were. "How old are they?" I asked. "This one is 9, the other 10," he replied. "How many hours do they work?" "Twelve," was the answer. "How much do they get a night?" "We all three together get 60 cents. They get 10 cents each and I 40."

I watched them as they left their slave-pen in the morning and saw them gather their rags around their frail forms to hide them from the wintry blast. Half-fed, half-clothed, half-housed, they toil on, while the poodle dogs of their masters are petted and coddled and sleep on pillows of down, and the capitalistic judges jail the agitators that would dare to help these helpless ones to better their condition.

Gibson is another of those little sections of hell with which the South is covered. The weaving of gingham is the principal work. The town is owned by a banker who possesses both people and mills. One of his slaves told me she had received one dollar for her labor for one year. Every weekly pay day her employer gave her a dollar. On Monday she deposited that dollar in the "pluck-me" store to secure food enough to last until the next pay day, and so on week after week.

There was once a law on the statute books of Alabama prohibiting the employment of children under twelve years of age more than eight hours each day. The Gadston Company would not build their mill until they were promised that this law should be repealed.

When the repeal came up for the final reading I find by an examination of the records of the House that there were sixty members present. Of these, fifty-seven voted for the repeal and but three against. To the everlasting credit of young Manning, who was a member of that House, let it be stated that he both spoke and voted against the repeal.

I asked one member of the House why he voted to murder the children, and he replied that he did not think they could earn enough to support themselves if they only worked eight hours. These are the kind of tools the intelligent workingmen put in office.

The Phoenix mill in Georgia were considering the possibility of a cut in wages something over a year ago, but after making one attempt they reconsidered and started a savings bank instead. At the end of six months the board of directors met and found out that the poor wretches who were creating wealth for them were saving 10 per cent of their wages. Whereupon they promptly cut them that 10 per cent, and the result was the '96 strike. I wonder how long the American people will remain silent under such conditions as these.

Almost every one of my shop-mates in these mills was a victim of some disease or other. All are worked to the limit of existence. The weavers are expected to weave so many yards of cloth each working day. To come short of this estimate jeopardizes their job. The factory operator loses all energy either of body or of mind. The brain is so crushed as to be incapable of thinking, and one who mingles with these people soon discovers that their minds like their bodies are wrecked. Loss of sleep and loss of rest gives rise to abnormal appetites, indigestion, shrinkage of stature, bent backs and aching hearts.

Such a factory system is one of torture and murder as dreadful as a long-drawn-out Turkish massacre, and is a disgrace to any race or age. As the picture rises before me I shudder for the future of a nation that is building up a moneyed aristocracy out of the life-blood of the children of the proletariat. It seems as if our flag is a funeral bandage splotched with blood. The whole picture is one of the most horrible avarice, selfishness and cruelty and is fraught with present horror and promise of future degeneration. The mother, over-worked and under-fed, gives birth to tired and worn-out human beings.

I can see no way out save in a complete overthrow of the capitalistic system, and to me the father who casts a vote for the continuance of that system is as much of a murderer as if he took a pistol and shot his own children. But I see all around me signs of the dawning of a new day of socialism, and with my faithful comrades everywhere I will work and hope and pray for the coming of that better day.

[*International Socialist Review* I (1900–01), 539-41.]

The Strike in Scranton

(Mother Jones makes the following statement concerning the strike of the 5,000 silk mill hands in Scranton, Pennsylvania.)

Most of them are little tots ranging from 8 to 14 years of age. The poverty of the parents compels them to swear that these babies are of the age when they can be legally worked by the master class. In one mill I found children who toiled twenty-four long, weary days of ten hours each; and at the end of that time received $2 apiece. The vampire who runs the plant felt deeply aggrieved because his little slaves went on strike. He complained that he had built and paid for a new mill and cleared $10,000 in two years, and just as he was getting his head above water, the ungrateful little wretches run away! And then some people say there is no hell! And others that there is no wage slavery! Why, I have got a trunk full of evidence showing that miners were plucked of all their earnings, and didn't have a dollar from one end of the year to the other. This is capitalism with a vengeance, the robber system that is upheld by those who vote Republican and Democratic tickets.

Boss Davis, the ringleader of the plute cannibals, has offered this compromise: If the strikers allow him to measure their work and take his word for it, he will pay them 25 cents a week more. If they won't allow him to measure, they must go back at the old rate. It's a scheme with robbery on its face, and the little ones won't yield.

[*St. Louis Labor,* 13 April 1901.]

268

A Picture of American Freedom in West Virginia

Some months ago a little group of miners from the State of Illinois decided to face the storm and go to the assistance of their fellow-workmen in the old slave state of West Virginia. They hoped that they might somehow lend a hand to break at least one link in the horrible corporation chains with which the miners of that state are bound. Wherever the conditions of these poor slaves of the caves is worst there is where I always seek to be, and so I accompanied the boys to West Virginia.

They billed a meeting for me at Mt. Carbon, where the Tianawha Coal and Coke Company have their works. The moment I alighted from the train the corporation dogs set up a howl. They wired for the "squire" to come at once. He soon arrived with a constable and said: "Tell that woman she cannot speak here tonight; if she tries it I will jail her." If you come from Illinois you are a foreigner in West Virginia and are entitled to no protection or rights under the law — that is, if you are interested in the welfare of your oppressed fellow beings. If you come in the interest of a band of English parasites you are a genuine American citizen and the whole state is at your disposal. So the squire notified me that if I attempted to speak there would be trouble. I replied that I was not hunting for trouble, but that if it came in that way I would not run away from it. I told him that the soil of Virginia had been stained with the blood of the men who marched with Washington and Lafayette to found a government where the right of free speech should always exist. "I am going to speak here to-night," I continued. "When I violate the law, and not until then will you have any right to interfere." At this point he and the constable started out for the county seat with the remark that he would find out what the law was on that point. For all I have been able to hear they are still hunting for the law, for I have never heard from them since. The company having called off their dogs of war I held my meeting to a large crowd of miners.

But after all the company came out ahead. They notified the hotel not to take any of us in or give us anything to eat. Thereupon a miner and his wife gave me shelter for the night. The next morning they were notified to leave their miserable little shack which belonged to the company. He was at once discharged and with his wife and babe went back to Illinois, where, as a result of a long and bitter struggle the miners have succeeded in regaining a little liberty.

§ § §

Up on New River last winter I was going to hold a meeting when the mine owner notified me that as he owned half the river which I had to cross to get to the meeting place, I could not hold the meeting. I concluded that God Almighty owned the other half of the river and probably had a share or two of stock in the operator's half. So I crossed over, held my meeting on a Sunday afternoon with a big crowd. The operator was present at the meeting, bought a copy of "Merrie England," and I hope has been a fairer and wiser man since then.

§   §   §

One of the saddest pictures I have among the many sad ones in my memory is that of a little band of unorganized miners who had struck against unbearable conditions. It was in a little town on the Tianawha where I spent an Easter. When the miners laid down their tools the company closed their "pluck me" store and started to starve them out. While they were working the poor wretches had to trade at the company store and when the payday came their account at the store was deducted from their check. The result was that many a payday there was only a corporation bill-head in their pay envelope to take home to the wife and babies. Enslaved and helpless if they dared to make a protest or a move to help themselves, they were at once discharged and their names placed on a black list. Ten tons of coal must go to the company each year for house rent; two tons to the company doctor who prescribes a "pill every five hours" for all diseases alike. You must have this corporation doctor when sick whether you want him or not. Two tons must go to the blacksmith for sharpening tools; two tons more for the water which they use and which they must carry from a spring half-way up the mountain side, and ten tons more for powder and oil. All this must be paid before a penny comes with which to get things to eat and wear. When one hears their sad tales, looks upon the faces of their disheartened wives and children, and learns of their blasted hopes, and lives with no ray of sunshine, one is not surprised that they all have a disheartened appearance, as if there was nothing on earth to live for.

Every rain storm pours through the roof of the corporation shacks and wets the miner and his family. They must enter the mine early every morning and work from ten to twelve hours a day amid the poisonous gases. Then a crowd of temperance parasites will come along and warn the miners against wasting their money for drink. I have seen those miners drop down exhausted and unconscious from the effects of the poisonous gases amid which they were forced to work. The mine inspector gets his appointment through a political pull and never makes anything but a sham inspection. He walks down "broadway" with the mining boss, but never goes into "smoke alley" where the men are dropping from gas poisoning. Then he walks out to the railroad track and writes his report to the government telling how fine things are.

§   §   §

I sat down on the side of the railroad track the other day to talk to an old miner. "Mother Jones," said the poor fellow, "I have been working in this mine for thirty-three years. I came here when it first opened and have worked faithfully ever since. They have got every penny I ever made. There has never been a ray of sunshine in my life. It has been all shadow. To-day I have not a penny in the world. I never drank. I have worked hard and steady." Just then he suddenly rose and walked away saying, "Here comes the superintendent. If he saw me speak to you I would lose my job."

§   §   §

As I look around and see the condition of these miners who produce the wealth of the nation, and the injustice practiced on these helpless people, I tremble for the future of a nation whose legislation legalizes such infamy.

[*International Socialist Review* 2 (1901–02), 177–79.]

The Coal Miners of the Old Dominion

A few Sundays ago I attended church in a place called McDonald, on Loop Creek, in West Virginia. In the course of his sermon the preacher gave the following as a conversation that had recently taken place between him and a miner.

"I met a man last week," said the preacher, "who used to be a very good church member. When I asked him what he was doing at the present time he said that he was organizing his fellow craftsmen of the mines."

Then, according to the preacher, the following discussion took place:

"What is the object of such a union?" asked the preacher.

"To better our condition," replied the miner.

"But the miners are in a prosperous condition now."

"There is where we differ."

"Do you think you will succeed?"

"I am going to try."

Commenting on this conversation to his congregation the preacher said: "Now I question if such a man can meet with any success. If he were only a college graduate he might be able to teach these miners something and in this way give them light, but as the miners of this creek are in a prosperous condition at the present time I do not see what such a man can do for them." Yet this man was professing to preach the doctrines of the Carpenter of Nazareth. Let us compare his condition with that of the "prosperous" miners and perhaps we can see why he talked as he did. At this same service he read his report for the previous six months. For his share of the wealth these miners had produced during that time he had received $847.67, of which $46 had been given for missionary purposes. Besides receiving this money he had been frequently wined and dined by the mine operators and probably had a free pass on the railroad. What had he done for the miners during that time? He had spoken to them twenty-six times, for which he received $32.41 a talk, and if they were all like the one I heard he was at no expense either in time, brains or money to prepare them. During all this time the "prosperous" miners were working ten hours a day beneath the ground amid poisonous gases and crumbling rocks. If they were fortunate enough to be allowed to toil every working day throughout the year they would have received in return for 3,080 hours of most exhausting toil less than $400.

Jesus, whose doctrines this man claimed to be preaching, took twelve from among the laborers of his time (no college graduates among them) and with them founded an organization that revolutionized the society amid which it rose. Just so in our day the organization of the workers must be the first step to the overthrow of capitalism.

§ § §

Then my mind turned to the thousands of "trap boys," with no sunshine ever coming into their lives. These children of the miners put in fourteen hours a day beneath the ground for sixty cents, keeping their lone watch in the tombs of the earth with never a human soul to speak to them. The only sign of life around them is when the mules come down with coal. Then as they open the trap doors to let the mules out a gush of cold air rushes in chilling their little bodies to the bone. Standing in the wet mud up to their knees there are times when they are almost frozen and when at last late at night they are permitted to come out into God's fresh air they are sometimes so exhausted that they have to be carried to the corporation shack they call a home.

The parents of these boys have known no other life than that of endless toil. Now those who have robbed and plundered the parents are beginning the same story with the present generation. These boys are sometimes not more than nine or ten years of age. Yet in the interests of distant bond and stockholders these babes must be imprisoned through the long beautiful daylight in the dark and dismal caverns of the earth. Savage cannibals at least put their victims out of their misery before beginning their terrible meal, but the cannibals of today feast their poodle dogs at the seashore upon the life blood of these helpless children of the mines. A portion of this blood-stained plunder goes to the support of educational incubators called universities, that hatch out just such ministerial fowls as the one referred to.

The miner with whom this minister had been talking had been blacklisted up and down the creek for daring to ask for a chance to let his boy go to school instead of into the mines. This miner could have told the minister more about the great industrial tragedy in the midst of which he was living, in five minutes, than all his college training had taught him.

§ § §

At the bidding of these same stock and bondholders, often living in a foreign land, the school houses of Virginia are closed to those who build them and to whom they belong by every right. The miners pay taxes, build the school and support the officers, but if they dare even to stand upon the school house steps a snip of a mine boss comes along with a pistol in hand and orders them off. "_____ free speech," said one of them to me when I protested, "we do not need any free speech. You get off the earth." Not only the school rooms, but every church or public hall is locked against us. On every school board you will find at least one company clerk or mining boss, and it is the business of this henchman of the mine owners to see to it that the school buildings are not used for public meetings by the miners.

Yet these same school buildings are used by the operators for any kind of meeting they choose and any demoralizing, degrading show that comes along has free access to them, as well as all political meetings of the old capitalist parties. But when the labor agitator, or trade union organizer comes along trying to make it possible for the miner's children to go to school, the school houses are tightly closed.

§ § §

In some of these camps the miners are forced to pay as much as $9 a barrel for flour, fourteen cents a pound for sugar, eighteen cents a pound for fat pork, and $8 to $10 a month rent for a company shack, the roof of which is so poor that when it rains the bed is moved from place to place in the attempt to find a dry spot. Many a miner works his whole life and never handles a cent of money. All he earns must be spent in the "Pluck me." Every miner has one dollar stopped for a company doctor. With 1200 men working in a mine and a young doctor paid $300 a year, this means a nice little lump for the company. And this is the Divine system the preacher was defending.

§ § §

In the closing hours of the baby year of the twentieth century I stood on the soil that gave birth to a Patrick Henry who could say, "Give me liberty or give me death," and a Jefferson, the truth of whose prophecy that the greatest tyranny and danger to American liberty would come from the judges on the bench, has been so often shown in the last few years. I had just left West Virginia with all its horrors, and as I was whirled along on the railroad I wondered if when I stood on the soil stained with the blood of so many revolutionary heroes, I would once more really breathe the air of freedom. Well, this is the first breath I received. I arrived in the northern part of Wise County, Virginia, over the L. & N. R. R., to find a message waiting me from the superintendent of the mines saying that if I came down to the Dorcas mine to talk to the miners of his company he would shoot me. I told him to shoot away, and that I did not propose to be scared out by the growling of any English bull-dog of capitalism. Here is the oath which every miner is forced to take before he can go into a mine or get an opportunity to live. (The name of the miner is omitted for obvious reasons.)

"I, John Brown, a Justice of the Peace, in and for the County of Wise and the State of Virginia, do hereby certify that ———

———— has this day personally appeared before me and made statement on oath, that he would not in any way aid or abet the labor organization, known as the United Mine Workers of America, or any other labor organization calculated to bring about trouble between the Virginia Iron, Coal and Coke Company, and its employes, in or near the vicinity of Tom's Creek, Wise County, Virginia.

Witness my hand and seal, this 19th day of December, 1901.

———— ————, J. P."

The superintendent should remember that the shooting of John Brown did not stop the onward march of the Civil War and the emancipation of the blacks, and should know that the shooting of Mother Jones will never stop the onward march of the United Mine Workers toward the goal of emancipation of the white slaves from capitalistic oppression. The laborers will move onward in their work until every child has an opportunity to enjoy God's bright and sunlight and until some Happy New Year shall bring to every toiler's home the joyful news of freedom from all masters.

[*International Socialist Review* 2 (1901–02), 575–78.]

The Dawning of a New Era

"To our imprisoned comrades in Idaho I have this to say: I am as ready to die with you now as I have been ready to fight with you in the past."
—Mother Jones.

In the history of the country — I go farther, in the history of the world — there is nothing more criminal and heartless than the kidnaping of Moyer, Haywood and Pettibone and walling them in alive without the shadow of a charge against them. Two governors, in league with the money power, are guilty of this crime. We who know these men know them to be innocent and we also know that they are worthy to receive our loyal support and that they shall have it to the end.

This diabolical deed, accomplished at night, upon honest workingmen is enough to set one's brain in a whirl and stir one's soul to revolt.

King Ruzvlt entered no word of protest, but indirectly approved and backed up this attack upon organized labor.

When Gooding said: "These men shall never leave Idaho alive" he said more than he intended. That is what he meant, but he has since realized that it was unfortunate for him to blurt it out.

General Miles says he can bring 250 honest citizens into court to swear that the beef trust murdered three thousand American soldiers by feeding them poisoned beef.

The mine owners, with the aid of United States deputy marshals, murdered seven miners in the dead of night on Stanaford Mountain, W. Va., February 23, 1903.

These are two typical incidents which show the murderous march of King Capital. Life counts for less than nothing. But let it be noted that it is always the life of labor.

Whether it be the beef trust to grind out profit, the Standard Oil trust to contribute to education one day and raise the price of oil the next, the smelter trust to suffocate its employees in the poison fumes of its infernos, or the mine owners' trust to have its hirelings blow up the workers to fasten crime on their organization, it is all the same, and it is always labor that furnishes the victims.

But this will not always be so. One of these days there is going to be a great awakening. I can already see the beginnings of it. Go where we will the workers are beginning to stand up and talk out loud. They are feeling the thrill of manhood; they are tired of cringing and crawling; they

276

are just realizing what they are and what they can be; and the change from slavery to freedom, from misery to splendid manhood is coming more swiftly than we know or the plutocrats dream.

There has been no conspiracy to kidnap the members of the beef trust for poisoning the soldiers, or the members of the Mine Owners' association for shooting and otherwise killing their miners. Such devilish things are never hatched in the brain of honest labor. All these crimes are spawned by the abnormal brain that is itself born of exploitation and thrives upon spoils wrung from misery.

One point in the Moyer, Haywood and Pettibone case we must not lose sight of; and that is, that Gooding, the governor of the state and at the same time the tool of the money power, declared to the world that they should not leave Idaho alive.

The whole conspiracy is locked up in this confession made in an unguarded moment.

Such a thing as a fair trial never entered Gooding's head. He had his orders from the power that rules in Idaho, as elsewhere in the capitalist system, and his one thought was to obey that order, catch our boys and kill them. That is the only thing he had in mind from the start. Such tools as Gooding, having no ability of their own, nor manhood, depend wholly upon their plutocratic masters and obey their orders implicitly to hold their jobs or to get better ones, and this applies particularly to hirelings of a political character.

When Gooding shouted that our boys should not leave Idaho alive he unintentionally issued a challenge to the working class of the United States. He did not intend this, but this has been the effect; and such an awakening has been produced that many times since the governor has found it expedient to explain that he had no intention of attacking "legitimate" unions of workingmen, but that his only purpose was to punish crime, and that Moyer, Haywood and Pettibone should have a perfectly fair trial.

This comes with poor grace from a governor who is at the same time a kidnaper: an executive of a state who at the very moment he is making these professions has one heel upon the law and the other upon the necks of his victims.

Gooding's protestations at this hour must be taken with considerable salt. He has been forced to this position and does not occupy it naturally, and any ordinary eye can see through the transparency very clearly.

Now let the working men and women of the United States say to Gooding and those behind him: You have issued the challenge, you have started this fight, you have attacked our comrades, and now we shall rally to the rescue of our fellow-workers and fight it out to a finish on any line you choose.

We have the right on our side, they have the power, but one honest-hearted workingman, whose cause is just and whose conscience is clear, has more moral power, more real strength that counts, than a thousand hirelings in the cause of crime.

If workingmen are now true, as seems evident upon every hand, then the last bull pen has been built and the last soldiers have insulted and out-raged the wives and children of their imprisoned fathers, husbands and brothers.

I personally know Moyer, Haywood and Pettibone. They are the last men to be guilty of assassination. No one who knows them believes in his heart that they had anything to do with the crime for which they are now in jail. They are as innocent as any of us, and the mine owners know this as well as anybody.

But these men were a menace to the capitalist anarchists that ruled with blood and iron in Colorado and this is why the charge of murder must be fastened upon them and an end put to them forever.

The real murderer is McPartland. He put up the job with Guggenheim and his crowd to back him up, supply the funds, the special train and the hundred other factors in the conspiracy.

Let us protest from the Atlantic to the Pacific, from the lakes to the gulf. Let the workers everywhere arise and swear that this crime shall not be committed.

To our imprisoned comrades in Idaho I have this to say: I am as ready to die with you now as I have been to fight with you in the past.

[*The Appeal to Reason,* 23 February 1907.]

The Grave of Martin Irons

On the morning of April 16 I arrived at Eddy, Texas. I was received by Comrade Williams and his wife. After breakfast they drove me to Bruceville, accompanied by a few of the citizens, and a little later I found myself at the grave of one of labor's loyal champions. The world remembers little of him now, and that little only to do him cruel injustice. He sleeps almost forgotten, but the day of his resurrection will come as certain as the sunrise.

It was nineteen long years since I had last seen this loyal fellow-worker in the great cause; since I had clasped his honest hand; since I had heard his earnest voice pleading for the slaves who work for wages and produce to enrich their masters and deny themselves.

The grave was marked with a piece of iron. This rough souvenir suggests the name of the labor warrior who there fell into his last long sleep. No tender hand had planted any flowers upon the grave of Martin Irons, but a mocking bird was singing sweetly near his resting place and the wild flowers were scattering their springtime perfume to the breezes as if to rebuke man's cruel forgetfulness by the sweet and gentle breath and melody of Mother Nature.

It is fortunate that Martin Irons did not awaken when he fell asleep. The world had nothing but cruelty, scorn and suffering for him. He had been too true. Had he prated of the identity of interests between master and slave, his name would have been honored and he would have fared like a prince of the blood. He had the ability but refused to prostitute it.

Jay Gould would have paid him liberally, but Martin Irons refused to see him. All of Gould's millions were so much worthless chaff to him in the presence of his duty to labor.

When the great Missouri Pacific strike was crushed the whole burden of it fell upon his shoulders. All the papers vilified him, but he never complained. His own followers who, had they been true to him, would have won the strike, now turned upon him to slander him on account of their own cowardice.

But Martin Irons through it all remained the warrior. He had the heart of a child and the soul of a hero. The capitalist class made up its mind that it would be troubled with him no more and so he was hounded as if he had been a wild beast, deprived of employment, driven from place to place until he was literally starved into a pauper's grave.

But Martin Irons was a pauper in no other sense. In principle he was rich and royal. He kept his own company and his pride did not desert him. What must have been his opinion of the world; he did not say. He accepted his fate; he had been true.

No self-reproach added to his suffering and if the angels of love have not abandoned their mission they hover near where Martin Irons sleeps and in God's good time his name will be revived, the contumely will be effaced and his memory will shine resplendent in the galaxy of agitators, pioneers and warriors who died to make man free.

[*The Appeal to Reason,* 11 May 1907.]

Governor Comer's Alabama Cotton Mills

It had been thirteen years since I bid farewell to the workers in Alabama and went forth to other fields to fight their battles. I returned again in 1908 to see what they were doing for the welfare of their children. Governor Comer, being the chief star of the state, I went out to Avondale, on the outskirts of Birmingham, to take a glance at his slave pen. I found there somewhere between five and six hundred slaves. The governor in his generous nature could provide money for Jesus, reduced the wages of his slaves first 10 per cent and then 16. As the wretches were already up against starvation a few of them struck, and I accompanied an organizer and the editor of the *Labor Advocate* out there to help organize the slaves into a union of their craft. I addressed the body, and after I got through a large number became members of the Textile Workers' Union. I returned again inside of another week, held another meeting with them, and another large number joined. I was also going to complete my work on Monday, the 12th, but I had to leave for Southern Illinois. He has not yet charged any of them nor has he threatened to call an extra session of the legislature to pass the vagrancy bill in case they struck against the lash of reduction. Of all the God-cursed conditions that surround any gathering of slaves, or slave pen, Comer's mill district beats them all. As you look at them you immediately conclude they have been lashed too far, but they still have some spirit of revolt in them. They work all of thirteen hours a day. They are supposed to go in at 6 in the morning, but the machinery starts up soon after 5, and they have to be there. They are supposed to get 45 minutes for dinner, but the machinery starts up again after they are out for 20 minutes and they have to be at their post. When I was in Alabama, 13 years ago, they had no child labor law. Since then they passed a very lame one, so-called. They evade the law in this way: A child who has passed his or her twelfth year can take in his younger brothers or sisters from 6 years on and get them to work with him. They are not on the pay roll, but the pay for these little ones goes into the elder one's pay. So that when you look at the pay roll you think this one child makes quite a good bit, when perhaps there is two or three younger than him under the lash. Then the Governor runs a pill peddler, who is a nephew of the Governor, Dr. Comer; there is two cents of every dollar knocked off of the 600 slaves to pay this doctor. You see it's all in the family. Then they have a Sunday school, and the chief guy of the Sunday school has got a gold tooth in the front of his mouth, and when he is talking about

Jesus you can see him open up the mouth to show the golden calf, so the little ones will pay particular attention to what he says. I found them all suffering from chills and fever and malaria, and whatever change they have left goes to the patent medicine doctor. One woman told me her mother had gone into that mill and worked and took her four children in with her. She said: "I have been in the mill since I was 4 years old. I am now 34." She looked to me as if she were 60. She has a kindly nature if treated right, but her whole life and spirit was crushed out beneath the iron wheels of Comer's greed. When you think of the little ones that this mother brings forth you can see that society is cursed with an abnormal human being. She knew nothing but the whiz of machinery in the factory. As I talked to her, with many others, she said: "Oh, can you do something for us." The wives, the mothers, the children, all go in to produce dividends — profit, profit, profit. This brutal Governor is a pillar of the First Methodist Church in Birmingham, and on Sunday he gets up and sings, "O Lord, will you have another star for my crown when I get there?" What a job God Almighty must have in hiring mechanics to make stars for that black-hearted villain's crown when he gets there. I saw the little ones lying on the bed shaking with chills and I could hear them ask parents and masters what they were here for, what crime they had committed that they were brought here and sold to the dividend auctioneer. Men and women of America, when shall you stop your hypocritical actions. When in Alabama, 13 years ago, these women ran from four to five looms; today I find them running some 24 looms; and when you think of the high tension, when you think of the cruelty to their nerves, the glory of their lives are gone. The days when their labor was not a burden perhaps is over; now it is all a hot rush and worry and incessant sweat, as they scratch their bits of corn out of these hard days. Think of the picture of these young girls and children on their feet guiding that machinery for twelve or thirteen hours a day; running that machinery hour by hour, and in their fever at night I hear them moaning: "Oh, what will I do; I can't make the machine go; it won't wind." It is hell, worse than hell. Think of these children standing in the midst of these spindles, every thread of which must be incessantly watched so that it may be instantly pieced together, in a hot room amid its roaring machinery, so loud that one can not hear another, no matter how close they are at hand. Amid the whizzing wheels and bands and switch racks that would snatch off a limb for one second's carelessness; all this in hot air so that in summer a great thirst scorches their throat, the weavers are encircled by 24 terrific looms in a steamed atmosphere which is even worse than hell. The method of communication used is as if they were dumb animals, because at any moment a rebellious shuttle may shoot forth and knock an eye out. A loose shirt may be seized by a wheel or a strap and then the horrors of the accident can be better imagined than told. Their mentality is dwarfed, and if they say a word the cruel boss, who is a scab, goes after them. They tell me that when they get thirsty they can not get enough water to drink. They are all victims of some ailment. They are never free from headache. Owing to the necessity of cleaning machinery, they do not eat at noon hour. The unpleasant odor coming from the oil and grease, the rumbling of shafts and drums, the squeaking of wheels and spindles make them sick and languorous. They rise at 4 o'clock in the morning to prepare to enter that slave pen at 5:30. They are all pale, dyspeptic, hollow-chested, and it seems as if life has no charms for them. They can not go and seek other employment because the energy has been all used up from childhood in their particular line of industry. Mr. Roosevelt makes no allusion to these undesirable citizens who murder these children for gold. I believe that the God of Justice will yet rise and take it into his own hands and punish the devourers of children's lives for profit. This is the Democratic South, my friends—this is the Democratic administration; this is what Mr. Bryan and Mr. Gompers want to uphold. I stand for the overthrow of the entire system that murders childhood; I stand for the overthrow of a system that can give a $6,000 job to labor leaders who have betrayed these infants in their infancy. I stand for the teachings of Christ put into practice; not the teachings of capitalism and graft and murder. I stand for the day when this rotten structure will totter of its own vileness. I stand for the day when the baby child will live in God's fair land and enjoy its air, its food and its pleasures, when every mother will caress it warmly, when there will be no parasites, no slaves, when $2,000 won't be paid for a hat to cover the skull of the desirable citizen's daughter, when the child shall not be taxed for such diabolical infamy; when poodle dogs will not be caressed on the life-blood of innocent childhood; when these children of Comer's hell-hole will live in God's heaven without any master to dictate their lives.

The high temperature of the mills combined by an abnormal humidity of the air, produced by steaming, done by manufacturers, make bad material weave easier and tend to diminish the workers' powers of resisting disease. The humid atmosphere promotes perspiration, but makes evaporation from the skin more difficult, and in this condition the operator when he leaves the mill has to face a much reduced temperature, which produces serious chest affections. They are all narrow-chested and disheartened looking. I found very few of them who could read or write as I went to take their names to register them for their charter. I found they would come and ask me, "You write his or her name," whoever was running for office. No wonder the Governor could send his daughter to the seashore; no wonder he could have the audacity to drive miners back at the point of the bayonet; no wonder man and women commit suicide. They are too tired out at the end of the day to engage in any mental pursuit. They want something or some one to cheer them up.

As a new Rudyard Kipling would say:

> Comer, go reckon your dead
> By the forges red
> And the factories where your slaves spin.
> You've eaten their lives,
> Their babes and wives.
> For which Roosevelt says you're a desirable citizen.
> It was your legal right, your legal share,
> But if blood be the price of your god-cursed gold,
> God knows these slaves have paid it dear.

[*St. Louis Labor,* 24 October 1908.]

Oh! Ye Lovers of Liberty!

Brothers and Comrades: From the bastile of capitalism in Los Angeles comes the cry of our brave brothers, calling on you to stand for freedom, right and justice. I know and feel that the cries will not be in vain. You responded cheerfully to the needs of our comrades of the industrial revolution as they were voiced from Idaho, and I know you will be none the less responsive now, in behalf of our Mexican comrades.

If ever there was a time in history when it was imperative that men and women should promptly rally to the banner of freedom and justice, that time is now. Before, it was the power of the state and the nation that the capitalists were using for the destruction of the working class. Now, it is the United States government seconding the murderous despotism of Russia and the irresponsible dictatorship of Mexico. The fight has become international; yet it centers in the United States. If these foreign vultures of oppression win now, then our liberty goes.

For Diaz and American capitalism are partners, even as American capitalism and the Russian czar are partners. Pierpont Morgan goes to Russia and shakes hands with the czar; and now the czar comes to America demanding the surrender of political refugees. Mrs. Diaz, when visiting in Texas, is entertained by members of the Copper Queen syndicate whose headquarters are at 95 John Street, New York, and Elihu Root of New York is wined and dined by the tyrant dictator, Diaz, when in Mexico.

This tyrant, this fiend, beside whom King George was a gentleman and lover of the poor, has given to American capitalists concessions that are worth millions of dollars, and guarantees them peon labor that dare not ask higher wages under penalty of being shot for violating the law; and in return he asks that if political refugees escape to America, or if a Mexican dare to come to America and criticise him, they must be returned to him, that they may be shot.

Some sixty years ago the fugitive slave law was enacted, requiring slaves that escaped to free territory to be returned to their masters. This was all in the United States of America. Yet the people refused to obey that law and arose in such a mighty protest that within ten years the institution of slavery was swept from the earth. Now we have the dictator of Mexico, and the czar of Russia, tyrants both, both foreigners, trying to enforce a fugitive slave law in the United States of America — a law infinitely more vile than that of the fifties — and the federal government lends its aid to the outrage. It is time that the people arose in all their sovereign power and said their say.

In 1906, two brave leaders of the strike in Cananea, Diegues and Caldreom, were sentenced to fifteen years in a dungeon by the sea. A deserter from the American army, Kosterlitsky, waited with his troops across the border line for any strikers who might be handed over to him by agents of the Standard Oil company, and other reptile combinations. Already the prisons of Mexico are filled with men who were merely suspicioned of favoring the strikers, while the children of the victims are left to struggle and starve.

I happened to be in Douglas, Ariz., in August, 1907, when they kidnaped young Sarabia, threw him into an automobile, and, as he screamed for help, muzzled him, ran him across the line, and handed him over to the devourers of human flesh. Kidnaping seems to be becoming very fashionable with the members of the American oligarchy of wealth.

In this connection, I wish to say a good word for Governor Kibbie, who took quick action and had Sarabia brought back. He also would not furnish troops to the Copper Queen company during the strike at Bisbee, Ariz. He had a clear view of the economic conflict, and understood that it was not labor that was riotous, but the minions of capitalism. During my stay in Arizona I also had the pleasure of meeting Captain Wheeler on several occasions, and believe he wants to do as nearly right as the powers that be will permit him. I must give him credit for the part he played in the strike at Bisbee. Yet after doing full justice to all who deserve credit, the fact remains that the federal government is allied with the masters of the big corporations in trying to enforce international absolutism and to make slaves of the workers who shall be unable to escape their chains.

All honor to you, my brave comrades, Magon, Villarreal and Rivera, for the gallant fight you are making for human liberty. In days to come your names will be inscribed on the temple of liberty. When the wolves of capitalism shall have disappeared from the cities of our nation, when men shall be able to walk forth free without Oscar Lawlers and detectives dogging their footsteps, then the three Mexican comrades shall have their names written large as lovers of their race.

But, let me ask you, Attorney Lawler, of Los Angeles, if you can reconcile your conscience to the crushing out of liberty and the human desire for justice. The class you represent has murdered and oppressed men, women and children in the interests of cursed greed. They have jailed the men who fed them; they have maligned us, vilified us, buried us in dungeons, hung us on scaffolds, chopped us to pieces, nailed us to the cross of profits as they did the Laborer of Palestine nineteen centuries ago. Have you not, Attorney Lawler, of Los Angeles, nursed from your mother's breast the milk of human kindness? Will you stoop to stain your hands with the blood of these four brave lovers of liberty, by handing them over to that brutal dictator called Diaz?

Permit me, Attorney Lawler, of Los Angeles, to serve notice on you and your class that the working people of America are awake. You cannot make them slaves as are the peons of Mexico, slaves of the dictator whom you serve. Let me hand you the edict of the One you pretend to honor—"Thou shalt not kill."

We are serving notice on you. Your dungeons shall yet be turned into club rooms. We want peace, we want justice, we want that which is justly ours. By all that is good and holy we shall have them.

Men of America, women of America, rouse as you never roused before. Wipe from our jurisprudence the infamous fugitive slave law of this later day. Tear from our statute books the modern and most wicked Dred Scott decision which makes of your government a hunter of the oppressed and persecutor of the helpless.

[*The Appeal to Reason,* 23 January 1909.]

Mexico and Murder

I rise to ask the American people, have you read John K. Turner's article in the *American Magazine* for October on the frightful brutality of the Mexican government toward its people? If not, read it at once. Then ask your Christian ministers why they are silent in the face of this frightful tragedy at our very doors.

Why are they silent? Because they worship at the shrine of Mammon.

If the Revolutionary fathers could come back to earth, the first question they would ask would be what has become of the national pride? Did it die with the immortal Lincoln? Look at the frightful pictures in the *American Magazine.* Imagine these lashes falling on your flesh. See and feel the blood dripping from your body. Go down to Belem prison and see the shocking pictures there. Then, men and women, ask yourselves, "Am I my brother's keeper?" Look at their lacerated bodies, their hopeless lives.

They ask you, does God sleep? No, he does not. He will wipe out injustice with suffering, wrong with blood, and sin with death. The disgraceful phase of it all is that we stand and see the public officials whom we pay, become bloodhounds and man-grabbers in the service of bloody Diaz.

It looks as if this government of the people and for the people and by the people, so-called, has become general scavenger for the most ferocious murderer on the face of God's earth. We have in our jails and prisons some of the bravest revolutionists, perhaps the world has known. Leavenworth, Kan., holds three of these brave political refugees. Yuma, Arizona, holds three more. That brave soul who swam the river across the Del Rio last year was arrested, tried in the federal court and turned loose; re-arrested under the emigration laws and turned loose by the bureau in Washington; re-arrested for the benefit of the hungry jackal who is thirsting for human blood and placed in jail in Texas to await trial.

Why all this? Listen: The American capitalists have started a steel trust in Mexico capitalized at fifty million dollars, and a smelter trust at sixty million. Cheap labor of course.

Attorney General Wickersham is a large stockholder in the Mexican Central railroad, where Harriman, before he passed to the great beyond, held most of the preferred stock. Hearst owns three million acres of mineral lands adjoining the Standard Oil company. The capitalist pirates have robbed the people of this nation, now they are going into Mexico to carry out the advice of Carnegie, and "hire labor cheap and make millions."

Rob the Mexicans now and next China.

This young legal leper, Oscar Lawler, has men imprisoned for daring to protest against such tyranny and robbery. He held three revolutionists in jail in Los Angeles without trial for twenty months, contrary to law.

Will it be recorded in the days to come that we, the people of a Christian nation, stood for our president, the chief executive, taking the hand of the most brutal specimen of the human race that this age has produced?

How the immortal Lincoln would blush with shame and frown with contempt at the mention of such men as Lawler and Wickersham! Contrast these legal satraps with John K. Turner, who took his life in his hands to make the world better for mankind to live in. All honor to John K. Turner! The world will call you blessed.

President Taft was placed in power by the Wall Street robbers and he can not do as his natural instincts would urge him to do. When a man is nominated by the money power of Wall Street his independence is gone, his manhood is sacrificed and his love of liberty if he ever had any must be offered up on the altar of selfish ambition.

I know what Lincoln would say to that crew on Wall Street: "The nation first and you last!"

The people who make up this nation will some day wake from their slumber with horror. I hope it will not be too late.

[*The Appeal to Reason,* 23 October 1909.]

Girl Slaves of Milwaukee Breweries

It is the same old story, as pitiful as old, as true as pitiful.

When the whistle blows in the morning, it calls the girl slaves of the bottle washing department of the breweries, to don their wet shoes and rags, and hustle to the bastile to serve out their sentences.

It is indeed true, they are sentenced to hard, brutal labor, labor that gives no cheer, brings no recompense. Condemned for life to drudge daily in the wash-room with wet shoes and wet clothes, surrounded with foul mouthed, brutal foremen, whose orders and language would not look well in print, and would surely shock over-sensitive ears, or delicate nerves! And their crime? Involuntary poverty. It is hereditary. They are no more to blame for it than a horse is, for having the glanders. It is the accident of birth. This accident that throws so many girl workers into the surging, seething mass, known as the working class, is what forces them out of the cradle into servitude — to be willing (?) slaves of the mill, factory, department store, hell or bottling shop in Milwaukee's colossal breweries. Here they create wealth for the brewery barons that they may own palaces, theaters, automobiles, blooded stock, farms, banks and heaven knows what all, while the poor girls slave on, all day, in the vile smell of sour beer, lifting cases of empty and full bottles, weighing from 100 to 150 pounds, while wearing wet shoes and rags; for God knows they can not buy clothes on the miserable pittance doled out to them by their soulless master class. That these slaves of the dampness should contract rheumatism is a foregone conclusion. Rheumatism is one of the chronic ailments, and is closely followed by consumption. Consumption is well known to be only a disease of poverty. The Milwaukee law makers, of course, enacted an anti-spitting ordinance, to protect the public health, and the brewers contributed to the Red Cross society to make war on the shadow of tuberculosis, and all the while the big capitalists are setting out incubators to hatch out germs enough among the poor workers to destroy the nation. Should one of these poor girls slaves spit on the sidewalk, it would cost her more than she can make in two weeks' work. Such is the fine system of the present day affairs.

The foreman on these breweries regulates the time, even, that the girls may stay in the toilet room, and in the event of overstaying it gives him an opportunity he seems to be looking for, to indulge in indecent and foul language. Should the patient slave forget herself and take offense, it will cost her the job in that prison. And after all, bad as it is, it is all that she knows how to do. To deprive her of the job, means less crusts and worse rags in "the land of the free and the home of the brave." Many of the girls have no home nor parents, and are forced to feed and clothe and shelter themselves; and all this on an average of $3.00 per week. Ye Gods! What a horrible nightmare! What hope is there for decency, when unscrupulous wealth may exploit its producers so shamelessly?

No matter how cold, how stormy, how inclement the weather, many of these poor slaves must walk from their shacks to their work, for their miserable stipend precludes any possibility of squeezing a street car ride out of it. Is this civilization? If so, what, please, is barbarism?

As an illustration of what these poor girls must submit to, one about to become a mother told me, with tears in her eyes, that every other day a depraved specimen of mankind took delight in mesuring her girth, and passing such comments as befits such humorous (?) occasions.

While the wage paid is 75 and 85 cents a day, the poor slaves are not permitted to work more than three or four days a week, and the continual threat of idle days makes the slaves much more tractable and submissive than they otherwise would be. Often when their day's work is done, they are put to washing off the tables and the lunch-room floor, and other odd jobs for which there is not even the suggestion of compensation. Of course, abuse always follows power, and nowhere is it more in evidence than in this miserable treatment the brewers and their hireling accord their girl slaves.

The foreman also uses his influence through certain living mediums, near at hand, to neutralize any effort having in view the organization of these poor, helpless victims of an unholy and brutal profit system, and threats of discharge were made, should these girls attend my meetings.

One of these foremen actually carried a union card, but the writer of this article reported him to the union and had him deprived of it for using such foul language to the girls under him. I learned of him venting his spite by discharging several girls, and I went to the superintendent and told him the character of the foreman; on the strength of my charges he was called to the office, and when he was informed of the nature of the visit, he patted the superintendent familiarly on the back and whined out how loyal he was to the superintendent, the whole performance taking on the character of a servile lick-spittle. As he fawns on his superior, so he expects to play autocrat with his menials, and exacts the same cringing from those under him. Such is the petty boss, who holds the living of the working class girls in his hands.

The brewers themselves were always courteous when I called on them, but their underlings were not so tactful, evidently working under instructions. The only brewer who treated me rudely or denied me admittance was Mr. Blatz, who brusquely told me his feelings in the following words:

"The Brewer's Association of Milwaukee met when you first came to town, and decided not to permit these girls to organize." This Brewer's association is a strong union of all the brewery plutocrats, composed of Schlitz, Pabst, Miller and Blatz breweries, who are the principal employers of women. This union met and decided, as above stated, that these women should not be permitted to organize! I told Mr. Blatz that he could not shut me out of the halls of legislation, that as soon as the legislature assembles I shall appear there and put these conditions on record, and demand an investigation and the drafting of suitable laws to protect the womanhood of the state.

Organized labor and humanity demand protection for these helpless victims of insatiable greed, in the interest of the motherhood of our future state.

Will the people of this country at large, and the organized wage-workers in particular, tolerate and stand any longer for such conditions, as exist in the bottling establishments of these Milwaukee breweries? I hope not! Therefore, I ask all fair minded people to refrain from purchasing the product of these baron brewers until they change things for the better for these poor girls, working in their bottling establishments.

Exploited by the brewer! Insulted by the petty bosses! Deserted by the press, which completely ignored me and gave no helping hand to these poor girls' cause. Had they had a vote, however, their case would likely have attracted more attention from all sides. Poor peons of the brewer! Neglected by all the Gods! Deserted by all mankind! The present shorn of all that makes life worth living, the future hopeless, without a comforting star or glimmer! What avails our boasted greatness, built upon such human wreckage? What is civilization and progress to them? What "message" hears our holy brotherhood in the gorgeous temples of modern worship? What terrors has the over-investigated white slave traffic for the woman brewery worker of Milwaukee? What a prolific recruiting station for the red light district. For, after all, the white slave eats, drinks and wears good clothing, and to the hopeless, this means living, if it only lasts a minute. What has the beer slave to lose? — the petty boss will make her job cost her her virtue anyhow. This has come to be a price of a job everywhere, nowadays. Is it any wonder the white slave traffic abounds on all sides? No wonder the working class has lost all faith in God. Hell itself has no terrors worse than a term in industrial slavery. I will give these brewery lords of Milwaukee notice that my two months investigation and efforts to organize in spite of all obstacles placed in my way, will bear fruit, and the sooner they realize their duty, the better it will be for themselves. Will they do it?

[*New York Call,* 4 April 1910; also *The Appeal to Reason,* 9 April 1910.]

A Sacred Call to Action

There are in our federal prisons some eight or ten Mexican revolutionists who have been silently railroaded to the American bastiles at the behest of the worst tyrant which ever cursed God's earth, Diaz of Mexico.

Some humane congressmen have introduced a bill of inquiry asking the attorney general to explain why as revolutionists these men are held. I beg of you in the name of freedom to flood Congress with letters demanding that this investigation be pushed through Congress.

Don't fail! the cause of justice falls on you. You hear the pleading of your brothers from behind the capitalist bastiles.

Men and women, save those brave brothers of the Revolution!

[*St. Louis Labor*, 16 April 1910.]

What I Saw in the Anthracite Fields

My work in connection with the Mexican cases being completed at Washington, and feeling assured that the victims of this "bloodocracy" would not be rearrested on their liberation from prison, I decided to visit the boys in the anthracite regions, investigate conditions, and see what progress, if any, had been made in the way of organization and education since the last general strike. My visit to the anthracite regions which border on the inferno followed that of Roosevelt and his ex-labor leader, John Mitchell, who had visited the coal fields, so it is said, for the purpose of making some observations and investigations as to the condition of the slaves whose lifeblood is coined into profits that the few may riot in luxury. When Roosevelt and his bodyguard arrived at Scranton they were received by the Bishop of Scranton, who wined and dined them and who remarked during the meal that it was the first time in his life he had had the honor of sitting between two Presidents. On the right of the bishop sat Mr. Roosevelt, friend of the workingman. It was he who, in order to show his friendship, sent 2,000 guns to Colorado to shoot the miners into subjection and, if they did not obey, blow their brains out, and who, while president of the United States, sent hundreds of messages to Congress, but never one in the interest of the working class. Not even when the explosion in the Monongah mine sent 700 souls, the souls of wage slaves, into the shadows and shocked the civilized world, did he find it in his sterile conscience to send a message to Congress demanding protection for the men whose labor feeds the mammoth maw of industry and warms the fireside of the world. Roosevelt's real interest in the working class is only aroused when he seeks their votes. On the left of the bishop sat the $6,000 Civic Federation beauty, pet of the mine owners, decorated with diamonds, gifts from the coal barons.

What would Christ have said if he could have looked down upon this trinity of sleek parasites as they sat at the bishop's table gorging themselves with the richest of food and the finest of wines, while thousands of their brothers down in the valley had no where to lay their heads?

Roosevelt and Mitchell made their investigations of the anthracite regions mostly from the comfortable seats of a large touring car. Waiting press representatives at each point were told that prosperity was rampant throughout the coal fields, that the miners never enjoyed to such an extent the good things of life. What an infamous libel on the truth! Careful indeed was the labor scavenger, the well-groomed vassal of the Civic Federation, to avoid Latimer and other points where the misery and wretchedness of the miners defy exaggeration. Here is where twenty-one of his comrades rest in eternal peace, murdered victims of a murderous mine owners association! Upon the breast of these rugged heroes, true to their brothers, loyal to their class even unto death, there flashed no radiant gem as scintillating evidence of servility that thrift may follow fawning!

Had Roosevelt followed my trail through the anthracite regions he would have seen women old and young carrying sixteen gallons of water on their heads across the coal strippings for a distance of a mile. He would have seen the motherhood of the future dwarfed morally, mentally, physically and spiritually in the mills where they are required to work ten hours a day and walk three or four miles each way going and coming from their work for a niggardly pittance. He would have seen the victims of his commission, whose award was so favorable to the coal barons that they have forced upon the miners ever since poverty and degradation.

In Wilkes-Barre, where they were received by a prominent divine, the outside of the house was illuminated by sixty dollars' worth of electric lights, while the bloodsuckers were feasting inside. There were forty sky-pilots and some public officials at the table, but not a single workingman among them! Mr. Roosevelt was the guest of the distinguished divine all night, and in order that the monkey chaser might have rest they hid his shoes and would not allow him to arise until the sun had cast its charming rays into the room. While all this was going on, my attention was called to a most diabolical act of one of the coal company clerks, who stripped a young boy of eighteen of all his clothing for owing the company $4 that he was unable to pay just at that time, and the child was forced to go home in torn underclothing, walking over a mile before he got from under public gaze. There are many more horrifying sights that Roosevelt and his lapdog might have seen in their tour of investigation if they had so desired. Roosevelt's real mission to the anthracite regions was one of spectacular self-exploitation, while Mitchell simply poodled in the interest of his salary-paying master.

(Just before the fall of the Roman empire, I heard of such things happening.)

[*New York Call,* 14 November 1910.]

How they "Histed" the Sheriff over the Fence

The strike of 1900 in the anthracite district was perhaps won in the shortest time and with less violence than any other strike recorded in history. The women played a most important part in that strike; they organized and went out every night.

It was pathetic to see them; old women, with their heads white with years of sorrow and care; young women, with hearts beating with hope for a brighter day, joined forces and marched close up to the mines. In one instance we marched 15 miles in one night. During the march we stopped to rest. Few knew where we were going, but there were 5000 men in some mines which we wanted to call out and get them to join our forces.

HALTED BY TROOPS

One night 5000 women from different camps gathered together and marched 15 miles over the mountains to Coledale, Pa. We had a band along, so we played and sang patriotic songs as we marched to Lansford, and the people dashed out in their night gowns and said, "— —ll, it is that old woman and her army. They are going to clean us all up."

As we attempted to pass along the road the glitter of bayonets in the dead hour of night faced us. The Colonel yelled, "Halt!" and we obeyed orders, of course.

ALLOWED TO PASS

"You will not charge bayonets," said I, "not on this crowd. We are not fighting the Government. We are simply going to get 5000 of our brothers, who are still working, to join our forces."

The regiment was the crack 13th, of Pennsylvania. The militia saw that we did not have a single weapon in our hands, but were armed only with our voices, which we raised in defense of childhood yet to come. We were peaceful and law abiding, but we wanted justice, that was all. So finally the soldiers let us pass.

After a while we met the miners, some of them coming down to work on the cars. We took possession of the cars and cleaned them out, and the men went back home, and those fellows were among the first to lay down their tools in response to the call of 1902.

Then more than 5000 went to the hotels where the militia had ordered their breakfasts, took the food right out of the kitchen and ate it and allowed the militia to go without.

DROPPED OVER FENCE

We went on singing as the band played until we met the little Sheriff. He made a lot of fuss about our "disorderly" conduct. I guess he didn't like our singing, or the way the band played. Anyway he was awfully cross and flashed his star all the while he was trying to boss us.

The easiest way to get by him was to remove him from the road, we thought. That some of the women did by picking him up and dropping him down on the far side of the fence.

He was shaking like an aspen leaf as he got up and ran away.

[*Cincinnati Post*, 2 April 1912.]

Papa, Don't Cry

In 1902 one of our organizers went up into the mountains of West Virginia to organize the men. He returned in a few hours. I asked him why he came back so soon, and he said:

"The Superintendent got a gun and chased me down and told me not to come back there again. I didn't come out here to get killed, Mother."

I concluded to go up and meet that Superintendent. I got off at one of the little mining towns and stayed all night with the family of a miner, gathered up eight or 10 of the union miners and the next morning we started up the mountain.

ANNOUNCES MEETING

It was a six-mile walk, straight up, and it was noon when we got up there. I said to the boys, "Go down and tell the miners that I am going to have a meeting up here at 2 o'clock, and tell that superintendent that I will feel highly honored by his presence also."

While I was sitting on a rock a man came out of an old log cabin and motioned for me to come over. I went and shook hands with him, and found that he was a miner from Ohio. I went in and there I saw, oh, such a beautiful young girl lying on a pallet of straw with a clean patched quilt spread over her.

I think I never gazed on a more sublimely beautiful face than hers in my life. I turned to the father and asked:

"Mountain fever?" He said, "Yes, she is sick, but not fever, it is consumption."

"I could not make enough at the mines," he continued, "to take care of those six children" (four of them were sitting around the fire), "so we concluded to let the girl go down and work. I went down a month ago and brought her up. This is all I've got left of her. They worked her to death."

"BETTER SOME DAY"

He broke down, and she said from her dying pillow:

"Papa, don't cry, I'll be better some day."

There was a little bottle of medicine by her bed. She took it up and said, "Mother Jones, that cost a dollar." I said, "Well, what of it, if it does you good." And she replied, "Yes, but it would have bought the children so much."

We had the meeting. The superintendent did not show up, but a lot of his men did. We organized them all at the close of the meeting, and I bade them good-by and told them I would be back inside of 10 days.

I went over to bid the young girl good-by, and she looked at me and said: "Mother Jones, I used to go down that mountain and thought it fun, but I'll never go again. I will never see you again, Mother, good-by."

FATHER IS DISCHARGED

Next morning when the father went to the mine the Superintendent told him to take his time and leave. He said to him: "You entertained that woman agitator yesterday and you cannot work in our mines."

In vain did the father explain my visit to his dying daughter. He got his time, but no money. That company gives the men the time and keeps the cash. He went home broken-hearted and told the mother.

They had only three days in which to vacate the shack, for the company owns every shingle on it, and sometimes there are not so many shingles on it, either. The girl dropped back and died as the father told of his discharge and that they must move at once.

The father went to the outhouse and taking the boards from that made a coffin, wrapped his dead daughter in a sheet and laid her to rest in the mountain.

[*Cincinnati Post,* 3 April 1912.]

Miners' Strikes in the Kingdom of West Virginia

During the strike in West Virginia in 1901 and 1902 I went up Stanaford Mountain and held a meeting with the miners. I found them to be peaceful, law-abiding boys. There was no drinking, no gambling, no carousing. They even had a little schoolhouse of their own.

The afternoon we held the meeting a Deputy United States Marshal had been there and wanted to arrest some of them. They were supposed to have violated some injunction, but the men told him they had violated no law, and that they did not propose to have their brothers carted off like a crowd of criminals. They gave him so many minutes in which to leave town, and he left.

SHOOT AT CABINS

That night a big gang of special deputies went up the mountainside and shot up the miners' cabins after all were in bed and asleep. Several miners were killed and about 20 others were wounded. Mattresses, saturated with the life blood of these helpless innocent slaves, were hung out to dry the next day and were a shocking exhibit.

So mean were the owners of the mines that they refused to allow the body of one of the murdered boys, a leader of the union men, to be buried in the near-by graveyard, the ground of which was owned by the coal operators. He was buried in his father-in-law's back yard.

A few days later I found his widow watering the grave with her tears, while a little child, digging in the fresh clay, was crying over and over:
"Papa, tum back to see baby."

I learned the next morning from the telegrapher at Montgomery that there had been trouble in the mountain, and when I asked what the trouble was he said he did not know, but that some one had been killed. I went up with a few of the boys, and there I beheld the most horrible picture imaginable. The women were begging the deputies not to kill their children, and the reply was, "to − −ll with your children." It was a blood night. It was a fearful night!

WOMEN HOMELESS

Those women, left homeless, shelterless, with their little broods around them, asked me what to do, and in their insane frenzy they said to me:

300

"Oh, Mother Jones, bring him back to me!" I am almost afraid to tell the terrible thoughts I had that day.

Now you say, "Well, but these murderers at the mines were arrested."

I answer, "Yes, but they were all acquitted."

The Judge ordered the photographer to destroy the pictures which I had him take of these seven dead men.

I heard of a poor woman, with four children, who was in great distress. I collected $50 and a Catholic priest came out on the platform and gave me $5. I sent it to the mothers by a miner, and I said to him:

"Give the woman with the four orphans $30 of this, for the other women will be better able to get along than she." When the miner found that family they were hungry, they were cold, they were living in an old shack and they had no coal nor food in the house.

When the miner came back he said: "Mother, you ought to have seen that poor woman when I gave her the money."

She said: "Tell Mother Jones I have nothing to send her in return for her kindness but the tears and gratitude of the widow and the orphans, but when the good Lord calls me home I will ask Him to be good to Mother Jones."

[*Cincinnati Post,* 5 April 1912.]

How a Little Girl Put Deputies to Flight
with a Big Gun

During the 1897 strike I held a meeting at Plumb Creek, Pa., one of the camps where the striking miners were living in tents. The bright face of a little girl of 13 drew my attention to her. Each day as I was telling about the purposes of the strike and what a victory would mean to the miners and their families, most of whom had not had a good square meal for years, as I would portray the suffering of the women and children, this little girl's eyes would fill with tears.

One day the company, in a last desperate effort to break up the strike, sent Deputy Sheriffs, each with a big star pinned on his coat, around to corral the strikers and force them into the mine. They went to the tent where this girl, with her sisters and brothers and father lived.

The deputies went in and dragged the father out, but they had no more than got him started toward the wagon than the children, headed by the oldest girl, came a-running. The four small ones began screaming and crying, to which the deputies paid less attention than they would have to a stray cur's yelping.

The eldest girl ran into the tent and came out dragging an old shotgun. Only one end of it could she keep off the ground at a time, but that happened to be the business end of the gun, and the deputies caught themselves looking down into the double barrels.

"Now you just let go of my papa," the little girl cried hysterically, "and if you don't this gun will shoot every one of you bad men."

"The little fool might shoot, Bill," one deputy said to another. They let the father climb out of the wagon and then turned the team around and drove back to the Mine Superintendent for further instructions.

"Bring that kid to me!" he said.

A whole company of deputies went down and catching the girl in the road carried her to the mine company's office.

The Superintendent told her that he was going to send her to the Reform School for attempting to murder officers of the law.

"You can send me there if you want to, the old gun didn't have any hammer or trigger on it. Them fellows are all cowards anyhow. Gee! You ought to have seen 'em let loose of papa, 'cause they were scared I'd shoot daylight through them."

The Superintendent didn't send the little girl to the Reform School and they didn't try to kidnap any other strikers either. We all held a meeting and I made a crown which we placed upon the little girl's head. From then until the men won the strike, which they finally did, the girl was the heroine of all the mining country thereabouts.

[*Cincinnati Post,* 6 April 1912.]

Fashionable Society Scored

No nation can ever grow greater than its women. None ever has; none ever will. It is the women who decide the fate of a nation, and that has always been so, as history proves.

What tremendous power and responsibility, therefore, rests with womankind. I wonder if they realize it. In the poorer classes I think they do, or are coming to, but the attitude of the rich is appalling.

I called the other day to see Mrs. J. Borden Harriman at the Colony Club. While I sat in the reception room waiting to be received I watched the fashionable women come and go. Nearly all of them, if you asked them, would tell you proudly that they belonged to society. But if you asked them what society meant they could not answer you truthfully without covering themselves with shame.

I will tell you why they could not, or would not, answer: Because the word society, as applied to women of today, stands for idleness, fads, extravagance and display of wealth.

The women I saw parade before me were "bluffs." They glanced at me languidly, because that in society is the correct way to look at anybody not of their own class.

They posed and strutted before me like the poor, ignorant geese that they are, and probably imagined that I was impressed. I was, but not in the way they intended. I realized that they were posing and strutting because they had nothing else to occupy their minds, and so I pitied them. My pity was not without censure, however, because in these times of suffering the idle rich woman who parades her finery before the hungry and poverty-stricken is a modern inquisitor turning the thumb-screws of envy and despair into the very vitals of those who are in reality her sisters.

The high ideals of womanhood can never be realized in Colony clubs. The mission of woman is to develop human hearts and minds along charitable and sympathetic lines. The canker worm that is gnawing at the vitals of our womanhood is the failure of the rich woman to fulfill her mission in life. We are society-mad, and the craze—I am sorry to have to say it, but I realize that it is too true—is growing worse.

I look on Mrs. Harriman as an exceptional woman of her class, but even she has only scratched the surface of things as they really are. In Mrs. Harriman I find a woman of force and character. She could be the great factor in the education of women of her own set. By that I mean she could educate them to a realization of their duty in life and help

304

to turn them from their follies, vanities and shams to putting their time toward helping their unfortunate sisters.

Mrs. Harriman is groping and seeking the light, and with her ability to grasp great problems will do much toward bettering conditions wherever she may extend her work.

The hard part of Mrs. Harriman's task will be for her to overcome the effect of her environments, but she is very gifted and has an open mind, which is more than I can say for any others in her class that I have met.

As soon as every woman grasps the idea that every other woman is her sister, then we will begin to better conditions. For instance, I saw a girl in a store the other day ready to drop from weariness. Her fatigue was apparent, and yet I noticed a woman customer loaded down with expensive furs and jewels call on this girl to get down several heavy boxes of goods. Then, after glancing over them, she concluded she didn't want to buy anything. This rich woman wouldn't have asked her own sister to do that, but she didn't view the shop girl in that light. Oh, no; she was "only a shop girl."

I spoke to this girl after the woman had left and found that she worked about twelve hours a day, and for a dollar a day. Out of this she had to buy her clothes, her lunch and supply her carfare. What a life!

It is among the poor that you find that sisterly feeling I have spoken about, because the poor know what suffering is and means, and sympathize with others. You never see a well-dressed woman give up her seat in the subway to an old woman, do you? No, never; but I have often had a poor, tired shop girl rise with a smile and proffer me her seat because of my white hair.

WOMAN WHO DOESN'T NURSE HER OWN CHILD IS WRONG

The rich woman who had a mind to raise her child can't expect to get the right viewpoint of life. If they would raise their own babies their hearts would open and their feelings would become human. And the effect on the child is just as bad.

A nurse can't give mother's love to somebody else's child.

And while I am talking about children and mothers I want to say that if women are against war they can do much to prevent it by changing their methods of bringing up children. Every woman should train her child to have a horror of war. Any woman who buys a toy gun or pistol for her child ought to be put in a sanitarium. When you see a child parading about in a cardboard suit of armor and a gayly colored helmet, carrying a gun, you can say to yourself that some mother is filling her child's mind with thoughts of murder, for that is what that uniform and gun represent. I don't believe in drilling men or children for murder, and whenever I see a man in uniform walking around with a belt full of bullets, I say to my-self, "There goes a murderer."

The power of women is limitless. Look at what they are doing for shat-tered Belgium. A great work that, but why not do as much for their sisters over here. I didn't see the women rising en masse for their stricken sisters of Colorado, Calumet and West Virginia during the mine strike riots, and God knows they needed help as much as the Belgians, and do yet.

Let woman put aside her vanities for the real things of life. It nauseates me to see your average city woman. She is always overdressed, and al-though she wears gloves she is careful to leave her right hand bared so that she can display her fingers crowded to their utmost with jewels. When-ever I see that sort of a display I think of the gems as representing the blood of some crucified child. The woman of today, the woman of the "upper classes," I mean, is a sad commentary on civilization, as we are pleased to call it.

Everywhere I go in a city I see this same display of jewelry. The women even go to church on Sunday with their fingers and breasts ablaze with diamonds. This includes the wives of ministers themselves. We never heard of Christ wearing diamonds.

When one starts to investigate conditions the result is appalling. We are supposed to be progressing, but a little study in comparisons seems to point the other way. For instance, it is a fact that although this country is in its infancy, and has gained in wealth more in fifty years than any other country has in 700 years still we have more poverty in comparison with any of those old countries.

No human being in this country ever ought to go hungry, and there's something radically wrong somewhere when our jails are continually over-crowded. An immense amount of good can be done with playgrounds and supporting other means to give the poor outdoor exercise. Healthy bodies go toward making healthy minds and a healthy woman, though poor, can [work and?] do more to overcome their condition if minds and bodies are kept in a normal state.

I have always felt that no true state of civilization can ever be realized as long as we continue to have two classes of society. But that is a tre-mendous problem, and it will take a terrific amount of labor to remedy it. I think myself that we are bound to have a revolution here before these questions are straightened out. We were on the verge of it in the Colorado strike and the reason we did not have it then was not due to the good judgment of public officials, but to that of labor officials, who worked unceasingly to prevent it.

[*Miners Magazine,* 1 April 1915.]

306

ADDENDA
to *The Correspondence of Mother Jones*

BIOGRAPHICAL NOTES

INDEX

Addenda to
The Correspondence of Mother Jones

Since the publication of The Correspondence of Mother Jones, *the following communications have come to light that supplement that collection.*

To Socialist Party Delegates

[29 July 1901]

To comrades, greeting; I feel the responsibility placed upon you as a band of united braves.

Mother Jones

Printed telegram (*Proceedings of the Socialist Party Unity Convention Held at Indianapolis Beginning July 29, 1901*, typescript, microfilm edition of the Socialist Party of America Papers)

To Western Federation of Miners

San Francisco, California
May 26, 1904.

Miners in Convention
Denver, Colorado

Greeting. Honor to labor's martyr, President Moyer. The slumbering giant is fast awakening.

Mother Jones

Printed telegram (*Official Proceedings of the Twelfth Annual Convention, Western Federation of Miners of America*, fifth day, May 27, 1904)

To *The Appeal to Reason*

Mexico City
Oct. 4 [1911]

[To *The Appeal to Reason*
Girard, Kansas]

Just a line to let you know I have just returned from the palace where I have had a long audience with President De La Barra. At the close of my interview the Mexican guaranteed me protection and my right to organize the miners of Mexico. This is the first time that any one has ever been granted that privilege in the history of the Mexican nation. It is the greatest concession ever granted to any one representing the laboring class of any nation.

309

Addenda

I also spent an hour with President-elect Madero and he granted me the protection and aid from his government that I called for. I am the first person who has been permitted to carry the banner of industrial freedom to the long suffering peons of this nation.

Mother Jones

Printed letter (*The Appeal to Reason,* No. 829, 21 October 1911)

From J. S. Coxey

The Commonweal Army Headquarters
General J. S. Coxey
Massillon, Ohio
[April, 1914?]

To Mother Jones:

We are moved to address you as "Mother" with the sentiment and respect that we apply the term "Father" to that of an Almighty God.

For like his son, Christ, you have suffered, been and are imprisoned and have been tortured that the injustices inflicted upon humanity might be eradicated.

We commission you as colonel of the Army of the Commonweal of the West, whose captains and companies will meet you in Colorado and accept your command "on to Washington."

With sincere greetings,
J. S. Coxey
Murray Yontz, Major General

Printed Letter (*The Workers' Chronicle,* vol. 4, no. 24, 15 May 1914, p. 8, col. 1)

To Mrs. Edward Verdeckberg

Denver, Colo.,
July 30, 1914.

Mrs. Edward Verdeckberg
Denver, Colorado.
My Dear Mrs. Verdeckberg:

Permit me to express my deep appreciation of Colonel Verdeckberg's courtesy and kind treatment to me while I was a military prisoner in the Colorado bastile at Walsenburg.

This is the first opportunity I have had to convey to the Colonel my gratitude. He could have been very unkind and cruel to me, if he so wished, but fortunately, even in military uniform, I found the traits of a well-bred man, which indicates that he came from the training of a real woman.

Sincerely
Mother Jones

Typed letter, signed (Verdeckberg Collection, Colorado Historical Society)

To W. M. Rogers

Charleston, W. Va.,
June 4, 1918.

President W. M. Rogers,
Convention Hall
Parkersburg, W. Va.
Will be in about 5:00. Tell Frank[1] to meet me.

Mother Jones

Printed transcript of telegram (*Proceedings of the Eleventh Annual Session of the West Virginia Federation of Labor* [1918], p. 27)

1. Probably Frank Keeney, president of District 17, UMWA. Mother Jones addressed the convention that evening, but her remarks were only summarized.

From Cornelia Bryce Pinchot

July 16, 1924

Dear Mother Jones:

I don't know whether you have heard that the Pardon Board has pardoned Mr. Dolla—you remember, the miner about whom you talked to Mr. Pinchot—and he is now actually free.

I am very happy about it, as is Mr. Pinchot, and I know that you will be also.

I did enjoy meeting you in Washington last winter—and hope to see you again sometime.

Sincerely yours,
[Cornelia Pinchot]

Typed letter, copy (Cornelia Bryce Pinchot Papers, Library of Congress)

Addenda

To Cornelia Bryce Pinchot

2759 Marengo Street
Los Angeles, Calif.
July 31, 1924

Mrs. Gifford Pinchot,
The Executive Mansion,
Harrisburg, Pa.
My dear Mrs. Pinchot:

I received your very inspiring letter yesterday with regard to Mr. Dolla, and wish to extend my deep appreciation to you and the Governor for your very humane act. If we had more such Governors as Mr. Pinchot, we might look for better things for humanity. Iron bars have never settled any question, Mrs. Pinchot, and they never will. We must find some other method besides jails to remedy the present day ills.

I have no words to convey to you how deeply I appreciate the interest you and Governor Pinchot have taken in the family of this poor boy. It was so good of you to restore the provider to the mother and children. Many thanks to you, and tell the Governor I hope it will be my pleasure to meet him at some future time.

Very sincerely yours,
Mother Jones

Typed letter, signed (Cornelia Bryce Pinchot Papers, Library of Congress)

Biographical Notes

Addams, Jane (1860–1935), founder of Hull House in Chicago. Mother Jones served on her committee to aid in the defense of political refugees J. J. Pouren and Christian Rudowitz in 1909.

Altgeld, John Peter (1847–1902), reform governor of Illinois, 1893–97, whom Mother Jones admired.

Ammons, Elias M. (1860–1925), governor of Colorado, 1913–15. During his term, the Ludlow Massacre and other brutalities committed by armed guards, militia, and strikers attracted nationwide attention.

Anderson, Albert Barnes (1857–1938), federal district judge in Indiana, 1902–25. He presided over the dynamite transportation conspiracy trial in 1912 in which officers of the structural iron workers' union were convicted.

Baldwin, Al, member of the Baldwin-Felts Detective Agency, located in Bluefield, W. Va. For two generations, the two-family firm, fathers and sons, supplied detectives and guards for railroads and industries nationwide. Coal mine operators in West Virginia and Colorado employed hundreds of Baldwin-Felts mine guards in the strikes of 1912–14. The agency ceased operations after the death of Thomas L. Felts in 1937.

Bandholtz, Harry (1864–1925), professional soldier. Bandholtz, who served with distinction in the Philippines and in France during World War I, was appointed in 1921 commander of the military district of Washington, D.C., and immediately dispatched to command troops who intervened in the march on Logan by armed miners in West Virginia.

Barnes, Benjamin F. (1868–1909), assistant secretary to Theodore Roosevelt. After serving in administrative positions in the Post Office Department, he became a clerk on the White House staff. Roosevelt appointed him postmaster of Washington, D.C., in 1906.

Barnes, John Mahlon (1866–1934), national secretary of the Socialist Party of America, 1905–11. Mother Jones's charges against him of financial misconduct led to an investigation which resulted in her expulsion from the party in 1911.

Belk, Walter, a Baldwin-Felts guard and Colorado deputy sheriff. In 1915 Belk was acquitted of the murder of Gerald Lippiatt, a UMWA organizer.

Belmont, August (1853–1924), financier. Son of the founder of a major nineteenth-century bank, Belmont was frequently cited by Mother Jones as an embodiment of capitalism.

Bennett, W. R. (1864–?), circuit judge of Fayette County, W. Va., 1912.

Borah, William Edgar (1865–1940), senator from Idaho. Mother Jones admired Borah for his character and some of his progressive views; he was one of the senators to whom she appealed when she was imprisoned in Pratt, W. Va., in 1913.

Brophy, John (1883–1963), president of District 2, UMWA, 1916–26. One of John L. Lewis's rivals, in 1926 Brophy lost a contest for the presidency and later left the union. He was reconciled with Lewis in the 1930s and became national director of the CIO from 1935 to 1939.

Brown, J. W., an organizer for the Socialist Party, worked with Mother Jones in the Paint Creek strike. In February 1913 he was arrested with her and convicted by a military court, but later released by Governor Henry D. Hatfield.

Brown, John (1800–59), abolitionist. Mother Jones frequently expressed admiration for Brown's fight against slavery.

Bryan, James Wesley (1874–1956), lawyer. He served as a Progressive Republican representative from Washington in the Congress, 1913–15.

Cabell, Charles Arnold (1870–?), West Virginia coal operator. The president of the Carbon Coal Co., he was the leader of the operators of nonunion mines on Cabin Creek in 1912.

Cairns, Thomas Francis (1875–1949), president of District 17, UMWA, 1912–17, and later of the West Virginia Federation of Labor.

Cannon, Joseph D. (1871–1952), union official. An organizer for the Western Federation of Miners, he accompanied Mother Jones to Mexico when she met with President Francisco Madero in 1911. In the 1930s he held various offices in the CIO.

Cannon, Joseph Gurney (1836–1926), speaker of the house, 1901–11. A congressman from Illinois for fifty years, as speaker he exerted dictatorial control of the House of Representatives, provoking a Progressive revolt that altered the power of that office.

Carillo Puerto, Felipe (1872–1924), governor of Yucatan. A follower of Emiliano Zapata, Carillo embraced agrarian reform and women's rights. He was killed in the de la Huertista rebellion of 1924.

Carnegie, Andrew (1835–1919), financier. Mother Jones often attacked him as an embodiment of exploitative capitalism.

Chafin, Don (1887–1954), sheriff and political boss of Logan County, W. Va., during the march on Logan by armed miners in 1921. In addition to holding various county offices, he had extensive coal interests.

Chase, John (?–1918), Colorado national guard commander. An ophthalmologist in Denver, he commanded state troops during the Cripple Creek strike in 1903–04 and the 1913–14 coal strike. Neither Governor James H. Peabody nor Governor Elias M. Ammons was able to restrain his reliance on excessive force.

Clancy, Eugene A., member of the executive board of the structural iron workers' union. He and other union officials were convicted of complicity in the bombing of the *Los Angeles Times* in 1910. Mother Jones visited him in prison and pleaded with Woodrow Wilson for clemency for him.

Clark, James Beauchamp (1850–1921), speaker of the house, 1911–19. Mother Jones regarded Champ Clark as a sympathetic congressman and appealed to him for protection for some of her Mexican friends.

Cunningham, Dan, (1850–1942), deputy federal marshal in 1903, he led the raid that is sometimes called the Stanaford Mountain massacre, in which several striking miners were killed. In February 1913, as a deputy sheriff of Kanawha County, he arrested Mother Jones in Charleston, W. Va.

Dalzell, John (1845–1927), corporate lawyer and congressman from Pennsylvania.

A member of the Republican House leadership, along with Joseph Cannon, he presided over the congressional committee before which Mother Jones testified for Mexican revolutionaries in 1910.

Darrow, Clarence Seward (1857–1938), lawyer. Well known for his labor sympathies, Darrow was associated with Mother Jones before the turn of the century and wrote the introduction to her autobiography. He was counsel for William D. Haywood and the McNamara brothers, among other causes célèbres.

Davis, Ben, was an associate of Mother Jones in organizing in West Virginia in 1902; in 1905 he served as UMWA Executive Board member from District 17.

Debs, Eugene Victor (1855–1926), president of the American Railway Union, and later Socialist leader. Mother Jones regarded Debs as a friend from the time of their first meeting in the early 1890s. She supported his nomination for president at the Populist convention of 1896, and participated in his campaigns for the presidency on the Socialist ticket. When he was imprisoned during the First World War she personally pleaded with Woodrow Wilson for his release. She sometimes stayed with the Debs family when visiting Terre Haute.

Diaz, Porfirio (1830–1915), president of Mexico. By championing the cause of opponents of Diaz in the United States, Mother Jones remotely had a hand in the overthrow of the dictator in 1911.

Dick, Charles W. F. (1858–1945), Republican congressman and senator from Ohio, 1904–11. In a widely reported incident, Mother Jones publicly refused to shake his hand because he sponsored anti-labor legislation.

Dolan, Patrick, UMWA official. President of District 5, he lost his bid for the presidency of the UMWA in 1898 to John Mitchell. Mother Jones knew him from strikes in Pennsylvania before the turn of the century.

Donahue, Patrick J. (1849–1922), Catholic bishop of Wheeling, W. Va. In the Paint Creek strike of 1912–13, Bishop Donahue headed a special commission appointed by Governor William E. Glasscock to investigate conditions in the Kanawha coal field. His report pleased neither the operators nor the strikers and contributed nothing to a solution of the controversy.

Dorchy, August, vice-president of District 14, UMWA. In 1921, Dorchy had been convicted, along with Alexander Howat, president of District 14, of violating a Kansas law requiring arbitration in industrial disputes. John L. Lewis strengthened his hold on the presidency of the UMWA by ousting both Howat and Dorchy from their positions.

Dougherty, Miles, UMWA executive board member from District 9. He lost to John Mitchell in his race for the presidency of the UMWA in 1900.

Doyle, Ed, secretary-treasurer of District 15, UMWA, he was one of the leaders of the Colorado strike of 1913–14. In 1916 he accused the UMWA of betraying District 15, and was ousted from his position by President John P. White.

Dwyer, Lawrence ("Peggy"), UMWA official. A one-legged miner on nonunion Cabin Creek in 1912, he became an aggressive organizer, and eventually UMWA executive board member from District 29.

Easley, Ralph Montgomery (1856–1939). He organized and became secretary of the Civic Federation of Chicago, 1892–1900, and served many years as chairman of the executive council of the National Civic Federation after that organization was formed in 1900.

Biographical Notes

Elkins, Stephen B. (1841–1911), Republican senator from West Virginia, 1895–1911. His name is usually associated with railroad legislation, reflecting his financial interests. He exerted a dominant influence in West Virginia politics.

Elliott, Charles D. (1861–1938), U. S. marshal and newspaper publisher. Educated at West Virginia State College, he engaged in the lumbering business, was admitted to the bar, and became a secret service agent. Appointed U. S. marshal by McKinley and Roosevelt, he also served in the Spanish-American War and in the Philippines. As marshal in 1902 he arrested Mother Jones at Clarksburg and took her before Federal Judge John J. Jackson. Later, he owned and edited the *Parkersburg News.*

Fairley, William, union official. Born and educated in England, Fairley came to the United States as a youth and mined coal in Pennsylvania and Ohio until blacklisted. He moved to Alabama and became the first president of District 20, UMWA. He later served on the UMWA executive board.

Farrington, Frank (1873–1939), president of District 12, UMWA, 1914–26. He opposed John L. Lewis in his rise to power in the UMWA, lending his support successively to Lewis's rivals. He resigned his position after Lewis disclosed a secret contract Farrington had made with a coal company.

Fitzpatrick, John (1871–1946), union official. He served as president of the Chicago Federation of Labor for more than forty years, and participated in efforts to establish a labor party. Mother Jones named him as one of the executors of her will.

Flores Magón, Ricardo (1873–1922), Mexican revolutionary. Organizer of the Partido Liberal and publisher of *Regeneración,* he conducted his opposition to Diaz from the United States. Mother Jones took up his cause when he was arrested and imprisoned by American authorities in 1907. in 1911 he refused to join other Partido Liberal members in assisting the new regime of Francisco Madero, despite a personal plea from Mother Jones. He died in a U.S. prison, having been convicted of violating neutrality laws.

Flyzik, Martin J. As a miner in Pennsylvania, he was active in UMWA affairs and, after his removal to the state of Washington, became the president of District 10 from 1912 to 1918.

Foster, Martin David (1861–1919), physician and Democratic politician. A congressman from Illinois, 1907–19, he was a faithful supporter of the Wilson administration.

Foster, William Zebulon (1881–1961), labor leader. Mother Jones was closely associated with Foster in the unsuccessful effort to organize the steel industry in 1919. In his later incarnation as head of the Communist party in the United States, they had little contact.

Gary, Elbert Henry (1846–1927), lawyer and industrialist. Builder of the city of Gary, Indiana, he was an associate of J. P. Morgan in the organization and direction of the U.S. Steel Corp.

Germer, Adolph (1881–1966), labor official. Mother Jones was associated with Germer in both the Socialist party, of which he became national secretary from 1916–1919, and in the UMWA, where he held various offices. In the 1930s he became a major figure in the CIO.

Gildea, Charles, Pennsylvania coal miner. He served as District 7 representative on the UMWA executive board and as president of District 2, 1912. Mother Jones admired his aggressive unionism and went to his home in Hazleton, Pa., for a rest after an exhausting campaign for the Mexican revolutionaries in 1910.

Gillotti, Angelo, a coal miner in District 7, Pennsylvania.

Glasscock, William Ellsworth (1862–1925), governor of West Virginia, 1909–13. It was Glasscock's misfortune that he, a mild reformer, was governor of West Virginia when the long, violent Paint Creek strike took place. The crisis lasted during most of his final year in office, and his actions pleased neither miners nor operators.

Goebel, William (1856–1900), governor of Kentucky, 1900. The son of immigrant parents, he ran as a Democrat against incumbent Republican William S. Taylor. The result was contested, and during the dispute Goebel was killed by a shot fired from the office of the Republican Secretary of State Caleb Powers. Powers escaped legal blame, but two other men were convicted of the killing.

Goff, Nathan (1843–1920), West Virginia Republican leader. A faithful machine politician, he was briefly secretary of the navy, 1881, a member of Congress, 1883–89, and a federal judge, 1892–1913. As senator from West Virginia, 1913–19, he defended the imprisonment of Mother Jones in the Paint Creek strike, but failed to defeat the Kern Resolution for a Senate investigation of conditions in the coal field.

Gompers, Samuel (1850–1924), AFL president for nearly forty years. Mother Jones knew him, but disagreed with his conservative trade unionist views.

Gooding, Frank R. (1859–1928), rancher and politician. He was governor of Idaho, 1905–07, when Charles H. Moyer, William D. Haywood, and George A. Pettibone were seized in Colorado and brought to Idaho to be prosecuted, unsuccessfully, for complicity in the murder of exgovernor Frank Steunenburg. He later served in the United States Senate, 1921–38.

Gould, Helen Miller, philanthropist daughter of Jay Gould (1836–1892), railroad magnate and financier. Mother Jones usually invoked the Gould name to personify ill-gotten and arrogant wealth.

Green, William (1870–1952), union official. Mother Jones knew him well as president of District 6, UMWA, as secretary-treasurer of the UMWA, 1912–22, and as president of the AFL, 1924–52, and their relationship was marked by mutual affection and trust. When John L. Lewis became president of the UMWA, Green was the only official in headquarters in whom Mother Jones had any confidence.

Greene, William Cornell (1851–1911), entrepreneur. His meteoric career as a major financier was based on his extensive mineral holdings at Cananea in northern Mexico and in the American southwest. Mother Jones at various times worked with the Western Federation of Miners to organize the men in his mines and smelters.

Haddow, John, a UMWA organizer from Iowa.

Haggerty, Thomas T. (1865–1946), union official and coal mine operator. One of the founding members of the UMWA in 1890, he was an aggressive union organizer for more than thirty years, but resigned from the UMWA executive board in 1917 when his secret coal mine investments were revealed. He was Mother Jones's favorite coworker in organizing.

Hanna, Marcus Alonzo (1837-1904), Ohio industrialist. An active Republican leader, he promoted the candidacy of William McKinley for president. Mother Jones usually portrayed him as an enemy of the people who exemplified the power of money in American politics, and as an opponent of labor for his sponsorship of the National Civic Federation.

Harlin, Robert, UMWA official. He was president of District 10 (Washington), executive board member, statistician, and editor of the UMWA *Journal.* He lost his bid for the presidency of the UMWA when he ran against John L. Lewis in 1920.

Harmon, Judson (1846-1927), Ohio lawyer and Democratic politician. Although he belonged to the conservative wing of the Democratic party, his term as governor of Ohio from 1908-1912 saw the enactment of several Progressive measures. Mother Jones incorrectly charged him with sending federal troops to Illinois in 1895; his term as attorney general under Grover Cleveland did not begin until after that incident.

Harriman, Edward Henry (1848-1909), railroad magnate, best known for his struggle with James J. Hill for the control of the Chicago, Burlington, & Quincy railroad in 1901. Mother Jones often invoked his name as a malefactor of great wealth.

Harriman, Florence Jaffray (1870-1967), Democratic political figure. Born to wealth, she became interested in working conditions for women, and was the only woman member of the Commission on Industrial Relations, 1913-17. She served on the Democratic National Committee and as minister to Norway, 1937-41.

Hatfield, Henry Drury (1875-1962), governor of West Virginia, 1913-17, senator, 1929-35. He combined his medical practice with an active career in Republican politics. After succeeding William E. Glasscock as governor, he freed Mother Jones and other union leaders from prison and worked out a settlement between the embattled miners and operators in the Paint Creek strike.

Hatfield, Sid (1894-1921), chief of police in Matewan, W. Va. A sympathizer with the miners in their attempt to organize unions in southern West Virginia, he was involved in the killing of seven Baldwin-Felts guards in Matewan in 1920. A year later Baldwin-Felts guards killed him on the steps of the courthouse in Welch, W. Va.

Hawkins, Horace (1867-1947), lawyer in Denver, Colo. He was in general charge of the many legal defenses of UMWA members accused of crimes in Colorado in the 1913-14 strike, most of whom were eventually acquitted, but his fees and expenses put heavy demands on the UMWA treasury.

Hayes, Frank J. (1882-1948), UMWA officer. Active in union affairs in District 12 (Illinois), he was vice-president of the UMWA, 1910-17, and president, 1917-20. His weaknesses as an administrator and fondness for the bottle enabled John L. Lewis, his appointed vice-president, to assume many presidential duties, and eventually to replace him. For nearly half of her career with the UMWA, Hayes was Mother Jones's immediate superior; he let her set her own agenda.

Haywood, William Dudley (1869-1928), union official. Best known as one of the leaders of the IWW, "Big Bill" Haywood was also an officer of the Western

Federation of Miners and charged with murder in a sensational trial in Idaho. Mother Jones was closely associated with him in founding the IWW and in work with the WFM, 1904-06. In 1921, under indictment for sedition, Haywood fled to Russia, where he spent the rest of his life.

Henry, Patrick (1736-99), statesman. Mother Jones frequently invoked the name of Patrick Henry as a fighter against tyranny and a defender of free speech.

Houston, Harold W. (1872-?), West Virginia lawyer. He ran on the Socialist ticket for governor of West Virginia in 1912 and served as legal counsel for the UMWA for many years. Mother Jones knew him, perhaps through her Socialist ties, as early as 1900, and he accompanied her on her trip to make a speech in Princeton, W. Va., in 1920.

Howat, Alexander (1876-1945), president of District 14, UMWA. A Scot by birth, he emigrated to the United States and became a coal miner in Illinois and later in Kansas, where he was repeatedly elected president of District 14. He was jailed for defying the Kansas Industrial Relations Act in 1921, and John L. Lewis seized the chance to displace him. He was one of Lewis's strongest and most persistent rivals.

Huerta, Victoriano (1854-1916), president of Mexico, 1913-14. A general under Porfirio Diaz, he helped establish the revolutionary regime of Francisco Madero, but soon plotted successfully to overthrow it. In turn, his government was overturned by a combination of his enemies.

Huff, George Franklin (1842-1912), banker and president of the Keystone Coal and Coke Co., Greensburg, Pa. A Republican, he served in Congress from 1891 to 1897 and from 1903 to 1911.

Hugo, Victor Marie (1802-85), French author. On several occasions Mother Jones declared her admiration for Hugo's writings.

Hunt, George W. P. (1859-1934), governor of Arizona. First governor of the state, he was elected to six subsequent terms. Mother Jones knew him and admired him for his prolabor policies. She campaigned for him in 1916, one of the few elections he ever lost.

Iglesias, Santiago, Puerto Rican labor leader. He advised Samuel Gompers on Latin American affairs and was one of the moving spirits behind the Pan American Federation of Labor.

Ingalls, John James (1833-1900), lawyer, editor, and politician. As senator from Kansas, 1872-91, he became famous for his vitriolic "Bloody Shirt" oratory.

Irons, Martin (1833-1900), labor leader. An official of the Knights of Labor, he led an unsuccessful strike against the Missouri Pacific Railroad in 1886. Fellow Knights turned against him, employers blacklisted him, and he died in poverty. Mother Jones knew him well and often praised him as a pioneer of organized labor.

Jackson, John J. (1821-1907), federal judge. Appointed by Abraham Lincoln, he was well known for his conservative rulings. When Mother Jones was brought before him for violating his injunction in the Fairmont strike of 1902, he held her guilty, but refused to make a martyr of her by imposing a jail sentence.

Kaplan, David, a structural iron worker implicated in the bombing of the *Los Angeles Times* in 1910. Mother Jones worked for his defense and for his release from prison after he was convicted.

Keeney, Frank, union official. He helped Mother Jones organize Cabin Creek in 1912 and was president of District 17, 1917–24. Ousted by John L. Lewis, he joined Brophy, Howat, Walker, Farrington and other rivals in their opposition to the UMWA president.

Kern, John Worth (1849–1917), senator from Indiana. Well known for his labor sympathies, he offered the resolution which instituted an investigation of the coal industry in West Virginia and brought about the release of Mother Jones from prison in 1913. Mother Jones campaigned for his reelection in 1916, but he was defeated and died within the year.

King, William Lyon Mackenzie (1874–1950), prime minister of Canada. Before his emergence as a dominant figure in Canadian politics, he advised John D. Rockefeller, Jr., on labor policies. In two conferences with him in Colorado, Mother Jones may have influenced the industrial relations plan he later submitted to Rockefeller.

Kipling, Rudyard (1865–1936), English author. The "Kipling poem" quoted by Mother Jones in her speech of 15 August 1913 is actually a parody, by an unknown socialist, of the second canto of his "Song of the Dead."

Laing, John (1865–1943), coal mine operator. He ran several West Virginia mines, and served as the head of the state Department of Mines, 1908–13.

Lane, Harry (1855–1917), Democratic senator from Oregon, 1913–17. Mother Jones encouraged his daughter Nina in her socialist views.

Langdon, Emma (1875–1937), Colorado socialist and printer. The author of *The Cripple Creek Strike,* she had a long career as a social activist. Mother Jones nominated her for assistant secretary of the IWW at its founding convention.

Lawler, Oscar, assistant attorney general of the United States. The author of a controversial "lost" memorandum in the Ballinger-Pinchot affair in 1909, he supervised the prosecution in Los Angeles in 1910 of Mexican revolutionaries who were charged with violating U.S. neutrality laws.

Lawson, John, union official. One of the leaders of the Colorado strike of 1913–14, he was charged with murder, but his conviction was overturned by the Colorado Supreme Court. After the strike, President John P. White of the UMWA displaced him as president of District 15.

Lesseps, Ferdinand Marie de (1805–94), French diplomat and promoter. The moving spirit behind the building of the Suez Canal, 1859–69, he also attempted to build a Panama Canal, 1879–94. His Panama company was later taken over by the United States.

Lewis, John Llewellyn (1880–1969), president of the UMWA, 1920–60. A coal miner in his youth, he used his formidable talents to move rapidly to the presidency of the UMWA in 1920. In the next ten years he eliminated all rivals, and in his last three decades as president of the union he was the premier labor leader of the United States, defying courts and presidents with impunity. In 1935 he formed the CIO, and took it and the UMWA out of the AFL. Interpreters of his career have to reconcile his use of deception and force with his very real achievements for the UMWA and for organized labor generally. Mother Jones detested him.

Lewis, Thomas L. (1866–1939), president of the UMWA, 1908–11. He succeeded

John Mitchell, whose vice-president he had been. After his term of office he became a spokesman for the Kanawha Coal Operators Association.

Lloyd, Caroline (1859-1940), sister and biographer of Henry Demarest Lloyd.

Lloyd, Henry Demarest (1847-1903), author and reformer. He and Mother Jones were associated in reform politics in Chicago in the 1890s.

Lloyd George, David (1863-1945), British political leader. As prime minister, 1916-21, he directed the war effort and the peace settlement after World War I.

Lord, James Ravell (1878-1941), union official. For many years he headed the Mining Department of the AFL, until he was ousted by John L. Lewis.

Low, Seth (1850-1916), merchant, president of Columbia University, 1890-1901, reform mayor of both Brooklyn and New York City. Mother Jones encountered him when she led her children's crusade to Oyster Bay in 1903 and may have also had contact with him when he was a member of Woodrow Wilson's commission to supervise a settlement in the Colorado strike of 1913-14.

Lowden, Frank Orren (1861-1943), governor of Illinois, 1917-21. A Chicago lawyer, he was active in Republican politics and served in Congress from 1906 to 1911. He was a strong candidate for nomination to the presidency in the Republican convention of 1920.

Madero, Francisco Indalecio (1873-1913), president of Mexico, 1911-13. After the overthrow of Porfirio Diaz, he encouraged Mother Jones to organize Mexican workers. He was killed in the rebellion that Victoriano Huerta raised against him.

Manning, Joseph Columbus (1870-1928?), editor and politician. A founder of the Populist party in Alabama, he served briefly in the legislature. He later became a Republican.

Martine, James Edgar (1850-1925), Democratic senator from New Jersey, 1911-17. He was well known for his prolabor views.

Matti, Andrew, a coal miner from the anthracite region, District 7, UMWA.

McDonald, Duncan, coal miner and union official. He served in various offices in the Illinois UMWA and as president of the state federation of labor, 1919. In the 1920s his union career faltered, and he opened a bookshop and edited a labor journal.

McKay, Ed, a UMWA organizer from District 2.

McKell, Thomas Gaylord (1845-1904), coal mine operator at Loop Creek, Glen Jean, and Thurmond, W. Va. His son William (1871-1939) took over management of the McKell Coal & Coke Co. after his death.

Miles, Nelson Appleton (1839-1925), army officer. A youthful Civil War general, he commanded the American troops in the Spanish-American War and retired as a lieutenant-general in 1903.

Mitchell, John (1870-1919), president of the UMWA, 1898-1908. Mother Jones was an enthusiastic supporter of John Mitchell after he appointed her as an organizer for the UMWA in 1900, but broke with him over union policy in the Colorado strike of 1904, and criticised him strongly for his later association with the National Civic Federation.

Mitchell William (1879-1936), general and advocate of air power. In the miners' march on Logan in 1921, he saw an opportunity to display the efficacy of air power, but his planes were used only for reconnaissance.

Montgomery, Lawrence C. (1873-?), physician. After receiving his M.D. from the University of Cincinnati in 1897, he practiced medicine in the town in West Virginia named for his family and held local political offices.

Mooney, Fred (1888-1952), secretary-treasurer of District 17, UMWA, 1917-24. A protégé of Mother Jones, he accompanied her to Mexico in 1921. John L. Lewis ousted him from his union office.

Mooney, Thomas Joseph (1882-1942), socialist and member of the IWW. When he was convicted of murder after the explosion of a bomb at a Preparedness Day parade in 1916, his case became a cause célèbre. Mother Jones worked on his behalf until the end of her life. He was released in 1939.

Morgan, Anne (1873-1952), social worker. Daughter of J. P. Morgan, she supported several organizations for the betterment of working women and served on the welfare committee of the National Civic Federation. During World War I she organized relief units in France.

Morgan, Ephraim Franklin (1869-1950), Republican governor of West Virginia, 1921-24. He was later a solicitor in the Department of Commerce, 1927-33. Although he called in federal troops during the mine wars in 1921, Mother Jones retained a high regard for him.

Morgan, John Pierpont (1837-1913), financier. Mother Jones frequently reviled him as the leader of the oligarchy of wealth.

Morrison, Frank (1859-1949), secretary of the AFL, 1897-1939. A printer by trade, he spent most of his union career in the shadows of Samuel Gompers and William Green.

Moyer, Charles H. (?-1929), president of the Western Federation of Miners, 1902-26. Leader of the metal miners in the Cripple Creek strike in Colorado, 1903-04, and one of the founders of the IWW, he left the IWW in 1908 and took the WFM back into the AFL in 1911.

Murray, John (1865-1919), socialist. A follower of Tolstoi, he devoted his life to various causes and to socialism. He was particularly interested in the workers of Latin America and was one of the moving spirits in the formation of the Pan American Federation of Labor.

Murray, Philip (1886-1952), union official. He became vice-president of the UMWA under John L. Lewis. From 1942 to 1951, he was president of the United Steel Workers, and simultaneously president of the CIO. He and Mother Jones were both active in the attempt to organize the steel workers in 1919.

Nicholls, Thomas David (1870-1931), union official and congressman. He was president of District I, UMWA, 1899-1907, and an independent Democratic congressman from Pennsylvania, 1907-11. After retirement from Congress he raised chickens in Maryland.

Obregón, Alvaro (1880-1928), president of Mexico, 1920-24. He and others who were dissatisfied with the failure of Venustiano Carranza to implement the constitution of 1917 overthrew the government and began a program of reforms. He was in power when Mother Jones was the guest of the Mexican government.

Older, Cora Baggerly (1873?-1968), reporter and author. The wife of Fremont Older, editor of the *San Francisco Bulletin* and later of the *Call,* she interviewed

Mother Jones in her prison quarters in West Virginia in 1913 and publicized her plight.

Olson, Harry (1867–1935), chief justice of the municipal court of Chicago, 1906–30.

Palmer, Alexander Mitchell (1872–1936), attorney general of the United States, 1919–21. He was best known for carrying out arrests and deportations in the Red scare following World War I. Mother Jones interceded with him for imprisoned union members and asked him to ensure civil liberties in the steel strike of 1919.

Peabody, James Hamilton (1852–1917), governor of Colorado, 1903–05. The militia that he called out clashed violently and frequently with both the coal and metal miners in the strikes of 1903–04.

Perry, Edwin, union official from Iowa. Secretary-treasurer of the UMWA during the presidencies of Thomas L. Lewis and John P. White, he resigned in August 1913. William Green succeeded him.

Pettibone, George, Denver merchant closely associated with the Western Federation of Miners. In 1908 he was acquitted of charges of conspiracy to murder growing out of the WFM strike of 1906.

Pinchot, Gifford (1865–1946), forester and governor of Pennsylvania, 1923–27 and 1931–35. Mother Jones became acquainted with him and his wife, Cornelia, when she interceded for a miner imprisoned in Pennsylvania.

Pitt, Emmiline, labor mediator, fl. 1910–30. One of the earliest female graduates of the Pittsburgh Theological Seminary, she served as secretary of the Pittsburgh Labor Council, as special assistant to the Pennsylvania Commissioner of Labor, and as a mediator for the U.S. Department of Labor.

Poggiani, Joseph, UMWA organizer. He was business manager of the UMWA *Journal,* 1912–14, and editor of the Italian portion of the trilingual weekly. He worked with Mother Jones as an organizer in West Virginia and Colorado.

Pouren, J. J., a dissident Russian immigrant whose extradition was sought by the czarist government in 1909.

Powderly, Terence Vincent (1849–1924), labor leader. After he resigned as head of the Knights of Labor, he became an immigration official. He kept a room in his house in Washington for Mother Jones's use.

Rend, W. P., a coal mine operator with extensive interests in West Virginia.

Rice, Bernard, UMWA organizer who was jailed with Mother Jones in Parkersburg, W. Va., in 1902.

Roan, John M., manager of the Hocking Valley Coal Co., in 1902. He later became commissioner of the Ohio coal operators' association.

Rockefeller, John Davidson (1839–1937), founder of the Standard Oil Co. Mother Jones frequently attacked him as an embodiment of capitalism.

Rockefeller, John Davidson, Jr. (1874–1960), financier and philanthropist. He began to take over management of the family business empire in 1911. Mother Jones met him in 1915 and discussed conditions in his Colorado mines with him. Thereafter, they corresponded occasionally.

Roosevelt, Theodore (1858–1919), president of the United States, 1901–09. In 1902 he avoided a confrontation with Mother Jones when she led an army of working children to Oyster Bay to publicize the need for a national child labor act.

Rudowitz, Christian, a Russian radical who emigrated to the United States, and whose extradition was sought by the czarist government in 1908.

Ryan, Frank M., an official of the structural iron workers' union who was convicted of complicity in the bombing of the *Los Angeles Times* in 1910. Mother Jones visited him in prison and worked for his parole.

Ryan, William D., secretary-treasurer of District 12 and later of the international UMWA. At first a supporter of President Thomas L. Lewis, he turned against him and resigned in 1909.

Sarabia, Manuel, a member of the revolutionary Mexican Partido Liberal. He was kidnapped in Douglas, Ariz., and taken to Mexico in 1907, but Mother Jones was instrumental in securing his return to the United States.

Schmidt, Katherine, sister of Mathew Schmidt, who was convicted of complicity in the bombing of the *Los Angeles Times* in 1910. Mother Jones assisted her attempts to provide for her brother's defense, and, after his conviction, to secure his parole or pardon.

Schmidt, Mathew, youthful explosives expert who, with his friend David Kaplan, was charged with having prepared the bomb which exploded at the *Los Angeles Times* building in 1910. He eluded capture for several years, but was eventually convicted and imprisoned for life.

Schwab, Charles (1862-1939), industrialist. President of the U. S. Steel Co., he was often the object of verbal attacks by Mother Jones.

Scott, Nathan B. (1842-1924), Republican senator from West Virginia, 1899-1911. After discharge from the Union army in 1865, he became a glass manufacturer and banker in Wheeling. He moved from city council to state Senate, to the Republican National Committee. Following his career in the Senate he became a banker in Washington.

Sellins, Fanny (?-1919), organizer for District 5, UMWA. She was killed by armed guards at the Allegheny Steel Co. mine in West Natrona, Pennsylvania, during the steel strike, becoming a martyr for union members everywhere.

Smith, Sylvester Clark (1858-1913), Republican congressman. Born in Iowa, he taught school there and in California after moving west. He practiced law in Bakersfield, and became a state senator. He served in Congress, 1905-13.

Stanford, Jane Lathrop (1825-1905), philanthropist. She took a close personal interest in all the affairs of Leland Stanford University, which she and her husband established in memory of their son.

Sunday, William Ashley (1863-1935), evangelist. At one time a professional baseball player, he became one of the most famous preachers of his day.

Taft, William Howard (1857-1930), president of the United States, 1909-13. Mother Jones got along surprising well with Taft on the two occasions when she personally pleaded for clemency for federal prisoners.

Tarbell, Ida Minerva (1857-1944), author. One of the earliest of the muckraking journalists of the turn of the century, her *History of the Standard Oil Company,* 1904, furnished ammunition for Mother Jones and others to attack the ethics of contemporary businessmen and politicians.

Taylor, William Sylvester (1853-1928), governor of Kentucky, 1899-1900. Inaugurated in a disputed election, he resigned after his rival, William Goebel, was killed by a gunshot. Under indictment, he fled to Indianapolis, and, when his name was later cleared, practiced law there.

Tikas, Louis (?-1914), Greek-born leader of the strikers at Ludlow, Colo. He was beaten to death with a rifle by a lieutenant of the Colorado militia who was later reprimanded by his superiors.

Tincher, Thomas, coal miner. He was a member of Local 195, District 17, UMWA.

Tobin, Daniel Joseph (1875-1955), president of the International Brotherhood of Teamsters, 1907-52. A power in the AFL for many years, he also held government positions under both Woodrow Wilson and Franklin D. Roosevelt. He introduced Mother Jones to the delegates at the Pan American Federation of Labor in Mexico City in 1920.

Turner, John Kenneth (1879-1948), author. Born in Portland, Oreg., he became a printer and then a muckraking reporter. His *Barbarous Mexico* was a scathing indictment of the Diaz regime. With Mother Jones, he testified before a congressional committee in 1910.

Ulich, Robert, coal miner. A minor officer of District 15, UMWA, and of the Colorado Federation of Labor, he was accused of killing Mac Powell and held without bail or trial for seven months, but was finally acquitted.

Verdeckberg, Edward (1853-?), industrialist. Born to immigrant parents in Brooklyn, he was apprenticed to a jewelry enameller and followed that trade in New York and Colorado before founding the Denver Iron and Wire Works. He served in both the New York and Colorado national guard.

Villarreal, Antonio I. (1879-1944), Mexican revolutionist. Secretary of the Partido Liberal of Ricardo Flores Magón, he broke with him and joined the successful Madero rebellion, serving as a brigadier general and as consul general to Spain. He joined with Alvaro Obregón to overthrow Venustiano Carranza, and served as Obregón's secretary of agriculture.

Waite, Davis Hanson (1825-1901), governor of Colorado, 1893-94. After a roving life on the frontier as a merchant, lawyer, and editor, he settled in Colorado and edited a Populist paper in Aspen. He served only one term.

Walker, John Hunter (1872-1955), president of the Illinois Federation of Labor, 1913-30. Over the years he was Mother Jones's closest friend within the UMWA, beginning with his youthful organizing efforts in West Virginia in 1901 under her direction. As president of District 12, 1905-13, he was one of the most powerful leaders of the UMWA, but his three attempts at the presidency failed. He opposed John L. Lewis, who in 1933 annulled the charter of District 12 and replaced Walker, his last major rival within the union and again district president, with his own appointee.

Warren, Fred D. (1872-1959), journalist. He worked on several socialist publications, most notably as associate editor of *The Appeal to Reason.*

Watson, Clarence Wayland (1864-1940), coal mine operator. President and chairman of the board of the Consolidation Coal Company, he was elected senator from West Virginia in 1911, filling an unexpired term for two years.

White, John P. (1870-1934), president of the UMWA, 1912-17. A coal miner in Illinois and later in Iowa, he rose to the presidency of District 13, 1904-07 and 1909-12. He resigned from the UMWA to serve as labor advisor to Dr. Harry A.

Garfield of the war-time Fuel Administration. After the war, he held a managerial job with the Haynes Powder Co.

Whitford, Greeley Webster (1856–1940), judge. Born in Indiana, he moved west to Washington and then to Denver, where he served as city and federal prosecutor. He was district judge from 1907 to 1913, and 1919 to 1921, and judge of the Colorado Supreme Court, 1921–31.

Wickersham, George Woodward (1858–1936), attorney general of the United States, 1909–13. Born in Pittsburgh, he gained a law degree from the University of Pennsylvania and practiced briefly in Philadelphia before moving to New York where he enjoyed great success. He served in William Howard Taft's cabinet, and after 1913 was Taft's partner in a New York law firm.

Wilson, William Bauchop (1862–1934), secretary of labor, 1913–21. A Scottish immigrant, he went into the mines at nine years of age. He joined the Knights of Labor before becoming one of the founders of the UMWA, which he served as secretary-treasurer, 1900–08. A Democratic congressman from Pennsylvania, 1907–13, he became the first secretary of labor. Besides establishing the department, he became a key member of the Council of National Defense, 1916–21. After the war he returned to mining and farming in Pennsylvania, and in 1926 lost a bid for the U.S. Senate. He and Mother Jones enjoyed cordial relations from their first strike association in Pennsylvania in the 1890s until he retired from the Department of Labor.

Wood, Leonard (1860–1927), physician and general. He led the Rough Riders in the Spanish-American War, was military governor of Cuba, 1899–1902, a major-general in the Philippines, 1906–08, and chief of staff, 1910–14. Denied high command in World War I, he failed in pursuit of the Republican nomination for president in 1920. He spent his last years as governor-general of the Philippines.

Zancanelli, Louis, miner in District 15, UMWA, during the 1913–14, strike in Colorado. He was charged with the killing of George Belcher, a mine guard, and convicted in a second trial after the first resulted in a hung jury. In April 1917, the Colorado Supreme Court overturned his conviction of murder.

Index

Acme, W. Va., 91
Adams, John, 218
Addams, Jane, 24, 313
Alliance, Ohio, 259
Altgeld, John Peter, 88, 90, 313
American Federation of Labor (AFL), 24, 201, 232, 236–38
American Railway Union, 7
American Red Cross, 198
Ammons, Elias M., 52, 129, 132, 313
Anarchists, 48
Anderson, Albert Barnes, 201, 313
Anthracite coal field, 3, 15, 44, 142, 151, 152, 180, 294, 295
Anthracite strike: of 1900, 3, 296; of 1902, 3, 7, 16
Appeal to Reason, 278, 280, 287, 289, 309
Arnot, Pa., 180
Avondale, Ala., 281

Baldwin, Al, 229, 313
Baldwin-Felts Detective Agency, 57, 224, 229, 313
Bandholtz, Harry, 238, 239, 313
Barnes, Benjamin F., 61, 313
Barnes, John Mahlon, 44, 313
Belk, Walter, 180, 313
Belmont, August, 28, 37, 52, 74, 313
Bennett, W. R., 313
Bentley, W. Va., 191
Birmingham, Ala., 265, 282
Bisbee, Ariz., 25, 164, 286
Black Hills, S.D., 49
Blacks, 20–21, 64, 71, 77, 98, 102, 220, 221, 228, 230, 243, 275
Blair Mountain, W. Va., 238, 239
Bolsheviks, 198, 203, 213, 215, 230, 231, 233
Boomer, W. Va., 183
Borah, William Edgar, 115, 313
Boston, Mass., 122, 129, 200, 221, 230
Boycott, 29, 40, 139
Brewers' Association, 41, 42, 291
Brewery workers, 38, 42, 121, 139, 290, 291
British Columbia, 122, 150, 174

Brooklyn, N.Y., 62
Brophy, John, 248, 313
Brown, J. W., 69, 314
Brown, John, 175, 183, 256, 275, 314
Bruceville, Tex., 209, 279
Bryan, James Wesley, 143, 314
Bryan, William Jennings, 283
Buck Stove and Range case, 24, 35, 40
Burgess, Lillie Mae, 260
Burgess, Walter, 260
Butte, Mont., 57, 147, 156

C & O Railroad, 111, 112, 147
Cabell, Charles Arnold, 142, 314
Cabin Creek, W. Va., 57, 77, 78, 88–97, 107, 109, 111, 126, 147, 153, 177, 186, 187, 215, 225–27, 244–45, 250
Cairns, Thomas Francis, 109, 314
Calumet, Mich., 158, 176–78
Canada, 27, 58, 150, 236
Cananea, 27, 235, 286
Cannon, Joseph D., 56, 314
Cannon, Joseph Gurney, 28, 37, 314
Carillo Puerto, Felipe, 238, 314
Carnegie, Andrew, 52, 88, 99, 288, 314
Carnegie Hall, 116
Cedar Grove, W. Va., 107
Central America, 237
Central Competitive Field, 254
Chafin, Don, 238, 239, 314
Charleston, W. Va., 56, 57, 66, 76, 86, 88, 106, 108, 115, 124, 125, 136, 153, 169, 187, 189, 238
Chase, John, 129, 145, 155, 164, 314
Cherry, Ill., 37
Chicago Federation of Labor, 201
Chicago, Ill., 22, 57, 69, 92, 140, 156, 158, 161, 162, 170–72, 182, 183, 196, 259
Child labor laws, 22, 229, 266, 281
China, 35, 36, 47, 60, 93, 96, 142, 244, 289
Chinese Exclusion Act, 3, 13
Chinese immigration, 251, 252
Christianity, 21, 158, 161, 162, 195, 212, 220, 234, 236, 288, 289

Index

Cigar workers, 42
Cincinnati, Ohio, 40, 101, 187
Citizens' Alliance, 140
Civic Federation, 35, 37, 46, 51, 52, 74, 89, 102, 294
Civil War, 275
Clancy, Eugene A., 185, 314
Clark, James Beauchamp, 112, 314
Clarksburg, W. Va., 67, 86
Cleveland, Grover, 46
Cleveland, Ohio, 88, 90, 161, 201
Coal strike of 1919, 200
Coledale, Pa., 296
Colorado coal strike: of 1904, 37; of 1913, 130, 150, 156, 167, 174
Colorado Federation of Labor, 129
Colorado Fuel and Iron Company, 46, 55, 122, 123, 151
Columbus, Ohio, 44, 198, 218
Comer, Braxton B., 281-83
Commission on Industrial Relations, 156
Commonweal Army, 310
Confederación Regional Obrera Mexicana, 233
Confederate States of America, 49
Connellsville, Pa., 51
Constabulary laws, state, 256
Constitution of 1917, 232
Cooper Union, 35
Copper Queen Company, 25, 26, 285, 286
Cork, Ireland, 259
Coxey, Jacob S., 310
Cripple Creek strike, 22
Cunningham, Dan, 79, 314

Dalzell, John, 50, 112, 314
Danbury Hatters case, 35
Darrow, Clarence Seward, 162, 315
Davis, Ben, 53, 315
Dawson, N.M., 178
de la Barra, Francisco, 309
Deal, Walter, 105
Debs, Eugene Victor, 7, 185, 315
Denver, Colo., 65, 122, 128-30, 132, 141, 144, 145, 148, 150, 166
Department of Commerce and Labor, 35, 37, 38
Diaz, Porfirio, 24-31, 38, 48, 49, 50, 61, 157, 285, 286, 288, 293, 315
Dick, Charles W. F., 88, 99, 315
Dolan, Patrick, 50, 315

Donahue, Patrick J., 106, 113, 315
Dorchy, August, 257, 315
Dougherty, Miles, 28, 315
Douglas, Ariz., 26, 286
Doyle, Ed, 174, 315
Dred Scott decision, 287
Duquesne, Pa., 203, 204
Dwyer, Lawrence, 186, 206, 250, 315

Easley, Ralph Montgomery, 52, 315
Eddy, Tex., 279
El Paso, Tex., 49, 82, 122, 129, 185
Elkins, Stephen B., 88, 90, 93, 316
Elliott, Charles D., 18, 67-69, 86, 169, 316
England, 213, 231
Eskdale, W. Va., 88, 112, 115
Espionage Act, 196
Ethnicity, 68, 122, 123, 215, 217
Europe, 132, 141, 151, 154, 158, 201, 212, 231, 236

Fairley, William, 38, 316
Fairmont, W. Va., 183, 187
Fairmont Coal Company, 17
Fairmont coal field, 15, 110, 211, 242
Farmer-Labor Convention, 259
Farrington, Frank, 200, 254, 255, 316
Fayette, W. Va., 70
Field, Marshall, 140
Fitzpatrick, John, 201, 259, 316
Flanders, 212
Flores Magón, Ricardo, 24, 56, 286, 316
Flyzik, Martin J., 50, 181, 316
Fort Worth, Tex., 49
Foster, Martin David, 159, 316
Foster, William Zebulon, 201, 316
France, 36, 67, 196
Free speech, 269, 273
Freeland, Pa., 9
Frontenac, Kans., 146
Fuel Administration, 200
Fugitive slave law, 285, 287

Garment workers, 35, 37, 45, 51, 171, 182
Gary, Elbert Henry, 181, 203-05, 207, 210, 316
George III (king of England), 20, 25, 202, 220
Germany, 67

Germer, Adolph, 30, 50, 167, 170, 316
Gildea, Charles, 50, 316
Gillotti, Angelo, 50, 317
Glasscock, William E., 56, 57, 62, 69, 76, 88, 89, 90, 104, 106, 108, 109, 115, 125, 169, 183, 317
Glen Jean, W. Va., 79
Goebel, William, 54, 317
Goff, Nathan, 180, 317
Gompers, Samuel, 232, 235, 237, 283, 317
Gooding, Frank R., 276, 277, 317
Gould, Helen Miller, 85, 88, 94, 163, 317
Gould, Jay, 279
Grand Trunk Railroad, 141
Green, William, 24, 28, 30, 31, 167, 170, 172, 174, 178, 179, 190, 259, 317
Greenback party, 198
Greene, William Cornell, 27, 28, 317
Greensburg, Pa., 47
Guards, company, 56–99, 103, 109–14, 123–27, 129, 132, 138, 141, 150, 153, 158, 160–61, 176–77, 181, 183, 184, 190, 191, 220, 222–31, 245, 313
Guggenheim family, 42, 93

Haddow, John, 243, 317
Haggerty, Thomas T., 183, 317
Hanna, Marcus Alonzo, 7, 13, 35, 73, 74, 88, 92, 318
Harding, Warren G., 239
Harlin, Robert, 200, 254, 318
Harmon, Judson, 46, 318
Harper's Ferry, W. Va., 257
Harriman, Edward H., 28, 37, 288, 318
Harriman, Florence Jaffray, 28, 37, 52, 304, 305, 318
Harrison County, W. Va., 77
Hatfield, Henry D., 115, 116, 136, 169, 318
Hatfield, Sid, 238, 239, 318
Hawkins, Horace, 144–45, 318
Hayes, Frank, 44, 56, 156, 167, 169, 170, 172, 174, 186, 190, 192, 200, 201, 318
Haywood, William D., 156, 276–78, 318
Hazleton, Pa., 7, 151, 181
Hearst, William Randolph, 288
Henry, Patrick, 7, 11, 19, 65, 87, 203–05, 207, 210, 218, 229, 248, 274, 316, 318, 319
Hocking Valley, Ohio, 54
Holly Grove, W. Va., 57, 88, 106, 115

Holy Rollers, 82, 83, 245
Homestead, Pa., 99, 204, 214
Houston, Harold W., 104, 225, 249, 319
Howat, Alexander, 200, 254–58, 319
Huerfano County, Colo., 122, 129
Huerta, Victoriano, 219, 319
Huff, George Franklin, 50, 319
Hugo, Victor Marie, 87, 126, 319
Hunt, George W. P., 185, 319

Iglesias, Santiago, 232, 319
Indianapolis, Ind., 3, 15, 24, 32, 35, 85, 167, 174, 185, 200, 208, 238, 251, 254
Industrial Workers of the World (IWW), 22, 196, 203, 213, 230, 233
Ingalls, John James, 142, 319
Injunctions, 11, 15, 17, 18, 40, 127, 213, 300
International Association of Bridge and Structural Iron Workers, 185
Ireland, 213
Irons, Martin, 7, 183, 184, 208, 209, 279, 280, 319
Iron workers, 158, 258
Irwin coal field, 44, 50, 51, 53, 54
Italy, 67

Jackson, John J., 15, 18, 29, 42, 77, 86, 127–28, 319
Japan, 34
Jefferson, Thomas, 7, 153, 218, 228, 229, 231, 233, 248, 274
Jeffries Detective Agency, 27
Jones, Mary Harris: in coal strike of 1902, 15–20; in Colorado coal strike of 1913, 122–55; court martial of, 115; imprisonment of, 17, 18, 56, 61, 62, 64, 67, 80, 84, 86, 91, 96, 115–44, 171, 185, 186, 194, 195, 203–31; last public appearance of, 259–61; in Mexico, 232–37; in Paint Creek–Cabin Creek strike, 56–118; preservation of speeches by, xiii–xiv; role of, in UMWA, xvi, 3, 15, 44, 122, 129, 150, 167, 174, 185, 200, 208, 211, 224, 238, 251, 254; as speaker, xiii–xvi; in steel strike of 1919, 200–10; as writer, xvii
Joplin, Mo., 25, 164

Kanawha coal field, 15, 20, 56, 68, 70, 89, 211, 216

Index

Kanawha County, W. Va., 89
Kansas City, Mo., 162, 184
Kansas Industrial Court Law, 256
Kaplan, David, 157, 319
Kayford, W. Va., 112
Kaymoor, W. Va., 110
Keeney, Frank, 206, 207, 239, 311, 320
Kelly Creek, W. Va., 243
Kern, John Worth, 115, 116, 180, 185, 246, 320
Kibbey, Joseph H., 286
King, William Lyon Mackenzie, 156, 320
Kipling, Rudyard, 66, 100, 284, 320
Knights of Columbus, 198
Knights of Labor, 154, 183, 208, 251

Labor spies, 7, 11, 13, 32, 74, 134, 137, 146, 170
Lafayette, Marie Joseph Paul de, 269
Laing, John, 97, 98, 116, 320
Lane, Harry, 135, 320
Langdon, Emma, 22, 320
Laredo, Tex., 232
Latimer, Pa., 295
Latin America, 232
Lawler, Oscar, 286, 287, 289, 320
Lawson, John, 174, 176, 183, 320
Leavenworth, Kans., 36, 288
Lens Creek, W. Va., 238
Lesseps, Ferdinand Marie de, 320
Lewis, John L., 174, 186, 200–02, 206, 209–11, 243, 247–55, 258, 320
Lewis, Thomas L., 24, 27, 28, 30, 33, 43, 44, 54, 320
Liberty bonds, 198
Lincoln, Abraham, 15, 65, 67, 81, 87, 91, 151, 153, 178, 188, 202, 217, 221, 228, 229, 231, 248, 288, 289
Lively, W. Va., 108
Lloyd, Caroline, 122, 150, 321
Lloyd, Henry Demarest, 122, 321
Lloyd George, David, 212, 321
Logan County, W. Va., 211, 222, 238, 239, 250
Loop Creek, W. Va., 20, 272
Lord, James Ravell, 237, 321
Los Angeles, Calif., 56, 185, 211, 285–87, 289
Los Angeles Times, 185
Louisville, Ky., 127, 251
Low, Seth, 61, 321

Lowden, Frank, 197, 321
Ludlow, Colo., 130, 131, 138, 142, 150, 154, 155, 176, 177, 219, 226, 245

McDonald, Duncan, 167, 168, 170, 172, 272, 321
McDowell County, W. Va., 211, 229, 231, 250
Machine guns, 57, 59, 62, 69, 89, 129, 144, 161, 226, 227, 245
McKay, Ed, 50, 321
McKees Rocks, Pa., 37
McKell, Thomas Gaylord, 78, 79, 321
McKinley, William, 3, 7, 154
McPartland, James, 278
Madero, Francisco, 56, 219, 232, 235, 310, 321
Magón. See Flores Magón, Ricardo
Manning, Joseph Columbus, 266, 321
Marmet, W. Va., 239
Martial law, 110, 115, 130
Martine, James Edgar, 153, 321
Matewan, W. Va., 227, 246
Matti, Andrew, 50, 321
Metalliferous miners, 22
Mexican revolutionaries, 24, 32, 35, 44, 84, 112, 156, 289, 293
Mexico, 24–29, 32, 36, 42, 50, 56, 58, 61, 75, 76, 82, 122, 127, 129, 131, 132, 164, 178, 213, 219, 232–38, 248, 254, 285–88, 293, 309
Mexico City, D.F., 232
Miles, Nelson Appleton, 276, 321
Military courts, 56, 106
Military intelligence, 194, 211, 224
Militia, 7, 12, 22, 51–152 passim, 179, 181, 206, 225, 244, 245, 249, 252, 296
Milwaukee, Wis., 40, 83, 139, 290–92
Mine inspectors, 9
Mingo County, W. Va., 211, 226, 250
Missouri Federation of Labor, 209
Missouri Pacific Railroad, 279
Mitchell, John, 3, 4, 7, 15, 16, 17, 22, 29, 40, 122, 294, 295, 321
Mitchell, William, 238, 321
Monessen, Pa., 202, 203
Monongah mine disaster, 294
Montgomery, Lawrence C., 183, 322
Montgomery, W. Va., 61, 66, 70, 71, 73, 147, 189
Mooney, Fred, 237, 322

Mooney, Thomas J., 194, 196, 199, 259, 322
Morgan, Anne, 28, 74, 322
Morgan, Ephraim F., 239, 259, 322
Morgan, J. Pierpont, 27, 28, 37, 38, 53, 74, 102, 285, 322
Morrison, Frank, 24, 29, 40, 322
Mt. Carbon, W. Va., 269
Mt. Olive, Ill., 184, 260
Mt. San Rafael Hospital, 122, 129
Moyer, Charles, 30, 144, 156, 276–78, 309, 322
Mucklow, W. Va., 57, 115
Murray, John, 232, 322
Murray, Philip, 248, 322

Napoleon Bonaparte, 45
Nashville, W. Va., 71
New England, W. Va., 242
New Hope, W. Va., 240
New River coal field, 20, 68, 78, 86, 110, 112, 186, 211, 220, 226, 240, 270
Nicaragua, 61, 69
Nicholls, Thomas D., 24, 28, 49, 322
Norfolk and Western Railroad, 215, 222, 224
Nova Scotia, 174, 181

Obregón, Alvaro, 232, 233, 322
Older, Cora Baggerly, 136, 322
Olson, Harry, 171, 323
Omaha, Neb., 256
Orizaba, 238
Oyster Bay, N.Y., 22, 61, 181

Pacific Gas and Electric Company, 194
Paint Creek, W. Va., 56–58, 64, 66, 68, 73, 76, 77, 87, 88, 103, 107, 111, 115, 124, 147, 167, 187, 244–45
Paint Creek Colliery Company, 244
Palmer, A. Mitchell, 206, 215, 323
Pan American Federation of Labor, 232, 237, 238
Panama Canal, 61
Panther Creek, Pa., 12
Parkersburg, W. Va., 15, 18, 86
Partido Liberal, 24, 232
Parton, Mary Field, 259
Peabody, James H., 52, 88, 96, 228, 323
Pells Brewery, 121
Peoria, Ill., 194

Perry, Edwin, 179, 323
Pettibone, George, 156, 276–78, 323
Peytona, W. Va., 64
Phelps Dodge Copper Company, 134, 178
Philadelphia, Pa., 22, 181, 201, 229
Pinchot, Cornelia Bryce, 311, 312
Pinchot, Gifford, 259, 311, 312, 323
Pinkerton Detective Agency, 26, 89, 99, 184
Pitt, Emmiline, 53, 323
Pittsburg, Kans., 129, 130, 156
Pittsburgh, Pa., 51, 53, 123, 135, 136, 201, 204, 208, 215, 218, 220
Plumb Creek, Pa., 302
Pocahontas coal field, 189, 215, 229
Poggiani, Joe, 18, 242, 323
Poland, 213, 231
Political campaigning, 185
Populist party, 198
Portugal, 213
Pouren, J. J., 24, 30, 157, 323
Powderly, Emma, 259
Powderly, Terence V., 14, 36, 115, 174, 184, 209, 259, 323
Pratt, W. Va., 108
Preparedness Day parade, 194
Princeton, W. Va., 224, 249
Prohibition, 249, 260
Pueblo, Colo., 123

Quarantine, 22

Railroad workers, 25, 36, 49, 56, 60, 65, 112, 133, 147, 148, 158, 161, 228, 244, 256, 265
Red Ash mine, 8, 9
Red scare, 211, 215
Rend, W. P., 241, 323
Rice, Bernard, 16, 242, 323
Rio Grande Railroad, 29
Rivera, Librado, 286
Roan, John M., 244, 323
Rockefeller, John D., 28, 37, 102, 122, 130, 132, 143, 149, 154, 159, 161, 165, 178, 184, 229, 323
Rockefeller, John D., Jr., 151, 156, 165, 179, 182, 246, 323
Rogers, W. M., 311
Roosevelt, Theodore, 15, 22, 26, 27, 37, 52, 61, 63, 88, 92, 102, 116, 152, 172, 181, 276, 283, 294, 295, 323

Index

Root, Elihu, 285
Rudowitz, Christian, 24, 30, 157, 324
Russia, 11, 25, 27, 94, 102, 124, 213, 285
Russian emigres, 157
Ryan, Frank M., 185, 324
Ryan, William D., 324

Salvation Army, 25, 60, 63, 75, 82, 83,
    113, 198, 199, 234
San Antonio, Tex., 48
San Francisco, Calif., 133, 136, 153, 194,
    211, 218
Sandy Hook, N.Y., 27
Sarabia, Manuel, 26, 286, 324
Schmidt, Katherine, 157, 324
Schmidt, Mathew, 157, 324
Schwab, Charles, 210, 213, 225, 229, 324
Scott, Nathan B., 88, 90, 324
Scranton, Pa., 268, 294
Seattle, Wash., 122, 150, 200, 201, 213
Sellins, Fanny, 205, 324
Silver Spring, Md., 260
Slavery, 5, 20, 60, 77, 133, 183, 221, 222,
    228, 230, 251, 257, 275, 277, 285–87
Smelter workers, 26
Smith, Sylvester Clark, 112, 324
Socialism, 267
Socialist, 146, 155
Socialist camp meeting, 122
Socialist Party of America, 24, 56, 309
Solidarity, 17, 32, 202, 209, 225, 236,
    251
Sonora, 27
South America, 237
Southern Pacific Railroad, 26, 49, 112
Spain, 67
Springfield, Ill., 254
St. Louis, Mo., 27, 38, 208
Stanaford Mountain, W. Va., 79, 111,
    205, 241, 242, 276, 300
Standard Oil Company, 27, 28, 30, 32,
    43, 47, 99, 140, 142, 276, 286, 288
Stanford, Jane Lathrop, 12, 324
Steel organizing committee, 201
Steel strike of 1919, 200, 202, 208, 211,
    231
Steel workers, 28, 35, 46, 99, 112, 157,
    167, 168, 175, 194, 195, 201, 202, 206,
    208, 214, 217, 230, 231
Streetcar workers, 46, 51, 185
Sunday, William Ashley, 195, 324

Taft, William Howard, 24, 33, 36, 37,
    38, 42, 48, 61–63, 116, 289, 324
Tarbell, Ida Minerva, 156, 324
Taylor, William Sylvester, 54, 324
Temperance, 64, 75, 95, 113, 142, 157,
    158, 162, 171, 188, 246, 270
Textile workers, 9, 22, 51, 181, 229, 265,
    266, 268, 281; strike of, in Austria, 12
Thayer, W. Va., 241
Thurmond, W. Va., 79
Tikas, Louis, 131, 325
Tincher, Thomas, 325
Titanic, 93
Tobin, Daniel, 235, 237, 325
Trades Council of New York, 133
Trinidad, Colo., 121–24, 129, 150, 152,
    156, 160, 179
Turner, John Kenneth, 43, 289, 325
Tuscaloosa, Ala., 265

UMWA. See Jones, Mary Harris: role of,
    in UMWA
UMWA women's auxiliary, 3, 10
Union Pacific Railroad, 251
Ulich, Robert, 180, 325

Vancouver, B.C., 181
Verdeckberg, Edward, 144, 325
Verdeckberg, Mrs. Edward, 310
Victor-American Company, 122, 123,
    150
Villarreal, Antonio I., 232, 286, 325
Virden, Ill., 209

Waite, Davis H., 76, 88, 325
Walker, John H., 19, 20, 30, 36, 200,
    201, 224, 240, 241, 254, 255, 325
Wall Street, 27, 28, 42, 46, 48, 49, 61,
    62, 80, 113, 136, 181, 289
Walsenburg, Colo., 122, 129, 179, 310
War Labor Board, 186, 200
War savings stamps, 198
Warren, Fred, 54, 325
Washington, George, 25, 91, 188, 202,
    218, 228, 231, 269
Washington, D.C., 49, 115, 116, 122,
    129–32, 150, 156, 169, 198, 215, 230,
    249, 250, 259
Watson, Clarence W., 225, 325
Western Federation of Miners, 24, 30, 32,
    33, 50, 54, 56, 116, 156, 309

Westmoreland County, Pa., 47, 48, 181
West Virginia, investigation of conditions in, by U.S. Senate, 56
West Virginia Federation of Labor, 311
West Virginia National Guard, 78
Wheeling, W. Va., 106, 115
White, John P., 115, 117, 130, 134, 135, 138, 141, 143, 146, 148, 167–71, 174, 181, 182, 184, 186, 192, 200, 325
Whitford, Greeley W., 47, 62, 326
Wickersham, George W., 49, 288, 289, 326
Wilhelm II (kaiser), 212, 213, 220, 226
Wilkes-Barre, Pa., 295
Williamson, W. Va., 211, 214, 224, 240

Wilson, William B., 8, 24, 27, 28, 30, 49, 50, 115, 159, 174, 179, 180, 326
Wilson, Woodrow, 116, 134, 150, 153, 156, 174, 179, 185, 186, 188, 189, 201, 202, 203, 250
Winding Gulf Coal Company, 191
Wise County, Va., 243, 274
Women's suffrage, 95, 197, 219, 246
Wood, Leonard, 207, 326
World War I, 189, 211–12, 234

YMCA, 198, 199, 215, 234
Yontz, Murray, 310
Youngstown, Ohio, 167, 175, 182, 184
Yuma, Ariz., 288

Pittsburgh Series in Social and Labor History

Maurine Weiner Greenwald, Editor

And the Wolf Finally Came: The Decline of the American Steel Industry
John P. Hoerr

The Correspondence of Mother Jones
Edward M. Steel, Editor

Don't Call Me Boss: David L. Lawrence, Pittsburgh's Renaissance Mayor
Michael P. Weber

The Speeches and Writings of Mother Jones
Edward M. Steel, Editor

Women and the Trades
Elizabeth Beardsley Butler

Other titles in the series

The Emergence of a UAW Local, 1936–1939: A Study in Class and Culture
Peter Friedlander

Homestead: The Households of a Mill Town
Margaret F. Byington

The Homestead Strike of 1892
Arthur G. Burgoyne

Immigration and Industrialization: Ethnicity in an American Mill Town, 1870–1940
John Bodnar

Out of This Furnace
Thomas Bell

Steelmasters and Labor Reform, 1886–1923
Gerald G. Eggert

Steve Nelson, American Radical
Steve Nelson, James R. Barrett, & Rob Ruck

Working-Class Life: The "American Standard" in Comparative Perspective, 1899–1913
Peter R. Shergold